# Studies in Applied Interpersonal Communication

*To the family, friends, and students*
*who have asked,*
*"So what?"*

# Studies in Applied Interpersonal Communication

## Michael T. Motley editor
*University of California at Davis*

Los Angeles • London • New Delhi • Singapore

*For information:*

Sage Publications, Inc.
2455 Teller Road
Thousand Oaks,
 California 91320
E-mail: order@sagepub.com

Sage Publications India Pvt. Ltd.
B 1/I 1 Mohan Cooperative
 Industrial Area
Mathura Road, New Delhi 110 044
India

Sage Publications Ltd.
1 Oliver's Yard
55 City Road
London EC1Y 1SP
United Kingdom

Sage Publications Asia-Pacific Pte. Ltd.
33 Pekin Street #02-01
Far East Square
Singapore 048763

Printed in the United States of America

*Library of Congress Cataloging-in-Publication Data*

Studies in applied interpersonal communication / Michael T. Motley, editor.
  p. cm.
Includes bibliographical references and index.
ISBN 978-1-4129-4215-7 (cloth : alk. paper)
ISBN 978-1-4129-4216-4 (pbk. : alk. paper)
  1. Interpersonal communication. I. Motley, Michael T.

HM1166.S78 2008
302.2—dc22                      2007037957

This book is printed on acid-free paper.

08   09   10   11   12   10   9   8   7   6   5   4   3   2   1

| | |
|---|---|
| *Acquisitions Editor:* | Todd R. Armstrong |
| *Editorial Assistant:* | Katie Grim |
| *Production Editor:* | Astrid Virding |
| *Copy Editor:* | Barbara Coster |
| *Typesetter:* | C&M Digitals (P) Ltd. |
| *Proofreader:* | Scott Oney |
| *Marketing Manager:* | Carmel Schrire |

# Contents

## PART III: EVERYDAY SITUATIONS

# Introduction

A noticeable trend within the past few years in communication conferences and essays is the implication that we should prize the social relevance of our research. Recent convention themes such as "Taking It to the Streets," "Making a Difference," "Reaching Out," "The Engaged Discipline," "Celebrating Our Centrality," "Communicating Social Impact," and so forth suggest that we have much to offer the lay public and that our social relevance, or applicability, should be highlighted.

Of course, social relevance is a subjective concept that no doubt has different connotations for many of us. I am reminded, for example, of a faculty meeting at which my department, after a long discussion to find a common theme under which all of our research would fit, finally settled on the label *social relevance.* Here was a group of scholars studying subjects as diverse as Spanish medieval rhetoric, critical analysis of war monuments, and cognitive mechanisms of language encoding, each of whom found *social relevance* to be an apt umbrella term for his or her research—and, I suspect, at the same time questioning its aptness for certain others.

Given that social relevance is an apparently valued but apparently vague concept, I'd like to suggest the following continuum as a starting point for clarification—four levels of social relevance, from remote to direct:

1. First, we can consider research to be socially relevant if it is interesting. For example, the work being done by paleontologists to determine what caused the dinosaurs to become extinct has this kind of relevance—it's just plain interesting to lots of people. But this is a remote level of social relevance because there is virtually nothing we can do with the answer to affect or improve our everyday lives (as far as we know, at least). All of our communication research has this kind of relevance. That is to say, our work is indeed interesting. At the very least it is interesting to the researcher, a handful of colleagues, and a handful of graduate students. Sometimes it is interesting more widely. Finding that someone else is interested in our research can be said to constitute one kind of social relevance.

2. Next, we can consider research to be socially relevant if it gives us behind-the-scenes insights into common human experiences. Dream research in psychology is a nice example of this. We all experience dreams, so there is a sort of inherent fascination with their frequency, true duration versus perceived duration, and so forth. Research on the causes of everyday slips of the tongue would be an analogous example. But again, there is very little practical value here, since there is no way (yet) to apply the information. Most all communication research has this behind-the-scenes kind of social relevance, since communication is an everyday phenomenon. But most often our investigations into everyday communication phenomena yield very little that communicators can apply to their own interactions. This is in large part because our independent variables usually are things that the communicator cannot control (e.g., gender, personality traits, culture, experience), and our dependent variables usually have little to do with communication efficacy or outcomes.

3. A third kind of social relevance is represented by research that can indeed be applied to common communication problems, but in a general awareness or consciousness-raising sort of way. To the extent that this research suggests solutions to communication problems, the solution is usually in the form of changing one's perspective or orientation, as with, for example, appreciating differences in the other sex's communication styles or recognizing what constitutes constructive communication in conflict situations. As social relevance goes, this kind of information seems much more direct than the earlier categories. But often it has an "easier said than done" flavor, for often the implied change in perspective must itself be learned. For example, knowing that compromise is helpful is one thing; being willing to compromise, eliciting willingness from others, and then achieving compromise are different matters. As another example, it is one thing to be aware that in differences of values there are no rights and wrongs, but it may be a more difficult matter for the "neatnik" to accept his or her "slob" roommate's messes as a mere no-right-or-wrong difference in values. Still, however, while the application to everyday communication situations may be a bit difficult at this level of social relevance, at least it is there.

4. The final level of social relevance is represented by more specific prescriptive information (empirically supported) that advises communicators about how to deal with problematic communication situations—that is, precisely (within reason) what to say and do (or not say and do) in order to promote the probability of optimal results when specific communication difficulties arise. Almost certainly, this kind of advice has to be very context-specific, addressing very particular communication dilemmas and situations. But there are a number of very specific communication situations on which many communicators would welcome our field's informed advice. This would constitute a sort of ultimate (or at least most direct) social relevance, it seems.

It is the relative paucity of this sort of information that instigated this book. In interpersonal communication, we have very little prescriptive information to offer. Of that which we *can* offer, only a small fraction of it has been both empirically supported and from our own field. The 14 chapters of this book represent research that is applicable to the problems of everyday communicators—some of it being applicable at Level 3 and some at Level 4 of the social relevance/applicability continuum suggested above.

The relative dearth of "applied"—that is, pragmatically applicable—interpersonal-communication research is, of course, not because of our subject matter. It is obvious that real people experience real communication dilemmas, obvious that solutions would be appreciated, and obvious that our field could be of considerable help. What we usually have done in the past, however, is to identify a problem area and then become less concerned with providing practical solutions than with turning the problem inside out for optimal "understanding" by ourselves, our colleagues, and our graduate students.

My favorite example of this is the story of a student who has to give a speech in a few days, is experiencing extreme anxiety about it, and goes to his communication professor for help. The professor agrees to search for a solution among the hundreds of articles on anxiety in our journals, and reports back to the student a couple of days later: "According to the research, here's what you can do: smaller audiences mean less anxiety, so you can hope that part of your audience doesn't show up; more experience means less anxiety, so you can try to give a few extra speeches between now and the one you're worried about; several personality variables correlate, so you could get some psychotherapy before your speech," and so on. What this obviously apocryphal story illustrates so well, I think, is a tendency for our research to examine socially relevant *topics* but by looking at all kinds of associated variables *except the variables that communicators themselves can control or affect.*

Let me give one more example of this—a true story this time. It concerns a convention panel I attended titled "Communication and Bereavement." Here is a clearly relevant topic, I think. After all, I've had many students mention their difficulty in knowing whether and when to approach someone who has recently lost a loved one, and especially in knowing what to say. And I used to find these situations to be difficult myself. So I went to the "Communication and Bereavement" panel looking forward to getting practical answers—for myself and for my students—on appropriate and inappropriate communication behaviors during others' grief. But not a single one of the four papers on the panel dealt with that question in the least. There was a paper on the symbolism of various artifacts of funerals, another on the characteristics of eulogies, and two others I don't remember. But there was nothing on the practical question that ordinary communicators would be most anxious to have answered, nothing to advise us on when or what to say or do.

I particularly like this story in the present context because it exemplifies one reason that there is very little applicable information in our research. In this case, clearly, it is not because there are no relevant applications. And it is not because the more applicable or socially relevant research would be too difficult. Notice how incredibly simple it would be, despite the several variables that obviously would need to be accounted for, to do a very good study on when and how to (or not to) communicate with the bereaved. The reason that directly applicable answers were not provided by the panel is simply that—as with most of our research—the applied questions were not the questions selected to be asked. And not that there is anything wrong with that. That the authors of those four papers were asking very different questions is their prerogative, certainly. Likewise for the anxiety example. The main reason that solutions to public-speaking anxiety have been found only very recently is not because the decades of preceding research was necessary groundwork for eventual application, but rather that in all of that preceding research, finding a cure never was the researcher's primary goal. In short, it is clear that our subject matter is not immune to socially relevant application. Indeed, our subject matter often invites it. And certainly the public (who, in most cases, by the way, is the one paying us to do our research) invites it.

The familiar counterargument that it is unwise and improper to dispense unfounded prescriptive advice to communicators is completely legitimate, of course. But while prescription can be unfounded, it also can be well founded. The 14 chapters of this book report empirical investigations of natural dilemmas and problems faced by ordinary communicators and offer suggestions for dealing with them. The reader should be the judge as to whether that advice is justified by the accompanying empirical evidence. Obviously, only if the evidence justifies the conclusion should the reader follow the advice in his or her own communication experiences or share it with students and others. I am confident that both the casual and the careful reader will find the practical application conclusions of each of these chapters to be well founded. But see if you agree.

It is worth mentioning in this regard that each chapter was originally submitted for peer review in a more elaborate and more detailed journal-article-type version and then, once accepted, was trimmed and tailored for readability and clarity more appropriate to graduate and advanced undergraduate student readers. In some cases, information that is necessary for replication (or full explication) of these studies has been sacrificed for brevity and clarity, but the more complete and detailed version of each chapter is available upon request from its authors.

The book has been organized according to three kinds of situations, the boundaries of which are admittedly fuzzy: fairly *rare* but nevertheless serious communication dilemmas (e.g., handling unrequited romantic attraction in an ostensible friendship, handling a stalker), more *common* situations (e.g., repeated argument on the same topic, asymmetrical physical intimacy thresholds, giving advice, doing forgiveness), and virtually *everyday* situations (e.g., giving support, using humor, employing emotional maturity). Different readers and students will resonate to different communication dilemmas, of course. One person may be especially concerned with his or her use of guilt messages, for example, while the next person may not be. Likewise for using TV to help relationships, social support in dyads, facework in romantic relationships, and so forth. But—assuming that the person who thinks he or she has no communication problems probably has the biggest problem of them all—there should be something here for everyone. All the contributors hope that their chapters serve both to help a large number of people in related communication situations and to instigate *more* research that can be of practical applied value to everyday communicators.

SAGE Publications gratefully acknowledges the following reviewers:

Dennis C. Alexander, University of Utah; Melanie Booth-Butterfield, West Virginia University; Jerold A. Hale, University of Georgia; Jon A. Hess, University of Missouri-Columbia; Lawrence A. Hosman, University of Southern Mississippi; Beth A. Le Poire, California Lutheran University; Valerie Manusov, University of Washington; Virginia M. McDermott, The University of New Mexico; Philip Salem, Texas State University-San Marcos; and April Trees, St. Louis University.

# PART I

*Special Communication Situations*

# 1

# Managing Unwanted Pursuit

### Brian H. Spitzberg

### William R. Cupach

Desire is sometimes a dangerous thing. We feel strongly that the pursuit of the things we desire will somehow lead to our contentment *if* (and sometimes *only if*) we *get* what we desire. For some, however, the *pursuit* becomes part of the desire, an end to an end, rather than a means to an end. When this occurs, pursuit may reflect an obsession.

This chapter is about a particular type of obsession—the pursuit of a relationship when the object of pursuit distinctly does not want to be pursued. We examine the process of obsessional pursuit of intimacy with a person who expressly does not want to reciprocate such intimacy and what tactics this object of pursuit may use to prevent, stop, and avoid such pursuit. In the process of exploring this process, we reveal what a sample of college students perceives about the relative appropriateness and effectiveness of such tactics.

## The Nature of Obsessive Unwanted Pursuit

Think of all the relationships you have had in your life—family, friends, teachers, bosses, colleagues, classmates, shopkeepers, and passing acquaintances. Of all these, only a relatively few reach a level of prominence in your life. The vast majority of relationships we establish in a lifetime fade away. Some end after a passing encounter, and many others end after a period of weeks, months, years, or decades.

The pursuit of intimate relationships often holds a meaningful place in our lives. In a broad sense, intimacy is simply a form of closeness. This closeness may entail the sharing of information, the sharing of time, the sharing of sexual activity, or the sharing of tasks. Intimacy grows in some relationships and decays in most of those relationships.

For some people, however, a level of intimacy is desired with someone beyond what that person prefers. A friend wants to continue a friendship or become more of a best friend instead of a mere friend. A former dating partner wants the relationship to progress to something more serious and committed. An acquaintance wants to become a lover. Such persons may engage in a pattern of pursuit in order to achieve intimacy, even when the person being pursued is distinctly disinterested in allowing the relationship to progress to such a state. When such pursuit of intimacy is actively maintained over time and is expressly unwanted by the person being pursued, it can be considered a type of *obsessive relational intrusion* (Cupach & Spitzberg, 1998, 2004; Spitzberg, 2002b; Spitzberg & Cupach, 2007). When pursuit becomes sufficiently intense or persistent to cause fear or seem threatening, it constitutes a form of *stalking*.

In the United States, by conservative standards, about 2% of men and 8% of women will be stalked in their lifetime (Tjaden & Thoennes, 1998). Across many estimates, however, approximately a quarter of all people have experienced a campaign of unwanted harassment or pursuit (Cupach & Spitzberg, 1998; Spitzberg & Cupach, 2007). When examining just the experience of unwanted pursuit of *romantic* intimacy, studies of college samples indicate relatively little difference between men's and women's experiences. High percentages of both men and women, around 40% to 50%, have at some time experienced at least some unwanted and repeated pursuit activities in which a person wanted more of a relationship than the person being pursued wanted to give (see, e.g., Cupach & Spitzberg, 2004; Spitzberg, 2002b).

Stalking, therefore, may reflect the most extreme tip of a much larger iceberg. Not all unwanted pursuit ends up as stalking, but it is important to note that approximately 75% to 80% of all stalking develops out of prior relationships and half of all stalking emerges from relationships that involved some degree of prior romantic or sexual intimacy (Cupach & Spitzberg, 2004; Spitzberg, 2002b; Spitzberg & Cupach, 2007). The average stalking relationship lasts about 1.8 years. At least two important implications of such findings are that (1) people with whom we clearly do *not* want to share further intimacy often seem normal or interesting enough to fly under our relational radar, and (2) we often experience problems ending a relationship as cleanly and finally as we would prefer. In this context, it seems important to examine some of the reasons why we often find ourselves entangled in a situation of needing to disengage ourselves from a relationship more competently than we seem able to accomplish.

The victims, or objects of unwanted pursuit, are likely to experience a wide range of ills as a result of such campaigns of harassment. Stalking victimization, in particular, is associated with psychological maladjustment, stress, anxiety, depression, physical disorders, and disruption to one's economic, social, emotional, and physical health (see Cupach & Spitzberg, 2004; Spitzberg & Cupach, 2007). Some percentage of people, probably in spite of these harms, also find silver linings to their victimization, such as greater personal resilience, confidence, or trust in friends and family (Spitzberg & Rhea, 1999). Such resilience effects are probably more likely to occur when the victim attributes the cause of the original breakup to the other person (Tashiro & Frazier, 2003).

Unwanted pursuit and stalking take an almost infinite variety of forms. Research on the patterns of unwanted pursuit, however, permits a manageable classification of the varied pursuit behaviors. A review of over 30 studies of stalking and unwanted pursuit reveals that most unwanted pursuit tends to involve any of eight types of actions: hyperintimacy, interactional contacts, mediated contacts, surveillance, harassment, invasion, threat, and violence (Cupach & Spitzberg, 2004; Spitzberg & Cupach, 2007). The first step to managing unwanted pursuit is recognizing the types of behaviors that need to be managed. Therefore, a brief review of these behaviors is in order.

## The Process of Pursuit

*Hyperintimacy* behaviors involve excessive or exaggerated expressions of courtship and attempts at closeness. Sending a flower might be nice, but sending six dozen, or sending a flower every day for weeks, especially in the context of recipient disinterest, is excessive. Expressing attraction or liking in a card may be a nice gesture, but expressing a sense of fated destiny, or that no one else in the world could ever be fulfilling, after only a few dates seems desperate. Hyperintimacy behaviors represent a diverse set of activities, including expressions of affection, flirtation, ingratiation, and proposing relationship escalation. *Mediated contacts* represent attempts at unwanted pursuit through technology or other communication media, including letters, faxes, instant messaging (IM), e-mail, leaving notes, tokens, and of course, telephone calls. *Interactional contacts* consist of both direct and indirect attempts at proximal communication, including approaching in various contexts, intruding upon ongoing conversations, showing up at places, personal space invasions, getting involved in common activities, and harassing or involving third parties in the process of pursuit.

*Surveillance activities* reflect various attempts at keeping tabs on the object of pursuit. Such behaviors include loitering nearby, synchronizing schedules of activities, following, monitoring, and drive-by attempts to locate an object of pursuit. *Invasion activities* involve information or property theft, breaking and entering a domicile or office, and other forms of intrusive surveillance, such as bugging or inserting a global positioning system (GPS) device or code into a person's property.

*Harassment and intimidation* include a wide variety of actions that attempt to exert sufficient pressure, frustration, or annoyance to influence a person's behavior. Such activities include forms of verbal abuse, regulatory harassment (e.g., filing suit), administrative harassment (e.g., entering subscriptions for a person to unwanted magazines), reputational and network harassment (e.g., spreading rumors to or bothering associates of the object of pursuit), and simple unrelenting persistence of pursuit.

*Threats* are messages that imply a harm will come to someone based on that person's behaviors and under the control of the person issuing the threat (e.g., "If you don't get back together with me, I'll make your life miserable"). Threats can be made against the person, the person's valued others (e.g., family, friends, pets, property), or the person's livelihood (e.g., economic status, career). They can include forms of coercion (e.g., sexual, economic), the display of weapons, and even threats against self (e.g., suicide).

The final form of unwanted pursuit and stalking is *aggression and violence*, which consist of actions intended to harm another person. Aggression and violence include attempted and actual vandalism, endangerment, kidnapping, physical assault, sexual assault, rape, murder, and suicide.

## The Problems of Courtship and Relationship Rejection

The ordinary activities of affinity seeking, relationship pursuit, social rejection, and breaking up are tricky undertakings, fraught with opportunities for miscoordination, miscommunication, and misperception (Metts & Spitzberg, 1996). The meanings two people ascribe to their developing (or ongoing) relationship can be quite divergent, because relationships are tacitly constructed, not overtly codified. It is common for two persons' relationship intentions not to match and for the two individuals to be unaware of the mismatch. Jack and Jill can have several pleasant interactions in which Jill thinks they share a budding companionate friendship, whereas Jack sees escalating intimacy and future romance.

Further complicating the construction of a mutual relationship are the norms of positivity and politeness that characterize social interactions between people, particularly early in their acquaintanceship. In these interactions, individuals attempt to create highly favorable impressions of themselves and at the same time mutually support each other's identity (Goffman, 1959). Thus each person is drawing inferences about the other based on limited and positively exaggerated information. Because relationships develop incrementally and temporally, it can take time for one person to discover a mismatch in relational intentions. Similarly, the obsessiveness of a partner's relationship pursuit is often emergent— revealing itself in a cumulative pattern of persistent behavior that manifests itself over time. In this way, objects of obsessive pursuit may initially interpret affinity-seeking behaviors "as romantic pursuit or friendship-building, only later reinterpreting them as stalking" (Emerson, Ferris, & Gardner, 1998, p. 292). In Brewster's (2003) interviews of 187 women stalked by a former intimate partner, for example, she found "nearly all of the women (98%) mentioned that their relationship started out normally enough, but that their partners later became controlling" (p. 211). She also discovered about two thirds of the women could not remember exactly at what point in the relationship their partner became controlling, which illustrates the subtle and inherently ambiguous manner in which relationships unfold.

The norm of persistence in courtship activity also contributes to unwanted relationship pursuit. Our culture promotes the belief that "if at first you don't succeed, try, try again" and "quitters never win, and winners never quit." "The stereotype of the ardent pursuer eventually winning over the object of affection given sufficient effort is a familiar one, reinforced by the occasional experience of persistence paying off, as well as fictional portrayals in popular media" (Spitzberg & Cupach, 2001, p. 122). Thus persistent pursuers believe that desired relationships are obtained by exerting sufficient effort. They rationalize that escalated, intensified bids for intimacy and connection, even in the face of rejection, eventually will be rewarded with success (Cupach & Spitzberg, 2004; Spitzberg & Cupach, 2002a, 2003). They also hold the concomitant expectation that objects of affection play hard to get, in which case, relational rejection is actually interpreted as an invitation to persist in pursuing the relationship, despite the fact that the rejection is genuine.

The manner in which rejection is conveyed also tends to foster persistence of relationship pursuit. Rejectors often feel sympathy for those they are rejecting, and they feel guilty that rejection will be hurtful to the rejected person (Baumeister, Wotman, & Stillwell, 1993; Dunn, 2002). Consequently, rejectors routinely employ polite, face-saving, and sometimes indirect rejection messages in an attempt to let the rejected person down easy (e.g., Emerson et al., 1998; Folkes, 1982; Metts, Cupach, & Imahori, 1992). The rejected pursuer is encouraged by the soft rejection and holds out hope that relationship intentions can be reconciled. Particularly in the context of unrequited love and formerly intimate relationships, some perpetrators of unwanted pursuit perceive they were led on or misled by the rejecting partner who showed signs of reciprocal interest (Baumeister et al., 1993; Sheridan, Gillett, Davies, Blaauw, & Patel, 2003).

Some of the politeness of rejection owes to the fact that some rejectors feel ambivalence about their unwanted pursuit. In addition to experiencing annoyance and even some fear, rejectors simultaneously feel flattered and pleased by the attention they receive from would-be suitors. As Dunn (1999) has shown, the trappings of romance and courtship, such as flowers, gifts, and compliments, trigger "ambivalence and confusion, thus masking the intrusive, instrumental character of interaction that follows the expressed desire that such interaction cease" (p. 455).

## Managing Unwanted Pursuit

There is relatively little research that directly addresses what causes stalking to stop. Some studies have attempted to address the question, albeit in relatively simple ways. For example, several studies of stalking simply ask victims to guess why the pursuit stopped. In general, only a relatively small percentage of cases appear to stop because the victim directly asks the pursuer to stop (12%: Bjerregaard, 2000; 6%: Blackburn, 1999; 9%: Brewster, 2001; 37.5%: Dutton-Greene & Winstead, 2001). Some research indicates that different strategies work differently in stopping different types of unwanted pursuit. Blackburn (1999), for example, found that when victims were asked why they thought the pursuit stopped, different reasons emerged for different types of pursuit. For example, *calls* stopped because the stalker was told to stop (19%), the harassment was documented to someone (12%), the phone number was changed (23%), or the stalker got involved with someone else (8%). In contrast, *following* behaviors were thought to stop because of a restraining order (18%), the victim moved (18%), the police intervened (16%), the stalker got involved with someone else (8%), the harassment was documented (10%), the victim's routine activities changed (7%), or the stalker was told to stop (7%).

There are also differences in perspective—victims perceive somewhat different reasons than pursuers perceive. When Dutton-Greene and Winstead (2001) asked victims why the pursuit ceased, 37.5% attributed it to direct communication with the pursuer, 12.5% thought it was their own acts of avoidance, 12.5% thought it was a form of indirect communication (e.g., ignoring the pursuer), 6% thought it was simply a matter of giving the pursuer "time" to get over it, and 12.5% of the time the victims indicated that they actually renewed the relationship. In contrast, when pursuers were asked why they stopped, 46% said it was due to direct communication, 11.5% due to indirect communication, 11.5% due to the victim's avoidance, 8% because a third party intervened, 8% because enough time elapsed to get over it, and 4% because the relationship resumed.

Some tactics work well in some cases and appear to make matters worse in others. For example, in a small British sample of stalking victims, Sheridan (2001) found that 41% believed there were specific activities that helped reduce or end the pursuit, including legal interventions, ignoring the stalker, using a telephone trace, and physically threatening the stalker. In contrast, an equal proportion (41%) of victims indicated that certain actions *worsened* the situation, including legal intervention or the victim getting involved with someone else, paying attention to the pursuer, going into hiding, or having opposite-sex visitors or partners. Of those who believed the stalking had ended, 25% attributed it to moving, 14% to arrest of the pursuer, 11% to a new partner, and 11% to the pursuer moving on to a new victim (Sheridan, Davies, & Boon, 2001).

Walby and Allen (2004) found somewhat different results for male and female victims. When asked what caused the stalking to stop, changing the phone number or address (16% men, 24% women) or threat of legal intervention (19% men, 19% women), as well as informal third parties (e.g., friend, neighbor) getting involved (5% men, 12% women) and moving away (6% men, 9% women) were mentioned. As part of a study of multiple forms of interpersonal violence victimization, they also found that when women ended their relationship with their abuser, the violence stopped for 63%, improved for 8%, stayed relatively the same for 5%, and got worse for 3%. But more important, the violence only started when they split up and evolved into "something else, such as stalking and other harassment" among 18% of the victims (p. 65). Mechanic, Weaver, and Resick (2000) also found that "stalking behavior escalated among women who left their abusive partners" (p. 69). Ending a relationship is sometimes the way of stopping stalking, but it also is sometimes only the beginning.

In the largest study to date, of 8,000 men and 8,000 women in the United States, Tjaden and Thoennes (1998) found that of those who had been stalked, the most common victim-attributed reasons for the stalking stopping were as follows: the victim moved (19%), the stalker got a new love interest (18%), a police warning (15%), the victim talking with the pursuer (10%), arrest of the stalker (9%), the stalker moved (7%), the stalker got help or counseling (6%), the victim got a new love interest (4%), the stalker died (4%), the stalker was convicted (1%), and, 3% of the time, "it just stopped."

Not surprisingly, when police are asked why stalking stops, they tend to be focused more on formal and legal forms of intervention (Spitzberg, 2002a). In a sample of Australian police, Dussuyer (2000) found that 41% of police attributed the ending of stalking to formal judicial processes and another 17% attributed the end to cautioning. Cautioning, sometimes referred to as a "knock-and-talk," tends to involve uniformed officers making it clear to pursuers that their activities are unwanted and verging on law enforcement intervention, along with all its consequences.

## A Taxonomy of Coping Responses

A systematic review of over 30 studies of victim responses to stalkers reveals five basic types (i.e., strategies) of responses (i.e., tactics) to unwanted pursuit (Cupach & Spitzberg, 2004; Spitzberg & Cupach, 2007). These types of response can be thought of in terms of function and *direction,* that is, the direction the victim is taking to deal with the problem. A person may move inward toward the self, outward toward others, toward the pursuer, against the pursuer, or away from the pursuer. These basic directions organize an extensive repertoire of responses.

*Moving inward* occurs when a victim of unwanted pursuit seeks to resolve or cope with the problem by turning to self for resilience, reframing, or a reevaluation of the situation. It is the least interpersonally communicative of the categories and is likely to include activities such as meditation, exercise, taking drugs or drinking, and so forth.

*Moving outward* involves seeking assistance or advice from third parties. These third parties may be fairly informal, such as friends or family, and they may have more formal or expert relevance to the situation, such as police, counselors, religious authorities, or protection order clinics. Research indicates that almost 60% of people who experience stalking tell friends or family, 52% contact police, 42% contact someone in a service-related capacity (e.g., a counselor or teacher), and fully 82% disclose their plight to at least someone (Spitzberg, 2006).

*Moving toward* the pursuer includes any actions intended to negotiate a more preferred form of relationship, including an ending of the relationship or pursuit. The key is that the victim is interacting directly with the pursuer, seeking through reason, persuasion, and negotiation to move the relationship to a more acceptable form.

*Moving against* behaviors reflect attempts to deter or incapacitate the pursuer. Such actions as threatening the pursuer, pursuing legal action against the pursuer, or engaging in aggression against the pursuer all represent attempts to increase the actual or expected costs or punishment to the pursuer of engaging in ongoing pursuit.

Finally, *moving away* behaviors represent any efforts that increase a victim's inaccessibility to the pursuer. When victims change their phone number or e-mail address, take their Web pages off-line, change their routes and routines, screen calls, ask acquaintances not to share personal information with anyone, or even limit social activities, such actions represent efforts at "being where the pursuer is not."

Examples of these practical types of response are listed in Table 1.1. These examples are drawn from an extensive literature on actual stalking victims, although some may be more typical than others, depending on the severity of the unwanted pursuit. Given that the average case of stalking lasts close to 2 years (Cupach & Spitzberg, 2004; Spitzberg & Cupach, 2007; Tjaden & Thoennes, 1998), it seems obvious that the typical victim ends up trying many coping responses and that these responses may well cut across these categories. It also seems obvious that many tactics of managing unwanted pursuit often fail, at least in the short term. As the research reviewed above indicates, no tactics seem to emerge as consistently effective in diminishing the unwanted pursuit. Therefore, it is important to investigate whether there are interactional tactics that could competently manage such unwanted pursuit. Given the politeness and face-management binds that surround the deescalation of relationships, it is important to examine such tactics in the context of their interpersonal competence.

*(Text continues on page 18)*

**Table 1.1**   Tactics of Managing Unwanted Pursuit Appropriateness and Effectiveness Ratings for Entire Sample and by Sex ($N = 148$)

| Tactic | I-A Total Mean App | I-B Total Mean Eff | II-A Female App | II-B Male App | III-A Female Eff | III-B Male Eff |
|---|---|---|---|---|---|---|
| **MOVING INWARD** | 3.78 | 3.58*** | 3.87 | 3.58 | 3.69 | 3.30 |
| IGNORE THE PROBLEM (e.g., wait, assume problem will go away on its own) | 3.83 | 3.45** | 3.88 | 3.63 | 3.57 | 3.17 |
| MINIMIZE THE PROBLEM IN YOUR OWN MIND (e.g., rationalize that the problem is less significant or serious than it actually is) | 3.81 | 3.63 | 3.87 | 3.71 | 3.75 | 3.34 |
| DENY THE PROBLEM (e.g., refuse to acknowledge the problem at all; rationalize alternative explanations for experiences) | 3.00 | 2.91 | 3.07 | 2.86 | 2.94 | 2.89 |
| BLAME YOURSELF (e.g., attribute responsibility for problems to self-actions or perceptions) | 3.01 | 2.55*** | 2.97 | 3.20 | 2.49 | 2.83 |
| SEEK THERAPIES (e.g., invest time and effort in hobbies, drugs, exercise, medicine, therapeutic activities such as massage, meditation, exercise, watching television, Internet) | 4.55 | 4.36* | 4.84 | 3.74** | 4.71 | 3.37*** |
| SEEK MEANING IN GENERAL (e.g., invest time and effort in making sense of your situation, trying to find a reason) | 5.15 | 4.88* | 5.32 | 4.77 | 5.03 | 4.54 |

*(Continued)*

Table 1.1 (Continued)

| Tactic | I-A<br>Total Mean App | I-B<br>Total Mean Eff | II-A<br>Female App | II-B<br>Male App | III-A<br>Female Eff | III-B<br>Male Eff |
|---|---|---|---|---|---|---|
| SEEK MEANING IN CONTEXT (e.g., invest time and effort in religion, philosophy, education, literature) | 4.82 | 4.55** | 4.92 | 4.63 | 4.73 | 4.11 |
| ENGAGE IN SELF-DESTRUCTIVE ESCAPISM (e.g., using drugs or alcohol, doing addictive things, attempting suicide) | 2.08 | 2.27 | 2.11 | 2.06 | 2.34 | 2.11 |
| MOVING OUTWARD | 4.50 | 4.62* | 4.69 | 3.82*** | 4.83 | 4.07* |
| SEEK SYMPATHY FROM OTHERS (e.g., cry, explain personal problems caused by the pursuer) | 4.19 | 4.22 | 4.42 | 3.57** | 4.50 | 3.46** |
| ENGAGE SOCIAL SUPPORT (e.g., seek or obtain emotional or instrumental support from friends, family, counselor) | 5.36 | 5.22 | 5.56 | 4.89* | 5.45 | 4.66* |
| ENGAGE DIRECT INVOLVEMENT OF OTHERS (e.g., seek or obtain protection or deterrence through signals of relationships with or by friends, family, colleagues) | 4.64 | 4.65 | 4.90 | 3.94*** | 4.95 | 3.83*** |
| ENGAGE LEGAL/LAW ENFORCEMENT INPUT (e.g., seek or obtain input from victim's advocate, report to public attorney, police, domestic violence unit, social worker) | 4.29 | 4.61** | 4.55 | 3.57** | 4.73 | 4.37 |

| Tactic | I-A Total Mean App | I-B Total Mean Eff | II-A Female App | II-B Male App | III-A Female Eff | III-B Male Eff |
|---|---|---|---|---|---|---|
| ATTEMPT TO END THE RELATIONSHIP (e.g., claim relationship is over, provide relationship ultimatum or define boundaries) | 5.53 | 5.17** | 5.79 | 4.86* | 5.21 | 5.20 |
| DIMINISH THE SERIOUSNESS OF THE SITUATION (e.g., tease or joke with the pursuer, make light of the pursuer's actions) | 3.74 | 3.62 | 3.82 | 3.57 | 3.64 | 3.66 |
| DECEIVE THE PURSUER (e.g., flirt or hint at interest to get out of immediate situation, arrange or suggest future meetings with no intent to keep date) | 2.60 | 2.82 | 2.63 | 2.57 | 2.77 | 3.09 |
| USE PROBLEM-SOLVING NEGOTIATION (i.e., confront pursuer with responsibility for actions and alternative approaches to achieve objectives) | 4.99 | 4.76** | 5.05 | 4.91 | 4.80 | 4.74 |
| NEGOTIATE RELATIONSHIP DEFINITION (i.e., discuss pursuer's own preferred relationship objectives: e.g., just be friends, reconciliation of previous relationship) | 5.35 | 4.84*** | 5.45 | 5.20 | 4.96 | 4.60 |
| BARGAIN (e.g., offer compromises, promises, or other rewards to get pursuer to alter behavior) | 3.54 | 3.50 | 3.56 | 3.57 | 3.54 | 3.49 |

(Continued)

Table 1.1 (Continued)

| Tactic | I-A<br>Total Mean App | I-B<br>Total Mean Eff | II-A<br>Female App | II-B<br>Male App | III-A<br>Female Eff | III-B<br>Male Eff |
|---|---|---|---|---|---|---|
| ACCEPT PROMISES (e.g., believe or hope that discussions about pursuer behaving more appropriately will work) | 4.11 | 3.61*** | 4.08 | 4.34 | 3.70 | 3.46 |
| MOVING AGAINST | 3.61 | 3.92*** | 3.77 | 3.16** | 3.91 | 4.09 |
| USE VERBAL AGGRESSION (e.g., yell at, criticize, insult, make fun of, show anger, annoyance, frustration, use harsh or hostile voice, write a strongly worded e-mail) | 2.84 | 3.32*** | 2.88 | 2.83 | 3.14 | 4.00* |
| ATTEMPT TO DETER FUTURE BEHAVIOR (e.g., carry air horn or Mace, show weapon, get self-defense training, put security stickers on car and home windows) | 3.96 | 4.24 | 4.22 | 3.21** | 4.33 | 4.06 |
| USE ELECTRONIC RETALIATORY RESPONSES (e.g., sabotaging pursuer's Web site, spamming pursuer's e-mail, sending viruses to pursuer's e-mail) | 2.37 | 2.90*** | 2.44 | 2.20 | 2.81 | 3.26 |
| USE PROTECTIVE RESPONSES TO CURRENT BEHAVIOR (e.g., call police, seek restraining order, press charges, sue) | 4.47 | 4.69 | 4.65 | 4.00* | 4.67 | 4.89 |
| USE ELECTRONIC PROTECTIVE RESPONSES (e.g., contact online service to block e-mail access, enhance firewalls in computer, sabotaging pursuer's Web site) | 4.08 | 4.16 | 4.22 | 3.74 | 4.32 | 3.77 |

| Tactic | I-A<br>Total Mean App | I-B<br>Total Mean Eff | II-A<br>Female App | II-B<br>Male App | III-A<br>Female Eff | III-B<br>Male Eff |
|---|---|---|---|---|---|---|
| ISSUE VERBAL WARNINGS/THREATS (e.g., articulate punishments or sanctions that the pursuer will experience if pursuit continues, threaten with the police or violence) | 3.88 | 4.02 | 4.13 | 3.17** | 4.04 | 4.09 |
| USE PHYSICAL VIOLENCE (e.g., hit, shove, use a weapon, throw an object, blackmail, restrain, beat up) | 2.03 | 2.79*** | 2.04 | 2.06 | 2.46 | 3.91** |
| BUILD A LEGAL CASE (e.g., save voicemail/e-mail, save gifts/notes, keep log of phone calls, try to entrap pursuer) | 4.43 | 4.59 | 4.72 | 3.60*** | 4.71 | 4.34 |
| PURSUE A LEGAL CASE (e.g., sue, swear out a complaint, hire a lawyer, pursue indictment on harassment or stalking charges) | 4.33 | 4.65* | 4.64 | 3.46** | 4.75 | 4.46 |

NOTE: When Levine's test for equality of variances indicated a significant difference in variance, the adjusted $p$ value was used. Correlated $t$ tests were used to compare overall sample ratings (column I-A vs. I-B), and independent $t$ tests were used for the comparisons of male versus female ratings of tactics (columns II-A vs. II-B and III-A vs. III-B).

$*p < .05. **p < .01. ***p < .001.$

*Interpersonal competence* is the perceived ability to interact in a way that is appropriate and effective (Spitzberg, 2000; Spitzberg & Cupach, 1984, 2002b). *Appropriateness* is the perception that a message or message interchange is legitimate or acceptable within the valued rules and expectations of the context in which they are performed. *Effectiveness*, in contrast, is the perception that a message or message interchange has achieved relatively valued objectives for the communicator. Appropriate messages can be ineffective (e.g., being polite in a flirtation situation but not getting the person's phone number), effective messages can be inappropriate (e.g., yelling and name-calling at roommates to clean their room may gain compliance), and of course, some messages are both inappropriate and ineffective (e.g., criticizing a person's appearance in an initial flirtation situation). Optimally competent communication occurs when messages are both appropriate and effective.

Appropriateness and effectiveness are obviously interrelated. The more inappropriate messages are, the less likely they are to be effective. The more ineffective messages are, the more likely they are to be viewed as inappropriate in some sense. In contrast, when a person is appropriate, it is likely to facilitate the evaluation of the person's effectiveness, and vice versa. Thus these are interrelated but distinct dimensions of interpersonal competence.

People generally consider themselves possessed of relatively high levels of communication competence, and in everyday interaction this is probably a reasonable assumption. However, when challenging interpersonal contexts arise (e.g., conflict, assertion, job interviews), competent performance is a far rarer commodity. Unwanted pursuit, with its various face-management dilemmas and disjunctive interests, constitutes a challenging context.

For example, Jason, Reichler, Easton, Neal, and Wilson (1984) interviewed women who had been harassed after a relationship breakup and found that "the more assertive the attempts to end the relationship, the more months women were subjected to harassment ($r = .29$, $p < .05$), and the more frequently the harassment occurred ($r = .39$, $p < .01$), the more threatening ($r = .48$, $p < .01$) and disruptive ($r = .44$, $p < .01$) the effects" (p. 266). Impolite rejection messages tend to produce more guilt and hurt in the receiver (Young, 2002). Cupach and Metts (2002) found that when someone is directly and unilaterally "dumped," the rejected person is more likely to continue to attempt reconciliation than when the relationship is more mutually deescalated. It seems that direct, assertive attempts can backfire. But if direct, assertive responses are not particularly effective, what is? The following study is an attempt to investigate the extent to which various interactional responses to unwanted pursuit are viewed as competent.

## A Study of the Competence of Coping

An online survey was completed by 148 college students (112 females, 35 males, and 1 unidentified) at San Diego State University. The survey consisted of two main sections. The first section asked respondents to consider whether or not they had ever been on the receiving end of a pattern of unwanted pursuit. Specifically, they were prompted to consider the following instruction:

> We are interested specifically in situations in which you already know a person to some extent, and that person seeks to have a MORE INTIMATE relationship with you than you are comfortable having or returning. In such a situation, you are likely to engage in one or more behaviors or communication messages in an attempt to get this person to stop pursuing a relationship with you.

Respondents who could think of such an instance were then prompted to recall that relationship in greater detail. Respondents who could think of no such experience were asked to complete the survey in terms of their perceptions of how one *might* respond to such a relationship.

Respondents were then introduced to two rating scales, one for appropriateness and one for effectiveness. They were instructed that "appropriate behavior shows respect for the other person's views as well as your own, whereas inappropriate behavior violates some rule or expectation about what is supposed to happen. That is, the inappropriate-appropriate rating represents the extent to which the behavior seems to protect, or threaten, the other person's 'face' or desired impression and self-respect." In comparison, "effective behavior accomplishes a person's preferred outcome in a situation, whereas ineffective behavior fails to achieve such preferences. That is, the ineffective-effective rating represents the extent to which the behavior seems to achieve, or fail to achieve, your own personal goals of ending the relationship, or at least stopping the pursuit of greater intimacy." They were then asked to make these judgments on a series of behaviors for attempting to manage or end unwanted relationship pursuit (1 = *very inappropriate*, 7 = *very appropriate*; 1 = *very ineffective*, 7 = *very effective*). Respondents were then presented with 40 pairs of the items in Table 1.1.

The second section of the survey assessed the extent to which the respondent had ever actually been pursued in unwanted ways. This assessment used a list of 11 typical unwanted pursuit behaviors (e.g., followed or spied on you; sent you unsolicited letters or written correspondence; made unsolicited phone calls to you; stood outside your home, school, or workplace; threatened you in some way). For each activity, the respondent answered first whether or not the behavior had ever been experienced in a context of unwanted pursuit (yes or no), and if the answer was yes, respondents were asked to rate the frequency with which it had been experienced (1 = *once*, 2 = *2 to 3 times*, 3 = *4 to 5 times*, 4 = *> 5 times*).

## Results

In this sample of Southern California college students, 74% reported that at some point in their lifetime after the age of 13, "at least one person has engaged in repeated behavior in which she or he was pursuing greater intimacy" with the respondent than the respondent wanted. Among this 74%, 34% reported that this repeated behavior made them "feel afraid or fearful." Of this same group, 31% considered what they experienced to be "stalking." When the entire sample was asked if they had ever been stalked, 35% said yes (37.5% of females, 26% of males).

Table 1.1 displays three sets of comparisons. The first two data columns (I-A and I-B) represent the mean appropriateness and mean effectiveness ratings across the entire sample of each coping tactic and of the average ratings of tactics within each strategy category. The second pair of data columns (II-A and II-B) represent a contrast of female and male ratings of appropriateness of each coping tactic and strategy, whereas the last two columns (III-A and III-B) contrast female and male ratings of tactic and strategy effectiveness.

A few important factors stand out. First, given that these tactics were rated on a 7-point scale, the vast majority of tactics are perceived as low to moderate in competence. The most competent tactics (seek meaning in general, engage social support, control the interaction, distance yourself, attempt to end the relationship, negotiate relationship definition) are just barely above the midpoint of the rating scale. No tactics or strategies are perceived as consistently or highly competent.

Second, the majority of tactics do not differ significantly between their perceived appropriateness or effectiveness. Where differences do occur, however, there are potentially important differences. For example, there is a tendency for people to view moving inward and moving with tactics as more appropriate than effective, and moving outward and moving against as more effective than appropriate. The only moving away tactic that differed in overall ratings was relocation, which was perceived as more effective than appropriate. In general, moving inward and moving against were the least competent, and moving outward, moving away, and moving with tactics and strategies were moderately competent.

Third, across all ratings, when there is a difference between men and women in their perception of competence, women tend to perceive tactics and strategies as more competent than men. This pattern appears to hold for both dimensions of evaluation, except when it comes to aggression. Compared with women, men perceived (a) the use of nonverbal aggression and physical violence as more effective and (b) building or pursuing a legal case as more appropriate.

## Practical Applications: Playing It Safe

At first glance, the implications of the research reviewed and newly reported here are discouraging. Stalking and unwanted pursuit tend to occur over long periods of time *despite* the various forms of resistance enacted by the object of this unwanted pursuit. Victims engage in multiple forms of coping in an effort to manage both their personal and their relational complications created by the campaigns of harassment to which they are subjected. None of these tactics or strategies appears to work consistently in a highly competent manner. There are, however, a number of practical implications that arise from the findings.

First, the research reviewed indicates that involvement of the legal system (Lemmey, 1999; Melton, 2004), whether police or legal action (e.g., restraining order, seeking prosecution), tends to decrease the level of pursuit. Specifically, restraining orders are unlikely to exacerbate the harassment and appear to work about half the time. Prior research indicates that restraining orders lower the risk of violence among victims (McFarlane et al., 2004; Meloy, Cowett, Parker, Hofland, & Friedland, 1997). In this sample, using protective responses (including restraining orders) was perceived as moderately competent. Thus although involvement of the legal system carries certain risks, it appears on balance to be a safer move than not involving the legal system.

Second, females tend to perceive almost all tactics of managing unwanted pursuit as more competent than males do, with the exception of aggression. In general, males are enculturated to pursue heterosexual romantic relationships and females are enculturated to be highly selective in determining which pursuers gain access to sexual intimacy (Metts & Spitzberg, 1996). Under this assumption, females would tend to perceive resistance behaviors as more competent in courtship contexts, whereas males would view them as less competent. For the most part, our results agree with this societal script. The practical implication is that females may assume the competence of various tactics, not realizing that sometimes they need to short-circuit the courtship process by jumping to more extreme tactics (e.g., moving away, moving against) earlier and more directly. By relying on standard scripts, women may attempt to preserve their own appearance of competence at the cost of prolonging the unwanted pursuit.

Third, given that most unwanted pursuit emerges from preexisting relationships, in which some level of intimacy can often be assumed, the process of ending the relationship may be prolonged in part because of a tendency to "let the person down easy" or to "preserve a friendship." Such objectives are laudable and may well work much of the time in normal relationships, but in unwanted pursuit relationships, a more direct and resolute approach to relationship termination is likely to be more effective, even if it is not perceived as more appropriate. The most consistent advice from experienced security consultants as well as scholars essentially boils down to three recommendations: harden the target, keep others apprised, and avoid the pursuer as completely as possible.

*Hardening the target* involves enhancing one's security and invisibility. Getting unlisted phone numbers, changing to a post office box instead of a publicly accessible mailbox, changing locks, using caution in letting personal information out (including, for example, what information is provided on a Web site like MySpace.com), and investing in a security system all represent tactics of moving away, limiting the interactional access that the pursuer has to a victim's life.

*Keeping others apprised* involves systematic notification of one's social and occupational networks as well as notification of law enforcement. Let friends, family, coworkers, school administrators, gym staff, and so forth know that the pursuer is a persona non grata. Give them a photograph of the person if available. Report any specific acts of harassment to police so a file can be started. Keep meticulous records, or even keep a diary of the events and episodes, so that notification can proceed with detail and credibility.

*Avoidance* involves shutting the interaction down to an absolute minimum. At some point a clear, concise, and extremely direct message needs to be sent indicating that "this relationship is over and no further contact of any kind is appropriate. If further contact is attempted, law enforcement will be contacted." After the delivery of such a message, all efforts by the pursuer at engaging in interaction should then be treated by the victim as episodes to avoid or shut down as completely as possible. Do not answer phone calls, IM, or e-mails. Do not return messages or items left on doorsteps or windshields. If the person appears, ignore the person, turn away, do not engage in interaction, and do not attempt to account for such behavior. Simply treat the pursuer as a nonentity as much as possible.

Such tactics, all of which are extensions of the moving away strategy, may seem harsh and lacking in appropriateness, especially in the context of a previously intimate relationship. Furthermore, their collective effectiveness is not really known. They do, however, represent much of the collective wisdom of practitioners, counselors, law enforcement, and scholars. The communicative problematic of such behavior is obvious—we are enculturated not to be rude or incompetent. We are taught to be polite and engage others who seek to communicate with us. When such communication turns coercive and harassing, however, it may be worthwhile to accept a more severe communicative ethic of denial of access and systematic avoidance, backed by the prospect of third-party or legal intervention. Just as it has become vital in sexual compliance-gaining situations for "no" to mean "no," it becomes vital that in relationships "no more" means "no more." For such meanings to be commonly accepted, cultural practices and expectations will need to change, and such changes begin at the personal and interpersonal level.

# References

Baumeister, R. F., Wotman, S. R., & Stillwell, A. M. (1993). Unrequited love: On heartbreak, anger, guilt, scriptlessness, and humiliation. *Journal of Personality and Social Psychology, 64,* 377–394.

Bjerregaard, B. (2000). An empirical study of stalking victimization. *Violence and Victims, 15,* 389–406.

Blackburn, E. J. (1999). *"Forever yours": Rates of stalking victimization, risk factors and traumatic responses among college women.* Unpublished doctoral dissertation, University of Massachusetts, Boston.

Brewster, M. P. (2001). Legal help-seeking experiences of former intimate-stalking victims. *Criminal Justice Policy Review, 12,* 91–112.

Brewster, M. P. (2003). The criminal justice system's response to stalking. In M. P. Brewster (Ed.), *Stalking: Psychology, risk factors, interventions, and law* (pp. 207–217). Kingston, NJ: Civic Research Institute.

Cupach, W. R., & Metts, S. (2002, July). *The persistence of reconciliation attempts following the dissolution of romantic relationships.* Paper presented at the 11th International Conference on Personal Relationships, Dalhousie University, Halifax, Nova Scotia, Canada.

Cupach, W. R., & Spitzberg, B. H. (1998). Obsessive relational intrusion and stalking. In B. H. Spitzberg & W. R. Cupach (Eds.), *The dark side of close relationships* (pp. 233–263). Mahwah, NJ: Lawrence Erlbaum.

Cupach, W. R., & Spitzberg, B. H. (2004). *The dark side of relationship pursuit: From attraction to obsession and stalking.* Mahwah, NJ: Lawrence Erlbaum.

Dunn, J. L. (1999). What love has to do with it: The cultural construction of emotion and sorority women's responses to forcible interaction. *Social Problems, 46,* 440–459.

Dunn, J. L. (2002). *Courting disaster: Intimate stalking, culture, and criminal justice.* New York: Aldine de Gruyter.

Dussuyer, I. (2000, December). *Is stalking legislation effective in protecting victims?* Paper presented to the Criminal Justice Responses Conference, Australian Institute of Criminology, Sydney, Australia.

Dutton-Greene, L. B., & Winstead, B. A. (2001, July). *Factors associated with the occurrence and cessation of obsessive relational intrusion.* Paper presented at the joint conference of the International Network on Personal Relationships and the International Society for the Study of Personal Relationships, Prescott, AZ.

Emerson, R. M., Ferris, K. O., & Gardner, C. B. (1998). On being stalked. *Social Problems, 45,* 289–314.

Folkes, V. S. (1982). Communicating the reasons for social rejection. *Journal of Experimental Social Psychology, 18,* 235–252.

Goffman, E. (1959). *The presentation of self in everyday life.* Garden City, NY: Doubleday.

Jason, L. A., Reichler, A., Easton, J., Neal, A., & Wilson, M. (1984). Female harassment after ending a relationship: A preliminary study. *Alternative Lifestyles, 6,* 259–269.

Lemmey, D. (1999). *Stalking of battered women before and after seeking criminal justice help.* Unpublished doctoral dissertation, Nursing Program, Texas Women's University, Denton.

McFarlane, J., Malecha, A., Gist, J., Watson, K., Batten, E., Hall, I., et al. (2004). Protection orders and intimate partner violence: An 18-month study of 150 black, Hispanic, and white women. *American Journal of Public Health, 94,* 613–618.

Mechanic, M. B., Weaver, T. L., & Resick, P. A. (2000). Intimate partner violence and stalking behavior: Exploration of patterns and correlates in a sample of acutely battered women. *Violence and Victims, 15,* 55–72.

Meloy, J. R., Cowett, P. Y., Parker, S. B., Hofland, B., & Friedland, A. (1997). Domestic protection orders and the prediction of subsequent criminality and violence toward protectees. *Psychotherapy, 34,* 447–458.

Melton, H. C. (2004). Stalking in the context of domestic violence: Findings on the criminal justice system. *Women & Criminal Justice, 15,* 33–58.

Metts, S., Cupach, W. R., & Imahori, T. T. (1992). Perceptions of sexual compliance-resisting messages in three types of cross-sex relationships. *Western Journal of Speech Communication, 56,* 1–17.

Metts, S., & Spitzberg, B. H. (1996). Sexual communication: A script-based approach. In B. R. Burleson (Ed.), *Communication yearbook 19* (pp. 49–92). Thousand Oaks, CA: Sage.

Sheridan, L. (2001). The course and nature of stalking: An in-depth victim survey. *Journal of Threat Assessment, 1,* 61–79.

Sheridan, L., Davies, G. M., & Boon, J. C. (2001). The course and nature of stalking: A victim perspective. *Howard Journal of Criminal Justice, 40,* 215–234.

Sheridan, L., Gillett, R., Davies, G. M., Blaauw, E., & Patel, D. (2003). "There's no smoke without fire": Are male ex-partners perceived as more "entitled" to stalk than acquaintance or stranger stalkers? *British Journal of Psychology, 94,* 87–98.

Spitzberg, B. H. (2000). What is good communication? *Journal of the Association for Communication Administration, 29,* 103–119.

Spitzberg, B. H. (2002a). In the shadow of the stalker: The problem of policing unwanted pursuit. In H. Giles (Ed.), *Law enforcement, communication, and the community* (pp. 173–200). Amsterdam: John Benjamins.

Spitzberg, B. H. (2002b). The tactical topography of stalking victimization and management. *Trauma, Violence, & Abuse, 3,* 261–288.

Spitzberg, B. H. (2006, June). *Policing unwanted pursuit.* Paper presented at the International Communication Association Conference, Dresden, Germany.

Spitzberg, B. H., & Cupach, W. R. (1984). *Interpersonal communication competence.* Beverly Hills, CA: Sage.

Spitzberg, B. H., & Cupach, W. R. (2001). Paradoxes of pursuit: Toward a relational model of stalking-related phenomena. In J. Davis (Ed.), *Stalking crimes and victim protection: Prevention, intervention, threat assessment, and case management* (pp. 97–136). Boca Raton, FL: CRC Press.

Spitzberg, B. H., & Cupach, W. R. (2002a). The inappropriateness of relational intrusion. In R. Goodwin & D. Cramer (Eds.), *Inappropriate relationships: The unconventional, the disapproved, and the forbidden* (pp. 191–219). Mahwah, NJ: Lawrence Erlbaum.

Spitzberg, B. H., & Cupach, W. R. (2002b). Interpersonal skills. In M. L. Knapp & J. R. Daly (Eds.), *Handbook of interpersonal communication* (3rd ed., pp. 564–611). Newbury Park, CA: Sage.

Spitzberg, B. H., & Cupach, W. R. (2003). What mad pursuit? Obsessive relational intrusion and stalking-related phenomena. *Aggression and Violent Behavior: A Review Journal, 8,* 345–375.

Spitzberg, B. H., & Cupach, W. R. (2007). The state of the art of stalking: Taking stock of the emerging literature. *Aggression and Violent Behavior: A Review Journal, 12,* 64–86.

Spitzberg, B. H., & Rhea, J. (1999). Obsessive relational intrusion and sexual coercion victimization. *Journal of Interpersonal Violence, 14,* 3–20.

Tashiro, T., & Frazier, P. (2003). "I'll never be in a relationship like that again": Personal growth following romantic relationship breakups. *Personal Relationships, 10,* 113–128.

Tjaden, P., & Thoennes, N. (1998). *Stalking in America: Findings from the National Violence Against Women Survey.* Washington, DC: National Institute of Justice and Centers for Disease Control and Prevention (NCJ 169592).

Walby, S., & Allen, J. (2004, March). *Domestic violence, sexual assault and stalking: Findings from the British Crime Survey* (Home Office Research Study 276). London: Home Office Research, Development and Statistics Directorate.

Young, S. L. (2002, February). *Receiving rejection messages: Responses to perceived expectancy violations in communication about unrequited love.* Paper presented to the Western States Communication Association Conference, Long Beach, CA.

# 2

# Conditions That Determine the Fate of Friendships After Unrequited Romantic Disclosures

*Michael T. Motley*

*Larissa J. Faulkner*

*Heidi Reeder*

When one discloses romantic feelings to another and the partner recip-
rocates, there is the presumed potential for a blissful relationship. But
what if one discloses romantic inclinations that are not mutually felt? If the disclosing partner views the situation as "all or nothing," the relationship most
likely dissolves. But if the partners wish to maintain the relationship much as it
was before the unrequited disclosure, the outcome is much less certain. Usually,
the friendship dissolves shortly thereafter (Werking, 1997). But not always.

Thus it should be worthwhile to discover the factors that account for the
subsequent fate of the relationship. This is especially so if some of these are factors that can be controlled via communication behaviors of the partners themselves in order to facilitate a satisfactory outcome. The present study is an
initial investigation of the factors by which partners may affect the fate of their
friendship after an unrequited romantic disclosure.

The pervasion of unrequited romance episodes is suggested by our cultural
lore as well as by the limited formal research on the subject (e.g., Baumeister,
Wotman, & Stillwell, 1993). And it seems likely that these episodes will increase
in frequency within contemporary society. Male/female friendships are becoming more common as men and women interact more frequently via gender

heterogeneity in college classes, social activities, and work settings and as marriage is taking place at later ages. And what begins as friendship sometimes comes to feel romantic to at least one partner. Indeed, it may be expected that romantic or sexual attraction by at least one partner will develop in at least 10% to 40% of cross-sex friendships (e.g., Monsour, Harris, & Kurzwell, 1994) and that the attraction will be one-way in many of these cases (e.g., Baumeister et al., 1993).

It is clear also that the discovery of unrequited romantic attraction within friendships is problematic. Indeed, the decision of whether and how to disclose romantic feelings in an ostensibly platonic friendship is among the most common "serious communication dilemmas" reported by college students (Motley, 1992).

Presumably, one of the reasons that it is often difficult to discuss one's feelings within an evolving relationship is that we recognize the possibility and potential awkwardness of asymmetry. And this is almost certainly the case when romantic feelings develop within a friendship. The romantically inclined partner may recognize that, should the feelings not be mutual, rejection by a friend could be even more unpleasant than usual. Similarly, while rejecting another's romantic feelings is usually unpleasant, it should be especially so when rejecting a friend (e.g., Kenny & Nasby, 1980). Of course, another way in which unrequited romantic attraction is even more problematic within friendships than otherwise is that the awkwardness of the disclosure and rejection threatens the friendship. Indeed, many who have experienced these episodes consider the loss of the friendship to have been more unfortunate than the rejection of romantic feelings (Baumeister et al., 1993).

But while unrequited romantic disclosures within friendships usually ruin the friendship (Werking, 1997), this outcome need not be automatic. It should be possible, if both partners so desire, to return—albeit perhaps after a short period of awkwardness—to some variation of the friendship that existed before the disclosure. In the case of unrequited romance that emerges from satisfactory friendships, one would think that reestablishing and continuing the friendship usually would be desirable. It is curious, therefore, that the outcome is usually negative. Certainly, it could be valuable to discover what factors account for the exceptions where friendships are maintained.

An observation by Baumeister et al. (1993) may partially explain the negative outcomes in these situations and at the same time suggests another likely reason for the reluctance to disclose romantic feelings when symmetry is uncertain: while films, novels, and songs provide many examples of "scripts" for how to enact mutual love, there are few available scripts or templates for how to behave in unrequited romance situations. Granted, Baumeister et al. show a few scripts to be available for the rejected would-be lover, but a close inspection of their examples reveals all of these to be of the negative variety of relationship dissolution. It appears that no scripts are available to help the unrequited lover who may want to repair or maintain an earlier form of the relationship. And in the case of the rejector, again there are virtually no models or scripts of any kind—relationship repair or otherwise (Baumeister et al., 1993). Given the absence of relevant scripts and socialization, it is not surprising that romantic disclosures within friendships are approached with trepidation nor surprising that they often destroy the friendship.

In summary, unrequited romantic attraction within ostensible friendships is common and becoming more so. And it is problematic, both before the disclosure and after, largely because of potential damage to the friendship. A dissolved friendship is indeed the most common outcome, probably due largely to the absence of scripts or other socializations for handling these inherently awkward episodes. But the fact that some friendships do survive unrequited romantic attraction suggests that some partners are able to improvise effective repair and maintenance behaviors. If it happens that partners within friendships that last employ different communication strategies and behaviors than partners within friendships that dissolve, then those differences could provide a foundation for relevant friendship-maintenance scripts in unrequited romance situations. Thus, it should be worthwhile to ask the following:

*Research Question: What behaviors differentiate friendships that dissolve after unrequited romantic disclosures from those that survive?*

We will be examining friendships wherein *romantic attraction has developed* in one partner, *is disclosed,* and *is not reciprocated.* And within this unrequited-romantic-disclosure context, we will compare friendships that *dissolve* with those that *last* after the asymmetry is discovered.

The study is driven in large part by a pragmatic, applied interest in the common problem of unrequited romantic attraction within ostensible friendships. That is to say, from the perspective of friendship partners, the study ideally would answer the question of how best to enact communication and other relational behaviors in order to maintain a friendship after an unrequited-romantic-disclosure episode. That is, the study might begin to fill the void of viable scripts or guidelines for unrequited-romantic-disclosure situations. Similarly, from the perspective of relationship researchers, the study attempts to determine the factors that affect the fate of friendships within the specific context of unrequited romantic attraction. We would expect that some of these may parallel general friendship repair behaviors, while others may be unique to the unrequited-romantic-attraction situation. The study intentionally explores the latter possibility, eschewing a priori predictions from research on more general relational or friendship repair contexts, per the assumption that applied-communication problems usually demand context-specific research (e.g., Motley, 1997) and per observations that relational maintenance strategies vary situationally (Jaesub, 1998).

The typical procedure in friendship maintenance/repair studies is to ask participants what they would do, hypothetically, to maintain or repair a friendship under various independent-variable conditions, with participants' selection of a priori strategies as the dependent variable. The present study draws instead on participants' actual experience with their own naturally generated strategies or behaviors. Our assumption was that if relational maintenance strategies are often context-specific, then the unrequited-romantic-disclosure context may be sufficiently unique to warrant a more exploratory approach. Moreover, while it is common in studies of scripts to ignore efficacy as a primary concern (e.g., Battaglia, Richard, Datteri, & Lord, 1998; Rose & Frieze, 1993), the present study attempts to determine whether promising scripts can be generated by identifying behaviors reported to have been effective within real-life situations.

## Method

OVERVIEW

The study is reported in two main parts. Part I was a preliminary examination, via open-ended questionnaire, of the factors that participants considered to have been crucial to the fate of the friendship after a recent unrequited-romantic-disclosure episode. From participants' responses, several conditions were identified as perceived "causes" of the friendships having lasted or dissolved. These conditions became the basis for Part II (in three subparts), wherein new participants reported on a past unrequited-romantic-disclosure episode within an ostensibly platonic friendship. In Part II.A, participants reported on the relative presence of the conditions generated by Part I. Part II.B sought the same participants' impressions of the relative importance of the conditions' presence or absence in determining the eventual fate of the friendship. Part II.C used open-ended items to seek the same participants' identification of specific verbal and nonverbal behaviors by which the various conditions were manifested.

In all parts of the study, participants reported via questionnaire on various characteristics of a single recent relationship—an ostensibly platonic male/female friendship[1] wherein one partner disclosed romantic inclinations that were not mutual for the other partner. We were interested from the outset, of course, in contrasts between behaviors within friendships that lasted after the unrequited disclosure versus behaviors within friendships that did not. But we were interested also in separating the behaviors of the romantically inclined versus platonically inclined partners, on the assumption that their perspectives might not agree. Thus each participant reported on a recent relationship for one of the following target situations:

1. *Participant disclosed* romantic inclinations; partner's feelings were platonic; friendship *lasted.*

2. Partner disclosed romantic inclinations; *participant's feelings were platonic;* friendship *lasted.*

3. *Participant disclosed* romantic inclinations; partner's feelings were platonic; friendship *dissolved.*

4. Partner disclosed romantic inclinations; *participant's feelings were platonic;* friendship *dissolved.*

## PART I

Part I was an exploratory effort to identify the behaviors critical to the fate (lasted/dissolved) of the friendships, so that these could be used as a priori variables in Part II. A simple questionnaire asked participants ($N = 90$ college students similar to those described below) to recall a single recent instance of one of the four target situations and to explain in open-ended fashion the main factors they believed to have been responsible for the friendship having lasted or dissolved after the unrequited disclosure. Participants who had experienced none of the target situations were dismissed. Those who had experienced more than one situation reported on only one—this selected by the experimenters to ensure roughly equivalent representation across the four situations.

Participants offered 153 explanations of factors responsible for the fates of their friendships. These were coded into various common groups or categories, using Strauss and Corbin's (1990) open-coding procedure, and the usable categories were employed in Part II as potential variables or conditions for more direct comparisons across the four target situations.[2]

While the study is especially interested in verbal and nonverbal *behaviors* critical to the fate of these postdisclosure friendships, Part I unexpectedly yielded virtually no specific behaviors as explanations for the fate of the friendships. Instead, explanations were in the form of what we will call *conditions,* or features, of the experience—for example, the presence or absence of perceived pressure to change one's feelings after the disclosures or the perception that the partner could (or could not) handle the asymmetry. Seventeen conditions emerged from the coding process. A complete list of these is presented below within the report on Part II. Related *behaviors* are pursued in Part II as well.

## PART II

### Participants

Participants in Part II were 140 native-English-speaking students of various communication courses (all levels) at the  University of California,

Davis. Participants were assigned to groups corresponding to one of the four target situations on the basis of a simple screening questionnaire asking, yes/no, whether the participant had experienced any of the four target situations within the past 3 years. Those who could not identify with any of the situations were dismissed. Participants who identified with only one situation were assigned to the corresponding group. Those who identified with more than one situation were assigned randomly to one of the relevant groups. Group *n*'s were as follows: (a) participant *romantically* inclined, friendship *lasted, n* = 32; (b) participant *platonic,* friendship *lasted, n* = 37; (c) participant *romantic,* friendship *dissolved, n* = 23; (d) participant *platonic,* friendship *dissolved, n* = 48.[3]

### Questionnaire

Participants completed questionnaires that were identical across groups except for minor editing to fit the four target situations.[4] Primary questionnaire items investigated three matters:

*Subpart A.* Questions sought perceptions of the relative presence or absence of the various conditions identified by Part I as being central to the fate of friendships in unrequited-romantic-disclosure situations. Seventeen potential conditions were investigated. For example, "After your partner's disclosure, did you *feel pressured to act or feel differently than before?*" (Remaining condition items are presented in Table 2.1.) Responses were via 7-point, *definitely-no/definitely-yes* scales.

*Subpart B.* Each of these questions had a companion item to assess the following: "*How big a role did this play in the fact that the friendship [lasted/dissolved]?*" Responses were via a 7-point scale—*definitely [did NOT/DID]* play a role.

*Subpart C.* Each of these sets included one or more open-ended items asking what verbal or nonverbal behaviors promoted or manifested the presence or absence of the condition, for example, "*Regardless of your answer to [Part A], can you recall anything in particular that your partner said or did (or didn't say or do) that made you feel any pressure to change? If so, please describe it here.*" And "*. . . that reduced any pressure for you to change.*"

### Analysis—Part II

For Part II.A the question was, in effect, which conditions would be identified as present or absent when participants were asked to consider all of them as a priori items, and for which conditions there was a difference between lasted or dissolved outcomes or between romantic or platonic partners' perspectives. Thus, a two-way ANOVA (Outcome × Viewpoint) was performed on the relative presence reported for each condition.

*Results and Discussion—Part II.A*

The conditions alluded to above are listed in Table 2.1, along with results of their ANOVA comparisons. Notice first that for most of these variables, the main effect on the outcome variable was statistically significant. That is to say, for most cases, the presence or absence of the condition was significantly different between the friendship-lasted and the friendship-dissolved situations. For the perspective variable—that is, responses by romantically versus platonically inclined partners—significant main effects were observed for a few conditions, as well.

Conditions that are significantly more prominent when the postdisclosure friendships *lasted* than when they dissolved include the following: (a) the platonic partner actively pursued the friendship after the unrequited disclosure; (b) likewise for the romantically inclined partner; (c) the platonic partner truly wanted to remain friends despite the asymmetry; (d) likewise for the romantic; (e) the relationship had a solid foundation of openness and honesty prior to the disclosure; (f) the friendship was solid or long established prior to the disclosure; and (g) the romantically inclined partner was able to accept (i.e., could "handle it") that the romantic feelings were not mutual.

Conditions that are significantly more prominent in friendships that *dissolved* include the following: (a) the platonic partner felt embarrassed or awkward around the other; (b) likewise for the romantic partner; (c) the romantically inclined partner was hurt that the feelings were not mutual; and (d) the platonic partner felt pressured to act differently after the disclosure than before.

In short, this phase of the study confirmed a number of differences between postdisclosure friendships that last and those that dissolve with respect to the relative presence of the target conditions. For most of these conditions, the difference is significant across lasted and dissolved friendships on the whole, and that was the primary question. In a few cases, moreover, the relative presence of the condition varies according to the partner's perspective or according to viewpoint/outcome interactions, and some of these differences shed additional light on contrasts between postdisclosure friendships that last and those that dissolve.

*Part II.B*

The fact that conditions differ between postdisclosure friendships that last and those that dissolve does not necessarily mean that the differences are indeed responsible for the fate of the friendship. While it would be very difficult to test directly whether these conditions *cause* postdisclosure friendships to last or dissolve, it is feasible to at least examine participants' impressions of the effects. This was the objective in the next phase of the study, Part II.B.

**Table 2.1**    ANOVA Results and Correlations Between Relative Presence of Condition and Its Perceived Role in the Fate of Friendship

| Condition | F(1, 118) Outcome | | F(1, 118) Viewpoint | | Correlations Dissolved Friendships | | Correlations Lasted Friendships | |
|---|---|---|---|---|---|---|---|---|
| | D > L | L > D | R > P | P > R | R-D (df = 21) | P-D (df = 46) | R-L (df = 30) | P-L (df = 35) |
| 1. P actively pursued the friendship after the episode | | ** | | | −.69** | −.67** | .80** | .52** |
| 2. P honestly wanted to remain friends after the episode | | ** | | | −.29 | −.72** | .77** | .70** |
| 3. P later felt uncomfortable, embarrassed, or awkward around R | ** | | | | .80** | .69** | −.41* | −.46** |
| 4. R actively pursued the friendship after the episode | | ** | | | −.02 | −.43** | .72** | .66** |
| 5. R honestly wanted to remain friends after the episode | | ** | | | −.50** | −.49** | .61** | .87** |
| 6. The relationship had a solid foundation of openness and honesty prior to R's disclosure | | ** | | | −.26 | −.39** | .62** | .68** |
| 7. R later felt uncomfortable, embarrassed, or awkward around P | ** | | | | .93** | .34* | −.38* | −.45** |
| 8. R accepted that it wasn't mutual; could "handle it" | | ** | ** | | −.52** | −.58** | .10 | .49** |
| 9. After the disclosure, P felt pressured to act or feel differently than before | ** | | | ** | .84** | .74** | −.33* | −.44** |
| 10. The friendship was strong, solid, or long established before R's disclosure | | ** | | | −.19 | −.39** | .72** | .79** |

| Condition | F(1, 118) Outcome D > L | F(1, 118) Outcome L > D | F(1, 118) Viewpoint R > P | F(1, 118) Viewpoint P > R | Correlations Dissolved Friendships R-D (df = 21) | Correlations Dissolved Friendships P-D (df = 46) | Correlations Lasted Friendships R-L (df = 30) | Correlations Lasted Friendships P-L (df = 35) |
|---|---|---|---|---|---|---|---|---|
| 11. R was hurt to discover that the feelings were not mutual | * | | | | .50** | .52** | −.54** | −.49** |
| 12. P had "led R on" before the disclosure | | | | ** | .38* | .43** | .05 | −.30* |
| 13. P accepted it; could "handle it" | | | | * | −.42* | −.31* | .50** | .46** |
| 14. After the episode, R still pursued a romantic relationship | | | | | .47* | .61** | −.36* | −.41* |
| 15. P "led R on" after the disclosure | | | | | .78** | .30* | .35* | −.11 |
| 16. R continued to hope that P would develop mutual romantic feelings | | | | | .11 | .43** | −.04 | −.24 |
| 17. There was frequent contact between P and R via mutual friends, work, and so on | | | | | .45* | −.16 | .69** | .50** |

NOTE: Most ANOVA means were in the 3.9–5.6 range (7-point scale; 1 = *definitely no*, 7 = *definitely yes*). Means available upon request. P = platonically inclined partner, R = romantically inclined partner, D = dissolved friendship, L = lasted friendship. (Positive correlation indicates perception of *larger* role in L or D fate when condition is *present*; negative correlation indicates perception of larger role when condition is *absent*.)

Correlations via Pearson r; *p < .05. **p < .01.

*Analysis—Part II.B*

Recall that after asking whether the above conditions were present or absent, the questionnaire asked the participants' impressions of the role this played in determining the fate of the friendship. For example, the questionnaire item *"After your partner's disclosure, did you feel pressured to act or feel differently than before? [1–7 scale]"* was followed immediately by *"How big a role do you think this . . . played in the fact that the friendship [lasted/dissolved]? [1–7 scale]."* The idea was to examine correlations between these two items for each of the conditions. Strong positive correlations would correspond to a condition being perceived as playing a larger role when present; negative correlations would correspond to a larger role when absent.

*Results and Discussion—Part II.B*

Correlation results are presented in Table 2.1. Notice that for every condition that yielded a significant outcome main effect earlier (Table 2.1, ##1–11), significant correlations are found in at least three of the four target situations, and with the expected polarities. That is to say, these conditions were perceived as having influenced the fate of the friendship, and in all cases the direction of the influence is as would be expected. For example, we saw earlier that the platonic partner's active pursuit of the friendship was fairly strong in friendships that lasted, and we see now that the strong pursuit is perceived to have played a large role in that outcome (i.e., via the positive correlations for Table 2.1, #1). In dissolved friendships, however, the platonic partners' pursuit of the friendship apparently was relatively weak, and this weak pursuit was perceived to have been influential for the friendship dissolving (i.e., negative correlations for Table 2.1, #1). And so on for at least conditions 1–11 of Table 2.1.

To summarize these results, the following conditions are perceived as having a "positive" effect on the fate of friendships after unrequited romantic disclosures (i.e., both their relative *presence in lasting friendships* and their relative *absence in dissolved friendships* are perceived as having played a large role in those outcomes): the romantically inclined partner (a) actively pursued the friendship, (b) honestly wanted to remain friends, and (c) accepted that the feelings were not mutual; the platonically inclined partner (d) actively pursued the friendship, (e) honestly wanted to remain friends, and (f) was able to accept the asymmetry; and the friendship itself (g) had been solid and (h) had been open before the episode (namely, Table 2.1, ##4, 5, 8, 1, 2, 13, 10, and 6, respectively).

The following conditions appear to have a "negative" effect on the fate of postdisclosure friendships (i.e., both their relative *presence in dissolved* friendships and their relative *absence in continued* friendships were perceived to have played a large role in those outcomes): the platonically inclined partner (a) was embarrassed or awkward after the disclosure, (b) felt pressured to change after the episode, and (c) seemed to have "led on" his or her partner before the disclosure; the romantically inclined partner (d) was embarrassed or uncomfortable after the episode, (e) was hurt that the feelings were not mutual, (f) appeared to have continued to push for a romantic relationship, and (g) continued to hope that his or her partner would develop romantic feelings (Table 2.1, ##3, 9, 12, 7, 11, 14, and 16, respectively).

Curiously, there are two conditions whose presence is positively correlated both to friendships having dissolved and to friendships having lasted: first, for the romantically inclined partner to have been led on *after* the disclosure/ rejection episode is perceived to have affected the outcome of both continued and dissolved friendships (data in subsequent phases of the study will account for this by suggesting that partners were led on in different ways for the lasted and dissolved situations), and second, involuntary contact between the partners was perceived to have contributed to the outcome by participants in both outcome groups. Probably the involuntary contact itself plays more a supporting role than a primary role, exacerbating the awkwardness or facilitating the repair, depending upon how the other conditions are played out.

The perceived causal conditions of Table 2.1 are not necessarily true causal conditions, of course. Indeed, the attributions may be suspect in a few cases. One might postulate, for example, that when partners truly want to remain friends after unrequited romantic disclosures, this does indeed help the friendship to survive the event (e.g., Table 2.1, ##2 and 5). But one may just as easily explain the correlation by speculating that participants who look back on failed friendships might be inclined to rationalize, post hoc, that a desire for friendship was weak on their part or their partner's and to assign a major outcome role to what might be a false recollection.

Moreover, even when the attributed causal conditions are intuitively sensible, there are sometimes competing interpretations. For example, let us assume that participants are accurate in having perceived a causal link between a well-established and solid predisclosure friendship and its postdisclosure endurance (e.g., Table 2.1, #10). We may wonder whether this is because relational foundation and history help a friendship to weather an uncomfortable unrequited disclosure episode, or whether it makes the episode less uncomfortable, or whether it makes the platonically inclined partner more likely to anticipate and prepare for the disclosure, or any combination of these and perhaps other possibilities.

In most cases, however, the causal attributions of Table 2.1 seem to be fairly unambiguous. It stands to reason, for example, that active postdisclosure pursuit of the friendship would be recalled with reasonable clarity and that it would indeed help to repair or sustain the friendship (i.e., Table 2.1, ##1 and 4). Most of the causal attributions appear to be similarly straightforward.

The results reflect participants' perceptions of reality rather than experimenter-manipulated or experimenter-observed reality, of course. Certainly, however, there is a sense in which participants' perceptions of the corresponding conditions are almost certainly critical to the fate of the friendship. For example, one's *perception* of how well the partner is accepting the asymmetry situation may be at least as important as his or her *true* coping abilities, which is also the case for perceptions of the partner's postdisclosure discomfort, pressure to change toward symmetry, and so on.

Thus far, the study identifies conditions perceived to have positive and negative influences on friendships after unrequited romantic disclosure episodes. But this provides only part of the answer to either the researcher who wants to understand friendship repair within the unrequited romantic disclosure context or to the individual who finds himself or herself in a corresponding real-life situation.

It is not uncommon for practical implications of communication research to operate at the level of conditions, attitudes, general objectives, and so forth. And sometimes that may be necessary and appropriate. But within the present study, it is one thing to know which *conditions* have positive and negative effects but quite another to know how these conditions are *manifested* between partners. For example, when we find ourselves in a real-life unrequited-romantic-disclosure situation, it may be comforting to know that we are indeed able to handle the situation, do indeed wish to retain the friendship, and so forth. According to Part II.B, all of these conditions are thought to be helpful if the friendship is to be repaired and maintained.

But the simple presence of these conditions may not be enough to affect the outcome. Presumably, these conditions need to be communicated to, or least manifested to, our partner. And presumably this is done not via mere internalization of the conditions but rather via overt *behaviors* of some sort. The next phase of the study tries to identify those behaviors.

### Part II.C

As suggested earlier, although we were seeking critical behaviors in Part I, participants reported conditions instead. Parts II.A and II.B have examined the extent to which those conditions appear to be critical. Part II.C attempts to identify the specific verbal and nonverbal *behaviors* by which the critical conditions are promoted, manifested, and communicated between partners in unrequited-romantic-attraction episodes.

### Analysis—Part II.C

Recall that the questionnaire included open-ended items seeking information on how each condition is manifested and communicated. Most of the items were designed to be completed independently of participants' responses on companion parts. For example, *"[Regardless of your answer to the companion items] can you recall anything in particular that your partner said or did (or didn't say or do) that made you feel any pressure to change? If so, please describe it here*" and "*Likewise, can you recall anything in particular . . . that reduced any pressure for you to change? If so, please describe it here.*" The strategy was to collect relevant behavioral manifestations from participants regardless of their presence or absence or role responses.

In all, the questionnaire asked for behaviors associated with 26 conditions— the 17 conditions of Table 2.1, plus variations.[5] (These will be presented via Table 2.3.) The 141 participants provided a total of 1,750 comments describing or identifying relevant behaviors.[6] These were coded by one of the coauthors into 33 categories using Strauss and Corbin's (1990) open-coding procedure and verified by another coauthor with 98% agreement (41 codings challenged). The coders reached agreement on revised codings for all but eight of the challenged items, and a third coder resolved these. The resulting behavior categories are presented in Table 2.2, along with examples and total frequencies of occurrence (e.g., frequencies across all conditions and situations).

Table 2.2      Behavior Manifestation Categories and Examples

---

A. **Disclosure re past relationships** ($f = 9$). *We were very candid and open about things like past lovers.*

B. **Spent a lot of time together** ($f = 12$). *We had spent quite a bit of time together up to that point.*

C. **Honesty, high disclosure (personal disclosure), open re "everything," feelings, personal things, etc.** ($f = 40$). *We'd tell each other everything.*

D. **The rejection itself (P said there was/would be no romantic feelings)** ($f = 93$). *That I told him that I wanted to just be friends./I told him I appreciated his roses and stuff but I wasn't interested.*

E. **Partners treated one another as very good friends do: special favors, supported each other, made sacrifices, etc.** ($f = 68$). *He had concern for my well-being./Just him being there for me.*

G. **Knew each other only briefly/slightly** ($f = 31$). *I hadn't known him for long./ We were still getting to know each other.*

I. **One avoided, ignored, or reduced contact with other** ($f = 166$). *I didn't initiate contact as much./She stopped coming by.*

J. **Had known each other/been friends for a long time** ($f = 17$). *We had known each other for 4 years./We were friends for almost 2 years before.*

K. **P blamed absence of romantic feelings on self (or on something other than R) or blamed self for R's misperception** ($f = 26$). *He said that he takes part of the blame./Placed blame on myself and said I wasn't ready for a relationship.*

L. **Not open, didn't discuss feelings** ($f = 13$). *We talked about casual things, not about feelings./We never talked about our feelings.*

M. **Told others about R's disclosure, R's feelings** ($f = 14$). *Told everyone what happened./He told his friends of his interest.*

---

*(Continued)*

Table 2.2 (Continued)

N.  Other/I acted embarrassed, awkward ($f = 17$). *He was awkward around me, which led me to be awkward around him./She was obviously uncomfortable.*

O.  (Re)affirmed friendship, told each other we were friends, that the friendship was important, etc. ($f = 152$). *I told him that I still wanted to be friends./After he disclosed his "crush" to me I said, "We're still buddies, right?"/I told her I would always have feelings for her and that it would hurt me more to not have her as a friend than as a girlfriend.*

P.  Disclosure/acceptance re present relationships/started dating others/ suggested partner start seeing others ($f = 108$). *Every time either of us would have problems with the opposite sex, we could talk to each other.*

R.  Acted like it never happened, dropped it, went on as before, didn't pressure ($f = 148$). *Pretended it didn't happen./We completely dropped the matter./Friendly, acted as though nothing changed in friendship.*

S.  P indicated romantic feelings may develop later ($f = 24$). *I just said, "You never know, maybe in the future my feelings will change."*

T.  Acted friendly ($f = 61$). *Acted friendly toward her—invited her along on group activities./I also attended his games and tried to talk to him more.*

U.  R kept pressuring, pursuing romance, didn't drop it, kept hoping, didn't give up ($f = 96$). *He continued to try to touch me./He kept coming on to me.*

V.  The disclosure itself ($f = 13$). *Maybe that I disclosed my affection toward him.*

W.  Said it was okay (that feelings weren't mutual)/talked about it openly ($f = 98$). *Said I understood./She did say that she was okay with the way things were./He would reassure me that he didn't care that I wasn't in love with him and would love me anyway./He stated that it would be hard, but he could bring himself to accept it.*

X.  Called, got together, maintained contact ($f = 208$). *He called and came by and tried to keep contact./Pursued conversations and interactions.*

Y.  Said did not want to be friends ($f = 12$). *He asserted that he would not be interested in me as a friend./He said he couldn't handle being friends anymore.*

AA. Sexual behaviors, overtures, suggestions, flirting, affectionate behaviors ($f = 72$). *I continued to flirt with her/him pursuing intimacy.*

CC. Acted less close ($f = 21$). *She would act a lot colder and less interested./ Didn't ask me out.*

DD. Reduced/avoided affectionate/sexual behaviors ($f = 14$). *He stopped the touchy-feely things./Denied any sexual tension, treated her like a sister.*

EE. Acted bothered/uncomfortable/complained ($f = 29$). *I was slightly sullen after he rejected me./Told me once how hard it was.*

FF. P had or acknowledged romantic feelings for R in the past ($f = 11$). *He was aware that I was once attracted to him, but I thought we developed more of a friendship./I had become uncertain as to whether I did or didn't like him romantically.*

NOTE: P = platonically inclined partner, R = romantically inclined partner. Low-frequency categories irrelevant to the remaining discussion have been omitted but are available from the authors.

The primary analysis involved tabulating, separately for each of the four situation groups, the frequency with which each behavior was associated with each condition (i.e., the number of times any particular behavior was mentioned as having manifested a given condition). While these data do not lend themselves to formal comparison via statistical tests, they are rich for purposes of qualitative descriptive analysis—especially where the relative frequencies for a particular behavior differ for dissolved versus maintained friendships.

The complete data set was organized so that for each of the four target situations, frequencies were recorded for all 33 behaviors within each of the 26 conditions (i.e., $4 \times 26 \times 33$ cells). Most of these frequencies were zero, of course. Within the various situation/condition categories, the typical number of behaviors with frequencies greater than zero was about nine (thus, approximately $4 \times 26 \times 9$ cells with "hits"). Clearly, to present these entire arrays here would be cumbersome and inefficient. While our own initial analysis was performed on the entire set of arrays (i.e., $4 \times 26 \times \sim 9$ cells), often with reference back to the raw data transcribed comments, we have devised Table 2.3 to represent a summary of the primary observations. Table 2.3 includes behaviors (coded as in Table 2.2) that account for at least 10% (arbitrarily determined) of all dissolved or all lasted *behaviors* reported for a given condition. The most frequent behaviors for each condition are featured.[7]

### Results—Part II.C

There are various ways in which Table 2.3 presents the dynamics of unrequited romance situations as being more complex than Table 2.1 suggests. It is apparent from the open-ended responses, for example, that even within friendships that endure unrequited romantic disclosures, the situation is not without at least temporary discomfort. For example, even in friendships that last, the disclosure and "rejection" of romantic inclinations is often embarrassing and awkward (i.e., notice the relative frequencies for Table 2.3, ##5D, 7V, and 20EE). Apparently, when a postdisclosure friendship lasts, it is not because it is so stable as to feel no noticeable effect from the "rejection" of a romantic disclosure. Rather, friendships that last apparently do so on the basis of conditions and behaviors, by both parties, that accompany or follow the inherently awkward disclosure/rejection episode.

As for identifying the optimal behaviors for ensuring an enduring friendship, the picture is not without ostensible contradictions, some of which are at least partially resolved upon closer inspection. For example, it is intuitively surprising to see that the pursuit of romance via sexual overtones is reported with relatively equal frequency for friendships that lasted and those that dissolved (i.e., #13AA). An examination of the raw-data participant comments sheds light on this, however: for dissolved friendships, in every case where

Table 2.3    Most Common Behaviors Within Conditions

1. **HOW P OR R INDICATED THAT THE RELATIONSHIP WAS STRONG. ($\Sigma f$'s = D: 48, L: 24)**
   E. Treated as Good Friends (D: 28%, L: 25%)
   C. High Personal Disclosure (D: 16%, L: 34%)                Also B & J

2. **HOW P OR R INDICATED THAT THE RELATIONSHIP WAS WEAK. ($\Sigma f$'s = D: 8, L: 18)**
   G. Brief History (D: 59%, L: 100%)

3. **HOW P/R DEMONSTRATED THAT THE RELATIONSHIP HAD HIGH OPENNESS/HONESTY. ($\Sigma f$'s = D: 29, L: 16)**
   C. High Personal Disclosure (D: 82%, L: 21%)
   P. Disclosure re Present Relationship (D: 0%, L: 28%)        Also A & J

4. **HOW EITHER DEMONSTRATED THAT THE RELATIONSHIP HAD LOW OPENNESS/HONESTY. ($\Sigma f$'s = D: 5, L: 18)**
   G. Brief History (D: 25%, L: 80%)
   L. Low Openness (D: 51%, L: 0%)

5. **WHAT P DID/SAID TO CAUSE OR INCREASE R'S EMBARRASSMENT. ($\Sigma f$'s = D: 32, L: 42)**
   D. The Rejection Itself (D: 22%, L: 33%)
   P. Disclosure re Present Relationship (D: 3%, L: 27%)
   I. Reduced Contact (D: 29%, L: 17%)
   Also M, N, & R

6. **WHAT P DID/SAID TO PREVENT/DECREASE R'S EMBARRASSMENT. ($\Sigma f$'s = D: 44, L: 37)**
   K. P Blamed Self/Not R (D: 13%, L: 15%)
   R. Dropped It (D: 18%, L: 24%)
   O. Reaffirmed the Friendship (D: 16%, L: 39%)
   Also W & T

7. **WHAT R DID/SAID TO CAUSE OR INCREASE P'S EMBARRASSMENT. ($\Sigma f$'s = D: 28, L: 45)**
   I. Reduced Contact (D: 15%, L: 20%)
   U. R Kept After Romance (D: 48%, L: 18%)
   Also M, EE, & V

8. **WHAT R DID/SAID TO PREVENT/DECREASE P'S EMBARRASSMENT. ($\Sigma f$'s = D: 44, L: 27)**
   R. Dropped It (D: 8%, L: 32%)
   W. Said It Was Okay (D: 47%, L: 23%)
   O. Reaffirmed the Friendship (D: 8%, L: 22%)
   Also I & T

9. **HOW R COMMUNICATED THAT HE OR SHE WANTED TO REMAIN FRIENDS. ($\Sigma f$'s = D: 49, L: 42 )**
   O. Reaffirmed the Friendship (D: 28%, L: 47%)
   X. Maintained Contact (D: 54%, L: 41%)               Also T

10. HOW R COMMUNICATED THAT HE OR SHE DID NOT WANT TO REMAIN FRIENDS. ($\sum f$'s = D: 9, L: 29)
    I.   Reduced Contact (D: 69%, L: 28%)
    Y.   Said Didn't Want Friendship (D: 13%, L: 0%)

11. HOW P COMMUNICATED THAT HE OR SHE WANTED TO REMAIN FRIENDS. ($\sum f$'s = D: 58, L: 33)
    O.   Reaffirmed the Friendship (D: 26%, L: 34%)          R. Dropped It (D: 5%, L: 14%)
    X.   Maintained Contact (D: 48%, L: 45%)

12. HOW P COMMUNICATED THAT HE OR SHE DID NOT WANT TO REMAIN FRIENDS. ($\sum f$'s = D: 11, L: 32)
    I.   Reduced Contact (D: 76%, L: 71%)

13. HOW R INDICATED THAT HE OR SHE WAS CONTINUING TO PURSUE A ROMANCE. ($\sum f$'s = D: 24, L: 32)
    U.   R Kept After Romance (D: 34%, L: 35%)
    AA.  Sexual Behavior/Overtures (D: 32%, L: 39%)          Also X

14. HOW R INDICATED THAT HE OR SHE WAS NOT PURSUING A ROMANCE. ($\sum f$'s = D: 29, L: 31)
    I.   Reduced Contact (D: 35%, L: 3%)                      Also P
    R.   Dropped It (D: 12%, L: 50%)

15. WHAT R DID/SAID THAT PRESSURED P. ($\sum f$'s = D: 14, L: 24)
    AA.  Sexual Behavior/Overtures (D: 19%, L: 6%)
    U.   R Kept After Romance (D: 52%, L: 41%)                Also N

16. WHAT R DID/SAID THAT ELIMINATED/REDUCED PRESSURE ON P. ($\sum f$'s = D: 25, L: 24)
    R.   Dropped It (D: 22%, L: 28%)                          Also O & P
    W.   Said It Was Okay (D: 28%, L: 28%)

17. HOW P LED R ON. ($\sum f$'s = D: 37, L: 47)
    AA.  Sexual Behavior/Overtures (D: 42%, L: 48%)
    T.   Acted Friendly (D: 27%, L: 29%)                      Also E & FF

18. HOW P INDICATED (POSTEPISODE) HE OR SHE VIEWED THE RELATIONSHIP PLATONICALLY. ($\sum f$'s = D: 22, L: 39)
    P.   Disclosure re Present Relationship (D: 16%, L: 28%)
    DD.  Reduced Sexual/Romantic Behavior (D: 12%, L: 21%)    Also D, E, & CC

*(Continued)*

Table 2.3 (Continued)

19. **HOW R INDICATED THAT HE OR SHE COULD ACCEPT IT.** ($\sum f$'s = D: 47, L: 29)
   R.   Dropped It (D: 42%, L: 36%)                    Also P
   W.   Said It Was Okay (D: 41%, L: 42%)

20. **HOW R INDICATED THAT HE/SHE COULD NOT ACCEPT IT.** ($\sum f$'s = D: 19, L: 34)
   U.   R Kept After Romance (D: 40%, L: 26%)          Also I
   EE.  Acted Bothered (D: 28%, L: 26%)

21. **WAYS THAT P CAUSED/AMPLIFIED R'S BEING HURT.** ($\sum f$'s = D: 28, L: 48)
   D.   The Rejection Itself (D: 40%, L: 53%)
   I.   Reduced Contact (D: 27%, L: 22%)

22. **WAYS THAT P PREVENTED/REDUCED R'S BEING HURT.** ($\sum f$'s = D: 41, L: 32)
   O.   Reaffirmed the Friendship (D: 34%, L: 25%)
   X.   Maintained Contact (D: 16%, L: 14%)            Also K & W

23. **HOW P INDICATED THAT HE OR SHE MIGHT DEVELOP ROMANTIC FEELINGS LATER.** ($\sum f$'s = D: 22, L: 22)
   S.   P Hints re Future Romance (D: 47%, L: 23%)
   AA.  Sexual Behavior/Overtures (D: 20%, L: 34%)     Also E & FF

24. **HOW P INDICATED THAT HE OR SHE WAS UNLIKELY TO DEVELOP ROMANTIC FEELINGS.** ($\sum f$'s = D: 26, L: 40)
   D.   The Rejection Itself (D: 36%, L: 34%)
   P.   Disclosure re Present Relationship (D: 26%, L: 31%)   Also I & R

25. **HOW R INDICATED (POSTEPISODE) ACTIVE PURSUIT OF THE FRIENDSHIP.** ($\sum f$'s = D: 45, L: 35)
   X.   Maintained Contact (D: 49%, L: 54%)
   R.   Dropped It (D: 15%, L: 22%)                    Also I

26. **HOW P INDICATED (POSTEPISODE) ACTIVE PURSUIT OF THE FRIENDSHIP.** ($\sum f$'s = D: 40, L: 32)
   X.   Maintained Contact (D: 44%, L: 66%)
   R.   Dropped It (D: 8%, L: 20%)                     Also I

NOTE: P = platonically inclined, R = romantically inclined, D = dissolved, L = lasted. Table 2.3 presents only those behaviors accounting for at least 10% of behaviors reported in D or L groups for a given condition. Behavior code letters are from Table 2.2.

participants reported that the romantic partner continued pursuit via sexual overtures, the overtures described were in the form of *physical* behaviors (e.g., "She kept making out with me," "Getting physically close," "Trying to maneuver me into situations where physical closeness was likely"). For lasting friendships, on the other hand, all but one of the responses described sexual overtures in the form of *verbal* innuendo (e.g., "Sexual jokes and stories," "Hypothetical statements about us getting physical," "He would jokingly make suggestive comments about having sex"). It is thus tempting to speculate that some sort of sexual overture threshold operates in these unrequited situations whereby physical overtures are more likely to damage the friendship than are verbal flirting and innuendo.

As another example, the consequences of disclosing one's (or accepting the partner's) other relationships appear inconsistent across conditions. Apparently the effect is more likely to be positive for the friendship when the other relationship is acknowledged or accepted *before* or *after* the disclosure, but is more likely negative when done *at the time* of disclosure (i.e., see ##14, 16, and 18 vs. #5). Similarly, it is curious that while it is generally interpreted positively when the matter is dropped and ostensibly forgotten, the interpretation is sometimes negative (e.g., Items ##8, 14, 16, 19, 25, 6, 24, and 26 vs. Item #5R). We would speculate that dropping the matter does not supersede first reaffirming the friendship and assuring one another that the situation and asymmetry are okay.

Perhaps the most crucial feature of Table 2.3 for our purposes is that certain behaviors do seem to be more common for positive conditions and others more common to negative conditions. By collapsing these data across all positive or negative conditions, we can identify behaviors that are reported much more often in positive conditions than in negative conditions and, at the same time, more often in lasted than in dissolved friendships.[8] These presumably "most positive" behaviors include dropping the matter, continuing as before the episode; reaffirming the friendship, explicitly reminding the partner that the friendship is important; disclosure and acceptance regarding the partner's existing or new relationships; having known one another as friends for a long time before the disclosure; having spent a lot of time together before the disclosure; and treating one another as special friends do, including special favors and sacrifices.

Conversely, we may identify behaviors that are reported much more often for negative than for positive conditions and, at the same time, more often in dissolved than in lasting friendships. These presumably "most negative" behaviors include avoiding or reducing contact with the partner, pressure on the platonic partner to develop romantic feelings, acting friendly, being closed regarding personal matters and feelings, doing mean things, suggesting that the friendship can or should be sacrificed, and shallowness or inconsistency.

# Discussion

This study sought to determine the behaviors that account for the fate of friendships wherein one partner discloses romantic attraction that is not shared by the other. Part I attempted to identify critical behaviors via open-ended reports by participants who had experienced unrequited-romantic-attraction episodes within friendships. But this phase yielded friendship maintenance conditions rather than specific behaviors. Part II used those conditions as a priori items of interest, testing for (a) their relative presence or absence in lasting versus dissolved friendships, (b) participants' perception of the conditions' importance in determining the fate of the friendship, and (c) open-ended identification of specific behaviors by which the conditions were manifested or promoted. Qualitative coding and matching of these behaviors with key conditions yielded the identification of certain "positive" and "negative" behaviors that appeared to be associated with desirable (for friendship maintenance) and undesirable conditions, respectively. The overall impression is that in virtually all cases, unrequited-romantic-attraction episodes within friendships are awkward for both partners and are at least temporarily disruptive to the friendship. Apparently, friendships survive or dissolve largely as a result of (or at least in concert with) particular behaviors and conditions established by the partners.

## PRACTICAL APPLICATIONS

If the participants in this study are typical, it is extremely common for people, by age 20 or so, to have experienced one or more episodes of unrequited romantic attraction within a friendship. In the majority of these cases, the awkwardness of the situation leads to a dissolution of the friendship, even when both partners would have preferred otherwise. Being without social scripts to guide their behaviors, partners are necessarily left to their own devices. Apparently, however, this improvisation often yields ineffective or counterproductive behaviors, and the friendship dissolves. Sometimes, however, partners improvise behaviors that save the friendship.

Assuming that this study has identified some of the conditions associated with saved and dissolved friendships, these can be highlighted to represent guidelines for friends who find themselves experiencing unrequited romance situations in the future.

Specifically, the study suggests the following guidelines if the friendship is to be maintained:

1. *Pursue the friendship and make clear that maintaining it is important to you.* This is facilitated by verbally reaffirming the friendship, by maintaining or

reestablishing earlier patterns of contact, and then by dropping the episode from further discussion.

2. *Make clear that you have accepted and can handle the asymmetry situation.* This is facilitated by (a) verbally acknowledging acceptance of the asymmetry, disclosure, and rejection and then by (b) dropping the matter.

3. *Try not to manifest discomfort or embarrassment.* This can be facilitated by maintaining earlier contact patterns and by dropping the matter.

4. If you were the romantically inclined partner, *try to avoid your partner's perception that you are pressuring him or her toward romantic feelings.* This can be facilitated by reducing sexual overtures and flirting, by accepting the partner's subsequent romantic interest in others, and by abandoning romantic intentions.

5. Other generally inadvisable behaviors include complaining of the asymmetry, the platonic partner suggesting the possibility of future mutual attraction, and telling friends about the disclosure/rejection episode.

6. Moreover, the prognosis for a repaired friendship presumably is better if certain conditions were present before the rejection episode, namely, (a) having known one another as friends for a long time before the episode and (b) having spent a lot of time together before the episode.

## OTHER IMPLICATIONS

Given evidence of positive and negative roles for these behaviors within the specific context of unrequited romance, it may be worth investigating the degree to which they generalize to a wider range of friendship repair contexts. Intuitively, several seem likely to be specific to the unrequited attraction context. For example, it seems unlikely that other friendship repair contexts would call for key behaviors such as disclosure of one's subsequent interest in others, avoiding increased flirtation, suggesting future romantic feelings, and so forth.

On the other hand, some of the key behaviors noted in this study might generalize to most any friendship repair situation, and some of them have been noted elsewhere, for example, reaffirming the friendship (Canary, Stafford, Hause, & Wallace, 1993) and continuing prior social interaction patterns (e.g., Fehr, 1996). Similarly, some of the key unrequited attraction behaviors probably have analogous behaviors in other contexts after minor contextual revision. For example, the effect of verbal reassurance that one is okay with romantic asymmetry probably is paralleled in verbal reassurance that one is okay with most any difference that accounts for disruption of a friendship, and likewise, perhaps, for dropping the matter once it has been discussed, not complaining about the situation, and so forth. In any case, the potential role of these behaviors or their analogues in other friendship repair contexts, perhaps even in other conflict contexts more generally, is worthy of further investigation.

## CAVEATS AND FUTURE RESEARCH

This study has identified several behaviors as positive (likely to help maintain the friendship) and several as negative (likely to dissolve the friendship) for unrequited romance situations within friendships. But while the data comparisons—lasted versus dissolved friendships and positive versus negative conditions—are intuitively impressive for many of these behaviors, the overall picture is incomplete. In particular, the relative frequencies tallied for the behaviors are simply the frequencies with which participants thought to report the behaviors in response to open-ended queries. While it may be that the most frequently reported behaviors are indeed those that most frequently occurred, it may be instead that the frequently reported behaviors were merely those most salient. Conversely, lower-frequency behaviors may have been experienced by many participants, though recalled or reported by few.

Thus future research on friendship maintenance and repair behaviors after unrequited romantic attraction should treat the conclusions and implied prescriptions of the present study as a priori hypotheses. There would be ethical problems with most true experimental tests of these hypotheses, of course. One could, however, test a priori predictions for "positive" and "negative" behaviors regarding their relative frequency of occurrence in lasted or dissolved friendships, or one could test predictions regarding the perceived influence of these behaviors, as a priori variables, upon presumably critical friendship repair conditions. These kinds of studies seem to be the appropriate extension of the findings made here.

## Conclusion

This study examined unrequited romantic attraction within ostensibly platonic friendships and was interested especially in behaviors differentiating friendships that survive an unrequited-romantic-attraction episode from friendships that do not. The theoretical concern was the identification of methods, conditions, and behaviors that might inform general friendship repair research. The pragmatic motivation was to identify behaviors that can be advised for persons who experience unrequited attraction episodes and wish to maintain the friendship.

Sets of apparently advisable and inadvisable behaviors were identified. The qualitative and interpretative nature of the study demands that the advice be cautious, and additional research certainly is called for in order to offer more confident advice.

Future research notwithstanding, maintaining a friendship after an unrequited-romantic-attraction disclosure has been a relatively scriptless situation, with partners left to improvise their own responses. And in most cases this has resulted in dissolved friendships. Thus we would hope that individuals involved in real-life episodes should welcome the advice implied by the present study, tentative though it may be.

## Notes

1. Questionnaires were worded to allow responses for parallel same-sex situations (namely, *"Imagine a time when you and **a member of the sex that you date** had developed a friendship, and where . . ."*). But demographic data on the sex of the participants and their partners indicated that all participants were describing heterosexual relationships.

2. Pilot data were coded by two of the coauthors into various categories. Seventeen functional categories emerged. Intercoder reliability was 97%. Differences were resolved via discussion.

3. The screening data are of some interest in their own right. Of 184 potential participants, 78% had experienced at least one unrequited-romantic-attraction episode within a friendship, about 70% of these more than once, with dissolution of the friendship being the more common consequence. Frequency breakdowns for each target situation are available upon request.

4. Instructions were as follows (e.g., for participant platonic/lasted, with bold type indicating edit points for the other target situations): *"You have indicated that you have experienced the following situation within the past 3 years: (a) You and a member of the sex that you date have developed a friendship; (b) It becomes more than platonic for **him/her. He/she** begins to develop romantic feelings for **you;** (c) At some point **he/she** discloses romantic feelings to **you;** (d) The feelings are not mutual. **You** disclose that you do not have romantic feelings for **him/her;** (e) The friendship **continues relatively unaltered for a good while.** In these situations sometimes the friendship lasts and sometimes it dissolves. We are interested in determining the factors responsible for your friendship having **lasted.** Please answer the following accordingly."*

5. By asking participants for manifestations that both exacerbated and relieved certain conditions, the number of "conditions" to be analyzed is expanded from 17 in Table 2.1 to 26 in Table 2.3. For example, Table 2.1 displays a single condition regarding whether the romantic partner was embarrassed, while Table 2.3 displays data for two subconditions—*increasing* this embarrassment and *decreasing* this embarrassment. The same is true for several other conditions.

6. With 141 participants and 26 comment opportunities, there could have been as many as 3,666 total comments. The difference—that is, the "missing" comments—is overwhelmingly due to individual participants not responding on select items (presumably because they were unable to recall manifestations, especially for low-presence conditions) rather than blanket omissions of the open-ended segments by given participants.

7. Omitted percentages on less frequent behaviors are available upon request.

8. Collapsing specific behaviors across all positive and negative conditions was performed as a separate analysis. Details and specific results are available upon request.

# References

Battaglia, D. M., Richard, F. D., Datteri, D. L., & Lord, C. G. (1998). Breaking up is (relatively) easy to do: A script for the dissolution of close relationships. *Journal of Social and Personal Relationships, 15,* 829–845.

Baumeister, R. F., Wotman, S. R., & Stillwell, A. M. (1993). Unrequited love: On heartbreak, anger, guilt, scriptlessness, and humiliation. *Journal of Personality and Social Psychology, 64,* 377–394.

Canary, D. J., Stafford, L., Hause, K. S., & Wallace, L. A. (1993). An inductive analysis of relational maintenance strategies: Comparisons among lovers, relatives, friends, and others. *Communication Research Reports, 10,* 5–14.

Fehr, B. (1996). *Friendship processes.* Thousand Oaks, CA: Sage.

Jaesub, L. (1998). Effective maintenance communication in superior-subordinate relationships. *Western Journal of Communication, 62,* 181–209.

Kenny, D. A., & Nasby, W. (1980). Splitting the reciprocity correlation. *Journal of Personal and Social Psychology, 38,* 249–256.

Monsour, M., Harris, B., & Kurzwell, N. (1994). Challenges confronting cross-sex friendships: "Much ado about nothing?" *Sex Roles, 31,* 55–77.

Motley, M. T. (1992). Mindfulness in solving communicators' dilemmas. *Communication Monographs, 59,* 306–314.

Motley, M. T. (1997). *Obstacles to socially relevant (applied) research in interpersonal communication.* Keynote address presented at the 23rd Conference in Communication, Fresno State University, CA.

Rose, S., & Frieze, I. H. (1993). Young singles' contemporary dating scripts. *Sex Roles, 28,* 499–509.

Strauss, A., & Corbin, J. (1990). *Basics of qualitative research.* Thousand Oaks, CA: Sage.

Werking, K. J. (1997). *We're just good friends: Women and men in nonromantic relationships.* New York: Guilford Press.

# 3

## Interactive Aspects of Interpersonal Guilt

### Relational Pragmatics and Consequences

*Lisa A. Miczo*

*Judee K. Burgoon*

nterpersonal guilt occurs when people feel bad because their behavior has affected a partner in some negative way. Frequently, people use guilt trips to try to make a partner feel guilty for some relational transgression (Tangney, 1992). What makes this interesting is that the very act of inducing guilt may itself have negative relational consequences (Vangelisti & Sprague, 1998). Yet most people will probably admit to risking these consequences to make someone feel guilty. Thus it is important to understand how and why guilt messages are used and what ramifications those messages have for the partners and the relationship.

The power of guilt cuts a wide swath. Even brief encounters with salespeople can instigate guilt (Dahl, Honea, & Manchanda, 2005), guilt may last for decades after a relational transgression (Ingersoll-Dayton & Krause, 2005), and merely anticipating guilt is enough to influence people's behaviors (e.g., Lindsey, 2005). Baumeister, Reis, and Delespaul (1995) found that people experience roughly 2 hours of mild guilt a day, 5 hours of moderate to severe guilt a week, and 3½ hours of severe guilt in a month. Plainly, guilt is prevalent in our lives.

This chapter examines guilt associated with those interpersonal transgressions that are perceived to have harmed a relational partner. Much of the research on the role of guilt within interpersonal relationships has involved retrospective accounts or focused on only one partner (the guilt message sender or receiver). This method has often been chosen because of the difficulty of studying guilt in a laboratory setting. Nevertheless, how people feel and respond immediately in guilt interactions is likely to differ from how they remember them (i.e., after having the chance to mull over the conversation). Focusing on one individual's account also misses the interplay between partners during these guilt trips. Unlike previous studies, this investigation takes a transactional approach to interpersonal guilt. It probes the perception and consequences of guilt messages from the perspective of both partners in established relationships. Also explored are the impacts of specific relationship type (friend or romantic partner), relational closeness and relational satisfaction on the experience of guilt, perceived appropriateness of the guilt message, and perceived effectiveness of the guilt message.

## Defining Guilt

Guilt is a psychological state that motivates a person to somehow "set things right" (Lindsey-Hartz, De Rivera, & Mascolo, 1995, p. 289; see also Lazarus, 1991). For example, missing a loved one's birthday may motivate one to give a belated gift that is certain to be especially well liked. Guilt over a betrayed confidence might compel a person to apologize and refrain from indiscretions in the future. In cases such as these, guilt may be decidedly unpleasant for the one experiencing it, but its consequences prove beneficial to the one who prompted it and to the relationship.

## Outcomes of Guilt Messages

Research on guilt within close relationships is relatively recent. Among the forerunners in this research are Baumeister, Stillwell, and Heatherton (1994, 1995a, 1995b). They study participants' personal narratives about guilt episodes—situations where they have angered someone and later felt guilty, have been induced by someone else to feel guilty, or have attempted to induce guilt in someone else. Their focus is guilt messages—messages that evoke guilt in a receiver. Baumeister et al. take a functional perspective on guilt, arguing that guilt messages serve a purpose for the sender (guilt elicitor). They have identified three primary functions of guilt messages. One function is to enhance patterns of behavior, meaning to enforce social or communal norms. For instance, a wife whose husband has left her standing at a public event may use a guilt message to motivate him to stay close when they are out socially. Guilt is intended to reinforce his public display of respect for his wife. A second function, and by far the most common (Vangelisti, Daly, & Rudnick, 1991), is to influence a relational partner. For example, guilt may prod a reluctant partner to visit one's in-laws or attend a child's athletic events. A third function is to redistribute emotional distress. A brother's expression of guilt for betraying a confidence, for example, may make his sister feel better because he feels bad about the harm he caused.

A guilt message, then, has the potential to accomplish multiple goals for the guilt elicitor. A successful guilt message may motivate a partner to behave in ways that will strengthen the relationship (e.g., participating more in domestic chores or child care) while also providing comfort to a hurt or angry partner by showing guilt and remorse and by engaging in remedial strategies. These functions point to some positive consequences for the guilt inducer (the sender) but ignore the big picture of the negative consequences that can also occur.

Sommer and Baumeister (1997) note three ways in which inducing guilt may cause damage to a relationship: (1) a partner may feel manipulated, (2) a partner may retaliate with negative remarks about the inducer, and (3) a partner who is made to feel guilty repeatedly may devalue himself or herself. Thus while a guilt message may serve positive functions for the sender, it may have negative effects on the receiver and on the relationship. This almost certainly explains why guilt messages carry negative connotations. Guilt messages are often seen as aversive because guilt inducement actually exploits the bond of closeness between partners (Baumeister et al., 1994). To influence a partner this way is "illicit and objectionable" (Baumeister et al., 1995b, p. 183). As a result, people are prone to *deny using* guilt messages on their relational partners, despite their claims that they are the *recipients of them* (emphasis added; Vangelisti et al., 1991). So guilt messages present a dilemma for communicators in terms of competence.

## Communication Competence and Guilt Message Usage

Two primary criteria are associated with communication competence: appropriateness and effectiveness (Spitzberg & Cupach, 1984). Appropriateness deals with meeting the conversational expectations (norms/standards) of a communication interaction, whereas effectiveness concerns communicators' ability to achieve their desired outcomes for that interaction. A persuasion attempt may be entirely appropriate in terms of wording, gestures, and tone but completely ineffective. Conversely, a boss may be effective in getting a subordinate to stay late to work but is seen as overly demanding (inappropriate). Spitzberg, Canary, and Cupach (1994) argue that while a message may fulfill one of these requirements and not the other, both components are fundamental for communication competence. Guilt poses a conflict between these components. That is, while people may prefer (or say they prefer) to refrain from using guilt messages because they are considered objectionable, nevertheless they use them because of their potential for effectiveness. The result is messages with unstable qualities as far as their effects. In some circumstances, they may function to improve relationships; in others they may produce only negative outcomes. Thus studying the use of and responses to guilt messages in terms of competence criteria is key to understanding the Jekyll and Hyde nature of interpersonal guilt.

To confirm the perceived (in)appropriateness of guilt messages in the context of a live interaction, we predict the following:

*Hypothesis 1: A guilt message will be judged less conversationally appropriate than a simple discussion (of a relational transgression).*

In addition, two exploratory questions are posed to investigate guilt message effectiveness. The first examines senders' perceptions of guilt message effectiveness; the second examines receivers' perceptions to determine partners' perceptual alignment.

*Research Question 1: Do guilt elicitors perceive receivers' responses to the interaction to be more or less positive than receivers' responses in a no-guilt condition?*

*Research Question 2: Do receivers of guilt messages report more or less positive responses to the interaction than receivers in a no-guilt condition?*

## Influence of Relationship Type and Closeness on Perceptions of Guilt Messages

A recurring theme in the guilt literature is that guilt messages are used most often in intimate relationships (e.g., Tangney, 1992; Vangelisti et al., 1991). One explanation is that closer partners are given more latitude in their communication practices. Yet another is that partners perceive interpersonal guilt to be more acceptable in closer relationships. Both of these assumptions support directly testing the influence of closeness on perceptions of guilt message appropriateness. A pilot study provided some evidence that relationship type does moderate guilt message utilization. Results from a small sample indicated romantics and adult children (parent/child relationships) were somewhat more likely to use guilt messages than friends and siblings (Allspach, 1999). To (partially) test the assumption that relationship type and closeness affect guilt usage and perceptions, a second and third hypothesis were formulated:

*Hypothesis 2: Partners in friendships will perceive guilt messages as less conversationally appropriate than will partners in romantic relationships.*

*Hypothesis 3: Partners' ratings of closeness will be positively related to perceived appropriateness of guilt messages.*

Finally, two research questions explored the impact of relationship type and closeness on actual likelihood of using a guilt message:

*Research Question 3: Does relationship type (e.g., friends/romantics) affect typicality of guilt message use on a partner?*

*Research Question 4: Do relational closeness and satisfaction affect typicality of guilt message use on a partner?*

METHOD

*Participants*

The sample consisted of 84 dyads (students paired with a friend or romantic partner who they were asked to bring). Students were solicited from communication courses at a large southwestern university and offered extra credit for participating; a minimum 2-month relational history was required. In all, 42 romantic and 42 friend dyads were recruited.

Within each dyad, the student was assigned the role of designated sender/guilt elicitor. There were 23 male and 61 female elicitors total. Elicitors ranged in age from 18 to 32, with approximately 90% between 19 and 23 years of age ($M = 21.57$, $SD = 2.10$). Among receivers, 42 were male and 42 were female. Receivers ranged in age from 18 to 50 ($M = 22.83$, $SD = 5.07$). Length of relationships ranged from 5 to 180 months (or 15 years), with a mean of 3.28 years (39.39 months). There was no significant difference between average length of relationship for romantics and friends, $t(82) = -0.18$, $p > .05$, *ns* ($M = 3.34$, $SD = 2.66$ vs. $M = 3.23$, $SD = 2.79$).

The sex-composition breakdown for romantic dyads (sender/receiver) resulted in 13 male/female dyads and 29 female/male dyads. The sex-composition breakdown for friendship dyads (sender/receiver) was 8 male/male dyads, 4 female/male dyads, 2 male/female dyads, and 28 female/female dyads.

*Procedures and Measures*

Upon arrival at the lab, participants completed consent forms and were informed that their conversations would be videotaped. Equal numbers of romantic and friend dyads were randomly assigned to experimental and control conditions.

Participants were separated to complete preinteraction measures that examined participants' individual perceptions of their relational closeness and satisfaction with their partners. Closeness, operationalized as interdependence, was measured via a 25-item Likert-type scale compiled by Stern (1994) out of previous measures and found to have very good internal consistency for each of the subcomponents of global interdependence (affective: sender $\alpha = .82$, receiver $\alpha = .76$; behavioral: sender $\alpha = .85$, receiver $\alpha = .80$; cognitive: sender $\alpha = .88$, receiver $\alpha = .77$) and for overall interdependence (sender $\alpha = .93$, receiver $\alpha = .89$). Sample items include "I feel very close to my partner" (affective),

"I do a wide variety of activities with my partner" (behavioral), and "The information I get from my partner is important to me" (cognitive), with responses ranging from 1 to 7, higher ratings representing more agreement. The Hendrick, Dicke, and Hendrick (1998) five-item relationship assessment scale was used to examine relational satisfaction[1] (e.g., "In general, how satisfied are you with your [relationship]?" and "How good do you feel your [relationship] is compared to most?" (sender $\alpha = .70$, receiver $\alpha = .86$).

Following administration of the preinteraction questionnaire, participants were provided a list of "grievance" topics (topics over which relational partners often report experiencing conflict or grievance). The list provided to participants included selfish actions, commitment to the relationship, lack of time or effort put into the relationship, infidelity or betrayal, failing to meet an obligation, conflict relating to sex, benefiting at the partner's expense, insensitivity, verbal insults, dishonesty, and a blank allowing participants to report additional grievances. This approach has been found to increase involvement in discussions (e.g., Downey, Freitas, Michaelis, & Khouri, 1998; Gottman, Swanson, & Murray, 1999). Still separated from their partners, participants selected up to five current or recently experienced relationship grievances and rated these items in terms of severity (least to most severe). Participants designated as receivers reviewed an identical list and identified topics reflecting problems they thought their partner (the sender) was having with them.

The lists were compared for topics chosen and severity ratings. To limit variability in receivers' discussion experiences, the experimenter chose matching topics that were rated most severe, giving preference to sender ratings. If no matches emerged, the topic rated most severe by the sender was chosen (23 cases, 27%).

Before sender and receiver were reunited, senders in the guilt condition received instructions. They were asked to discuss the selected grievance topic with the partner for 10 minutes, with the objective of coming to some resolution of the issue, and to use a guilt message during the discussion. Specifically, they were told:

> Research shows that guilt is often used as a strategy to resolve areas of dispute or conflict within a relationship because people often feel guilt about doing things (or in some cases not doing things) that end up causing their relational partner harm or hurt. We would like you to use this strategy; that is, we would like you to make your partner/friend feel guilty about the topic chosen.

Senders were given no specific instructions regarding the actual message, as it was believed their relational history made them more knowledgeable about messages likely to induce guilt in their partners. However, they were cautioned to converse in as natural a way as possible. In the control condition, senders were simply asked to discuss the topic with their partners for 10 minutes with the purpose of coming to some kind of resolution. They were given no further instructions as to content.

Senders and receivers were reunited in a room furnished like a living room, with senders seated in a chair and receivers seated on a love seat on an adjoining wall, such that both were captured by video camera. Following the interaction, partners were separated to complete postinteraction questionnaires. Both partners rated their perceptions of the "elicitor's" conversational appropriateness using a 20-item, 7-point Likert-type scale, where higher ratings indicate more appropriateness (e.g., "Everything I said was appropriate," "She/he did not violate any of my expectations in the conversation" [Canary & Spitzberg, 1987]; sender $\alpha = .89$, receiver $\alpha = .92$). In addition, elicitors rated their efforts to induce guilt in their partners using seven 7-point Likert-type items, where higher ratings indicate more effort (e.g., "I tried to make my partner feel guilty," "I believe I came up with an effective guilt message during the course of our conversation"; $\alpha = .82$), and receivers reported on guilt actually experienced as a result of the conversation. This was measured via a modified 8-item version of the Kugler and Jones (1992) 7-point Likert-type state-guilt measure, with higher ratings indicating more guilt ($\alpha = .82$). Both partners also completed a 14-item, 7-point Likert-type measure designed to capture guilt-message responses that have been identified in the literature (e.g., Baumeister et al., 1995a). The items measured anticipated positive or negative outcomes based on the actual interaction (e.g., "My partner showed that he or she felt bad about what he or she had done" scored as a positive effect of guilt induction in that the partner demonstrates regret and perhaps even motivation toward reparative behavior, and "I am resentful because of the discussion we just had"; sender $\alpha = .80$, receiver $\alpha = .72$). Items were scored so that higher scores indicated more positive outcomes. Both partners also responded to an item measuring how typical it was for the elicitor in the interaction to use a guilt message on the receiver. Instruments administered to senders and receivers were identical except for wording changes corresponding to role (sender/receiver). After completing postinteraction measures, participants were debriefed and allowed to ask questions concerning the study.

## RESULTS

Senders in the experimental condition reported significantly stronger attempts to make their partners feel guilty ($M = 4.04$, $SD = 1.17$, 7-point scale) than those in the control condition ($M = 2.77$, $SD = 1.07$), $t(82) = -5.19$, $p < .001$. A $t$ test revealed no significant difference across relationship types in senders' self-reported attempts to make their partners feel guilty, $t(82) = 1.45$, $p > .05$, ns. Guilt message attempts by experimental senders were corroborated by objective coders who, blind to the conditions, correctly identified experimental senders by their videotaped attempts to elicit guilt 76% to 79% of the time (producing a kappa of .67, described by Fleiss, 1981, as "good"). However, coder ratings indicated that some participants in the control condition used a guilt message on their partners of their own volition. To address this issue, a third coder was employed to resolve all differences between the two initial coders regarding guilt message usage. Coders' ratings were then examined to determine guilt message usage by senders in both the control and manipulation conditions. Based on final coder ratings of the 42 senders designated to the control group, coders agreed that 12 (28.6%) used a guilt message with their partners of their own accord. Of the 42 intended guilt elicitors in the experimental group, coders agreed that 6 (14.3%) did not use a guilt message, despite having been instructed to do so. As a result of this outcome, a decision was made to regroup participants into condition categories based on whether or not the message sender was coded as having actually used a guilt message in the interaction. *All results reported below represent statistical analyses of the two groups based on this categorization.* In addition, supplementary analyses examining the subset of the control group who freely chose to use a guilt message were conducted and are reported following the results for the formal hypotheses and research questions.

The results of the manipulation check for guilt experienced by receivers whose senders used a guilt message were complex. Receivers of guilt messages reported feeling a moderate level of guilt in the interaction, $M = 4.57$, $SD = 1.14$, on a Likert-type scale of 1 to 7, with 7 representing higher guilt, but surprisingly, receivers in the control condition reported experiencing slightly more guilt in the interaction, $M = 4.98$, $SD = 1.30$; $t(82) = 1.51$, *ns*. While this difference is not statistically significant, it is noteworthy that a moderate level of experienced guilt was reported even by receivers who did not hear guilt messages. Although the purpose of the design was to elicit guilt in the experimental group, the hypotheses and research questions nevertheless focus on *responses to guilt messages.* As these were based upon whether a guilt message was used rather than upon whether guilt, per se, was experienced by the receiver, the following analyses are justified.

### Hypotheses Tests

*Perceived conversational appropriateness of guilt messages:* Hypothesis 1 (H1) predicted conversations containing guilt messages would be viewed as less conversationally appropriate than conversations that do not, while Hypothesis 2 (H2) predicted that perceptions of conversational appropriateness of guilt messages would differ based on relationship type. To test these hypotheses, two 2 (condition: guilt/no guilt) × 2 (relationship type: romantic/friend) ANOVAs were conducted, with sender and receiver ratings of senders' conversational appropriateness as the dependent variables. For senders, the main effect for guilt was not significant (although $M = 4.64$ and $M = 4.92$ for guilt and nonguilt conditions, respectively), $F(1, 80) = 2.32$, *ns*. For receivers, the main effect was significant, $F(1, 80) = 5.82$, $p < .05$, with receivers who heard guilt messages rating the conversation as significantly less appropriate ($M = 5.45$) than receivers who did not ($M = 5.96$; range of possible scores = 1–7). Thus, H1 was partially supported.

The second hypothesis concerned the interaction between condition and relationship type. This interaction effect was not significant for senders, $F(1, 80) = 1.05$, *ns*, or for receivers, $F(1, 80) = 0.77$, *ns*. Thus, H2 was not supported.

*Closeness and perceived conversational appropriateness:* Hypothesis 3 (H3) predicted a positive association between closeness and perceived appropriateness of guilt messages. For each subject in the experimental condition, we examined the three components of closeness (affective, behavioral, and cognitive interdependence) for their association with elicitors', receivers', and (as a means of examining the correlation between partners' ratings) dyads' averaged ratings of elicitors' conversational appropriateness. No statistically significant correlations were found in romantic dyads. However, significant correlations emerged for friends, namely, the correlation between receivers' ratings of cognitive interdependence and dyads' averaged ratings of conversational appropriateness, $r(21) = .65$, $p = .001$, between receivers' ratings of cognitive interdependence and of elicitors' conversational appropriateness, $r(21) = .48$, $p < .05$, and, separately, senders' ratings of appropriateness, $r(21) = .59$, $p < .01$. Therefore, while this hypothesis was not fully supported, results suggest that in friendships, receivers' appropriateness ratings of guilt messages increase as cognitive interdependence increases.

### Research Questions

*Elicitors' perceptions of receivers' responses to guilt messages:* Research Question 1 (RQ1) addressed whether senders who used guilt messages perceived their partners' responses to be less positive than senders who used no guilt messages. The postinteraction measure of overall quality of receivers' responses was used to address this question. A 2 (guilt message/no guilt message) × 2 (friends/romantics) ANOVA on senders' ratings of receivers' responses (positive or negative) produced a significant main effect for condition, $F(1, 80) = 7.49$, $p < .01$. Senders in the guilt-message condition reported significantly less positive receiver responses than senders in the no-guilt condition ($M = 4.83$ vs. $M = 5.33$). There were no significant results for relationship type or for the interaction of condition by relationship type.

*Receivers' reports of their responses to guilt messages:* Research Question 2 (RQ2) addressed whether receivers' ratings of the interaction were less positive when guilt messages were present than when they were absent. A 2 (guilt message/no guilt message) × 2 (friends/significant others) ANOVA on receivers' ratings of the interaction (positive/negative) produced no significant main effects or interaction. Thus it appears that guilt message senders may have exaggerated their receivers' relatively negative response.

*Typicality of guilt message usage by senders:* Research Question 3 (RQ3) examined whether relationship type affects partners' ratings of how typical it is for senders to use a guilt message on their partner. A one-way ANOVA revealed no significant difference across relationship types in senders' perceptions of how typical it was for them to use a guilt message on their partner; however, results for receivers' perceptions demonstrated a significant difference. Receivers in the friendship group perceived it was much less typical of senders to use a guilt message than did receivers in the romantic group, Welch's $F(1, 44.72) = 11.82$, $p < .01$ ($M = 1.86$, $SD = 1.20$ vs. $M = 3.37$, $SD = 1.84$, range 1–7).

*Closeness, relationship satisfaction and guilt message usage:* Research Question 4 (RQ4) addressed whether typicality of guilt usage would vary as a function of closeness/interdependence or relational satisfaction. No significant correlations emerged between senders' or receivers' ratings of closeness (interdependence) and ratings of how typical it was for senders in these relationships to use guilt messages. In terms of relational satisfaction, a Pearson product-moment correlation between senders' relational satisfaction with their partner and their perception of how typical it was for them to use a guilt message on their partner was nonsignificant. However, senders' relational satisfaction was significantly and negatively associated with receivers' ratings of senders' typicality of guilt usage, $r(48) = -.30$, $p < .05$. Plainly, senders reported higher relational satisfaction with partners who attributed less guilt message use to them. Receivers' satisfaction with the relationship and their perceptions that their partner typically used guilt messages were also negatively associated but only nearly significant, $r(48) = -.27$, $p = .06$. When the sample was broken down by gender, significant correlations between these variables emerged for females: $r(35) = -.38$, $p < .05$ for sender satisfaction by receivers' ratings of typicality, and $r(35) = -.35$, $p < .05$ for receivers' satisfaction and their ratings of typicality, respectively. To consider the possibility of gender differences in typicality, 2 (sender sex) × 2 (receiver sex) ANOVAs were conducted on sender and receiver ratings of typicality of guilt messages. No significant main or interaction effects emerged for these comparisons.

## SUPPLEMENTARY ANALYSES

The finding that fully 28% of the senders in the initial control condition chose to use guilt inducement of their own volition affords some additional analyses for this investigation, albeit done conservatively. Each of the 12 participants originally assigned to the control condition as senders who elected to use guilt messages were females, 10 (83.3%) of whom were in female/male dyads. Of those 10 senders in female/male dyads, 8 (80%) were in romantic dyads. These data suggest that females in opposite-sex relationships, particularly romantic relationships, are more prone to use guilt messages.

An additional supplementary analysis of these female guilt message users yielded one particularly noteworthy result. A comparison of female senders in the control condition who chose to use a guilt message, versus those who did not, found guilt message users to be significantly less satisfied with their relationship, $t$ with Levene's correction (13.66) = 2.66, $p < .05$ ($M = 4.38$ vs. $M = 4.83$). No significant differences in senders' self-reports of typical guilt use emerged between these groups, nor were there any significant differences in reported closeness with partners. For partners of these females, there were no significant differences across groups for satisfaction, closeness, or receivers' perceptions of how typical it was for their partners to use a guilt message. Finally, ANOVAs examining potential differences in receivers' evaluations of the interaction for this subsample of the initial control group (guilt message/no guilt message) resulted in no significant main effect or interaction effects for either the sender or the receiver.

# Discussion

## GUILT MESSAGES AND CONVERSATIONAL APPROPRIATENESS

This investigation examined conversational appropriateness and guilt elicitation attempts from a number of different angles. First, it was confirmed that as a communication technique, a guilt message is seen as less appropriate by receivers than other techniques (more specifically, in this study, addressing the conflict issue without a guilt message). Thus the study bolsters research evidence demonstrating that people generally have a negative view of guilt message use. It supports research that cautions communicators about the negative responses guilt messages may elicit, despite their potential for positive outcomes (e.g., Baumeister et al., 1994, 1995a, 1995b). It also demonstrates that receivers of guilt messages may view them as incompetent communication attempts because they fail the appropriateness requirement. As an example, while we might be successful in "guilting" a spouse into forgoing an outing with friends so as to attend a family reunion, resentment over the pressure used and a loss of perceived communicator competence may result.

Intriguingly, in further exploring the above results, this study revealed that perceptions of conversational appropriateness also appear to be influenced by partner role in interactions (sender/receiver). Using paired-sample $t$ tests, exploratory analyses of both the entire sample and guilt message/no guilt message groups separately demonstrated that senders rated their own conversational appropriateness significantly lower than did receivers.[2] Thus while receivers view guilt messages as less appropriate in and of themselves, it would seem that merely bringing up concern or unhappiness with a relational partner's transgression is perceived as face-threatening enough by senders for them to rate their conversations as lower in appropriateness. These results are fascinating for their commentary on relational communication, for they hint at a holistic view of relationships (by partners in the sender role) that communication about relational problems is stigmatized, inappropriate, and, using Spitzberg and Cupach's (1984) definition, incompetent.

Relationship type was also investigated for its association with perceived conversational appropriateness of guilt messages by comparing friendship and romantic relationships. Results indicated no difference in perceived guilt message appropriateness across these relational contexts for the full sample. Nevertheless, results from supplementary analyses found that 75% of the females using guilt messages voluntarily were in romantic relationships, which offers evidence that relationship type may indeed set the tone for guilt message utilization. Furthermore, as an additional means of teasing out relationship characteristics that affect partners' use of and responses to guilt messages, the potential association between closeness/interdependence and partners' perceptions of guilt messages' appropriateness, was explored, with somewhat unexpected results. Romantics reported more closeness than friends,[3] but no significant correlation emerged between closeness/interdependence and conversational appropriateness ratings of guilt messages. However, for friends there was a correlation between receivers' cognitive interdependence and both elicitors' and receivers' ratings of elicitors' conversational appropriateness (and separately, partners' averaged ratings of conversational appropriateness). These results indicate closeness and relational type may each factor into decisions by relational partners to evaluate guilt messages more forgivingly on the appropriateness dimension.

## GUILT MESSAGES AND EFFECTIVENESS

Two of the study's research questions explored broadly the effectiveness of guilt messages by examining partners' perceptions of responses to guilt messages within interactions. Not surprisingly, partners who attempted to make their partner feel guilty predicted less positive outcomes from the interaction than partners who simply discussed the grievance. However, it should be noted that while these means were significantly different, senders from both groups predicted moderately positive outcomes (on a scale of 1–7, group means were 4.83 and 5.33, respectively). Thus in the context of moderate-intensity guilt messages, it can be said from these data that partners perceive outcomes to be more positive than negative, despite anticipating less positive attitudinal and behavioral outcomes based on their partners' reactions in the interaction (e.g., mild resentment by partners, some likelihood of reciprocity of the guilt message). In this way, results parallel research by Baumeister et al. (1995b) that emphasized the functionality of guilt messages for the sender and speak to guilt message effectiveness in offering more (perceived/anticipated) benefits than costs. Similarly, partners receiving a guilt message did not report significantly less positive responses than did partners who did not receive a guilt message, though the means for receivers in the no-guilt condition were in the hypothesized direction with slightly higher ratings (representing more positive responses) than receivers in the guilt condition ($M = 5.51$, $SD = 0.71$ vs. $M = 5.19$, $SD = 0.85$ on a scale of 1–7).

## GUILT MESSAGES AND COMMUNICATION COMPETENCE

Taken together (in the context of these data demonstrating moderate-intensity guilt messages), the above results go some way in explaining why people may choose to use guilt messages in spite of their less than stellar reputation. For senders, they appear to offer more positive than negative outcomes, and although they suffer from questionable appropriateness from the receivers' point of view, their appropriateness doesn't significantly differ from the perceived appropriateness of simple discussion of a relational problem. For receivers, we see a similar picture, with receivers actually rating guilt messages higher in appropriateness than do senders. In fact, despite a significant difference between guilt/no-guilt groups, it would be questionable to say receivers saw guilt messages as inappropriate ($M = 5.45$ vs. $M = 5.96$ on a scale of 1–7) rather than less appropriate. The same could be said for receivers' perceptions of interaction outcomes, with no significant differences between guilt and no-guilt groups, and ratings of outcomes decidedly positive ($M = 5.51$ vs. $M = 5.19$ on a scale of 1–7). These data seem to attest to guilt messages being a viable option for relational partners; however, this picture is incomplete without an examination of relationship variables.

## RELATIONSHIP VARIABLES AND
## TYPICALITY OF GUILT MESSAGE USAGE

Of interest to relationship researchers are the dynamics of relationships, the interconnected variables that cause partners to do what they do. The current results yielded some unique insights into senders who volitionally chose to use a guilt message on their partners. Based on the evidence in this study, females appear more likely to use guilt messages in opposite-sex relationships (particularly romantic relationships). Of key interest is that those females *who chose to use a guilt message of their own volition* were significantly less satisfied in their relationships. This is in line with arguments that females are more likely to use guilt (than males) as a result of perceived inequity or lack of power (Baumeister, Sommer, & Cicora, 1996; Sommer & Baumeister, 1997). In addition, results from the guilt message condition data set indicated that for females, relational satisfaction (and separately, partners' satisfaction with the relationship) was significantly and negatively correlated with female senders' use of guilt messages as reported by receiver partners. As such, relational satisfaction demonstrated a measurable negative association with both females' propensity to use guilt and their perception that guilt messages are used by their partners. It may be that their use of guilt messages is part of the nag/withdrawal pattern that often characterizes dissatisfied relationships: the women complain, men perceive their complaints as nagging, they withdraw, and the women try harder to get their grievances heard. The result is a destructive relational communication spiral.

Though there is evidence that females are more prone to experience guilt (e.g., Bybee, 1998; Lutwak & Ferrari, 1996), no significant sex differences for experienced guilt emerged from these data.[4] Closeness, measured as interdependence, did not demonstrate a strong association with partners' tendency to use guilt messages, though there was a significant negative association between females' perceptions that their partners used guilt messages and their reported cognitive interdependence with their partners. Overall, these data suggest that for females, interpersonal guilt is tied to the perceived state of their relationship.

Relationship type was explored for its association with typical guilt usage in friendships and romantic relationships. Partner role (sender/receiver) seemed to influence these results, with senders reporting no greater likelihood of using guilt messages in one relationship type than another. Senders are likely demonstrating self-presentation efforts, in that they do not want to be seen as using an inappropriate communication strategy. However, receivers in friendships reported guilt messages as significantly more typical than did receivers in romantic relationships. Though all means were below the midpoint of the scale, friends' ratings were nearly twice as high as receivers' ratings in romantic couples. Receivers rate guilt messages as more typical in friendships, although they do not rate them significantly different in terms of appropriateness (than do receivers in romantic relationships). Moreover, receivers in friendships who reported their cognitive interdependence with their partners to be higher actually rated the appropriateness of their partners' guilt messages higher as well. As such, results from friendship data paint a picture of relational partners who experience cognitive, intellectual closeness (mutual understanding of the way one another think and believe), allowing more leeway in the use of guilt messages, perhaps indicating stronger empathy with partners who resort to using guilt.

# Limitations and Directions for Future Research

This investigation of guilt messages within the context of live interactions between established partners was not without its challenges. One primary issue concerned the experimental manipulation. Even in accommodating partners' choices to use (or not use) a guilt message, receivers in the reconfigured groups representing guilt/no guilt message conditions demonstrated no significant differences in their reported experience of guilt. The difficulty of reliably inducing an emotion (e.g., guilt, fear) using tested messages has been experienced by previous researchers; it was thought that allowing relational partners to craft their own messages (based on personal knowledge of their partners) might circumvent some of these difficulties, but this method demonstrated similar weaknesses. In addition, while senders in the reconfigured no-guilt condition were not rated by coders as using a guilt message, the type of message actually used is in question. In the original control group, senders were instructed to simply discuss the relational transgression with the purpose of coming to some resolution, and, based on our familiarity with the audio/videotapes, many of these senders followed these instructions in a fairly straightforward fashion. However, other conversational strategies (e.g., use of humor) were not examined in the above analyses. Sex differences in the sample may also have contributed some bias; this sample included over twice as many females as males. Friendship pairs were mainly female/female pairs, and romantic couples were mainly female-sender/male-receiver pairs. A design more balanced in terms of same-sex male friendships and male-sender/female-receiver romantic couples would be ideal.

# Practical Applications

What practical advice can be given to relational partners regarding interpersonal guilt? To begin, a discussion of interpersonal guilt from a communication competence perspective is useful. While messages can be appropriate without being effective or effective without being appropriate, without both components, competence suffers, and guilt messages may test both of these components to the limit. These participants' responses demonstrate that guilt messages are not seen as equally legitimate or as appropriate as more general discussion of a problem. Much like deceptive messages, while guilt messages are not uncommon in interpersonal relationships, most people view them negatively and prefer not to *be the recipient* of them or to *be associated* with using them. Thus with respect to appropriateness, guilt messages are certainly questionable.

Regarding effectiveness, both senders and receivers rated receivers' responses to guilt messages as somewhat positive. With a theoretic midpoint of 4 (on a scale of 1–7), guilt-condition senders rated receivers' responses as slightly positive ($M = 4.83$), and guilt-condition receivers rated their own responses somewhat more positively ($M = 5.19$). However, if we allow that one way to measure effectiveness would be to measure partners' overall responses and anticipated outcomes, then guilt messages certainly don't perform very strongly. Moreover, potential negative effects (such as resentment and feelings of being exploited) have a relational price tag. On the other hand, senders in the no-guilt condition, instructed to simply discuss the grievance topic, reported significantly more positive responses from their receivers. In addition, partners who received no guilt message actually reported experiencing slightly more guilt from the relational-grievance discussion. So while guilt inducers may have to deal with defensiveness and resentment as a consequence of their guilt messages, this study would suggest that simply airing one's feelings about a relational transgression appears to be enough to trigger guilt/self-reflection by relational partners. Thus from a relational perspective, these data indicate not only that guilt messages are less than ideal but that they only weakly meet standards of effectiveness. They carry with them negative relational implications; thus their potential to result in positive outcomes (e.g., strengthening the relationship, and social influence, as in Baumeister et al., 1995a) appears to be handicapped. Our results indicate that a more competent approach to relational conflict would be to simply discuss one's grievance with a partner.

Receivers of guilt messages should benefit from trying to understand a partner's motivation in using a guilt message rather than another approach. In this investigation, partners who chose to use guilt messages on their own were significantly less satisfied than those who did not. So the use of guilt messages by a partner should serve as a signal to the recipient that the sender may be using guilt because of dissatisfaction with the relationship. Specific reasons that have been reported for partners using guilt messages include frustration, hurt, or lack of or inequitable power. Therefore, partners who use guilt messages may very well be signaling, intentionally or not, that the relationship is in trouble, at least from their standpoint. As such, guilt trips by relational partners can function as a heads-up for receivers that they better consider the state of the relationship.

Based on these issues, a number of recommendations can be made for relational partners.

1. *Openly discuss issues.* This study demonstrated that partners are likely to respond to open discussion of a conflict topic. Receivers actually reported higher average ratings of experienced guilt when they *did not* receive a guilt message. Having a partner bring up the relational transgression with the goal of coming to some resolution was enough to jump-start the other's conscience and get him or her to reflect on the issue at hand. Partners are less likely to feel exploited or resentful if relational conflicts are addressed in a way that is perceived

as more appropriate, such as using an integrative conflict-resolution strategy whereby both partners attempt to resolve the conflict in a way that takes each person's interests into account.

2. *Resist the temptation to use guilt.* Research suggests that persuasive messages that receivers find threatening may activate a variety of defense mechanisms (see Block, 2005; Witte, 1992). In terms of face threat, guilt messages pack a double blow. Guilt messages threaten positive face (the desire to be respected, valued, included) in that they communicate a negative evaluation of a partner. Guilt messages also threaten negative face (the desire for autonomy) in that they put pressure to bear on receivers to act differently than they would of their own accord. Kubany and Watson (2003) describe two separate paths a person experiencing guilt may take in response to the emotion: guilt reduction and guilt avoidance. While a person trying to reduce guilt may be motivated to change his or her ways, there is nothing to ensure that he or she won't also perceive the message to be a poor reflection on the relationship or the partner who used it. In the case of those who engage in guilt avoidance, the denial of guilt should effectively undercut any catalytic properties the message may have had, thereby rendering it weak at best, useless at worst. And having put a relational partner in this defensive stance, the likelihood of successfully getting through to him or her with a second, different strategy seems even less likely. Avoid these relational pitfalls.

3. *Take stock of things when a relational partner tries to influence you with a guilt message.* Rather than immediately bristling when a partner uses a guilt trip on you, ask yourself why your partner felt he or she needed to induce guilt in the first place. Senders in this study found guilt messages to be less conversationally appropriate than did the actual recipients of them. This demonstrates awareness on the part of relational partners of violating (or at least stretching) communication appropriateness norms when sending guilt messages. So their willingness to take this risk is, apparently in their minds, justified. Is your partner feeling hurt? Does your partner feel frustrated by a lack of power or equity in the relationship? Has your partner communicated in other ways that he or she is dissatisfied? By identifying the motivation underlying his or her use of a guilt message, you should gain understanding of your partner's perspective of the relationship itself and ideally be able to address the big picture rather than simply reacting to the immediate message. For example, if your mother is trying to make you feel guilty about neglecting her and your father, at least consider whether maybe you *have* been neglecting them. Ask how many times you've seen them in the past couple of years and whether that is within the range of what is normal for others you know, whether it seems appropriate based on your circumstances and theirs, and so forth.

## Conclusion

The present study examined established partners using guilt messages about real relational concerns. Overall, the results portray guilt as a communication strategy with numerous flaws. While it is no secret that good relationships take work, it seems that we are prone to wanting to take shortcuts. Guilt messages appear to function as shortcuts for relational partners who either resist using a more productive strategy or, having tried other strategies and failed, are desperate to find one that might work for them. In either case, the well-being of the relationship is an issue. Prior to taking this shortcut, partners should ask themselves if a guilt trip is likely to take them to a relational destination they'll be happy with in the long run. If it's not, don't make the trip.

## Notes

1.  The original 5-point semantic differential scale demonstrated greater reliability when one item ("To what extent does your [partner] meet your expectations?") was deleted.

2.  Results for paired $t$ test analyses of senders' and receivers' ratings of senders' conversational appropriateness: $t(83) = -7.10$, $p < .01$, $M = 4.76$, $SD = 0.97$ for senders and $M = 5.66$, $SD = 0.96$ for receivers, no guilt condition $t(35) = -5.55$, $p < .01$, $M = 4.92$, $SD = 0.95$ for senders and $M = 5.94$, $SD = 0.80$ for receivers, and guilt condition $t(47) = -4.65$, $p < .01$, $M = 4.64$, $SD = 0.98$ for senders, and $M = 5.94$, $SD = 1.02$ for receivers.

3.  ANOVA results comparing friends and significant others for partners' averaged ratings of relational interdependence: $F(1, 82) = 13.27$, $p < .01$, $M = 6.16$, $SD = 0.53$ for significant others versus $M = 5.71$, $SD = 0.58$ for friends. Significant group differences also resulted for senders' ratings of relational, affective, behavioral, and cognitive interdependence and receivers' ratings of relational ($p = .046$) and behavioral interdependence, but not for receivers' ratings of affective or cognitive interdependence.

4.  ANOVA results comparing males and females for guilt experienced in guilt message condition: $F(1, 46) = 2.96$, $p > .05$, $M = 4.70$, $SD = 1.38$ for males versus $M = 4.45$, $SD = 0.91$ for females.

## References

Allspach, L. E. (1999, November). *Guilt trips: What are the relational destinations?* Paper presented at the annual meeting of the National Communication Association, Chicago.

Baumeister, R. F., Reis, H. T., & Delespaul, P. A. E. G. (1995). Participative and experiential correlates of guilt in daily life. *Personality and Social Psychology Bulletin, 21,* 1256–1268.

Baumeister, R. F., Sommer, K. L., & Cicora, K. E. (1996). Inequity and iniquity in marriage. *Social Justice Research, 9,* 199–212.

Baumeister, R. F., Stillwell, A. M., & Heatherton, T. F. (1994). Guilt: An interpersonal approach. *Psychological Bulletin, 115,* 243–267.

Baumeister, R. F., Stillwell, A. M., & Heatherton, T. F. (1995a). Interpersonal aspects of guilt: Evidence from narrative studies. In J. P. Tangney & K. W. Fischer (Eds.), *Self-conscious emotions: The psychology of shame, guilt, embarrassment, and pride* (pp. 255–273). New York: Guilford Press.

Baumeister, R. F., Stillwell, A. M., & Heatherton, T. F. (1995b). Personal narratives about guilt: Role in action control and interpersonal relationships. *Basic and Applied Social Psychology, 17,* 173–198.

Block, L. G. (2005). Self-referenced fear and guilt appeals: The moderating role of self-construal. *Journal of Applied Social Psychology, 35,* 2290–2309.

Bybee, J. (1998). The emergence of gender differences in guilt during adolescence. In J. Bybee (Ed.), *Guilt and children* (pp. 113–125). San Diego: Academic Press.

Canary, D. J., & Spitzberg, B. H. (1987). Appropriateness and effectiveness perceptions of conflict strategies. *Human Communication Research, 14,* 93–118.

Dahl, D., Honea, H., & Manchanda, R. (2005). Three Rs of interpersonal consumer guilt: Relationship, reciprocity, reparation. *Journal of Consumer Psychology, 15,* 307–315.

Downey, G., Freitas, A. L., Michaelis, B., & Khouri, G. (1998). The self-fulfilling prophecy in close relationships: Rejection sensitivity and rejection by romantic partners. *Journal of Personality and Social Psychology, 75,* 545–560.

Fleiss, J. L. (1981). *Statistical methods for rates and proportions.* New York: Wiley.

Gottman, J., Swanson, C., & Murray, J. (1999). The mathematics of marital conflict: Dynamic mathematical nonlinear modeling of newlywed marital interaction. *Journal of Family Psychology, 13,* 3–19.

Hendrick, S., Dicke, A., & Hendrick, C. (1998). The relationship assessment scale. *Journal of Social and Personal Relationships, 15,* 137–142.

Ingersoll-Dayton, B., & Krause, N. (2005). Self-forgiveness: A component of mental health in later life. *Research on Aging, 27,* 267–289.

Kubany, E. S., & Watson, S. B. (2003). Guilt: Elaboration of a multidimensional model. *Psychological Record, 53,* 51–90.

Kugler, K., & Jones, W. H. (1992). On conceptualizing and assessing guilt. *Journal of Personality and Social Psychology, 62,* 318–327.

Lazarus, R. S. (1991). *Emotion and adaptation.* New York: Oxford University Press.

Lindsey, L. L. M. (2005). Anticipated guilt as behavioral motivation: An examination of appeals to help unknown others through bone marrow donation. *Human Communication Research, 31,* 453–481.

Lindsey-Hartz, J., De Rivera, J., & Mascolo, M. F. (1995). Differentiating guilt and shame and their effects on motivation. In J. P. Tangney & K. W. Fischer (Eds.), *Self-conscious emotions: The psychology of shame, guilt, embarrassment, and pride* (pp. 274–300). New York: Guilford Press.

Lutwak, N., & Ferrari, J. R. (1996). Moral affect and cognitive processes differentiating shame from guilt among men and women. *Personality and Individual Differences, 21,* 891–896.

Sommer, K. L., & Baumeister, R. F. (1997). Making someone feel guilty: Causes, strategies, and consequences. In R. M. Kowalski (Ed.), *Aversive interpersonal behaviors* (pp. 31–55). New York: Plenum Press.

Spitzberg, B. H., Canary, D. J., & Cupach, W. R. (1994). A competence-based approach to the study of interpersonal conflict. In D. D. Cahn (Ed.), *Conflict in personal relationships* (pp. 183–202). Hillsdale, NJ: Lawrence Erlbaum.

Spitzberg, B. H., & Cupach, W. R. (1984). *Interpersonal communication competence.* Beverly Hills, CA: Sage.

Stern, L. A. (1994). *Confrontation between friends.* Unpublished doctoral dissertation, University of Arizona, Tucson.

Tangney, J. P. (1992). Situational determinants of shame and guilt in young adulthood. *Personality and Social Psychology Bulletin, 18,* 199–206.

Vangelisti, A. L., Daly, J. A., & Rudnick, J. R. (1991). Making people feel guilty in conversations: Techniques and correlates. *Human Communication Research, 18,* 3–39.

Vangelisti, A. L., & Sprague, R. J. (1998). Guilt and hurt: Similarities, distinctions, and conversational strategies. In P. A. Anderson & J. K. Guerrero (Eds.), *Handbook of communication and emotion: Research, theory, applications, and contexts* (pp. 123–154). San Diego: Academic Press.

Witte, K. (1992). Putting the fear back into fear appeals: The extended parallel process model. *Communication Monographs, 59,* 329–349.

---

AUTHORS' NOTE: This study was conducted as part of L. Miczo's dissertation research under the direction of J. Burgoon. The former would like to thank Chris Segrin for his invaluable aid and incredible generosity with this project, including, but not limited to, use of his research assistants and other resources.

# 4

# Behaviors That Determine the Fate of Friendships After Unrequited Romantic Disclosures

*Michael T. Motley*

*Heidi Reeder*

*Larissa J. Faulkner*

P latonic opposite-sex friendships often are among our most valued relationships (e.g., Baumeister, Wotman, & Stillwell, 1993). It is not surprising that romantic attraction sometimes develops within these initially platonic friendships, and it is not surprising that often the attraction is not mutual. The disclosure of romantic feelings that develop within a platonic friendship is risky. It is possible that the feelings are not mutual, and in that case, while the friendship may survive the asymmetry, it is more likely that it will not (Motley, Faulkner, & Reeder, 2008; Werking, 1997).

By age 20 or so, about 80% of today's population has experienced unrequited romantic attraction within an ostensibly platonic friendship, typically more than once. These experiences are problematic both before and after the disclosure and rejection. Deciding whether to reveal romantic attraction for a friend is among the most common serious communication dilemmas reported by college students (Motley, 1992), presumably because of partners' general reluctance to discuss the relationship (e.g., Baxter, 1988), the fear of asymmetry (Hill, Rubin, & Peplau, 1976), and fear of damage to the friendship in case of asymmetry (e.g., Werking, 1997). And once the disclosure is made, unrequited romantic attraction is awkward for both partners, at least for a while

(Motley et al., 2008). Among other problems, the romantically inclined partner almost always has felt led on and is surprised, embarrassed, and of course disappointed by the rejection. And almost always, the platonically inclined partner feels pressured to reciprocate the attraction, feels awkward rejecting the attraction, and feels guilty for having disappointed a friend.

To exacerbate the discomfort of the disclosure/rejection episode, the partners are on their own to determine how to deal with the situation and must operate without the benefit of predetermined "scripts" to guide their behavior. That is to say, while movies, songs, novels, and so forth provide many examples of scripts for behaviors common to *mutual* romance, there are very few for *unrequited* romance, and almost all of these are for negative relationship-dissolution outcomes. There are virtually no guidelines available for either the unrequited lover who wants to repair and maintain the friendship despite the rejection nor for the "rejecter" who, while not romantically attracted to the partner, wishes to reestablish and maintain the friendship (Baumeister et al., 1993).

If unrequited romantic attraction within friendships causes awkwardness and embarrassment for the partners, but there are no guidelines with which to navigate the experience, then it is not surprising that most cases end with a dissolved friendship. But since some friendships do indeed survive the episode, it is obvious that losing the friendship is not inevitable. Apparently, some individuals or couples find ways of dealing with the initial awkwardness, ways of putting the episode behind them, and ways of reestablishing a mutual friendship. These people operate without scripts too, of course, but manage to improvise behaviors that salvage the friendship.

If there are particular behaviors that are unique to salvaged friendships after unrequited attraction episodes, and if they can be identified, then perhaps we could offer guidelines for future unrequited attraction episodes. That is to say, the practical answer to what one "should do" in case of unrequited attraction within a friendship probably lies in the difference between what friends typically have done when the friendship dissolved versus what friends have done when the friendship lasted.

Our interest in differentiating partners' behaviors in friendships that last versus those that dissolve after disclosures of unrequited attraction began with an earlier study (Motley et al., 2008) described in Chapter 2. Using subjects who reported on a past unrequited attraction-in-friendship episode they had experienced, the earlier study first identified a number of *conditions* that participants believed to be instrumental in determining the subsequent fate (lasted/dissolved) of their friendship (e.g., partner appeared able to accept asymmetry, participant felt pressured to develop romantic feelings, participant/partner stayed embarrassed). Then the study identified *behaviors* that participants believed to be the means by which those conditions were communicated and manifested. By comparing participants in both roles—platonic versus romantically inclined—across both friendship fates (lasted vs. dissolved), it was possible to identify a dozen or so behaviors that are perceived to be more common to one friendship fate than to the other. The conservative interpretation is that we identified behaviors that seem especially likely to occur within either friendships that last or those that dissolve. The liberal interpretation is that the behaviors may actually be responsible for the fate of the friendship. In this case they would represent a list of practical do's and don'ts for those who wish to keep the friendship together after one of these unrequited-romantic-attraction episodes.

The conclusions of our earlier study must be viewed cautiously, however. The target conditions and optimal behaviors emerged from qualitative, interpretative analysis of exploratory open-ended questionnaire items to identify the critical behaviors for specific conditions. While the study compared the frequency with which certain behaviors were *recalled,* there was no assurance that this recall reflected the true relative presence of the behaviors rather than merely their salience or memorability.

To put it another way, a consequence of the exploratory qualitative approach of the earlier study is that its conclusions technically are merely informed hypotheses rather than tested claims. The purpose of the present study is to go further toward testing those hypotheses.

The earlier study identified "positive" behaviors that seem to be present in friendships that survive unrequited attraction episodes and "negative" behaviors that seem to be present within friendships that dissolve. While these behaviors emerged from open-ended questionnaire items in the earlier study, the present study will treat them as a priori targets of interest for two kinds of hypotheses:

*Hypothesis 1: Behaviors identified in our earlier study as "positive" behaviors will be reported to have been present significantly more frequently for friendships that survived unrequited attraction episodes than for friendships that did not (while the opposite will be true for "negative" behaviors).*

*Hypothesis 2: The perceived effect of target behaviors upon critical conditions will be such that "positive behaviors" are perceived to have facilitated "positive conditions" significantly more commonly than to have facilitated "negative conditions" (while the opposite will be true for "negative behaviors").*

## Method

### PARTICIPANTS

Participants were 98 native-English-speaking students of various upper-division communication courses at the University of California, Davis.

*Groupings:* Each participant reported via questionnaire about a single recent unrequited-romantic-attraction-within-friendship episode for one of the following target situations:

1. *Participant* disclosed *romantic* inclinations; partner's feelings were platonic; friendship lasted.

2. Partner disclosed romantic inclinations; *participant's* feelings were *platonic;* friendship *lasted.*

3. *Participant* disclosed *romantic* inclinations; partner's feelings were platonic; friendship *dissolved.*

4. Partner disclosed romantic inclinations; *participant's* feelings were *platonic;* friendship *dissolved.*

Participants were assigned to a group that represented one of the four target situations via a simple screening questionnaire asking, yes or no, whether the participant had experienced any of the four target situations within the past 3 years. Those who could not identify with any of the situations were dismissed. Participants who identified with only one situation were assigned to the corresponding group. Those who identified with more than one situation were assigned randomly to one of the relevant groups. Group $n$'s were as follows: participant romantically inclined and friendship lasted = 24, participant platonic and friendship lasted = 25, participant romantic and friendship dissolved = 24, participant platonic and friendship dissolved = 25.

## QUESTIONNAIRE

Participants completed questionnaires that were identical across groups except for minor editing to fit the four target situations (e.g., switching "lasted" for "dissolved," switching "you" for "your partner"). Primary questionnaire items investigated two matters:

### Part I

Based on the earlier study, 19 behaviors were selected as a priori items hypothesized to differ on their reported presence between the lasted and dissolved groups. Essentially, these behaviors were the ones identified in the earlier study as having potential for a strong positive or negative effect upon the eventual fate of the friendship. These behaviors are listed in Table 4.1. The questionnaire asked participants to answer a number of questions within the context of the single unrequited-romantic-attraction episode corresponding to their group assignment.

Table 4.1        Target Behaviors

---

1.  P (re)affirmed friendship, told R that the friendship was important (+)
2.  R (re)affirmed friendship, told P that the friendship was important (+)
3.  R said it was okay (that feelings weren't mutual) and talked about it openly (+)
4.  P said it was okay (that feelings weren't mutual) and talked about it openly (+)
5.  R called, got together, maintained earlier patterns of contact (+)
6.  P called, got together, maintained earlier patterns of contact (+)
7.  R dropped the subject of romantic attraction, acted like nothing happened (+)
8.  R complained, acted bothered/uncomfortable (−)
9.  P avoided, ignored, or reduced contact with R (−)
10. R avoided, ignored, or reduced contact with P (−)
11. P acknowledged blame or acceptance re R's assumption of mutual romantic attraction (+)
12. P indicated that romantic feelings for R may develop later (−)
13. P said a new romantic interest in another was reason for rejecting R (−)
14. P told others about R's disclosure, R's feelings (−)
15. R accepted P's subsequent attraction to others/another (+)
16. R told P of his or her subsequent interest in others (+)
17. P told R of his or her subsequent interest in others (+)
18. R reduced flirtation and sexual innuendo (+)
19. P reduced flirtation and sexual innuendo (+)

---

NOTE: P = platonically inclined partner, R = romantically inclined partner; + = presumed "positive" behaviors, − = presumed "negative" behaviors.

For each target behavior, participants were first asked simply whether the behavior had occurred in conjunction with their disclosure/rejection episode. Responses were either yes or no. The prediction, of course, was that yes responses to positive behaviors would be more frequent in lasted friendships, while yes responses to negative behaviors would be more common to dissolved friendships. These 19 yes/no questions regarding the presence of target behaviors will be treated as Part I of the study.

*Part II*

Each of the 19 yes/no questions about the presence of a particular behavior was accompanied by three to five follow-up questions. One of these asked whether the reported presence or absence of the target behavior was perceived to have played a major role in the eventual *fate of the friendship* (rated on a 1–7 Likert-type scale). The remaining subquestions asked whether the reported presence or absence of the target behavior served to manifest certain of the key maintenance/repair conditions suggested by our earlier study, for example, "*Do you feel that this (your answer to [the preceding item]) reduced or increased the embarrassment or awkwardness for your partner"* (1–7 Likert scale), *"Do you feel that it showed whether he/she was able or unable to 'handle' or 'live with' the situation"* (1–7 Likert scale), and so forth.[1] These items will be discussed as Part II.[2]

## ANALYSIS—PART I

Participants' yes or no (present/absent) responses on the 19 target behaviors were coded as "correct/incorrect" responses—assuming a lasting friendship as the goal and assuming the "positive/negative" characterizations above. That is to say, "yes" responses on "positive" behaviors and "no" responses on "negative" behaviors were coded as "correct," or consistent with the hypothesis. "Correct" responses were assigned a value of 1, "incorrect" responses a value of 0. Thus for each of the 19 target behaviors, the potential range of presence/absence group means was 0.0 to 1.0.

Conceptually, Part I represents 19 separate hypotheses wherein the mean for each behavior is predicted to be significantly larger (i.e., more participants giving "correct" responses) for participants reporting on friendships that lasted than for those reporting on friendships that dissolved. Analysis consisted of a 2 × 2 ANOVA (*outcome:* lasted/dissolved, and *partner:* romantic/platonic) for each of the 19 behaviors.[3]

## RESULTS AND DISCUSSION—PART I

Results are summarized in Table 4.2. Main effects on the outcome variable represent the primary predictions. For all but one of the behaviors examined (#11), overall differences between lasting and dissolved friendships were in the predicted direction (i.e., higher scores for the former). For all but two of these behaviors (##7 and 12), the differences were statistically significant. But in both of those cases, at least one pairwise subgroup difference was statistically significant in the predicted direction.

In short, almost all of the behaviors hypothesized earlier to be "positive" behaviors were reported to be more often present in friendships that lasted after an unrequited-romantic-disclosure episode than in friendships that dissolved. And the behaviors identified as "negative" were found to be more often present in friendships that dissolved than in friendships that lasted.

### Secondary Observations

While differences on the partner variable were of less a priori concern, Table 4.2 shows a few interesting differences and trends. For example, for almost all behaviors, platonic/romantic partners' perspectives are much more similar in

**Table 4.2** Presence of Behaviors Across Situations—Means and F Values

| Behaviors | Means | | | | F(1, 94) | | | Subgroup Differences P | | | |
|---|---|---|---|---|---|---|---|---|---|---|---|
| | | | | | Outcome | Viewpoint | O × V | | | | |
| | RL | PL | RD | PD | p | p | p | RD/RL | PD/PL | RD/PD | RL/PL |
| 1. R reaffirmed friendship (+) | .96 | .84 | .13 | .32 | **** | | * | **** | **** | | |
| 2. P reaffirmed friendship (+) | .79 | .88 | .29 | .52 | **** | | | *** | ** | ** | |
| 3. R acknowledged OK (+) | .75 | .76 | .58 | .20 | **** | * | * | | *** | ** | |
| 4. P acknowledged OK (+) | .79 | .88 | .21 | .48 | **** | * | | **** | ** | * | |
| 5. R returned to earlier contact patterns (+) | .58 | .56 | .08 | .44 | *** | | * | ** | | ** | |
| 6. P returned to earlier contact patterns (+) | .63 | .60 | .08 | .32 | **** | | | *** | * | | |
| 7. R dropped discussion of romantic interest (+) | .75 | .72 | .75 | .44 | | | | | * | * | |
| 8. R complained, acted bothered (−) | .79 | .76 | .75 | .32 | ** | ** | * | | ** | *** | |

*(Continued)*

**Table 4.2** (Continued)

| Behaviors | Means | | | | F(1, 94) | | | Subgroup Differences | | | |
| | RL | PL | RD | PD | Outcome p | Viewpoint p | O × V p | RD/RL | PD/PL | RD/PD | RL/PL |
|---|---|---|---|---|---|---|---|---|---|---|---|
| 9. R avoided contact/ communication (−) | .50 | .76 | .12 | .32 | **** | ** | | ** | ** | | * |
| 10. P avoided contact/ communication (−) | .71 | .72 | .21 | .20 | **** | | | *** | *** | | |
| 11. P acknowledged R's assumption justified (+) | .62 | .52 | .63 | .56 | | | | | | | |
| 12. P suggested future romantic interest (−) | .71 | .84 | .50 | .80 | | * | | | | * | |
| 13. P new romantic interest as reason (−) | .75 | .88 | .50 | .64 | ** | | | | | | |
| 14. P told friends of episode (−) | .96 | .56 | .63 | .16 | **** | **** | | ** | *** | *** | ** |
| 15. R accepted P's new romantic targets (+) | .83 | .89 | .55 | .18 | **** | ** | *** | *** | **** | **** | |

| Behaviors | Means | | | | F(1, 94) | | | Subgroup Differences | | | |
|---|---|---|---|---|---|---|---|---|---|---|---|
| | | | | | Outcome | Viewpoint | O × V | P | | | |
| | RL | PL | RD | PD | p | p | p | RD/RL | PD/PL | RD/PD | RL/PL |
| 16. R told of new romantic targets (+) | .55 | .82 | .33 | .09 | **** | | *** | * | **** | ** | ** |
| 17. P told of new romantic targets (+) | .93 | .53 | .33 | .17 | **** | **** | | **** | *** | | **** |
| 18. R decreased flirtation and innuendo (+) | .95 | .92 | .58 | .71 | **** | | | *** | * | | |
| 19. P decreased flirtation and innuendo (+) | .92 | .96 | .75 | .93 | * | * | | * | | * | |

NOTE: R = romantically inclined partner, P = platonically inclined partner; D = dissolved friendship, L = lasted friendship. A priori alpha = .05; p values are for comparison (*, **, ***, **** = .05, .01, .001, .0001, respectively). Pairwise comparisons via Newman-Kuels. F values available upon request.

friendships that lasted than in those that dissolved. (That is, for subgroup means and tests, the agreement between romantic/platonic partners is usually greater in friendships that lasted and lesser in those that dissolved.) Moreover, the interactions and pairwise comparisons amplify a pattern hinted at in the earlier study regarding the relative "charity" of romantic/platonic partners' attributions in lasted and dissolved friendships. In particular, within the dissolved friendships, significant partner-viewpoint differences (in all cases except Table 4.2, #5) occur because the actors of the target behaviors give themselves more credit for having behaved "correctly" (i.e., higher mean scores) than do the partners. In lasted friendships, on the other hand, significant romantic/platonic differences (except #14) occur because the observing partners give the actors of the target behavior more credit than do the actors themselves. For example, as for whether romantically inclined partners displayed the positive behavior of mentioning their new targets of romantic attraction after the episode, more romantic than platonic partners answered affirmatively in dissolved friendships, while more platonic than romantic partners answered affirmatively in lasted relationships (i.e., Table 4.2, #16). In general, it appears that actors of the target behaviors in the dissolved friendships are more naive or presumptuous, while those in the lasted friendships are more sensitive, or that the "observing" partners are relatively critical in dissolved friendships, while those in the lasted friendships are more charitable. Of course, these data may simply reflect the difference between subjects looking back on relatively negative and positive social events. But it is interesting to speculate that if these charity differences were present at the time of the episode, for example, as personality or style differences, they may in part account for the fate of the friendship or the tendency toward positive and negative behaviors.

In summary, Part I reinforces the identification of behaviors that are more common to lasting or dissolved friendships after unrequited-romantic-attraction episodes. The question of *how* the behaviors operate, at least with respect to promoting the critical conditions of corresponding friendship repair efforts, is investigated in Part II.

## ANALYSIS—PART II

Recall that on the questionnaire, each presence/absence question about a particular behavior was followed by two to four Likert-type scale questions about the extent to which the behavior's presence or absence was perceived to promote certain presumably associated conditions (e.g., *"Do you feel that [the absence/presence of the behavior] reduced or increased* **the embarrassment** *for [the romantically-inclined partner]?"*). Subjects' responses were grouped by lasted/dissolved outcomes and by platonic/romantic perspectives, as above, but also by the yes/no presence-of-behavior responses that served as the dependent measure for Part I above.

Thus data were analyzed via separate $2 \times 2 \times 2$ ANOVAs for each behavior/ condition item: *Presence of Behavior* (present/absent) $\times$ Friendship Outcome (lasted/dissolved) $\times$ Partner Perspective (romantic/platonic).[4] To repeat, dependent measures were Likert-scale (1–7) responses on whether the presence or absence of a given *behavior* was perceived as signaling or promoting a particular friendship repair *condition.*

Main effects on the presence variable were of primary a priori interest. That is to say, if a given behavior does indeed operate to promote a certain friendship repair condition, then Likert scale manifestation scores (i.e., the dependent measure) should differ in a predictable direction between participants who report the behavior to have been present and those who do not.

## RESULTS—PART II

Results are summarized in Table 4.3. Likert scale scores have been converted where necessary so that higher means represent the affirmative end of the scale, given the condition's wording on the table; for example, a 7.0 would now represent "very much" for both "showed friendship to be important" and "showed friendship to be *un*important."[5]

For purposes of display in Table 4.3, groupings on the presence/absence variable were converted to presumed "correct/incorrect" behaviors for friendship repair. That is, "correct" behavior ("√" in Table 4.3) corresponds simultaneously to both "yes" on positive behaviors and "no" on negative behaviors; and "incorrect behavior" ("X") corresponds to "yes" on negative behaviors and "no" on positive behaviors. Thus higher means on desirable conditions would be expected for subjects reporting "√" behaviors, and higher means on undesirable conditions would be expected for subjects reporting "X" behaviors.

Table 4.3 includes, for each target behavior, the conditions for which significant main effects were found on the √/X variable. All differences are in the predicted direction, with one exception, to be discussed below. That is, the presence of presumed positive behaviors generally was perceived to promote desirable conditions, compared with their absence, while the presence of negative behaviors promoted undesirable conditions. Clearly, most of the target behaviors may operate to promote more than one critical condition, though for most of these behaviors the relationship appears stronger to some associated conditions than to others.

As a whole, Table 4.3 offers a view of *how* positive and negative behaviors operate to affect the fate of male/female friendships after unrequited-romantic-attraction episodes. There are very few major surprises in the Table 4.3 data. Most of the behavior/condition relationships are consistent with those suggested by the qualitative analysis of our earlier study, and the few that represent new observations are intuitively sensible.

(*Text continues on page 87*)

Table 4.3    Perceived Effect of Behaviors on Conditions

| Behavior and Conditions | Means | | | | √ vs. X p | Main Effects F(1, 90) L vs. D p | P vs. R p |
|---|---|---|---|---|---|---|---|
| | √LR XLR | √LP XLP | √DR XDR | √DP XDP | | | |
| **R reaffirmed friendship (+)** | | | | | | | |
| Showed friendship to be important | 6.4 5.0 | 6.1 3.5 | 5.0 3.6 | 5.6 3.5 | √ > X**** | L > D** | |
| Decreased P's embarrassment | 4.9 4.0 | 5.4 2.5 | 2.7 3.5 | 3.4 2.3 | √ > X* | L > D** | |
| **P reaffirmed friendship (+)** | | | | | | | |
| Showed friendship to be important | 6.5 3.2 | 5.9 4.0 | 5.3 3.2 | 5.2 2.8 | √ > X***** | L > D** | |
| Decreased R's embarrassment | 4.9 3.2 | 5.2 3.3 | 5.0 2.9 | 4.3 3.0 | √ > X***** | | |
| Showed P able to handle it | 6.3 4.6 | 5.6 4.0 | 4.6 3.4 | 5.2 3.4 | √ > X****** | L > D*** | |
| Decreased P's embarrassment | 4.8 4.0 | 5.1 2.3 | 3.6 4.0 | 3.8 3.6 | √ > X** | | |

| Behavior and Conditions | Means | | | | Main Effects F(1, 90) | | |
|---|---|---|---|---|---|---|---|
| | √LR XLR | √LP XLP | √DR XDR | √DP XDP | √ vs. X p | L vs. D p | P vs. R p |
| **R acknowledged situation OK (+)** | Subsequent means available upon request. | | | | | | |
| Showed R able to handle it | | | | | √ > X***** | L > D** | R > P**** |
| Decreased P's embarrassment | | | | | √ > X***** | L > D*** | |
| Showed friendship to be important | | | | | √ > X***** | L > D*** | R > P**** |
| Decreased R's embarrassment | | | | | √ > X**** | | |
| **P acknowledged situation OK (+)** | | | | | | | |
| Showed P able to handle it | | | | | √ > X***** | L > D** | |
| Showed friendship to be important | | | | | √ > X**** | L > D***** | |
| Decreased R's awkwardness | | | | | √ > X*** | L > D* | |
| **R tried to return to earlier contact patterns (+)** | | | | | | | |
| Showed friendship to be important | | | | | √ > X***** | L > D***** | |
| Showed R able to handle it | | | | | √ > X**** | L > D***** | |
| Decreased P's discomfort | | | | | √ > X* | L > D** | R > P** |

(Continued)

Table 4.3 (Continued)

| Behavior and Conditions | Means | | | | Main Effects F(1, 90) | | |
|---|---|---|---|---|---|---|---|
| | √LR XLR | √LP XLP | √DR XDR | √DP XDP | √ vs. X p | L vs. D p | P vs. R p |
| **P tried to return to earlier contact patterns (+)** | | | | | | | |
| Showed friendship to be important | | | | | √ > X***** | | |
| Decreased R's discomfort | | | | | √ > X**** | L > D** | |
| Showed P able to handle it | | | | | √ > X**** | | |
| Decreased P's discomfort | | | | | √ > X** | L > D* | |
| **R dropped mention of asymmetry (+)** | | | | | | | |
| Reduced pressure felt by P | | | | | √ > X***** | L > D** | R > P* |
| Showed R able to handle it | | | | | √ > X***** | L > D** | |
| Showed friendship to be important | | | | | √ > X*** | L > D** | |
| **R complained of asymmetry (−)** | | | | | | | |
| Showed R unable to handle it | | | | | X > √***** | D > L*** | P > R**** |
| Increased pressure felt by P | | | | | X > √***** | D > L** | |
| **R avoided contact (−)** | | | | | | | |
| Showed friendship to be unimportant | | | | | X > √**** | D > L***** | |
| Showed R unable to handle it | | | | | X > √**** | D > L**** | P > R*** |

| Behavior and Conditions | Means | | | | √ vs. X $p$ | Main Effects F(1, 90) L vs. D $p$ | P vs. R $p$ |
|---|---|---|---|---|---|---|---|
| | √LR XLR | √LP XLP | √DR XDR | √DP XDP | | | |
| **P avoided contact (−)** | | | | | | | |
| Showed friendship to be unimportant | | | | | X > √***** | D > L***** | |
| Showed P unable to handle it | | | | | X > √***** | D > L** | |
| Increased R's embarrassment | | | | | X > √** | D > L*** | |
| **P acknowledged R justified to expect symmetry (+)** | | | | | | | |
| Reduced R's discomfort | | | | | √ > X*** | D > L* | |
| **P suggested future symmetry (−)** | | | | | | | |
| Increased R's discomfort | | | | | √ > X***** | D > L** | |
| Made it hard for R to return to friendship | | | | | X > √***** | D > L* | |
| **P's reason for rejection was new romantic target (−)** | | | | | | | |
| Made friendship less genuine | | | | | X > √**** | D > L***** | |
| Showed friendship to be unimportant | | | | | X > √** | D > L*** | |
| **P told friends about episode (−)** | | | | | | | |
| Increased R's embarrassment | | | | | X > √***** | D > L* | |
| Made it harder for R to deal with episode | | | | | X > √***** | | |
| Showed friendship to be unimportant | | | | | X > √***** | D > L*** | |

(Continued)

Table 4.3 (Continued)

| Behavior and Conditions | Means | | | | Main Effects F(1, 90) | | |
|---|---|---|---|---|---|---|---|
| | √LR XLR | √LP XLP | √DR XDR | √DP XDP | √ vs. X p | L vs. D p | P vs. R p |
| R accepted P's romantic interest in others (+) | | | | | | | |
| Reduced P's perceived pressure | | | | | √ > X***** | | |
| Showed friendship to be important | | | | | √ > X** | | R > P** |
| R disclosed subsequent interest in others (+) | | | | | | | |
| Decreased pressure on P | | | | | √ > X***** | | |
| Showed friendship to be genuine | | | | | √ > X** | L > D* | |
| P disclosed subsequent interest in others (+) | | | | | | | |
| Made R feel less "led on" | | | | | √ > X*** | | |
| R increased flirtation (−) | | | | | | | |
| Increased pressure on P | | | | | X > √** | | |
| P increased flirtation (−) | | | | | | | |
| Made R feel "led on" | | | | | X > √* | | |

NOTE: *p* values provided for significant differences only. A priori alpha = .05; *p* values are for comparison (*, **, ***, ****, ***** = .05, .01, .001, .0001, .00001, respectively). R = romantically inclined partner, P = platonically inclined partner; D = dissolved friendship, L = lasted friendship. √ "correct" behavior, X = "incorrect" F values, means, and interaction effects available upon request.

Two Table 4.3 curiosities seem worthy of mention, however. One has to do with the behavior whereby the *platonic individual,* in rejecting the romantic attraction, *acknowledges that the partner was justified in having assumed symmetry.* Recall that Part I (e.g., Table 4.2) showed this to be the only behavior of the 19 investigated for which there was no difference in frequency between any main groups or subgroups (having been reported as present by about half the participants in all groups). While the behavior apparently is no more common to lasting friendships than to dissolved friendships, Table 4.3 suggests that it is indeed a "positive" behavior in the sense that it clearly is perceived to reduce the romantic partner's discomfort when it does occur. A second curious result is observed with the behavior by which the *platonic partner rejects the romantic inclinations while suggesting that he or she may very well develop a romantic attraction at some future time.* Earlier phases of our research suggest this to be a negative behavior (e.g., see Table 4.2), so we would not expect it to manifest or promote positive conditions. Yet Table 4.3 shows that the behavior clearly is perceived to reduce the romantic partner's discomfort. (This is the only case in the entire Part II analysis, including conditions deleted from Table 4.3, where a negative behavior promoted a desirable condition, or the reverse.) On the other hand, Table 4.3 suggests that this behavior makes it much more difficult for the romantically inclined individual to return to a friendship mode. Thus it appears that the behavior may be accompanied by a short-term gain followed by a long-term loss with respect to its effect on friendship maintenance. Except for these two curious but understandable results, relationships between target behaviors and friendship repair conditions, as summarized by Table 4.3, seem straightforward.

### Supplementary Analyses

The questionnaire included additional items regarding the relationship, recall of the episode, demographics, and so forth, some of which are worth reporting briefly.

Recall that the questionnaire asked the subjects to rate, for each behavior, the role of its presence or absence in determining the fate of the friendship. These data were analyzed as were the other data in Part II (i.e., $2 \times 2 \times 2$ ANOVAs). Each of the target behaviors was perceived by at least one subgroup as critical to the fate of the friendship. Means representing the $\sqrt{}/X \times$ Lasted/Dissolved interactions showed that partners in lasted friendships generally consider it to have been crucial when positive behaviors did occur and when negative behaviors did not. The same was true for partners in dissolved friendships.[6]

Recall that in all parts of the study, participants reported on an episode that occurred within the last 3 years. Our intention with this time window was to allow enough time to have passed to ensure that "lasted" friendships had indeed lasted while not allowing so much time that the behaviors and conditions would be recalled incorrectly. As a crude measure of the latter, the questionnaire contained two items: (1) *How well do you remember the episode?* (mean response [1–7 Likert scale, 7 = *very well*] was 6.15, with no significant difference between main groups or subgroups) and (2) *How confident are you in the accuracy of your responses to the above questions?* (mean response [1–7 Likert scale, 7 = *very confident*] was 5.98, with no significant difference between main groups or subgroups). Apparently, most participants consider their recollection of the episode to be fresh and consider their memory of the episode to be valid.[7]

## Discussion

This study continues earlier investigation of the relational dilemma whereby a friendship is threatened by one partner's revelation of romantic attraction for the other, followed by the other's rejection of romantic advancement. Having noted that some friendships survive these unrequited attraction episodes, while most do not, our primary question all along has been whether particular behaviors could be identified as likely to contribute to repairing, maintaining, and prolonging the friendship, while other behaviors could be identified as likely to contribute to the dissolution of the friendship. And one of our primary motives all along has been to provide real-life opposite-sex friends with prescriptive guidelines for maintaining the friendship, if that is their preference, in future unrequited-romantic-attraction experiences.

Our earlier research was able to identify friendship maintenance *conditions* that people perceived to be crucial to the fate of their friendships after past unrequited attraction episodes and to generate a set of behaviors that could be hypothesized to facilitate those conditions. But the earlier study fell short of being able to say that "positive" behaviors—those thought to contribute to friendships lasting—were actually more common in friendships that lasted than in those that dissolved (or conversely for "negative" behaviors), because subjects reported via open-ended recall rather than via a priori prompts.

The present study examined these behaviors and behavior/condition relationships as a priori items, testing (a) whether positive and negative behaviors are indeed more common, respectively, within lasting and dissolved friendships, and (b) subjects' impressions of the degree to which particular behaviors are perceived to promote critical friendship repair conditions.

For the most part, the behaviors hypothesized to contribute to an enduring friendship were indeed significantly more common to friendships that lasted than to those that dissolved, while those hypothesized to hurt the friendship were significantly more common in friendships that dissolved. And for the most part, the perceived relationship between behaviors and friendship repair conditions was as had been expected. The clear impression is that when romantic attraction is disclosed and rejected within a friendship, the result is awkwardness and embarrassment for both partners in virtually all cases, but the eventual fate of the friendship is largely a result of particular behaviors performed by the partners.

## PRACTICAL APPLICATIONS

Given that part of the difficulty of disclosing one's romantic feelings within an ostensible friendship apparently comes from the absence of scripts with which to maintain the friendship in the event of asymmetry, the study appears to be of pragmatic value in providing prospective guidelines for unrequited-romantic-attraction episodes. That is to say, the findings may be taken as providing a tentative list of do's and don'ts when real-life friends experience these attraction/rejection episodes—a list to be shared via interpersonal communication textbooks, classroom lectures, the popular press, and so forth. While the study's suggested guidelines should not be taken as directly tested prescriptions, they are backed up by strong evidence of their relative presence and perceived consequences in lasting and dissolved friendships.

In particular, the following postepisode behaviors seem to be advisable for *either* partner; that is, they were found to be associated with *lasting* friendships when performed by *either* partner:

1. *Verbal affirmation of the importance of the friendship.* This behavior shows the friendship to be of high priority and also reduces the other partner's embarrassment and awkwardness over the disclosure/rejection episode.

2. *Verbal acknowledgment that one is okay with the disclosure/rejection episode and the friendship/romance asymmetry inherent within it.* This shows that one is able to handle the episode, shows the friendship to be of high priority, and decreases the other partner's embarrassment.

3. *A return to preepisode patterns and routines of social contact (seeing one another, phoning, etc.).* Given the awkwardness of disclosure/rejection episodes, it may be tempting for partners to avoid one another for a while, perhaps not realizing that the other is likely to interpret the avoidance in any of several negative ways (e.g., signaling that the avoidant partner is unable to handle the situation, signaling that the avoidant partner wants to terminate the friendship). The study suggests that timely reestablishment of earlier social contact patterns serves to decrease the other's embarrassment, to demonstrate that the friendship is still valued, and to show one's ability to handle the situation or asymmetry.

4. *Disclosure of one's subsequent interest in others.* When the romantically inclined partner mentions a new interest in someone else, the platonically inclined partner feels relieved of his or her perceived pressure toward symmetry. Apparently, the disclosure confirms a return to the friendship mode, since

such disclosures are known to be common to friends and uncommon to romantic targets. When the platonically inclined partner discloses interest in another, it reduces the romantically inclined partner's feelings of being led on to expect romantic feelings to be developing.

5. *Decrease (or at least no increase) in the preepisode level of flirtation and sexual innuendo.* While a certain degree of sexual frankness, flirtation, and innuendo is reported as one of the particular features of healthy opposite-sex friendships, it appears helpful to the friendship to taper off a bit after an unrequited attraction episode. The earlier levels make the platonically inclined partner feel more pressure toward symmetry and provide the romantically inclined partner with evidence of being led on to expect romantic symmetry.

As for behaviors within the domain of one partner or the other, the following are associated with (i.e., presumably advisable for) lasting friendships:

1. *The romantically inclined partner drops the matter of asymmetry.* While one cannot flip a switch to turn off one's romantic attraction toward another, it apparently helps to turn off one's comments (and perhaps other signs) about the attraction. Doing so reduces pressure felt by the partner, shows that one is able to handle the asymmetry, and validates the importance of the friendship.

2. *The platonically inclined partner acknowledges the other to be justified in having expected his or her romantic feelings to be mutual.* This serves to reduce the partner's discomfort with the disclosure/rejection episode.

3. *The romantically inclined partner accepts the other's new romantic interests.* This reduces the pressure toward symmetry felt by the platonically inclined partner and also shows that the romantically inclined partner values the friendship.

On the other hand, certain behaviors appear to be inadvisable or at least are "negative" behaviors associated with friendships that *dissolve* after unrequited romantic disclosures:

1. *Either partner avoids social contact with the other.* While it is intuitively understandable that the awkwardness and embarrassment of the episode might incline the partners to avoid one another for a while, this behavior apparently carries consequences of implying the friendship to be unimportant, of implying that one is unable to handle the situation, and of increasing embarrassment at least for the romantically inclined partner.

2. *The romantically inclined partner complains about the absence of mutually romantic feelings.* It was implied above that it is unwise to even continue mentioning asymmetry, so it makes sense that actually complaining about it would

exacerbate the negative conditions of showing that one is unable to deal with the situation and of increasing pressure on the partner.

3. *The platonically inclined partner suggests that mutual romantic feelings may develop in the future.* It may seem kind to reject another's romantic interest by suggesting that mutual attraction, while absent at the moment, is not out of the question for the future. Apparently, if the partner recognizes the suggestion as a mere ploy, it increases his or her embarrassment and discomfort; and if he or she believes the suggestion, the assumed potential for romantic symmetry makes it difficult for him or her to return to a friendship mode.

4. *The platonically inclined partner suggests that the romantic feelings cannot be reciprocated because of a new romantic target of his or her own.* While it is common to reject advances of various kinds by stating that one is already interested in someone else, it appears to be a poor rejection strategy within unrequited romance friendships. The information implies the friendship to have been insincere and unimportant, presumably because within true friendships one is expected to disclose one's interest in others.

5. *The platonically inclined partner tells friends about the episode (and the other finds out).* The data suggest that it is quite common—within both friendships that last and those that dissolve—for the platonically inclined partner to tell friends of the disclosure/rejection episode. What distinguishes between lasting and dissolved friendships is not the platonic partner's having told but rather the romantic partner's awareness that friends were told, in which case his or her embarrassment becomes more difficult and the platonic partner's commitment to the friendship seems questionable.

## Conclusion

The standard approach to the study of interpersonal communication strategies and behaviors is to examine variables such as personality, gender, and demographics as causal variables; to examine hypothetical strategies or behavioral choices as an outcome variable; and to ignore the efficacy variable. The present study examined behavior choice as a causal variable; examined efficacy as an outcome variable; and infers, but does not test, generalizability across personality and demographics. And while there is value in both approaches, further attention to the efficacy variable should be welcomed in communication research.

Still, we cannot be certain that the behavior/efficacy associations observed in this study are perfect, of course. To rely on participants' recall does not constitute a direct test of factors influencing the fate of friendships in unrequited romance situations. While true-life male/female friendship partners should welcome the practical advice suggested by the behavior/outcome associations of this study, we should prefer more direct tests guided by the present observations. For example, an obvious next step would be an intervention study with individuals who are considering disclosing romantic feelings within an existing friendship.[8]

In any case, the study brings us closer to an understanding of why, after unrequited romantic disclosures, some friendships last, while others dissolve. An applied interpretation of the findings provides one of very few available scripts or guidelines to behaviors for handling these situations in ways that are advantageous to the friendship. Sharing these guidelines via lectures, textbooks, and so forth seems likely to reduce the risk of disclosure and to increase the likelihood that friends may maintain their relationship when romantic attraction is not mutual.

## Notes

1. As an example of the exact questionnaire wording (for romantic/lasted in this case): "5.A. Did you try to return quickly to the same frequency and patterns of contact as before the disclosure? [Yes/No.] 5.B. Do you feel that this (your answer to 5.A) played an important role in the fact that the friendship lasted? [1–7 yes/no Likert scale.] 5.C. Do you feel that it (your answer to 5.A) reduced or increased the embarrassment or awkwardness for you? [1–7 increased/decreased Likert scale.] 5.D. Do you feel that it (your answer to 5.A) reduced or increased the embarrassment or awkwardness for your partner? [1–7 increased/decreased Likert scale.] 5.E. Do you feel that it showed whether you were able or unable to 'handle' or 'live with' the situation? [1–7 showed to be able/unable Likert scale.] 5.F. Do you feel that it served to show the importance or unimportance of the friendship? [1–7 showed to be important/unimportant Likert scale.]"

2. Rather than testing all candidate conditions suggested by Motley et al. (2008), only those suggested as primary associates of the behaviors were included. On occasion, we added conditions only remotely suggested by the earlier study and, in a few cases, even "filler" conditions with no apparent a priori link. The inclusion of these less likely associates was primarily to disguise the investigators' predictions so as to reduce subject effects.

3. Multiple ANOVAs appear justified, given evidence that the responses on all 19 behaviors were intercorrelated, as would be expected. Specifically, a $2 \times 2$ MANOVA on all 19 behaviors combined indicated significant main effect on the outcome variable, Wilk's lambda $(22, 73) = .19$, $p < .00001$, and for the outcome-by-partner interaction, Wilk's lambda $(22, 73) = .54$, $p = .0005$.

4. MANOVAs $(2 \times 2 \times 2)$ were performed on the collective conditions for each behavior. A significant main effect $(p < .0001)$ on the presence variable was observed in all cases. While collapsing the conditions via MANOVA does not especially inform the primary questions of Part II, the significant main effect does suggest legitimacy for multiple ANOVAs.

5. On the actual questionnaire, these would be the 1 and 7 ends of identically worded scales, of course. The conversion for Table 4.3 is to simplify the presentation via a consistent pattern.

6. Details of these results are available upon request.

7. Responses to additional supplementary questions indicate the following: (a) on average, the episodes on which participants reported had occurred approximately 1.29 years earlier, (b) participants' mean age at the time of the study = 21.04, (c) whereas neither subject sign-up nor screening questionnaires specified male/female friendships for unrequited attraction episodes, all participants' partners were of the opposite gender, and (d) participant $n$'s by gender within the main groups were: romantic/dissolved, male = 13, female = 11; platonic/dissolved, male = 14, female = 11; romantic/lasted, male = 14, female = 10; and platonic/lasted, male = 15, female = 10.

8. For example, participants could be divided into two groups—one receiving "advice" based upon the above predictions and the other receiving placebo information—with the groups compared on friendship maintenance at a later point (eliminating participants who never disclosed and those for whom the partner's feelings were mutual).

## References

Baumeister, R. F., Wotman, S. R., & Stillwell, A. M. (1993). Unrequited love: On heartbreak, anger, guilt, scriptlessness, and humiliation. *Journal of Personality and Social Psychology, 64,* 377–394.

Baxter, L. A. (1988). A dialectical perspective on communication strategies in relationship development. In S. W. Duck (Ed.), *A handbook of personal relationships* (pp. 257–273). New York: Wiley & Sons.

Hill, C. T., Rubin, Z., & Peplau, L. A. (1976). Break-ups before marriage: The end of 103 affairs. *Journal of Social Issues, 32,* 147–168.

Motley, M. T. (1992). Mindfulness in solving communicators' dilemmas. *Communication Monographs, 59,* 306–314.

Motley, M. T., Faulkner, L. J., & Reeder, H. (2008). Conditions that determine the fate of friendships after unrequited romantic disclosures. In M. T. Motley (Ed.), *Studies in applied interpersonal communication* (pp. 27–50). Thousand Oaks, CA: Sage.

Werking, K. J. (1997). *We're just good friends: Women and men in nonromantic relationships.* New York: Guilford Press.

# PART II

*Occasional Situations*

# 5

## Communication During Serial Arguments

### Connections With Individuals' Mental and Physical Well-Being

*Michael E. Roloff*

*Rachel M. Reznik*

Often individuals are unable to resolve an interpersonal conflict in a single episode and go on to have reoccurring argumentative episodes about that issue. Roloff and Johnson (2002) define such serial arguing as "argumentative episodes focused on a given issue that occur at least twice" (p. 108). Serial arguing often involves repeated communication sequences that adversely impact relationships and personal well-being (Johnson & Roloff, 2000; Malis & Roloff, 2006a, 2006b). In this chapter, we examine how destructive and constructive communication sequences enacted during episodes of serial arguing are related to psychological and physical health.

First, we examine literature focused on communication patterns enacted during serial arguing. We then review studies indicating that destructive communication processes are related to poor psychological and physical well-being. Next, we present evidence concerning the health impact of engaging in constructive conflict processes. From that analysis, we posit hypotheses and present a study that compares constructive and destructive conflict processes in serial arguments.

## Communication Patterns During Serial Arguments

Although serial argument episodes are focused on the same issue, the communication patterns evident within them can vary (Roloff & Johnson, 2002). In some cases, individuals engage in mutual hostility in which, across the serial episodes, they threaten, insult, and express their anger toward one another. Johnson and Roloff (2000) found that hostility occurring during serial arguments was positively related to individuals experiencing harm to their relationship. However, a constructive communication pattern, including expressing feelings and suggesting solutions, may occur during serial arguing that has a positive effect on solving relational problems. Constructive communication was positively related to individuals being optimistic about their serial arguments being resolvable (Johnson & Roloff, 1998).

There is evidence that mutual hostility and constructive communication may be related to stress and stress-related health problems in different ways.

### HOSTILITY AND WELL-BEING

When arguing, individuals often engage in verbal attacks. Resick et al. (1981) found that arguments, relative to nonconflict interactions, contain higher levels of criticism, disagreement, and sarcasm spoken at a higher level of volume. These behaviors can lead to problematic sequences enacted by both conversation partners. For example, distressed spouses, more so than those who are nondistressed, engage in cross-complaining, in which one spouse's relational complaint is met with a countercomplaint by the partner (Gottman, Markman, & Notarius, 1977). Hence one spouse might complain that his or her partner never helps around the house, and the other counters by noting that the spouse only spends money but does not generate any family income. Often the participants do not stay focused on a single complaint about the partner's behavior but rather escalate the conflict by adding different issues. Or when addressing a single problem, they fight back, which leads to problem escalation (Revenstorf, Vogel, Wegener, Hahlweg, & Schindler, 1980), with each partner rejecting the other's complaint while continuing to repeat his or her own complaint. For example, one spouse may complain, "You spend too much money," to which the partner replies, "You don't know what you are talking about." This pattern is then repeated throughout the conversation and for both partners' complaints. Perhaps the most damaging sequence has been termed the "four horsemen" and is a predictor of divorce (Gottman, 1994). In this case, a partner begins the argument with harsh criticism (e.g., "You are lazy"), which prompts defensiveness ("You are always criticizing me, I work really hard") that is followed by contempt ("Quit whining") and ends with stonewalling (silence).

Mutual hostility may be stressful. Verbal attacks are likely to be perceived as intentional and hurtful (Vangelisti & Young, 2000). Moreover, negativity expressed within interpersonal interactions is related to negative affect (Räikkönen, Matthews, Flory, & Owens, 1999), and negative interactions have a longer-lasting impact on one's feelings than positive exchanges (Newsom, Nishishiba, Morgan, & Rook, 2003). Indeed, individuals who experience criticism from their spouses are more likely to be distressed at a later point in time (Manne, 1999).

Hostility is linked to individuals' self-reports of illness (Lawler et al., 2003). Intensity of negative affect expressed during conflict is linked to decreases in immune functioning and increases in blood pressure (Kiecolt-Glaser et al., 1993). Similarly, individuals with a dominating conflict style experience more work-related stress as a result of increases in relational conflicts (Friedman, Tidd, Currall, & Tsai, 2000). Finally, aggression in adults is positively related to electrodermal activity (EDA) reactivity, which is a common measure of psychophysiological response (Lorber, 2004).

Although research has not directly related mutual hostility to personal health, we believe that it suggests the following hypothesis:

*Hypothesis 1: Mutual hostility will be positively related to stress and stress-related health problems.*

## CONSTRUCTIVE COMMUNICATION AND HEALTH

Some couples engage in constructive communication that prevents conflict escalation. For example, rather than cross-complaining or problem escalation, nondistressed spouses engage in validation loops in which they acknowledge each other's complaints and are willing to discuss them (Gottman et al., 1977). So when one spouse accuses the other of not helping around the house, the partner responds, "I understand; let's talk about how we can share the load." When doing so, they validate each other while avoiding conflict escalation.

Constructive communication may reduce stress. Although constructive relational partners are expressing their concerns and feelings, they are also focused on resolving the problem rather than winning the fight or hurting each other. By validating each other's viewpoint and offering to work together to address emotional complaints, they may emotionally soothe each other (Gottman, Coan, Carrere, & Swanson, 1998). Indeed, constructive disagreements, including problem solving and generating constructive solutions, is correlated with normalized blood pressure (Davidson, MacGregor, Stuhr, Dixon, & MacLean, 2000), suggesting that expressing disagreement in a constructive way has benefits for individuals' health. Indeed, Robles, Shaffer, Malarkey, and Kiecolt-Glaser (2006) state that the absence of constructive communication during interactions interrupts individuals' "normal physiological regulation" (p. 322). Thus the presence of constructive communication such as suggesting solutions and being supportive of the partner during conflict encourages "adaptive physiological responses to interpersonal conflict" (Robles et al., 2006, p. 305).

Hence we expect that constructive communication has a calming effect on disputants.

*Hypothesis 2: Constructive communication will be negatively related to stress and stress-related health problems.*

## INTERPLAY OF CONSTRUCTIVE AND DESTRUCTIVE COMMUNICATION

Both constructive and destructive conflict strategies can occur in the same interaction. For example, individuals may begin an argument with a highly confrontational, negative tone and then become more conciliatory if the partner is responsive. Or they can begin the conversation with a conciliatory tone and become more negative if encountering resistance. We know of no research investigating the possible interplay between destructive and constructive conflict strategies in serial arguments and their association with physical and mental health.

Thus far, we have predicted that destructive conflict strategies will have a negative impact, and constructive strategies a positive impact, on individuals' health. However, there is consistent evidence indicating that the deleterious effects of bad events on individuals are of greater magnitude than the beneficial effects of good events (see Baumeister, Bratslavsky, Finkenauer, & Vohs, 2001). For example, Gottman (1991) reports that to offset the relational harm of one negative statement, spouses must engage in at least five positive statements. Also, negative social interactions have greater impact on individuals' well-being than do their positive social interactions (Rook, 1984). Finally, conflict can involve harsh criticism and negative affect that undermines a partner's mental health, and this effect is greater than when partners are socially supportive (Vinokur & van Ryn, 1993).

Based on the aforementioned evidence, one might expect that the negative impact of destructive conflict would be much stronger than the positive impact of constructive conflict. However, we believe that the effect is more complex. Because hostility and constructive communication can co-occur, hostility might alter the relationship between constructive communication and stress. The initial reaction to a partner's destructive behavior is to reciprocate; thus individuals must exert self-control in order to respond constructively (Finkel & Campbell, 2001). This self-control may become a source of stress as individuals inhibit their natural tendencies to attack back and shift their focus to constructing a positive response. If so, the positive effect of constructive conflict strategies would be diminished as the frequency of hostility increases. We expect a two-way interaction of constructive communication and hostility on well-being.

*Hypothesis 3: Hostility will moderate the relationship between constructive communication and stress-related health problems such that the negative relationship between constructive communication and stress problems will decrease as hostility increases.*

# Method

## PARTICIPANTS

Undergraduate students at a medium-sized, private, midwestern university received course credit for participating in this study. In total, 219 participants completed the questionnaires. Participants were allowed to report on either a current dating relationship or one that had terminated. Roughly the same number chose each type (broken up: $n = 106, 49\%$; intact: $n = 112, 51\%$; 1 participant did not indicate the state of the relationship). Of the 219 questionnaires, 82 were completed by men (37%) and 137 were completed by women (63%). The participants' mean age was 19.8 years ($SD = 1.18$).

## PROCEDURE

Upon arrival at a lab, participants signed consent forms, completed questionnaires, and were briefed.

## MEASURES: PREDICTORS

As part of a larger study on serial arguing, participants reported on a serial argument that had occurred in either a current or a previous dating relationship. The following definition was provided to help them recall such an incident: "A serial argument exists when individuals argue or engage in conflict about the same topic over time, during which they participate in several (at least two) arguments about the topic." Then participants were asked to think of a recent episode of a serial argument and to answer questions about the communication they and their partners enacted during the episode as well as measures of stress and stress-related problems that occurred afterward. Participants described the most recent argumentative episode because it should be easiest to recall, and research indicates that the most recent episode is similar to typical disagreements about the issue (Malis, 2006).

### *Mutual Hostility and Constructive Communication*

Items from Christensen's Communication Pattern Questionnaire (CPQ; Christensen & Heavey, 1993; Christensen & Sullaway, 1984) assessed destructive and constructive communication. Participants indicated (1 = *very little*, 7 = *very much*) the degree to which argumentative episodes were hostile—for example, "How much did both you and your partner call each other names, swear at each other, or verbally attack each other?" and "How much did you and your partner threaten each other with negative consequences"—(four items, $M = 2.65$, $SD = 1.33$, $\alpha = .78$), and the degree to which they engaged in constructive communication—for example, "How much did both you and your partner suggest possible solutions and compromises?" and "How much did you and your partner express your feelings to each other?"—(two items, $M = 4.59$, $SD = 1.51$, $\alpha = .68$).

## DEPENDENT MEASURES

### Stress

The Perceived Stress Scale (PSS; Cohen, Kamarck, & Mermelstein, 1983) assesses the degree to which situations in a person's life are stressful on 5-point scales (1 = *never*, 5 = *very often*). The scale was adapted for this study to assess the degree to which individuals felt life events were stressful right after their most recent episode of their serial argument (e.g., "After your last argument, how often have you felt nervous and 'stressed'?" $M = 2.63$, $SD = 0.62$, $\alpha = .88$).

We also measured stress-related illness (e.g., Lawler et al., 2003), anxiety (Bancila, Mittelmark, & Hetland, 2006; see National Institute of Mental Health [NIMH], 1999), sleep disruption (e.g., Brissette & Cohen, 2002), intrusive thoughts and hyperarousal (e.g., NIMH, 1999), and interference with life activities (e.g., Repetti, 1994).

### Anxiety and Sleep Disruption

The degree to which individuals experienced anxiety and sleep disruption after the most recent serial arguing episode was assessed via related questions. Responses were in a 4-point format (1 = *did not have*, 2 = *had but not diagnosed*, 3 = *diagnosed, but not treated*, 4 = *diagnosed and treated*; Rich, 1989). Respondents answered three items that indicated the degree to which they suffered from sleep problems after the most recent argumentative episode (problems sleeping, problems falling asleep, problems staying asleep) and four items that indicated the degree to which they suffered from anxiety after their most recent episode (worrying a lot, panic attacks, high anxiety, and anxiety disorder). Because very few participants reported being diagnosed (responses 3 and 4), the responses to each item were converted into a dichotomy (0 = *did not have*, 1 = *had*), regardless of whether diagnosed or treated. An index was formed from the responses to the three sleep items ($M = 0.89$, $SD = 1.14$, $\alpha = .81$) and the four anxiety items ($M = 0.22$, $SD = 0.29$, $\alpha = .73$).

*Distress*

Distress was measured with the Impact of Event Scale–Revised (IES-R; Weiss & Marmar, 1997). The IES "is a widely used questionnaire that quantifies the frequency of intrusive thoughts and avoidance behaviors" (Hall et al., 1997, p. 108), as well as hyperarousal due to a specific event. For the purposes of this study, the event is identified as the individuals' "most recent argument."

Participants indicated (1 = *not at all*, 5 = *extremely*) the degree to which, after the most recent episode, they suffered from intrusive thoughts, feelings, and images associated with the episode (e.g., "I thought about it when I didn't mean to," eight items, $M = 2.29$, $SD = 0.83$, $\alpha = .89$), felt hyperaroused (e.g., "I was jumpy and easily startled," six items, $M = 1.79$, $SD = 0.71$, $\alpha = .80$), and tried to avoid/suppress thoughts and feelings about the argument (e.g., "I tried not to think about it," eight items, $M = 2.33$, $SD = 0.80$, $\alpha = .83$).

*Health Interference*

To assess individuals' limitations due to their mental and physical health, items were adapted from the SF-36 (Ware & Sherbourne, 1992) and targeted participants' feelings following their most recent serial argument episode. The following three subscales were used: (1) experiencing interference with activities due to emotional problems, (2) experiencing interference with activities due to physical problems, and (3) pain interfering with daily activities. For the emotional interference, there were three items (1 = *not at all*, 5 = *extremely*) assessing the degree to which individuals had problems with their work, school, or other daily activities due to emotional problems ($M = 2.07$, $SD = 1.00$, $\alpha = .93$). Four items (1 = *not at all*, 5 = *extremely*) assessed how much participants' physical health has caused them to cut down on work, school, and other activities after their most recent argumentative episode ($M = 2.57$, $SD = 1.00$, $\alpha = .93$). The pain subscale consisted of two items assessing the degree to which participants felt pain (1 = *none*, 5 = *very severe*) and how much pain interfered with completing normal daily activities (1 = *not at all*, 5 = *extremely*; $M = 2.85$, $SD = 1.48$, $\alpha = .74$).

# Results

Bivariate correlations among the measures were computed, and then moderated regression analyses were used to test the hypotheses. Our two independent variables, mutual hostility and constructive communication, were not significantly correlated ($r = .11$, $p = .12$). The relationships between our dependent variables are summarized in Table 5.1. All of the dependent variables are correlated with one another, suggesting that the problems measured were interrelated and constitute a constellation of stress-related outcomes.

**Table 5.1**   Correlations Between Dependent Variables

| Variable | 1 | 2 | 3 | 4 | 5 | 6 | 7 | 8 | 9 |
|---|---|---|---|---|---|---|---|---|---|
| 1. Stress | — | .53*** | .60*** | .37*** | .33*** | .52*** | .51*** | .32*** | .31*** |
| 2. Intrusive thoughts | | — | .79*** | .58*** | .33*** | .39*** | .55*** | .45*** | .30*** |
| 3. Hyperarousal | | | — | .59*** | .45*** | .49*** | .64*** | .54*** | .32*** |
| 4. Avoidance | | | | — | .22* | .25*** | .51*** | .40*** | .34*** |
| 5. Sleep problems | | | | | — | .35*** | .27*** | .30*** | .24*** |
| 6. Anxiety | | | | | | — | .36*** | .31*** | .22** |
| 7. Interference with activities due to emotional problems | | | | | | | — | .66*** | .33*** |
| 8. Interference with activities due to physical problems | | | | | | | | — | .31*** |
| 9. Pain | | | | | | | | | — |

*p < .05. **p < .01. ***p < .001.

## EXPLORATORY ANALYSES TO ELUCIDATE POTENTIAL CONTROL VARIABLES

Because of the nature of our method, it is possible that our independent variables are correlated with other variables, and if so, these factors could confound the interpretation of the statistics used to test our hypotheses. We focused on five factors: relationship status, frequency of episodes, cause of the argument, gender, and who initiated the argument. Only two were significantly correlated. First, because approximately half of the sample reported on failed relationships, we determined whether those in intact versus terminated relationships might show different patterns of communication during their arguments. To some extent they did. Respondents whose relationship had terminated were significantly more likely, $t(216) = 2.20$, $r^2 = .02$, $p < .05$, to report that they engaged in mutual hostility during argumentative episodes ($M = 2.86$, $SD = 1.30$) than were those whose relationships were still intact ($M = 2.46$, $SD = 1.32$). However, relational status was not significantly related to mutual constructive communication.

Second, argument frequency was examined because it implies an inability to manage one's serial argument, and this could make partners more volatile during episodes. Respondents were asked at two different points in the questionnaire to estimate how many same-topic argumentative episodes had occurred, and the two responses were averaged. Respondents reported about a serial argument in which they had disagreed on an average of 12.18 occasions ($SD = 18.47$). On average, respondents indicated that they had been arguing about this issue for 9 months ($SD = 10.8$). Frequency was significantly and positively correlated with mutual hostility ($r = .25$, $p < .001$), but it was not significantly related to constructive communication.

Because relational status and argument frequency were significantly related to mutual hostility, we statistically controlled for these variables when testing our hypotheses.

## HYPOTHESIS TESTING

We tested our hypotheses with moderated regression. On Step 1, we entered our two control variables: relational status (terminated = 0, intact = 1) and the number of argumentative episodes that had occurred. On Step 2, we entered hostility and constructive communication. On Step 3, we entered the interaction term of hostility and constructive communication. Standardized regression weights ($\beta$) are reported for the tests of Hypotheses 1 and 2, but when testing Hypothesis 3, unstandardized regression coefficients ($B$) are reported for interaction terms (Aiken & West, 1991). When the interaction term was statistically significant, we analyzed its form by examining the relationship between constructive communication and the dependent variable at low (1 $SD$

below the *M*), average (*M*), and high (1 *SD* above the *M*) levels of hostility (Aiken & West, 1991). One-tailed *t* tests were employed for all hypothesized relationships.

See Table 5.2 for a summary of the nine regression analyses. Although not hypothesized, when entered on the first step, the control variables accounted for a significant increment of variance when predicting five of the nine dependent variables: intrusive thoughts, hyperarousal, avoidance, interference with activities due to emotional problems, and pain. For all nine dependent variables, the additive model containing mutual hostility and constructive communication accounted for a significant increment of variance. In only three cases (intrusive thoughts, hyperarousal, and interference with daily activities due to emotional problems) did the interaction term of mutual hostility and constructive communication account for a significant increment of variance.

### Control Variables

Relational status was significantly related to three dependent variables. Individuals whose relationship had ended reported more intrusive thoughts (*M* = 2.42, *SD* = 0.81), more avoidance (*M* = 2.55, *SD* = 0.80), and more pain (*M* = 3.22, *SD* = 1.44) than did those whose relationship was intact: intrusive thoughts: *M* = 2.17, *SD* = 0.83; avoidance: *M* = 2.12, *SD* = 0.75; pain: *M* = 2.51, *SD* = 1.43. Frequency of episodes was positively related to hyperarousal, life interference due to emotional problems, and pain (see Table 5.2). The more episodes the participants reported, the more likely they were to experience hyperarousal, interference with daily activities due to emotional problems, and pain.

### Hypothesis 1

Hypothesis 1 predicted that mutual hostility would be positively related to stress and stress-related problems. Consistent support is found for the hypothesis across eight of the dependent measures. The regression weight for hostility is positive and statistically significant when predicting stress, hyperarousal, avoidance, sleep problems, anxiety, interference with activities due to emotional problems, interference with activities due to physical problems, and physical pain. The regression weight for intrusive thoughts was positive but only approached statistical significance, $\beta = .13$, $t(207) = 1.92$, $p = .06$ (see Table 5.2). Thus the more individuals engaged in hostility during their serial arguments, the more likely they experienced stress, a hyperaroused state, avoidance, problems sleeping, anxiety, interference with daily life due to both emotional and physical problems, pain, and intrusive thoughts.

*(Text continues on page 111)*

**Table 5.2** Summary of Regression Analysis of Communication on Control Variables, Hostility, and Constructive Communication

| Variable | df | $R^2$ | $R^2\Delta$ | $F\Delta$ | $t$ | $\beta$ | $B$ |
|---|---|---|---|---|---|---|---|
| *Stress* | | | | | | | |
| Step 1: Control variables | 2, 207 | .00 | .00 | 0.47 | | | |
| Relational status | | | | | 0.06 | .00 | |
| Number | | | | | 0.97 | .07 | |
| Step 2: Predictor variables | 4, 205 | .06 | .06 | 5.99** | | | |
| Hostility | | | | | 3.46*** | .25 | |
| Constructive | | | | | -0.72 | -.05 | |
| Step 3: Interaction term | 5, 204 | .08 | .02 | 3.39 | 1.84 | | .05 |
| *Intrusive thoughts* | | | | | | | |
| Step 1: Control variables | 2, 207 | .05 | .05 | 5.16** | | | |
| Relational status | | | | | -2.42* | -.17 | |
| Number | | | | | 1.92 | .13 | |
| Step 2: Predictor variables | 4, 205 | .12 | .07 | 8.54*** | | | |
| Hostility | | | | | 3.87*** | .27 | |
| Constructive | | | | | 0.80 | .05 | |
| Step 3: Interaction term | 5, 204 | .15 | .03 | 6.18* | 2.49* | | .08 |
| *Hyperarousal* | | | | | | | |
| Step 1: Control variables | 2, 207 | .03 | .03 | 3.55* | | | |
| Relational status | | | | | -0.93 | -.06 | |
| Number | | | | | 2.42* | .17 | |

*(Continued)*

**Table 5.2** (Continued)

| Variable | df | $R^2$ | $R^2\Delta$ | $F\Delta$ | t | β | B |
|---|---|---|---|---|---|---|---|
| *Hyperarousal* | | | | | | | |
| Step 2: Predictor variables | 4, 205 | .14 | .11 | 12.71*** | | | |
| Hostility | | | | | 4.87*** | .33 | |
| Constructive | | | | | −2.09* | −.14 | |
| Step 3: Interaction term | 5, 204 | .16 | .02 | 4.04* | 2.01* | | .06 |
| *Avoidance* | | | | | | | |
| Step 1: Control variables | 2, 207 | .09 | .09 | 10.15*** | | | |
| Relational status | | | | | −4.04*** | −.27 | |
| Number | | | | | 1.66 | .11 | |
| Step 2: Predictor variables | 4, 205 | .19 | .10 | 12.48*** | | | |
| Hostility | | | | | 4.89*** | .33 | |
| Constructive | | | | | −1.81* | −.11 | |
| Step 3: Interaction term | 5, 204 | .20 | .01 | 2.62 | 1.62 | | .05 |
| *Sleep problems* | | | | | | | |
| Step 1: Control variables | 2, 202 | .01 | .01 | 0.63 | | | |
| Relational status | | | | | −0.78 | −.06 | |
| Number | | | | | 0.75 | .05 | |
| Step 2: Predictor variables | 4, 200 | .02 | .02 | 1.64 | | | |
| Hostility | | | | | 1.67* | .12 | |
| Constructive | | | | | −1.00 | −.07 | |
| Step 3: Interaction term | 5, 199 | .03 | .01 | 2.08 | 1.44 | | .07 |

| Variable | df | $R^2$ | $R^2\Delta$ | $F\Delta$ | t | β | B |
|---|---|---|---|---|---|---|---|
| *Anxiety* | | | | | | | |
| Step 1: Control variables | 2, 200 | .01 | .01 | 1.32 | | | |
| Relational status | | | | | 0.49 | .03 | |
| Number | | | | | 1.58 | .11 | |
| Step 2: Predictor variables | 4, 198 | .05 | .04 | 3.85* | | | |
| Hostility | | | | | 2.52** | .19 | |
| Constructive | | | | | 0.70 | .05 | |
| Step 3: Interaction term | 5, 197 | .06 | .01 | 2.95 | 1.71 | | .02 |
| *Interference with activities due to emotional problems* | | | | | | | |
| Step 1: Control variables | 2, 207 | .03 | .03 | 3.43* | | | |
| Relational status | | | | | −0.94 | −.06 | |
| Number | | | | | 2.37* | .16 | |
| Step 2: Predictor variables | 4, 205 | .12 | .09 | 10.24*** | | | |
| Hostility | | | | | 4.52*** | .31 | |
| Constructive | | | | | −0.58 | −.04 | |
| Step 3: Interaction term | 5, 204 | .14 | .02 | 4.28* | 2.07* | | .08 |

*(Continued)*

**Table 5.2** (Continued)

| Variable | df | $R^2$ | $R^2\Delta$ | $F\Delta$ | $t$ | $\beta$ | $B$ |
|---|---|---|---|---|---|---|---|
| *Interference with activities due to physical problems* | | | | | | | |
| Step 1: Control variables | 2, 207 | .01 | .01 | 1.34 | | | |
| Relational status | | | | | −1.43 | −.10 | |
| Number | | | | | 0.66 | .05 | |
| Step 2: Predictor variables | 4, 205 | .06 | .05 | 5.04** | | | |
| Hostility | | | | | 3.15*** | .23 | |
| Constructive | | | | | −0.88 | −.06 | |
| Step 3: Interaction term | 5, 204 | .07 | .01 | 2.82 | 1.68 | | .06 |
| *Pain* | | | | | | | |
| Step 1: Control variables | 2, 207 | .11 | .11 | 13.07*** | | | |
| Relational status | | | | | −3.65*** | −.24 | |
| Number | | | | | 3.28*** | .22 | |
| Step 2: Predictor variables | 4, 205 | .23 | .12 | 15.33*** | | | |
| Hostility | | | | | 5.23*** | .36 | |
| Constructive | | | | | −1.23 | −.08 | |
| Step 3: Interaction term | 5, 204 | .23 | .00 | 1.14 | 1.07 | | .06 |

NOTE: Control variables = relational status, number of times argument occurred. Predictor variables = hostility, constructive communication. Interaction term = hostility multiplied by constructive communication.

*$p < .05$. **$p < .01$. ***$p < .001$.

*Hypothesis 2*

Hypothesis 2 predicted that constructive communication will be negatively related to stress and stress-related problems. Support for the hypothesis is only found in two of the regressions. Statistically significant negative regression coefficients were uncovered between constructive communication and hyper-arousal, and constructive communication and avoidance. Thus the more constructive communication that occurred during episodes, the less likely the participants felt hyperaroused and tried to avoid thoughts and feelings about the arguments.

*Hypothesis 3*

Hypothesis 3 predicted that hostility will moderate the relationship between constructive communication and stress-related problems such that the negative relationship between constructive communication and stress problems would decrease as hostility increased. Significant interactions only occurred when predicting intrusion, hyperarousal, and interference with activities due to emotional problems. With regard to intrusion, when entered on Step 3, the interaction term was statistically significant, $B = .08$, $t(204) = 2.49$, $p = .01$. When hostility was low, constructive communication was negatively and not significantly related to intrusion, $B = -.03$, $t(204) = -0.77$, $p = .44$. When hostility was at an average level, constructive communication was positively and marginally significantly related to intrusive thoughts, $B = .07$, $t(204) = 1.82$, $p = .07$. Finally, when hostility was high, constructive communication was positively and significantly related to intrusion, $B = .18$, $t(204) = 2.55$, $p = .01$.

With regard to hyperarousal, when entered on Step 3, the interaction term accounted for a significant amount of variance, $B = .06$, $t(204) = 2.01$, $p = .05$. When hostility was low, constructive communication was negatively and significantly related to hyperarousal, $B = -.11$, $t(204) = -2.88$, $p = .004$. When hostility was at an average level, constructive communication was negatively and not significantly related to hyperarousal, $B = -.03$, $t(204) = -1.01$, $p = .32$. When hostility was at a high level, constructive communication was positively and not significantly related to hyperarousal, $B = .04$, $t(204) = 0.66$, $p = .51$.

With regard to interference with daily activities due to emotional problems, when entered on Step 3, the interaction term accounted for a significant amount of variance, $B = .08$, $t(204) = 2.07$, $p = .04$. When hostility was low, constructive communication was marginally negatively related to interference, $B = -.09$, $t(204) = -1.69$, $p = .096$. When hostility was at an average level, constructive communication was positively and not significantly related to interference, $B = .02$, $t(204) = 0.38$, $p = .70$. When hostility was at a high level, constructive communication was also positively and not significantly related to interference, $B = .004$, $t(204) = 1.48$, $p = .14$.

In these cases, the interactions were disordinal (i.e., the direction of the relationship between constructive communication and the dependent variable changed from negative to positive as the degree of hostility increased). These results suggest that benefits of constructive communication largely disappear with increasing levels of mutual hostility.

## Discussion

Our first hypothesis was strongly supported. Hostility was positively related to eight of the mental and physical well-being indicators. The more likely people were to engage in mutual negative communication in the form of yelling at one another, threatening each other, calling each other names, swearing at each other, or verbally attacking each other during their serial argument episodes, the more likely they experienced stress, hyperarousal, avoiding thoughts about the encounter, problems sleeping, high anxiety, cutting down on daily activities, such as work, due to emotional problems, cutting down on daily activities due to physical health problems, and physical pain. These findings are consistent with other research on arguing and health (e.g., Kiecolt-Glaser et al., 1993). In addition, this evidence indicates that hostile communication during serial arguments can damage relational and personal health.

Although only two statistically significant relationships were uncovered for constructive communication, they were in the direction we hypothesized. Constructive communication was related to individuals experiencing less hyperarousal and less avoidance but not the other indicators of well-being. In three cases, we found evidence that the presence of hostile communication lessened the positive impact of constructive communication on intrusive thoughts, hyperarousal, and interference in daily activities due to emotional problems.

Overall, these results support the notion that bad is stronger than good (Baumeister et al., 2001). Mutual hostility reflects a pattern of hurtful behavior and was consistently a significant predictor of stress and stress-related problems, whereas constructive communication was not. Furthermore, in three cases, the presence of mutual hostility seemed to overwhelm the positive impact of constructive communication.

### APPLIED IMPLICATIONS

Given our findings, what should individuals do to reduce the likelihood of negative health consequences resulting from serial arguing? It is more important to reduce negative actions such as mutual hostility than it is to enact positive ones such as acting in a constructive manner. Mutual hostility can overwhelm and alter the impact of constructive communication. Unless a couple can control their negative emotional outbursts, there is little health benefit arising from dealing with the conflict in a seemingly rational and problem-solving manner.

Of course, this advice raises the question, How does one prevent mutual hostility? Three skills may be necessary to prevent mutual hostility. First, when initiating an episode, individuals must be able to avoid negative start-up. Sometimes individuals begin an argument in a highly intense and negative way (e.g., Gottman et al., 1998) that could set off defensive responses from the partner. This seems especially likely in a serial argument wherein frustration arising from unresolved prior episodes could prompt an individual to adopt a hostile tone from the beginning of a new episode. For example, one spouse may complain that the other does not do his or her share of housework, and the encounter ends in a standoff. Because the argument has not ended, the spouse who complains may continue to mull over the problem, which increases his or her anger, and especially so if the partner does not help out. That frustration could eventually result in an explosive encounter.

To avoid such spirals, individuals should be proactive. Since one partner's moods and behavior sometimes signal to the other partner that a serial argument is about to reemerge (Johnson & Roloff, 1998), individuals should discuss how to handle these arguments prior to a new episode. Hence if a couple has an ongoing argument about in-laws, and argumentative episodes emerge around holidays when they visit, the couple might talk about how to handle those problems prior to the visit, when they are less likely to be angry. Alternatively, if a problem occurs, individuals should discuss the problem early on before anger increases or wait to discuss it until after anger subsides. Gottman (1994) argues that prior to initiating a confrontation, partners should wait 5 to 15 minutes so as to calm down and to collect their thoughts. When doing so, they can confront their partners in a less aroused and more supportive state.

Second, individuals must develop skills aimed at constructively expressing their anger. Arguments may be initiated by anger and may also prompt angry responses (Baumeister, Stillwell, & Wotman, 1990). Indeed, hearing attitudes that contradict one's own increases physiological arousal more so than hearing attitudes that are consistent (Gormly, 1974), and when we listen to an argument between two individuals, one of whom we identify with, our level of anger increases (Dutton, Webb, & Ryan, 1994). The key may be to find ways of expressing that emotion in a fashion that does not anger the partner, which then sets off mutual hostility. One way is to avoid the use of the term "anger" and substitute terms that imply that one is "distressed" by the other's behavior. Kubany, Richard, Bauer, and Muraoka (1992) argued that "anger" implies antagonism toward another that resulted from injury or attack, whereas "distress" implies pain/stress and a request for help. A partner who says "I am angry with you because you didn't call last night" indicates that other person has hurt him or her and he or she is upset. When the partner says, "Last night you didn't call and I was worried about you," it expresses concern and the partner is making an indirect request that the person call. Consistent with this viewpoint, Kubany and colleagues' research showed that confrontational statements in which speakers indicated that they were angry with someone were perceived to evoke more negative and fewer positive emotional and behavioral responses than were statements that expressed distress. Moreover, some styles seem to help individuals cope with their own anger. Davidson et al. (2000) found that individuals who are prone to express their anger constructively (i.e., express their anger directly to another while trying to understand what caused their anger) had lower levels of hypertension than did those who expressed their anger less constructively. So instead of saying, "You really make me angry and you need to change," they say, "I am bothered by your actions; can you explain to me why you did that?" Although this style of expression was not part of the aforementioned research, we note that it may reduce the likelihood of mutual hostility, since partners are less likely to feel personally attacked.

Finally, individuals identify escalating sequences and engage in behavior that will avoid escalation. Individuals must be sufficiently aware of the danger signals so that they can break the reciprocal pattern of negative affect (Gottman et al., 1977), engage in emotional soothing to calm down the partner as well as themselves (Gottman et al., 1998), or suspend the interaction until they calm down (Nielsen, Pinsof, Rampage, Solomon, & Goldstein, 2004). Gottman and DeClaire (2001) recommend that individuals reflect about their *prior* interactions so as to identify the conditions that led them to become flooded with negative emotions. In addition to identifying what initiated the flooding, individuals need to identify things they have done in the past that have helped them to calm down. If, during an argument, individuals realize they are becoming flooded, they need to call a time-out for approximately 20 minutes during which they distract themselves from the argument and engage in stress reduction techniques prior to reengaging. Furthermore, individuals must also identify ways to emotionally soothe their partners. Gottman (1994) notes that humor is an effective soothing technique, and humor enacted by the wife seems to be especially effective at soothing her husband (Gottman et al., 1998).

## LIMITATIONS AND FUTURE DIRECTIONS

This research has limitations. The self-report methodologies employed to study the serial arguments are potentially biased and inaccurate. For example, individuals completing these self-report measures may have been subject to a social desirability bias and thus may have underreported their negative behavior. Also, because the measures involve relying on memory, these measures could be subject to recollection biases. To address these issues, future research should also use diary methods and role-plays that have partners reenact their argumentative episodes, which can then be coded by independent raters (Malis & Roloff, 2006a). It would also be useful to corroborate these results using physiological indicators of stress. Our sample also imposed limitations on the generalizability of our results. The present analysis only investigated the experiences of individuals in dating relationships. However, there is evidence that recurring arguments occur in other types of relationships, including families (Vuchinich, 1987) and roommate relationships (Trapp & Hoff, 1985). Finally, our cross-sectional design does not allow us to identify the direction of causality or the manner in which the effects build over time. Longitudinal designs are necessary to do that.

In spite of the need for methodological improvements, our findings suggest fruitful avenues for further research. One issue for future research concerns identifying the causal mechanisms that mediate the relationships between mutual hostility, stress, and stress-related problems. Although our data set does not allow us to definitively speak to that issue, we see several plausible processes emerging from our results. First, it is possible that the stress arising from mutual hostility stimulates postepisode cognitive processes that sustain rather than diminish the level of stress and hence weaken the immune system. Indeed, we found that mutual hostility and stress were positively related to having intrusive thoughts, as well as attempts to avoid thinking about the conflict, both of which were positively associated with health-related problems. Second, the stress arising from mutual hostility may set off a heightened sense of physiological arousal that is difficult to reduce after an episode. We found that mutual hostility was positively related to hyperarousal after the episode and that both of these were positively related to health problems. Of course, a third possibility is a combination of the first two. It is possible that mutual hostility stimulates highly stressful responses that are sustained or easily reactivated by cognitive responses that increase the likelihood of health-related problems.

A second issue for future research concerns how individuals can best achieve the various goals they have when engaged in serial arguing. Individuals report a complex set of goals that they want to achieve in serial arguing, including the desire to resolve the disagreement, preserve the relationship, and vent anger at their partners (Bevan, Hale, & Williams, 2004). Unfortunately, research has not related these goals to constructive or destructive communication patterns. However, our research suggests what they might be. Venting anger may be counterproductive. Should one's angry confrontation prompt the partner to reciprocate anger, one could become entrapped in a pattern of mutual hostility that creates resistance from the partner, harms the relationship, and negatively impacts their physical and psychological well-being. Unfortunately, we did not identify an alternative way of addressing ongoing relational problems that would avoid stress. Although engaging in constructive communication would seem to hold promise for resolving serial arguments without damaging the relationship, it does not seem to reduce stress and many stress-related health problems. It may be that serial arguments are inherently stressful and that little can be done during the interaction to offset it.

The key may be to focus on what can be done afterward to reduce stress-related problems. Indeed, research indicates that individuals might be able to reduce their stress-related health problems by maintaining an optimistic, upbeat outlook (Malis, 2006). However, researchers have not investigated whether staying optimistic can buffer against the stress created by mutual hostility. In fact, one study found little evidence that making optimistic comparisons (i.e., viewing one's relationship as improving) helps to reduce stress-related problems (Malis & Roloff, 2006b). Identifying coping devices that can reduce stress arising from serial arguing merits the attention of researchers.

Finally, our research has focused on mutual actions rather than asymmetrical ones. In other words, our research focused on the relationship between communication patterns and health when the patterns are enacted by both partners rather than only one during an argumentative episode. An important question for future research is focused on the health ramifications arising from one partner acting constructively while the other is hostile. Gottman et al. (1998) noted that during conflicts involving happily married couples, the wife often engages in actions that emotionally soothe her husband. In doing so, she prevents or reduces emotional flooding in her husband and he remains engaged in the conversation. However, they did not address the issue of whether this asymmetrical pattern might be harmful to the wife. In other words, she may be expending a great deal of energy while engaging in self-control, as well as perspective-taking, that might increase her stress level. In effect, she might be engaging in emotional labor that could harm her health.

In conclusion, communication during serial arguments has implications for both relational and individual well-being. Constructive communication is somewhat beneficial, while a mutual hostility is clearly detrimental for individuals' well-being. This research provides more insight into the links between communication during serial arguing and health, but more research needs to be done.

# References

Aiken, L. S., & West, S. G. (1991). *Multiple regression: Testing and interpreting interactions.* Thousand Oaks, CA: Sage.

Bancila, D., Mittelmark, M. B., & Hetland, J. (2006). The association of interpersonal stress with psychological distress in Romania. *European Psychologist, 11,* 39–49.

Baumeister, R. F., Bratslavsky, E., Finkenauer, C., & Vohs, K. D. (2001). Bad is stronger than good. *Review of General Psychology, 5,* 323–370.

Baumeister, R. F., Stillwell, A. M., & Wotman, S. R. (1990). Victim and perpetrator accounts of interpersonal conflict: Autobiographical narratives about anger. *Journal of Personality and Social Psychology, 59,* 991–1005.

Bevan, J. L., Hale, J. I., & Williams, S. L. (2004). Identifying and characterizing goals of dating partners engaging in serial argumentation. *Argumentation and Advocacy, 41,* 28–40.

Brissette, I., & Cohen, S. (2002). The contribution of individual differences in hostility to the associations between daily interpersonal conflict, affect and sleep. *Personality and Social Psychology Bulletin, 28,* 1265–1274.

Christensen, A., & Heavey, C. L. (1993). Gender differences in marital conflict: The demand/withdraw interaction pattern. In S. Oskamp & M. Costanzo (Eds.), *Gender issues in contemporary society* (pp. 113–141). Newbury Park, CA: Sage.

Christensen, A., & Sullaway, M. (1984). *Communication patterns questionnaire.* Unpublished manuscript, University of California, Los Angeles.

Cohen, S., Kamarck, T., & Mermelstein, R. (1983). A global measure of perceived stress. *Journal of Health and Social Behavior, 24,* 385–396.

Davidson, K., MacGregor, M. W., Stuhr, J., Dixon, K., & MacLean, D. (2000). Constructive anger verbal behavior predicts blood pressure in a population-based sample. *Health Psychology, 19,* 55–64.

Dutton, D. G., Webb, A. N., & Ryan, L. (1994). Gender differences in anger/anxiety reactions to witnessing dyadic family conflict. *Canadian Journal of Behavioural Science, 26,* 353–403.

Finkel, E. J., & Campbell, W. K. (2001). Self-control and accommodation in close relationships: An interference analysis. *Journal of Personality and Social Psychology, 81,* 263–277.

Friedman, R. A., Tidd, S. T., Currall, S. C., & Tsai, J. C. (2000). What goes around comes around: The impact of personal conflict style on work conflict and stress. *International Journal of Conflict Management, 11,* 32–55.

Gormly, J. (1974). A comparison of predictions from consistency and affect theories for arousal during interpersonal disagreement. *Journal of Personality and Social Psychology, 30,* 658–663.

Gottman, J. M. (1991). Predicting the longitudinal course of marriages. *Journal of Marital and Family Therapy, 17,* 3–7.

Gottman, J. M. (1994). *What predicts divorce? The relationship between marital processes and marital outcomes.* Hillsdale, NJ: Lawrence Erlbaum.

Gottman, J. M., Coan, J., Carrere, S., & Swanson, C. (1998). Predicting marital happiness and stability from newlywed interactions. *Journal of Marriage and the Family, 60,* 5–22.

Gottman, J. M., & DeClaire, J. (2001). *The relationship cure: A 5 step guide to strengthening your marriage, family and friendships.* New York: Three Rivers Press.

Gottman, J. M., Markman, H., & Notarius, C. (1977). The topography of marital conflict: A sequential analysis of verbal and nonverbal behavior. *Journal of Marriage and the Family, 39,* 461–477.

Hall, M., Buysse, D. J., Dew, M. A., Prigerson, H. G., Kupfer, D. J., & Reynolds, C. F., III. (1997). Intrusive thoughts and avoidance behaviors are associated with sleep disturbances in bereavement-related depression. *Depression and Anxiety, 6,* 106–112.

Johnson, K. L., & Roloff, M. E. (1998). Serial arguing and relational quality: Determinants and consequences of perceived resolvability. *Communication Research, 25,* 327–343.

Johnson, K. L., & Roloff, M. E. (2000). Correlates of the perceived resolvability and relational consequences of serial arguing in dating relationships: Argumentative features and the use of coping strategies. *Journal of Social and Personal Relationships, 17,* 676–686.

Kiecolt-Glaser, J. K., Malarkey, W. B., Chee, M. A., Newton, T., Cacioppo, J. T., Mao, H. Y., et al. (1993). Negative behavior during marital conflict is associated with immunological down-regulation. *Psychosomatic Medicine, 55,* 395–409.

Kubany, E. S., Richard, D. C., Bauer, G. B., & Muraoka, M. Y. (1992). Impact of assertive and accusatory communication of distress and anger: A verbal component analysis. *Aggressive Behavior, 18,* 337–347.

Lawler, K. A., Younger, J. W., Piferi, R. L., Billington, E., Jobe, R., Edmondson, K., et al. (2003). A change of heart: Cardiovascular correlates of forgiveness in response to interpersonal conflict. *Journal of Behavioral Medicine, 26,* 373–393.

Lorber, M. F. (2004). Psychophysiology of aggression, psychopathy, and conduct problems: A meta-analysis. *Psychological Bulletin, 130,* 531–552.

Malis, R. S. (2006). *Serial arguing in relationships: Implications for individuals' well-being.* Unpublished doctoral dissertation, Northwestern University, Chicago.

Malis, R. S., & Roloff, M. E. (2006a). Demand/withdraw patterns in serial arguing: Implications for well-being. *Human Communication Research, 32,* 198–216.

Malis, R. S., & Roloff, M. E. (2006b). Features of serial arguing and coping strategies: Links with stress and well-being. In R. M. Dailey & B. A. Le Poire (Eds.), *Applied interpersonal communication matters: Family, health, and community relations* (pp. 39–65). New York: Peter Lang.

Manne, S. L. (1999). Intrusive thoughts and psychological distress among cancer patients: The role of spouse avoidance and criticism. *Journal of Consulting and Clinical Psychology, 67,* 539–546.

National Institute of Mental Health. (1999). *Anxiety disorders research at the National Institute of Mental Health: Fact sheet.* Retrieved April 10, 2004, from http://www.nimh.nih.gov/publicat/anxresfact.cfm

Newsom, J. T., Nishishiba, M., Morgan, D. L., & Rook, K. S. (2003). The relative importance of three domains of positive and negative social exchanges: A longitudinal model with comparable measures. *Psychology and Aging, 18,* 746–754.

Nielsen, A., Pinsof, W., Rampage, C., Solomon, A. H., & Goldstein, S. (2004). Marriage 101: An integrated academic and experiential undergraduate marriage education course. *Family Relations, 53,* 485–495.

Räikkönen, K., Matthews, K. A., Flory, J. D., & Owens, J. F. (1999). Effects of hostility on ambulatory blood pressure and mood during daily living in healthy adults. *Health Psychology, 18,* 44–53.

Repetti, R. L. (1994). Short-term and long-term processes linking job stressors to father-child interaction. *Social Development, 3,* 1–15.

Resick, P. A., Barr, P. K., Sweet, J. J., Keiffer, D. M., Ruby, N. L., & Spiegel, D. K. (1981). Perceived and actual discriminators of conflict from accord in marital communication. *American Journal of Family Therapy, 9,* 58–68.

Revenstorf, D., Vogel, B., Wegener, R., Hahlweg, K., & Schindler, L. (1980). Escalation phenomena in interaction sequences: An empirical comparison of distressed and nondistressed couples. *Behavior Analysis and Modification, 4,* 97–115.

Rich, D. A. (1989). *Anomalous dominance, immune disorders, and ability patterns.* Unpublished doctoral dissertation, Bowling Green State University, Bowling Green, OH.

Robles, T. F., Shaffer, V. A., Malarkey, W. B., & Kiecolt-Glaser, J. K. (2006). Positive behaviors during martial conflict: Influences on stress hormones. *Journal of Social and Personal Relationships, 23,* 305–325.

Roloff, M. E., & Johnson, K. L. (2002). Serial arguing over the relational life course: Antecedents and consequences. In A. L. Vangelisti, H. T. Reis, & M. A. Fitzpatrick (Eds.), *Stability and change in relationships* (pp. 107–128). Cambridge, England: Cambridge University Press.

Rook, K. S. (1984). The negative side of social interaction: Impact on psychological well-being. *Journal of Personality and Social Psychology, 46,* 1097–1108.

Trapp, R., & Hoff, N. (1985). A model of serial argument in interpersonal relationships. *Argumentation and Advocacy, 22,* 1–11.

Vangelisti, A. L., & Young, S. L. (2000). When words hurt: The effects of perceived intentionality on interpersonal relationships. *Journal of Social and Personal Relationships, 17,* 393–424.

Vinokur, A. D., & van Ryn, M. (1993). Social support and undermining in close relationships: Their independent effects on the mental health of unemployed persons. *Journal of Personality and Social Psychology, 65,* 350–359.

Vuchinich, S. (1987). Starting and stopping spontaneous family conflicts. *Journal of Marriage and the Family, 49,* 591–601.

Ware, J. E., & Sherbourne, C. D. (1992). The MOS 36-item short form health survey (SF-36): I. Conceptual framework and item selection. *Medical Care, 30,* 473–483.

Weiss, D., & Marmar, C. (1997). The impact of event scale–revised. In J. Wilson & T. Keene (Eds.), *Assessing psychological trauma and PTSD* (pp. 399–411). New York: Guilford Press.

# 6

## Unwanted Escalation
## of Sexual Intimacy

### Pursuing a Miscommunication Explanation

*Michael T. Motley*

Within relationships, there are several variations of one partner wanting a different level of physical intimacy than the other. While any version of this asymmetry can be unfortunate, the most problematic, according to both common lore and social research, is the heterosexual dating situation in which the male wants to escalate physical intimacy beyond his partner's threshold. Sometimes, when she indicates that she wants to go no further, he ceases his advances. But sometimes he attempts to escalate the intimacy despite her wishes to the contrary.

These attempts—whether "successful" or not, and regardless of whether they occur at more preliminary or more advanced levels of intimacy—are almost always bothersome for the female, often extremely so. And they are extremely common. Among college women, for example, about 70% to 85% have had the experience, usually more than once, of a male attempting to escalate physical intimacy beyond the point that she has said "stop," and the large majority of these experiences have been unpleasant (Byers, 1988; Davis, George, & Norris, 2004; Kanin, 1957; Motley, 2008; O'Sullivan & Byers, 1992).

If she says "stop," then why does he try to take the intimacy further than she wants? Traditionally, there have been three explanations: (1) the "biological explanation" that hormones and physiology make males inherently more inclined toward escalated intimacy (e.g., Byers, 1988), (2) the "sociological explanation" that social roles, norms, peer scripts, and so forth incline males toward assertiveness or aggression regarding sexual intimacy (e.g., Muehlenhard & McCoy,

1991; Shotland & Goodstein, 1992), and (3) the "evolutionary-psychology explanation" that aggressive social roles, in sexual intimacy and otherwise, have long been inherent in male primates (e.g., Barash & Lipton, 1997).

Notice that these explanations are of little comfort to women who might appreciate a pragmatic solution to the problem. They say, in effect, that there is little they can do to prevent the situation because—for biological, sociological, or evolutionary reasons—men can be expected to pursue unwanted levels of sexual intimacy.

A more recent "communication explanation" for male pursuit of unwanted levels of intimacy suggests a solution, however. Motley and Reeder (1995) hypothesized that some of the common ways women say "stop" during physical intimacy—that is, women's "sexual resistance messages"—are misinterpreted by men to mean something other than to stop. In effect, a woman says something meaning "stop" (e.g., "It's getting late"), the man doesn't realize it meant "stop," so he continues to pursue intimacy beyond her threshold and—unlike as described in the biological, sociological, and evolutionary accounts—is oblivious to her having wanted to stop. Certainly, there are cases where the male is well aware that the female wants to stop yet pushes on nevertheless, inconsiderate of her wishes. There are cases where resistance messages are understood, but if it is true that there are cases where resistance messages are misunderstood, then part of the solution would be to increase men's understanding of women's resistance messages.

More specifically, the miscommunication explanation points out that women's resistance messages have varying degrees of directness. Some resistance messages are very direct. That is, the intended meaning and literal translation are the same—as in "Please don't do that," meaning "stop." But many common female resistance messages are indirect. An indirect message is one where the intended meaning and the literal translation are not the same, as in "It's stuffy in here," meaning "Please open a window." As an example from female sexual resistance messages, "It's getting late" is almost always intended to mean "stop," but that meaning must be derived indirectly, since it is not the literal translation. Thus while there is virtually no ambiguity or room for misunderstanding in direct resistance messages, it seems possible that women's indirect resistance messages might sometimes be misinterpreted to mean something other than "stop."

Indeed, research has supported this notion. While "stop" is by far the most likely male interpretation of women's *direct* resistance messages ("Please don't do that," "Let's stop," "I don't want to do this"), it is *not* the most common interpretation of women's *indirect* resistance messages, despite their intent. For example, when a woman attempts to indicate "stop" by saying "I'm not sure we're ready for this," the man is less likely to correctly interpret that she means "stop" and more likely to believe she means either (a) that she wants to go further but wants him to think that she doesn't usually go this far this fast or (b) that she wants to go further but wants him to reassure her that the relationship has reached the point where higher levels of intimacy are appropriate. With this particular example, he is more likely to misinterpret her message to mean some version of "go" than to correctly interpret "stop." And it is the same for several other common indirect resistance messages (Motley & Reeder, 1995).

These findings not only have explanatory value in partially accounting for males ignoring females' sexual resistance messages but also seem promising pragmatically. If men understand direct resistance messages ("Please stop," "I don't want to do this," etc.) but misunderstand indirect versions ("It's getting late," "I'm confused about this," etc.), then one implication is that we should advise women to eschew indirect resistance messages in favor of direct versions and should educate men as to the intended meaning of common indirect resistance messages.

This may be easier said than done, however. Women, at least through their mid-20s, are often reluctant to use direct resistance messages out of concern for negative relational consequences—thinking the partner will be hurt, angered, offended, and so forth—and believe these consequences to be less likely with indirect versions (which they expect to be understood as resistance messages). There is evidence, however, that women overestimate the relational consequences of resistance in general and also overestimate the relative advantage of indirect versions. The likelihood of the male partner being offended, angered, hurt, and so forth by any kind of resistance message apparently is far lower than most women imagine (Motley & Reeder, 1995). Nevertheless, the practical advice that women have much to gain (i.e., disambiguation of their resistance) and little to lose (i.e., very low probability of relational consequences) by favoring the more direct resistance messages is not always well received.

In this writer's experience, conference and classroom efforts to share the research findings on males' misinterpretation of resistance, and to urge women toward more direct resistance messages, are sometimes opposed. Despite the research evidence, a few female students and colleagues persist in believing that male partners are more likely to become upset ("He'll get mad," "He'll think I'm a bitch," etc.) upon hearing a direct resistance message than an indirect message. And even more students find it difficult to believe that males can assign meanings so different than their intended "stop."

With respect to the first of these challenges—the relational consequences of direct versus indirect resistance—the Motley and Reeder (1995) study was not as complete as it might have been. Males' reactions to three direct and three indirect messages were compared, with no significant difference on any of seven relational consequences (anger, hurt, disappointment, etc.). But the three indirect messages tested constitute only about one fourth of the common repertoire of indirect resistance messages, so it is possible that these were not representative and that different results would occur with different indirect resistance messages. This should be easy to test, however, simply by replicating the relevant parts of Motley and Reeder (1995) but using a more complete and representative set of indirect resistance messages. That will be one objective of the present study. Accordingly, consider the following hypotheses:

*Hypothesis 1: Women view negative relational consequences to be a more likely outcome of direct sexual resistance messages than of indirect sexual resistance messages.*

*Hypothesis 2: The likelihood of negative relational consequences from direct sexual resistance messages is perceived to be greater by women than by men.*

The second challenge by laypeople (or at least some female students) hearing about misinterpretations of indirect resistance messages is more difficult to answer. Essentially, the issue takes the form of incredulity over common male misinterpretations. There are always a few students who ask, in effect, "How on earth can guys think that when we're making out and I say, 'I'm seeing someone else,' that I mean 'So don't take the intimacy as a commitment,' instead of 'stop'?" Or "How can he think 'I'm not sure we're ready for this' means 'Tell me that it's okay to go that far at this point in the relationship' instead of 'stop'?" And so forth.

There is a sense in which this is asking a question that has challenged language philosophers for decades, namely, how do people correctly (or incorrectly, in our case) infer the intended meaning of indirect messages, since the intended meaning is not found in its literal meaning? This is not the place to review over a quarter century of thought on the question except to say briefly that none of the popular theories provides a satisfactory account of misinterpreted indirect messages of the sort we are discussing. Grice's (1975, 1989) notion that listeners infer an implicature based on assumptions about the speaker's veracity, efficiency, relevance, and so forth hardly explains a correct interpretation of "I'm confused about this," meaning "stop," and certainly does not explain the common misinterpretation (Motley & Reeder, 1995) whereby males take it to mean "I'm a 'nice girl' who doesn't usually go this far this fast." Tannen's (e.g., 1986, 1990) popular discussion of male and female indirectness addresses indirectness in terms of politeness and vagueness versus honesty and rudeness, assumes that differences result from individual or cultural styles, and does not ask how meaning is assigned to nonliteral messages. Gibbs's (e.g., 1999, 2002) direct-access account would imply that males—since they have access to the same background knowledge and contextual factors as females—should interpret indirect resistance messages correctly, not incorrectly. The configuration model of Cacciari and Tabossi (1988) works well for idiomatic and well-learned indirect messages—for example, "Do you know what time it is?" meaning "Please tell me what time it is"—but does not explain how we derive correct or incorrect meanings for new indirect messages (such as "It's getting late" meaning "stop" versus meaning "So let's skip the preliminaries").

While established treatments of indirect messages do not seem to provide an answer, an intuitively attractive possibility is suggested by ordinary accounts of meaning whereby messages are interpreted via (a) semantic meaning, that is, the literal meaning of the words, (b) personal knowledge meaning, that is, knowledge about the subject, object, speaker, context, and so forth, and (c) pragmatic meaning, which is a guess or assumption as to the sender's goal or intention (e.g., Motley, 1978; Osborn & Motley, 1999). Thus, for example, if Jack says to Jill, "My French fries are bland," semantic meaning tells her what French fries are, what "bland" means, and so forth; personal knowledge tells her that he probably thinks they need salt or catsup, not, say, maple syrup or lemon juice. And *pragmatic* meaning has her guessing why he is telling her this—does he want her to pass the salt, is he just making a declarative statement to make small talk, is he trying to discourage her from snitching his fries, is he trying to criticize the restaurant in general, or what? In the case of familiar indirect messages, the pragmatic meaning may have been learned (e.g., "Can you reach the salt?" meaning "Please pass the salt"). But in the case of unfamiliar messages in unfamiliar contexts, *it seems reasonable that our pragmatic-meaning guesses are determined in large part by speculating upon what we ourselves might have intended by the same statement in the same context.*

Thus part of the answer to "How could he think I mean anything but 'stop'?" might be "Because of what he would have meant if he had said the same thing in that situation" (or perhaps even, "Because of what he has meant when he has said the same thing in that situation"). If, for example, the only reason he can imagine *himself* saying "I'm seeing someone else" while making out is to mean "So please be discreet about this so that she won't find out," or if the last thing he would ever mean by "I'm seeing someone else" is "So let's stop," then his misinterpretation of her indirect message might be at least partially explained.

This admittedly intuitive answer seems to satisfy many skeptics about male misinterpretation of women's resistance messages. Moreover, it may shed light on the general theoretical question of how we attribute meaning to novel indirect messages. But it is untested and thus becomes a second issue for the present study. Specifically, consider the following:

*Hypothesis 3: Males' inferred meanings for women's indirect sexual resistance messages will be more similar to the meanings males would have intended by those same messages than to the meanings women intend.*

## Method, Analysis, and Results

The Motley and Reeder (1995) study began by identifying common female resistance messages via interviews and questionnaires asking college women to recall all of the things they have said to indicate their resistance when "you have been on a date with a male and have engaged in at least preliminary physical intimacy, or even more advanced intimacy [and where] you do not want to 'go further,' but you think he does," both in situations where they did and did not hope to see or date the male again. Sixteen common resistance messages were identified, as presented in Table 6.1. These were used in the present study.

## PART I

This chapter will present an abbreviated account of Part I. Details, for purposes of replication or explication, are available from the author.

Undergraduate students (45 male, 36 female) completed a disguised-purpose questionnaire asking that they imagine themselves in a physical intimacy situation during which the woman indicates that she does not want the intimacy to go further by uttering each of three direct and six indirect resistance messages (Table 6.1, Items a, b, c, e, f, h, m, o, p). For each message, participants indicated on a 7-point yes or no scale the likelihood that they (for males) or the male partner (for females) would become hurt, angry, offended, and so on by the resistance message.

Each participant received two "scores"—the mean of his or her three direct resistance messages and the mean of his or her six indirect resistance messages. These were compared via 2 (male/female) × 2 (direct/indirect) ANOVA.

Table 6.1      Common Female Resistance Messages

---

**Direct:**
  a. *Please don't do that.*
  b. *I don't want to do this.*
  c. *Let's stop this.*

**Less direct:**
  d. *We can do other things, but not that.*
  e. *I'm confused about this.*
  f. *I'm not sure we're ready for this yet.*
  g. *I can't do this unless you're committed to me.*
  h. *Are you sure you want to do this?*
  i. *It's against my religion.*
  j. *I'm saving myself for marriage.*
  k. *I don't think I know you well enough for this.*

**Indirect:**
  l. *Let's be friends.*
  m. *It's getting late.*
  n. *I'm having my period.*
  o. *I'm seeing someone else.*
  p. *I don't have protection.*

*Results*

Means are presented in Table 6.2. Note that all differences between means are in the predicted direction. The negative consequences imagined by females exceed those stated by males in every case, usually significantly so.

Hypothesis 1 predicts that women view male partners' reactions to be more negative (i.e., lower scores) for direct resistance messages than for indirect messages. The cell comparisons on Table 6.2 (direct vs. indirect for females) show that this prediction was supported in every case. Notice that when the same comparison is made for males—that is, consequences of direct versus indirect messages—the differences are in some cases not even in the direction that favors indirect messages (e.g., for becoming angry, thinking she's a bitch, and deciding to not date her again). In any case, the direct versus indirect differences for males are not statistically significant except for one consequence— his disappointment—which in the Motley and Reeder (1995) study was the least of women's concerns among the seven potential consequences examined. The implication is that while women perceive a significant relational advantage for men's responses to indirect (vs. direct) resistance messages, men do not actually respond accordingly.[1]

Hypothesis 2 predicts that for direct messages in particular, women's predictions of men's negative relational consequences exceeds the experienced consequences reported by men. Table 6.2 shows this prediction to be supported via significant differences in the predicted direction for every case (males vs. females for direct). (Indeed, even for indirect messages, the negative consequences imagined by women exceed those reported by men, usually significantly so.)

*Discussion*

Even with a different and more complete set of indirect resistance messages, this replication confirms the Motley and Reeder (1995) observations. Women consider certain negative relational consequences to be likely outcomes of their sexual resistance messages and view these as especially likely for direct resistance messages. This implies a relational advantage for indirect messages, and for some women this may compete with the clarity advantage of direct messages. It appears, however, that from the point of view of the male partner, the relational consequences predicted by women are exaggerated even for indirect resistance messages, but especially so for direct resistance messages.

The primary pragmatic implication is that if women, once aware of the relative ambiguity of indirect sexual resistance messages, remain inclined to opt for them out of concern for negative consequences from direct resistance messages, then that concern may be unnecessary. Apparently, women have more "freedom" than is realized to use direct messages. Males are much more likely to interpret direct resistance messages correctly as "stop" than they are indirect messages and

Table 6.2    Perceived Male Reactions to Resistance Messages

| Means | | | Main Effects and Interactions | $F(1, 79)$ | Cell Comparisons | | | |
|---|---|---|---|---|---|---|---|---|
| | | | | | Direct vs. Indirect | | Males vs. Females | |
| | | | | | For Males | For Females | For Direct | For Indirect |
| **Thinks she's a PRUDE** | | | | | | | | |
| | Direct | Indirect | Sex | 13.95 ** | | ** | ** | |
| Males | 4.50 | 5.01 | Directness | 63.44 ** | | | | |
| Females | 3.17 | 4.68 | S × D | 17.01 ** | | | | |
| **Be DISAPPOINTED** | | | | | | | | |
| | Direct | Indirect | Sex | 9.85 * | ** | ** | ** | ** |
| Males | 2.51 | 3.43 | Directness | 74.39 ** | | | | |
| Females | 1.82 | 2.71 | S × D | 0.03 | | | | |
| **Be OFFENDED** | | | | | | | | |
| | Direct | Indirect | Sex | 8.83 * | | ** | ** | |
| Males | 4.46 | 4.57 | Directness | 10.88 * | | | | |
| Females | 3.34 | 4.27 | S × D | 8.23 * | | | | |
| **Becomes ANGRY** | | | | | | | | |
| | Direct | Indirect | Sex | 18.97 ** | | ** | ** | ** |
| Males | 5.12 | 4.86 | Directness | 1.20 | | | | |
| Females | 3.67 | 4.28 | S × D | 14.40 ** | | | | |

| | Means | | Main Effects and Interactions | | Cell Comparisons | | | |
| | | | | | Direct vs. Indirect | | Males vs. Females | |
| | Direct | Indirect | | F(1, 79) | For Males | For Females | For Direct | For Indirect |
|---|---|---|---|---|---|---|---|---|
| **Thinks she's a BITCH** | | | | | | | | |
| Males | 5.63 | 5.37 | Sex | 5.71 | | ** | ** | * |
| Females | 4.78 | 5.06 | Directness | 0.50 | | | | |
| | | | S × D | 5.82 * | | | | |
| **Feels HURT** | | | | | | | | |
| Males | 4.47 | 4.64 | Sex | 5.05 | | ** | ** | |
| Females | 3.61 | 4.25 | Directness | 8.01 * | | | | |
| | | | S × D | 3.03 | | | | |
| **Decides NOT TO DATE her again** | | | | | | | | |
| Males | 5.27 | 4.96 | Sex | 13.28 ** | | ** | ** | ** |
| Females | 4.00 | 4.59 | Directness | 0.71 | | | | |
| | | | S × D | 16.26 ** | | | | |

NOTE: *Higher* scores represent judgments of *less perceived likelihood* for the relational consequences. Potential range of scores is 1–7. Cell comparisons are via Newman-Kuels.

*p < .05. **p < .01.

are comparatively less likely with direct messages to experience negative relational responses such as feeling upset, angry, hurt, and so forth.

## PART II

### Participants

Participants were 91 students of various undergraduate communication courses at the University of California, Davis, all of whom had lived in the United States for at least the past 15 years, none of whom had heard or read about earlier research on resistance messages, and none of whom had participated in Part I.

### Procedure

Participants completed one of three versions of a questionnaire providing four potential multiple-choice interpretations of all three direct and all 13 indirect messages identified earlier. The potential interpretations were the same ones used by Motley and Reeder (1995) with a few (~6) modifications based on conference and classroom discussions of likely resistance-message interpretations. In addition to the 16 resistance messages, 6 presumably encouraging or ambiguous filler items, with multiple-choice interpretations, were included to disguise the resistance message focus of the questionnaire (e.g., "That feels good," "You're turning me on," "That tickles").

The female version of the questionnaire was intended to measure women's intended meanings for the targeted resistance messages. The questionnaire asked the participant ($n = 30$) to imagine the same make-out situation as in Part I and recall whether she had said any of the 22 resistance and filler messages. In cases where the message was something that she had indeed said in the past, she was to indicate, by circling all the potential interpretations that apply, "what you meant when you said it." (For others, she was to indicate "what you probably would mean if you [were to say it in those circumstances]," but these responses were ignored in the present study so as to focus on actual rather than hypothetical meanings when women use the messages.) Participants also indicated whether the message was or was not something they had ever said in the target situation, so that analysis could focus on messages participants had actually used.

Response options for each resistance message included "You don't want to go further" plus three alternate interpretations, these varying from message to message, plus space to write in alternate meanings (which was uninformative on this and the other questionnaires). For example,

> 5. You say, "I'm seeing someone else." YOU MEANT, OR PROBABLY WOULD MEAN—
>
>   A. You want to go further but want him to know that it doesn't mean that you're committed to him.

*B. You want to go further but want him to be discreet, so that the other guy doesn't find out.*

*C. You want to go further but want him to realize, in case you end up "going together," that you may do this with someone else while you're seeing him.*

*D. You don't want to go further.*

*E. OTHER:* _____

*Also HAVE YOU SAID THIS WHILE MAKING OUT? (Circle One) HAVE HAVEN'T*

Males completed one of two remaining questionnaire versions, randomly assigned. One of these ($n = 31$) was designed to determine common male interpretations of women's sexual resistance messages. This questionnaire was matched to the female version except that for each of the 22 resistance and filler messages, the participant was to recall whether a female partner had ever said the message to him within the target scenario. If so, he was to indicate how he had interpreted the message, circling any interpretations that applied from the four potential interpretations for that message (e.g., in case he had heard the message more than once) or to write in a different interpretation. If not, he was to skip to the next item, this being designed to focus on actual male interpretations rather than speculations. (Sender-oriented wording of the female version was switched to receiver-oriented wording, for example, "You want . . . him . . ." → "She wants . . . you . . .")

Another group of males ($n = 30$) completed a version of the questionnaire virtually identical to the female version and designed to determine what males would mean by the same messages if they were to speak them themselves during physical intimacy. That is, they were asked to indicate whether they had ever spoken any of the 22 messages while making out with a female; if so, they were to indicate what they had meant, and if not, to indicate what they probably would mean if they were to say it.[2]

### Analysis

The objective of the analysis was to determine the extent to which males' interpretations of female indirect resistance messages differ from females' actual meanings and the extent to which those interpretations differ from males' meanings if they were to say the same thing in similar circumstances.

Each participant received a score representing the number of interpretations *other than "stop"* that he or she assigned to the indirect resistance messages. For each participant, the resistance messages actually spoken or heard were identified, the number of other-than-stop meanings/interpretations on these items were tallied (since participants could circle all that applied), and these frequencies were multiplied by the proportion of the 13 messages represented by the relevant items. Thus for 13 messages, each with three possible interpretations other than "stop," the potential range of scores was 0 to 39. This approach was used to score meanings and interpretations for women's use of the messages, men's interpretations upon hearing women use the messages, and men's own use of the messages (which was relatively rare). To score men's meanings *if* and when they were to speak these messages, a simple tabulation of all other-than-stop responses for all 13 messages was made for each participant (i.e., tallies on those messages he had spoken, if any, as well as those he had not, since on these, participants were to indicate what they probably would have meant).

### Results

Table 6.3 shows the means for this analysis. Males interpret females' indirect resistance messages to mean something other than "stop" far more frequently than women mean something other than "stop." (The female mean of 5.16 comes mostly from a few female participants having sometimes meant something other than "stop" *in addition to* sometimes meaning "stop" for certain messages.)

As predicted by Hypothesis 3, Table 6.3 shows that while males' other-than-stop interpretations of female resistance messages are quite different from females' actual meanings, they are not very different from the meanings males have intended on the relatively rare occasions where they have spoken the messages themselves nor very different from the meanings they project when imagining what they would mean if they were to speak these messages.

### Descriptive Analysis

Table 6.4 presents the relative frequency with which the various potential female meanings and male interpretations were assigned to women's resistance messages.[3] For comparison purposes, Motley and Reeder's (1995) data are included also.

**Table 6.3**   Means of Interpretation Scores for *Indirect* Resistance Messages

| Comparisons | Female's Meaning When She Says It | Male's Interp. When She's Said It | Male's Meaning When He's Said It | Male's Meaning If/When He'd Said It |
|---|---|---|---|---|
| Other-than-stop | 5.16 | 12.90 | 12.70 | 11.30 |
| | ------*------- | | | |
| | | ----------------ns---------------- | | |

NOTE: For other-than-stop scores, higher values indicate more instances of interpreting a resistance message to mean something other than "Stop." Possible range is 0–39. Differences evaluated via *t*-test, $df = 59$; * = $p < .01$, t > 2.40.

*(Text continues on page 137)*

**Table 6.4**   Relative Frequency of Meanings/Interpretations for Sexual Resistance Messages

| Male Interp. (M&R 1995) (N) % | Male Interp. (This Study) (N) % | Female Meaning (This Study) (N) % | Direct Female Resistance Messages |
|---|---|---|---|
| | (30) 93.1 | (25) 100.0 | "I don't want to do this." D. SDWTGF. |
| | (28) 100.0 | (20) 100.0 | "Let's stop this." D. SDWTGF. |
| | (30) 93.1 | (19) 94.7 | "Please don't do that." D. SDWTGF. |
| | | | *Less Than Direct Female Resistance Messages* |
| (52) 23.1 | (28) 39.3 | (21) 19.1 | "I'm not sure we're ready for this." A. SWTGF, but wants him to think/know that she usually only does this with guys she has known longer. |
| 37.2 | 78.6 | 23.8 | C. SWTGF, but wants him to reassure her that the relationship has reached the point where this is expected or appropriate. |
| 25.6 | 35.7 | 76.2 | D. SDWTGF. |
| (22) 30.0 | (25) 36.0 | (4) 0.0 | "This is against my religion." A. SWTGF, but wants him to think/know that she's a "nice girl" who doesn't do this with everyone. |
| 32.5 | 60.0 | 25.0 | B. SWTGF, but wants him to know that she has some moral reservations about it. |
| 12.5 | 24.0 | 0.0 | C. SWTGF, but wants him to reassure her that it's okay to go against her religion's views. |
| 25.0 | 40.0 | 75.0 | D. SDWTGF. |

*(Continued)*

**Table 6.4** (Continued)

| Male Interp. (M&R 1995) (N) % | Male Interp. (This Study) (N) % | Female Meaning (This Study) (N) % | Less Than Direct Female Resistance Messages |
|---|---|---|---|
| (39) | (27) | (11) | **"I don't think I know you well enough for this."** |
| 37.9 | 29.6 | 0.0 | A. SWTGF, but wants him to think that she usually only does this with guys she has known longer. |
| 27.7 | 37.0 | 0.0 | B. SWTGF, but wants him to reassure her that it's okay despite not knowing each other very long. |
| 25.8 | 63.0 | 90.9 | D. SDWTGF. |
| (47) | (29) | (6) | **"I'm confused about this."** |
| NA | 17.2 | 0.0 | A. SWTGF, but she's surprised that the two of them are making out like this. |
| 31.1 | 51.7 | 66.7 | B. SWTGF, but is confused about what it implies for the relationship. |
| 36.5 | 51.7 | 50.0 | C. SWTGF, but wants him to reassure her that it isn't purely physical. |
| 18.9 | 17.2 | 66.7 | D. SDWTGF. |
| (44) | (29) | (18) | **"We can do other things, but not that."** |
| 12.7 | 20.7 | 16.7 | A. SWTGF, but wants him to know that she doesn't let everyone else do "that." |
| 7.3 | 10.3 | 0.0 | B. SWTGF, but wants to wait until she's more turned on before doing "that." |
| 49.1 | 37.9 | 27.8 | C. SWTGF, but in other ways. |
| 30.9 | 41.4 | 61.1 | D. SDWTGF. |
| (30) | (27) | (6) | **"I'm saving myself for marriage."** |
| NA | 33.3 | 0.0 | B. SWTGF, but expects a commitment now. |
| 44.2 | 77.8 | 66.7 | D. SDWTGF. |
| (44) | (28) | (11) | **"Are you sure you want to do this?"** |
| 38.9 | 60.7 | 45.5 | A. SWTGF, but only if he really wants to. |

| Male Interp. (M&R 1995) (N) % | Male Interp. (This Study) (N) % | Female Meaning (This Study) (N) % | Less Than Direct Female Resistance Messages |
|---|---|---|---|
| 37.5 | 53.6 | 9.1 | B. SWTGF, but wants him to tell her how much he wants to. |
| NA | 57.1 | 27.3 | C. SWTGF, but wants to be able to say it was because *he* wanted to. |
| 5.6 | 17.9 | 27.3 | D. SDWTGF. |
| (45) | (27) | (8) | "I can't do this unless you're committed to me." |
| 29.6 | 40.7 | 12.5 | A. SWTGF, but wants him to know that she considers them to be committed to each other. |
| 33.8 | 44.4 | 12.5 | B. SWTGF, but wants to let him know that she will interpret it as a commitment. |
| 33.8 | 74.1 | 5.0 | C. SWTGF, but wants him to assure her that he's committed to her. |
| 2.8 | 11.1 | 37.5 | D. SDWTGF. |
|  |  |  | *Indirect Female Resistance Messages* |
| (47) | (30) | (8) | "I'm seeing someone else." |
| 29.6 | 30.0 | 12.5 | A. SWTGF, but wants him to know that it doesn't mean that she's committed. |
| 35.2 | 33.3 | 0.0 | B. SWTGF, but wants him to be discreet, so that the other guy doesn't find out. |
| 11.4 | 33.3 | 25.0 | C. SWTGF, but wants him to realize, in case they end up "going together," that she may do this with someone else while she's "seeing" him. |
| 23.9 | 43.3 | 75.0 | D. SDWTGF. |
| (49) | (30) | (24) | "It's getting late." |
| 14.7 | 23.3 | 0.0 | A. SWTGF, but wants to skip past the "preliminaries" and get to the "heavy stuff" because they're running out of time. |

*(Continued)*

**Table 6.4** (Continued)

| Male Interp. (M&R 1995) (N) % | Male Interp. (This Study) (N) % | Female Meaning (This Study) (N) % | Indirect Female Resistance Messages |
|---|---|---|---|
| 26.7 | 23.3 | 8.3 | C. SWTGF, but only if he doesn't mind how late it'll be if they continue. |
| 40.0 | 73.3 | 100.0 | D. SDWTGF. |
| (54) | (31) | (24) | **"I'm having my period."** |
| 30.9 | 35.5 | 12.5 | A. SWTGF, but wants to give a "heads up" on how to proceed. |
| NA | 12.9 | 4.2 | B. SWTGF, and wants him to know that it's a relatively "safe" time with respect to pregnancy risks. |
| 20.0 | 38.7 | 33.3 | C. SWTGF, but wants to adapt the intimacy behaviors accordingly. |
| 25.5 | 61.3 | 54.2 | D. SDWTGF. |
| (50) | (28) | (12) | **"Let's be friends."** |
| NA | 21.4 | 0.0 | A. SWTGF, and wants to see if a "friends with benefits" arrangement is okay with him. |
| 21.7 | 17.9 | 8.3 | B. SWTGF, but wants him to know that he's making no emotional commitment. |
| 18.8 | 17.9 | 8.3 | C. SWTGF, but wants him to assure her that it's okay for friends to do this. |
| 46.4 | 71.4 | 91.7 | D. SDWTGF. |
| (48) | (25) | (12) | **"I don't have protection."** |
| NA | 36.0 | 16.7 | A. SWTGF, but not as far as intercourse. |
| 47.5 | 44.0 | 50.0 | B. SWTGF, but only if he has protection. |
| 26.3 | 36.0 | 0.0 | C. SWTGF, but wants him to know that there'll be risks if they go all the way. |
| 16.3 | 32.0 | 50.0 | D. SDWTGF. |

NOTE: (Messages are presented by approximate directness categories. The actual questionnaire order was random.) M&R 1995 = Motley and Reeder (1995). SDWTGF = "She doesn't want to go further"; SWTGF = "She wants to go further." These abbreviations were **not** used on the questionnaires.

While these data do not allow probability tests, several observations are note-worthy. First, it is clear that males' interpretation of resistance messages is reasonably accurate for *direct* resistance messages. Second, it is clear that for most *indirect* resistance messages, men interpret "stop" far less frequently than women mean "stop." Third, while Motley and Reeder (1995) implied that all 13 of these indirect messages almost always mean "stop," Table 6.4 suggests that a few have fairly common meanings other than "stop." Indeed, one or two of them (e.g., "Are you sure you want to do this?") perhaps should not be labeled as a resistance message. This does not take away, however, from the primary observation that when women *do* mean "stop" via indirect messages, men are likely to interpret otherwise. Fourth, even for resistance messages that usually do mean "stop," there are rare instances where some women may mean something other than "stop." And fifth, the male interpretations in the present study, while still remarkably inaccurate, generally are not as inaccurate as those in the Motley and Reeder (1995) study. Implications of some of these observations will be discussed below.

### Discussion

Part II was instigated by the lay question of how males come up with some of their ostensibly far-fetched interpretations of messages that women intend as clear requests to halt their physical intimacy. In particular, we have examined the possibility that these male interpretations are derived by searching for a pragmatic meaning, guided in large part by imagining their own pragmatic meaning for the same message under similar circumstances. This explanation is supported by the similarity between the range of interpretations men give to women's resistance messages and the range of interpretations they would have as senders of the same messages. (In the case of female resistance messages, this explanation, of course, neither changes nor justifies the fact that, regardless of the source of the interpretations, they are usually wrong interpretations.)

## General Discussion

Inferring the complexities of reality from mere questionnaire responses is often suspect. Certainly, the questionnaires of the present study have omitted direct examination of certain factors that may be assumed to affect real-life responses to sexual resistance messages. It is obvious, for example, that real-life resistance messages are accompanied by nonverbal vocal and nonvocal cues that can sometimes help to disambiguate the pragmatic intention. Similarly, such factors as the couple's past intimacy levels (with others and with each other), the point to which the intimacy has advanced when resistance is attempted, and so forth can affect her intended meaning and his interpretation of the messages we have examined here. While this study did not examine these factors explicitly, it did attempt to account for them implicitly. By asking female participants what they *usually* have meant by the messages, and asking males how they *usually* have responded, the groups presumably were describing similar composites of real-life phenomena that included a natural range of nonverbal behaviors, intimacy thresholds, levels of past intimacy, and so forth. The study's design assumes that these variables balance out, both across the groups' experiences and across a normal range of resistance episodes.

It is worth noting that the male misinterpretations in the present study were not as dramatically misguided as in the Motley and Reeder (1995) study. Examples of the differences can be seen in Table 6.4. Three explanations come to mind. One is the possibility that some of the participants in this study had heard about the earlier study, along with hearing the "correct" interpretations (i.e., "stop") for indirect resistance messages. Even though the study excluded former students of courses known to have discussed the earlier study, it is possible that some participants had indeed heard about the earlier research from friends taking those courses. This possibility becomes more reasonable when noticing that the most dramatic shifts toward correct "stop" interpretations in the present study (compared with the 1995 study) happened on the very items that constitute the most common classroom examples at the participants' institution (namely, "It's getting late" and "I'm seeing someone else"). A second possibility for the shift toward fewer misinterpretations is that the 1995 study used male participants from two different institutions, half being from a reputed "party school" university and the other half being from the same relatively straitlaced institution as in the present study. It is possible that interpretations actually have not changed so much at the latter institution since 1995 and that the difference between the two studies is because of considerably more misunderstanding at the other institution. A third possibility is that times are changing such that men are much more sensitive to the meanings of women's sexual resistance messages today than in 1995. Assuming that the first two explanations probably have some validity (even if in combination with the third), the point is that the participants' responses in the present study may not be as representative as we would wish and may reflect less misinterpretation of resistance messages than actually exists.

## THEORETICAL IMPLICATIONS

This study sheds light on two questions that social scientists have asked for decades. One of these is the question of why, in heterosexual intimacy situations, do men so frequently attempt to escalate physical intimacy after the partner has indicated her unwillingness to do so? The present study does not rule out the traditional biological, sociological, and evolutionary-psychology explanations for this form of "male sexual aggression" (e.g., Kanin, 1957). But this study emphatically supports the alternative "miscommunication explanation." Strong evidence has been provided for a model whereby women sometimes try to communicate their resistance to continued or escalated intimacy via messages that are very likely to be misinterpreted by their male partner to mean something other than resistance (and, indeed, in some cases are even likely to be interpreted as a request for escalated intimacy). As discussed at some length by Motley and Reeder (1995), it is possible that miscommunication interacts with biological and sociological factors, but a key difference is that the miscommunication explanation suggests a course of action whereby episodes of unwanted escalation efforts might be reduced.

The second theoretical question illuminated by this study is that of how people solve for the pragmatic meaning of novel indirect messages. The specific variant in this study asked, in effect, How is it that he can think, for example, that during intimacy, "I'm seeing someone else" means "It's okay to escalate the intimacy if no one finds out," when in fact women virtually never mean this and almost always mean "stop"? The potential answer examined here is that perhaps the cognitive process of deciphering a novel indirect message is based largely on one's own likely meaning under similar circumstances, and "It's okay if no one finds out" is what he would have meant (or because "stop" is the last thing he would have meant). The study supports this explanation of deriving meaning for novel indirect messages, at least in the case of male misinterpretations of female indirect sexual resistance messages. The data summarized in Table 6.3 suggest both that males almost never mean "stop" when *they* say any of the indirect messages during physical intimacy and that the very large range of other-than-stop interpretations they attribute to women's indirect resistance messages duplicates the meanings they have had, or would have had, as senders of the same messages. (There may be a wishful thinking component as well, where, in addition to thinking in terms of his own meaning, his interpretation is further biased by hoping she means what he would mean.)

It seems intuitively likely that this approach to solving for the meaning of novel indirect messages goes beyond the specific context we have been concerned with here. For example, if two people are talking by cell phone and one says, "I don't think my battery has much charge left," the likelihood that the other will interpret this to mean (correctly or incorrectly) "So let's say goodbye and hang up now" (vs. "So let's keep talking, but don't be surprised if we're disconnected," etc.) may be higher if that is what he or she would have meant by the same statement, and perhaps even more so if he or she wanted to terminate the conversation anyway. This "introspection" account of how people attribute meaning to novel indirect messages generally may be worth pursuing via future research.

## PRACTICAL APPLICATIONS

This study has addressed a phenomenon that most young women experience and most find to be unpleasant, namely, the situation in which a man and woman are engaged in physical intimacy, she indicates to him that she wants to stop or go no further, yet he attempts to escalate the intimacy anyway. Both common lore and earlier scientific explanations have assumed that this happens with his complete awareness that he is violating her wishes. No doubt, that is sometimes the case, and unfortunately there may be little that can be done to reduce those violations. But this study suggests that these transgressions also often occur *without* his awareness. And if we assume that many, if not most, males will respect the line they believe to be their partner's threshold, especially if that threshold has been expressed, then this study does suggest ways to reduce these transgressions. Moreover, the suggestions are fairly simple and straightforward.

The primary suggestion to men is to become aware of the many ways that women can say "stop" without saying "stop." Not only should men become acquainted with the messages of Table 6.1 as ways that women indicate resistance but perhaps should give the benefit of the doubt to other ostensibly irrelevant or ambiguous statements that have not been identified here. When he asks himself during intimacy "Why did she say that?" he should not assume the answer that he derives by wondering what he would have meant himself. It might be helpful to adopt a sort of "when in doubt, ask" rule. Male responses such as "So it's getting late; does that mean you want to stay over, or does it mean I should take you home soon?" should be helpful. If in fact she does *not* want to stop, she presumably will let him know.

The first suggestion to women is to realize that direct resistance messages are likely to be interpreted correctly, but *indirect resistance messages are not.* It may be worthwhile for women to examine Table 6.4 in light of the specific messages with which they would be likely to attempt resistance and to notice the likely male misinterpretations of those messages (keeping in mind the possibility that typical misinterpretation frequencies may be closer to those of the 1995 data than to the present study).

Second, those who find it incredible that men would assign the interpretations of Table 6.4 should remember the strong possibility that their male partner is deciphering resistance messages according to the meaning he derives when imagining himself saying the same thing, and in most cases that probably is not "stop."

So far, the advice to women is to avoid indirect resistance messages and use direct resistance messages instead, because these are so much more likely to be interpreted as resistance. But there may be some who find this advice difficult to follow because of (a) the perception that direct ways of saying "stop" are too blunt, impolite, or forceful and (b) the notion that male partners will therefore be offended or put off by direct messages. The results presented in Table 6.2

suggest that this simply is not the case. Apparently, males accept direct resistance messages easily and without negativity and in some cases even more so than for indirect messages. It appears that there is little to lose and much to gain (i.e., clarity and effectiveness of resistance) for women to indicate their resistance more directly. Except for perhaps wishing that she wanted to go further, most men are fine with her saying simply, "Let's stop" or "Let's not do this" or "I don't feel comfortable doing this" or "I don't want to do this," and so forth.

Finally, for those who remain skeptical of the assertion that direct resistance messages are not offensive to males and who put a premium on politeness, an untested but intuitively attractive compromise can be suggested: if the assumption is that an indirect resistance message is more acceptable because it lets him down more gently, or some such, then it might be useful to combine the presumed softness of the preferred indirect message along with the disambiguity of a direct message. For example, instead of "You know, it's getting late," try "You know, it's getting late; *we need to stop.*" Presumably, that would avoid the possibility of his interpreting a direct "Let's stop" as being ". . . because I don't like you" or ". . . because I'm not attracted to you" or whatever reaction is trying to be avoided by not using a direct message, but at the same time would avoid his interpreting the simpler "It's getting late" as meaning ". . . so let's skip to the heavier stuff." The same applies to virtually any indirect message: "I'm confused about this, *so I'd like to stop,*" "I'm in a relationship with someone else, *so I need for us to stop,*" "I can't do this unless I'm in a committed relationship, *so I'd like to stop,*" and so forth.

The bottom line on the practical applications of the present study is that it may be possible to reduce the incidence of unwanted attempts to escalate intimacy. Many men need to realize the indirect ways that women try to indicate resistance, many women need to realize that indirect resistance messages are likely to be misinterpreted as something other than resistance, and many women need to realize that most males will not resent a clear expression of resistance.

## Conclusion

Some sexual aggression episodes are not a matter of misunderstanding, of course. And without an empirical intervention-type study, there is no direct evidence that the elimination of the misunderstandings highlighted by this study would seriously impact the unwanted physical escalation phenomenon. But it seems most reasonable to assume, given the results of this study, that a significant subset of unwanted escalation attempts occur where the male has unknowingly pursued intimacy beyond the threshold his partner has tried to express and that a significant subset of these could be avoided, without consequences to the relationship, if her initial resistance efforts were better understood.

## Notes

1. It is worth noting that for all seven relational consequences, the most negative male responses were on "I'm seeing someone else." This is probably because this revelation causes the male to feel that he has been led on.

2. Wording was adjusted, of course. "You want him to . . ." on the female version became "You want her to . . ." on this version, for example. The only substantive change necessary to an actual resistance message or interpretation was that the "I'm having my period" resistance message was changed to "Are you still having your period?" for this version of the questionnaire.

3. For simplicity, and to highlight misinterpretations, Table 6.4 omits responses on which fewer than 10% of the males interpreted incorrectly. The data are available upon request.

## References

Barash, D. P., & Lipton, J. E. (1997). *Making sense of sex: How genes and gender influence our relationships.* Washington, DC: Island Press.

Byers, E. S. (1988). Effects of sexual arousal on men's and women's behavior in sexual disagreement situations. *Journal of Sex Research, 25,* 235–254.

Cacciari, C., & Tabossi, P. (1988). The comprehension of idioms. *Journal of Memory and Language, 27,* 668–683.

Davis, K. C., George, W. H., & Norris, J. (2004). Women's responses to unwanted sexual advances: The role of alcohol and inhibition conflict. *Psychology of Women Quarterly, 28,* 333–343.

Gibbs, R. W. (1999). Interpreting what speakers say and implicate. *Brain and Language, 68,* 466–485.

Gibbs, R. W. (2002). A new look at literal meaning in understanding what is said and implied. *Journal of Pragmatics, 34,* 457–486.

Grice, H. (1975). Logic and conversation. In P. Cole & J. Morgan (Eds.), *Syntax and semantics: Vol. 3. Speech acts* (pp. 41–58). New York: Academic Press.

Grice, H. (1989). *Studies in the way of words.* Cambridge, MA: Harvard University Press.

Kanin, E. J. (1957). Male aggression in dating-courtship relationships. *American Journal of Sociology, 63,* 197–204.

Motley, M. T. (1978). *Orientations to language and communication.* Palo Alto, CA: Science Research Associates.

Motley, M. T. (2008). Verbal coercion to unwanted sexual intimacy: How coercion messages operate. In M. T. Motley (Ed.), *Studies in applied interpersonal communication* (pp. 185–203). Thousand Oaks, CA: Sage.

Motley, M. T., & Reeder H. M. (1995). Unwanted escalation of sexual intimacy: Male and female perceptions of connotations and relational consequences of resistance messages. *Communication Monographs, 62,* 355–382.

Muehlenhard, C. L., & McCoy, M. L. (1991). The sexual double standard and women's communication about sex. *Psychology of Women Quarterly, 15,* 447–461.

Osborn, S., & Motley, M. T. (1999). *Improving communication.* New York: Houghton Mifflin.

O'Sullivan, L. F., & Byers, E. S. (1992). College students' incorporation of initiator and restrictor roles in sexual dating interactions. *Journal of Sex Roles, 29,* 435–446.

Shotland, R. L., & Goodstein, L. (1992). Sexual precedence reduces the perceived legitimacy of sexual refusal: An examination of attributions concerning date rape and consensual sex. *Personality and Social Psychology Bulletin, 18,* 756–764.

Tannen, D. (1986). *That's not what I meant.* New York: Ballantine.

Tannen, D. (1990). *You just don't understand: Women and men in conversation.* New York: Ballantine.

# 7

# *"Good" and "Bad" Advice*

## How to Advise More Effectively

*Erina L. MacGeorge*

*Bo Feng*

*Elizabeth R. Thompson*

When people encounter family, friends, coworkers, or even acquaintances who are upset about something, a typical response is to give advice. In fact, advice—recommendations about what might be thought, said, or done to manage a problem—may be the most frequent single type of communication in supportive interactions (MacGeorge, Graves, Feng, Gillihan, & Burleson, 2004, Study 1). Advice may be a beneficial response. Recipients may obtain useful information, insight, or motivation, experience a reduction in stress and upset, and be soothed by the advice giver's evident care and concern (Dakof & Taylor, 1990; Goldsmith & Fitch, 1997). The advice giver may also benefit from an enhanced relationship with the recipient or feelings of self-esteem from having been helpful.

Unfortunately, these benefits are far from guaranteed. In fact, research (and everyday experience) suggests that advice can quite easily result in negative outcomes for both recipient and provider. Giving advice can exacerbate another person's stress and upset, undermine independent coping efforts, result in negative perceptions of the advice giver, and damage the relationship between the two parties (Goldsmith & Fitch, 1997; Lehman, Ellard, & Wortman, 1986). Alternatively, it may simply have little or no effect on the recipient and may take time that might have been more effectively used for other supportive behaviors.

If we define "good" advice as advice that is perceived positively by its recipient, facilitates the recipient's ability to cope with the problem, and is likely to be implemented, and "bad" advice as advice that fails to produce these outcomes, then the question becomes: How can support providers give good advice rather than bad? The ubiquity and consequentiality of advice makes this question an important one. At present, research literature on how people respond to advice is not abundant, nor has it been synthesized with a specific focus on giving good rather than bad advice. Accordingly, this chapter is divided into three sections. In the first, we describe the two major research paradigms that have been used to study advice. In the second, we present research-based ideas about giving good advice and also explore some of the limitations of this research. In the third, we present an original, multimethod study that extends the insights of the existing literature.

## Research on Advice: Paradigms and Outcome Variables

The total research literature on advice is relatively small, and most of it falls within one of two research traditions: work on supportive communication by communication and social-support scholars (for a review, see Burleson & MacGeorge, 2002) and work using the judge-advisor system (JAS), a paradigm initiated by psychologists focused on organizational psychology and decision making (for a review, see Bonaccio & Dalal, 2006).

Research on supportive communication has developed within the broader domain of social support research but is distinguished by a specific focus on the communication processes through which support is conveyed (Burleson & MacGeorge, 2002). Within this tradition, studies focused on advice are increasing (Feng & MacGeorge, 2006; MacGeorge, Feng, Butler, & Budarz, 2004) and have taken two primary forms. In one of these—experimental message-evaluation studies—participants evaluate advice messages created by the researcher to manipulate variables such as content, style, and source of the advice (Caplan & Samter, 1999; Goldsmith & MacGeorge, 2000; MacGeorge, Lichtman, & Pressey, 2002). In the other approach—naturalistic self-report studies—participants respond to questions about naturally occurring advice episodes (Feng & MacGeorge, 2006; Goldsmith & Fitch, 1997; MacGeorge, Feng, et al., 2004). Consistent with the focus on advice as a form of supportive communication, outcome variables across both types of studies have included (a) message quality (typically, a composite scale, including items assessing helpfulness, supportiveness, sensitivity, appropriateness, and effectiveness), (b) perceived message politeness or threat to face (i.e., to identity or self-esteem), or (c) facilitation of the recipient's coping. Increasingly, supportive-communication researchers have also recognized advice as a form of interpersonal persuasion (e.g., Wilson, Aleman, & Leatham, 1998) and have included assessments of receivers' intention to implement the advice (Feng, 2006; MacGeorge, Feng, et al., 2004).

JAS research is a subset of research on decision making that grew out of the recognition that individuals often seek input from others as they make decisions (Sniezek & Buckley, 1995). In this experimental research paradigm, the "judge" is the person who must make a decision and the "advisor" is the one who provides advice. Typically, judges in these studies are asked to choose answers on a multiple-choice test of knowledge in some domain (e.g., movies) or make a financial decision (e.g., how much a backpack is worth); they also receive advice before making a final decision. Advisors give answers (their advice) to the judges. Usually, the advisors are strangers to the judges, and in many studies they provide their advice in writing. In some studies, the advisors do not even exist; instead, judges are given descriptions of hypothetical advisors and advice created by the researchers. Frequently, the researcher manipulates judge perceptions of the advisor by providing information about the advisor's characteristics, such as level of expertise. Consistent with the focus on advice as an aid to decision making, the outcome variable in JAS research is advice utilization, operationalized as the degree of match between advisor recommendation and judge decision. However, associated outcomes have also been assessed, including trust in the advisor, confidence about the decision, and accuracy of the decision (e.g., correctness of the judge's responses to the test).

JAS research has not yet examined advice in the context of supportive interactions, and the method as employed in research thus far has limitations that affect generalization to the supportive interaction context (e.g., lack of relationship or interaction between advisor and recipient). However, this strongly experimental approach also has advantages: it allows rigorous manipulation of variables and provides an opportunity to observe advice utilization. Furthermore, despite the obvious differences between the supportive communication and JAS traditions of studying advice, the reported findings are complementary in many respects. Accordingly, the following observations about ways of giving better advice are drawn from both lines of research.

## Some Research-Based Advice About Giving Advice

We view the existing research as providing five types of recommendations for advice givers who want to give "good" advice. First, advice needs to be appropriate to the situation. Second, advice givers must choose whether and how to give advice based on their own characteristics as sources of advice. Third, advice givers need to give advice in a style that is respectful of recipients' "face" needs. Fourth, advice messages are viewed more positively if they adhere to several important standards of content. Fifth, certain characteristics of the recipient may influence how advice is received, and advice givers may be able to adapt to some of these. We address each of these issues in turn.

## Contextual Appropriateness: Needed, Wanted, and Well Timed?

Logically, the first thing a potential advice giver should consider is whether giving advice is appropriate in that interaction context. Research has identified three relevant aspects of the interaction: the nature of the problem and corresponding need for advice, the potential advice recipient's interest in being advised, and the sequencing of advice relative to other forms of supportive communication.

### NEED FOR ADVICE

Research indicates that giving effective advice begins not with the choice of words or the action to be advised but with the decision about whether and when to give the advice. If (a) someone has already undertaken the best available actions or (b) there is little that can be done about the problem, then advice is probably inappropriate and other forms of support are preferable. In the case of bereavement, for example, no effort on the part of the bereaved is going to restore the lost individual or immediately relieve grief, and advice in this situation is often viewed as particularly unhelpful (Lehman et al., 1986; Servaty-Seib & Burleson, 2007). To put it another way, research indicates that advice and other forms of instrumental support are viewed as most relevant to "controllable" problems—problems in which the situation is alterable or preventable (Cutrona & Russell, 1990).

### DESIRE FOR ADVICE

Support givers should also give serious consideration to whether their advice is wanted. Several studies indicate that unsolicited advice is more likely to be viewed as intrusive and unsupportive (Goldsmith, 2000; Goldsmith & Fitch, 1997). More recently, MacGeorge, Feng, et al. (2004) found that receptiveness to advice (defined as the extent to which advice was wanted by its recipient) was a strong predictor of perceived advice quality, facilitation of coping, and intention to implement the advised action. Ideally, then, advice givers should (a) wait until their advice is directly solicited or (b) wait until there are other indicators of interest in receiving advice (e.g., asking for information) (Goldsmith, 2000).

## INTERACTIONAL SEQUENCING OF ADVICE

Even when advice appears necessary and is directly solicited, support providers should still attend to the sequencing of advice relative to other types of supportive communication. Theorists have argued that providing emotional support before giving advice can reduce emotional distress, creating a conversational environment that is better suited to problem solving (Burleson & Goldsmith, 1998). Furthermore, it may be advantageous when support providers encourage recipients to discuss their problems (e.g., by asking questions such as "So, what exactly happened?") before giving advice. Feng (2006) found that advice offered following emotional support and problem analysis was evaluated more positively (on several dimensions) than advice that did not follow this sequential pattern.

# Sources of Advice: Who Are You, Anyway?

A growing body of research indicates that responses to advice are influenced by characteristics of the source (i.e., the advice giver). We review the research on three of these characteristics—expertise, confidence, and closeness—before discussing the implications of the research.

## EXPERTISE

Multiple studies demonstrate that people are more positive toward, inclined to follow, and confident about decisions based on the advice of those they perceive as being more expert than themselves (Bonaccio, 2006; Goldsmith & Fitch, 1997; Sniezek, Schrah, & Dalal, 2004; White, 2005). These findings recur across different ways of conceptualizing, manipulating, and measuring expertise, ranging from expertise as problem- or decision-specific knowledge (Goldsmith & Fitch, 1997; Sniezek & Van Swol, 2001) to global expertise as a composite of the advisor's age, education, income, knowledge, accomplishment, life experience, and wisdom relative to that of the advice recipient (Feng & MacGeorge, 2006).

## CONFIDENCE

Advisors' expression of confidence in their advice also emerges as an important influence on advice utilization and related outcomes (Sniezek & Van Swol, 2001; Van Swol & Sniezek, 2005). In JAS studies, advisors are frequently asked to indicate their confidence using a percentage (e.g., "I am 90% confident in this answer"); these confidence estimates are often among the strongest source variables predicting advice utilization (Van Swol & Sniezek, 2005). In ordinary interactions, confidence may be conveyed through statements such as "I'm certain about this." In one JAS study, frequency of such comments was positively associated with judges' trust of their advisors.

## CLOSENESS

Several studies indicate that people are more positive toward advice from people with whom they have a closer relationship. Sniezek and Van Swol (2001) found that classmates assigned to be judges (i.e., advice recipients) had more trust in their classmate advisors when they knew something of the advisor's background or had interacted with the advisor about class work. Similarly, Feng and MacGeorge (2006) found that relational closeness was a positive predictor of receptiveness to advice, with influence on a par with the advisor's expertise.

## THE IMPLICATIONS OF SOURCE CHARACTERISTICS

Overall, the research examining the source characteristics of expertise, confidence, and closeness indicates that those who want to give good advice must consider the advice recipient's perceptions of these characteristics. If an advice giver is perceived as lacking in expertise or confidence, the advice is less likely to be appreciated, or heeded. Alternatively, if the advice giver actually has expertise or confidence about which the recipient might be unaware, it could be important to provide information ("You know, I had a situation like this, and the thing that worked for me was . . ."). There is probably less that an advice giver can do to influence perceptions of closeness within the immediate context of a supportive interaction. Therefore, the primary implication of the research on closeness is that advice should be given sparingly in interactions with strangers and acquaintances.

# Style of Advice: Don't Boss or Belittle Me

In supportive communication research, many early studies of advice have focused on the style in which advice was presented, especially the extent to which advice messages protected or threatened the recipient's face, or public self-image (Brown & Levinson, 1987). Goldsmith (1994) argued that two types of face threat were especially problematic in advice-giving interactions. One of these is a threat to the advice recipient's autonomy. Recipients may perceive advice as putting too many constraints on their freedom of action ("She's ordering me around," "He's trying to take over my life"). The second type of face threat occurs when recipients feel that their competence has been called into question. Advice can be perceived as patronizing, critical, blaming, or even insulting, especially if it implies that the recipient can't fix his or her own problems or has created those problems. Goldsmith also argued that the language (i.e., style) with which the advice is presented may ameliorate threats to autonomy or competence. For example, advice given in the form of a suggestion ("One possibility is . . .") may be viewed as more respectful of autonomy.

Subsequent research has supported much of Goldsmith's original arguments. The perceived face threat associated with an advice message has a substantial influence on the perceived quality of advice (Goldsmith & MacGeorge, 2000). Furthermore, advice that is seen as less face threatening does more to facilitate coping with problems and is more likely to be implemented (Feng, 2006; MacGeorge, Feng, et al., 2004). Research has been less successful at identifying stylistic strategies that consistently reduce perceptions of face threat (Goldsmith & MacGeorge, 2000). However, studies do suggest that advice givers should try to avoid explicit or implicit attacks on recipients' sense of competence (e.g., avoid insulting, blaming, criticizing, or patronizing) (MacGeorge et al., 2002) and should try to convey that the choice of action is ultimately up to the recipient (Goldsmith & Fitch, 1997).

## Content of Advice: Give Me Something I Can Use

Recent research has given increased attention to the content of the advice messages and specifically to the recommended actions that are the content "core" of any advice message. Several recent studies have examined how recipients' perceptions of advice content (i.e., the advised actions) influence their responses to advice messages (Feng, 2006, Study 1; Hung & Feeley, 2005; MacGeorge, Feng, et al., 2004). In each of these studies, participants have answered survey items regarding a recent advice interaction. The findings show that several aspects of advice content affect how advice is evaluated, how much it is perceived to facilitate coping, and the intention to actually implement the advised action. Specifically, the outcomes of advice are more positive to the extent that the action being advised is rated as more (a) useful (i.e., comprehensible and relevant to the problem), (b) efficacious (likely to be effective at addressing the problem), (c) feasible (able to be accomplished by the recipient), and (d) not possessed of too many limitations or drawbacks. In addition, these studies suggest that efficacy and absence of limitations may be the most important influences. Thus advice givers should give some careful thought to the match between their advice and the advice recipient's likely perspective. Is the recipient going to understand the advice and see it as relevant to the situation? If not, advice givers should probably choose a different action to recommend, explain it differently, or do something other than giving advice. Is the advised action really likely to help with the recipient's problem, and is the recipient going to be able to accomplish that action? The importance of these two issues is underscored by considerable research on persuasion. In general, people will not initiate actions they do not believe to be efficacious or which they do not feel capable of doing (Witte, 1998). Will the advised action create any new difficulties if the recipient implements it? Advice givers must also consider any negative side effects of the actions they recommend, because actions with too many limitations or drawbacks will not be evaluated positively or implemented.

These findings might be interpreted pessimistically as saying that advice givers will only be successful if they choose advice content that falls within a fairly narrow range of recipient perceptions about efficacy, feasibility, and so forth. However, a recent experimental study (Feng & Burleson, 2007) indicates that advice givers can improve recipients' perceptions of advice efficacy, feasibility, and limitations by making explicit arguments about those characteristics of an advised action. Students who read messages advising various actions in response to a failed exam viewed each action as more efficacious when explicit arguments for efficacy were included rather than omitted. (For example, the explicit efficacy argument for talking to the professor was "You know, the professor is the best person to help you figure out what you need to do in order to do well on the next exam.") Advice with explicit argument also produced more intention to implement. Thus advice givers do need to adapt their advice to the perceptions of recipients, but they also have the opportunity to influence those perceptions.

## Recipient: Is It All About Me?

Intuitively, it seems reasonable that characteristics of the advice recipient, such as gender, culture, or personality, have influence on the evaluation and outcomes of advice. However, existing studies provide only weak support for this idea. Studies suggest that men and women are very similar in their overall evaluations of advice and are similarly influenced by advice content and style (for a review, see MacGeorge, Graves, et al., 2004). Cultural influences on responses to advice have been given insufficient attention, but one recent study (Feng, 2006, Study 1) found that Americans and Chinese responded similarly to characteristics of the advice giver and advice content, with the latter playing a more significant role than the former for both groups. A few personality traits (e.g., expressivity, need for cognition) have shown small effects on advice evaluations (Feng, 2006; MacGeorge, Graves, et al., 2004), but other traits, including several relevant to decision making, have shown no effects (Bonaccio, 2006).

Overall, these findings suggest that advice givers might be able to give advice without specific attempts to adapt to the gender or culture of the recipient, though the limited studies should dictate caution in making that interpretation (and the need for considerably more research with diverse cultures). With regard to personality factors, it is convenient pragmatically that the traits examined to date appear to have little influence, since it is often difficult for advice givers to assess these traits in natural advice-giving situations.

While receiver personality traits might be difficult for an advice giver to assess, there may be other influential receiver characteristics that are more pragmatically viable. One example is the level of distress a recipient is experiencing, which an advice giver could determine (at least roughly) from observation or by asking questions ("How are you feeling about all this?"). Studies of emotional support suggest that level of distress influences the evaluation of support messages (Burleson, 2008). Other recipient perceptions that may be relevant to advice evaluations include the seriousness of the problem or responsibility for the cause (Feng & MacGeorge, 2006).

## Summary and Critique

The research literature on advice has thus far identified a variety of contextual, source, style, content, and recipient factors that influence advice evaluation. Some of this literature provides important ideas about how support providers might improve their advice. Specifically, existing research indicates that advice givers should determine whether advice is needed or wanted and whether they have the appropriate expertise and relationship with the advice recipient to be giving advice. Research also suggests that advice should be given in ways that are respectful of the recipients' autonomy and competence and, perhaps most important, should attempt to recommend actions that are useful, feasible, efficacious, and not undermined by limitations.

Despite the value of these preliminary insights, there are numerous issues left to be addressed. One such issue is the "experiential validity" of the variables examined in the literature. In most studies, researchers have chosen a small subset of contextual, source, style, content, or recipient factors to manipulate or measure in order to test theoretically derived hypotheses. This approach is scientifically rigorous but not well designed to examine what people themselves identify as the factors that influence their responses to advice, the relative importance of those factors (again, from a participant perspective), or the extent to which researchers have neglected to consider factors that might help to better predict advice evaluation and related outcomes. The study we report here was specifically designed to elicit participants' reports of factors affecting their evaluations of advice as good or bad.

## Good and Bad Advice: What's the Difference?

Because prior research on advice has not examined participants' views of the key factors influencing their evaluations of advice, we designed a study with this issue as its primary focus. To facilitate participants' ability to identify factors that influence their responses to advice, we set up the study to elicit distinctions between good and bad advice, guided by the following research questions:

*Research Question 1: To what extent do participants report contextual, source, style, content, or recipient factors as key differences between advice messages they experienced as good versus bad?*

*Research Question 2: Do the specific factors mentioned by participants appear to be represented in the current literature, or do participants report specific differences between good and bad advice that are distinct from variables identified by researchers?*

## Method

### PARTICIPANTS AND PROCEDURES

Study participants ($N = 151$) were recruited from communication classes at a large midwestern university. Consistent with the fact that most of these classes enrolled upper-division students, the average age was 21 (21.3). A majority was female ($n = 97$, 64.2%). Most were communication majors ($n = 88$, 58.3%), but a range of other majors was represented. Students received a small amount of extra credit or research credit from their instructors for participating in the study.

After providing informed consent, participants were given a questionnaire packet. The first questionnaire in each packet requested demographic information (age, sex, ethnicity, major). This was followed by the instruction to recall a conversation in the past month in which they had discussed an upsetting problem in their lives with another person. Half of the participants were instructed to recall a conversation in which they had received good advice, whereas the other half recalled a conversation in which they had received bad advice.

Participants then responded to a series of questions about the advice episode, including when the episode occurred, the nature of the problem discussed ("Please provide a brief description of the problem you were experiencing"), the advice received ("Please think back to the advice you were given . . . and describe it briefly"), and the quality of the advice (measured on a quantitative scale, described below). After completing these questions, participants were instructed to recall a second conversation from the past month—the participants who began with good advice were asked to recollect bad advice, and vice versa. This instruction was followed by the same series of questions as well as a final item requesting that participants describe, from their perspective, "the most important difference" between the two pieces of advice. Most participants completed the packet in approximately 20 minutes.

## DESCRIPTIVE DATA ON THE ADVICE EPISODES

### Length of Time Since Advice Was Received

As a check on our request that participants attempt to recall conversations that had occurred in the preceding month, we asked them to report how long it had been since each advice interaction had occurred. For the instances of good advice, the median response was 2 weeks, and 89% of the advice interactions had occurred in the past month. For the instances of bad advice, the median response was also 2 weeks, with 87% of the interactions having occurred in the past month. These data suggest that participants were reporting, as requested, on relatively recent interactions.

### Types of Problems

To summarize the types of problems reported by the participants, we used the 10-category coding system reported by MacGeorge, Feng, et al. (2004), with the addition of a health category. Two of the coauthors independently coded a random sample of 30 problem descriptions (13.2% of the data); Cohen's kappa for this sample was .95, indicating excellent intercoder reliability. Disagreements were resolved by discussion, and another coauthor coded the remaining data. Of the 151 participants, 121 described the problem for which they received good advice, and 106 described the problem for which they received bad advice, for a total of 227 problem descriptions. The largest quantities of described problems involved romantic relationships (29.9%), academic matters (15.4%), career matters (11.5%), or friendships (10.1%). Family, living situation, financial, health, and "other" were also represented in roughly equivalent quantities; our participants did not report sexual or moral problems (the remaining categories from MacGeorge, Feng, et al., 2004).

### Quality of Advice

As a manipulation check on our instructions for participants to choose good and bad advice, we used an existing measure of advice quality (MacGeorge, Feng, et al., 2004) to assess whether the two types of advice differed in average perceived quality. The 5-point Likert-style items assessed perceptions of message helpfulness, appropriateness, sensitivity, supportiveness, and effectiveness (1 = *strongly disagree*, 5 = *strongly agree*). The five items exhibited good internal consistency for both good and bad advice (both α's were .87); thus the item sets were averaged to form indices for quality of good advice and quality of bad advice. A paired-samples $t$ test revealed that good advice was perceived as higher in quality ($M = 4.42$) than bad advice ($M = 2.70$), $t(125) = 14.62, p < .001$.

## Comparisons of Good and Bad Advice—Coding

In order to summarize the key differences between good and bad advice as reported by participants, we developed a coding system with five categories. Consistent with the types of variables examined in prior studies, we initially hoped to distinguish between participant comparisons made on the basis of context, source, style, content, or recipient factors. However, participants' comparisons were frequently ambiguous about whether a quality such as caring or rudeness was a feature of the person giving the advice or the advice message per se, making it nearly impossible to distinguish between source and style as influences on advice evaluation. Similarly, we found it challenging to determine whether participants were making distinctions on the basis of context (i.e., the interaction or the problem being experienced) or recipient (i.e., characteristics of the recipient). This was due, in part, to recipients' subjective perceptions of their problems, which were reported in ways that made it difficult to decide whether they should be viewed as objective characteristics of the problem (i.e., context) or qualities of the recipient in that situation (e.g., "The difference was the amount of fault that was mine"). We also found that some participants' responses framed differences between good and bad advice primarily in terms of outcome (i.e., this advice message produced a good outcome, that one didn't), and a few failed to make any clear distinction between the two pieces of advice. Accordingly, we created combined categories of source/style and recipient/context and categories of outcome and no difference.

After developing the coding system and selecting examples for the coding manual and this chapter (using approximately 10% of the data), two of the coauthors independently coded a random sample of 30 comparisons (20.4% of the total data); Cohen's kappa for this sample was .76, indicating acceptable intercoder reliability. Disagreements were resolved by discussion, and a third coauthor coded the remaining data.

## Results

To answer Research Question 1, we examined the frequencies with which participants distinguished between good and bad advice on the basis of source/style, content, recipient/context, or outcome, or made no distinction (definitions of these categories are given in Table 7.1). Of the 151 participants, 147 (97.4%) provided a comparison between the good and bad advice they had received. The results (frequencies) from coding these comparisons into categories (source/style, content, etc.) are reported in Table 7.1. Inspection of the data revealed that comparisons on the basis of source or style constituted the clear majority ($n = 78$, 51.7%). A chi-square test also indicated a significant difference between the frequencies for source/style, content, and recipient/context (eliminating the outcome and no-distinction categories that were not of research interest), $\chi^2(2) = 46.7$, $p < .001$.

Table 7.1     Comparison Coding Categories, Frequencies, and Percentages

| Category Name and Definition | Frequency | Percentage |
|---|---|---|
| Source/Style<br><br>The difference between the advice messages is identified as being primarily due to the source (provider) or style of the advice message. | 78 | 51.7 |
| Content<br><br>The difference between the advice messages is identified as having primarily to do with the qualities of the action that the recipient is advised to do. | 21 | 13.9 |
| Outcome<br><br>The difference between the advice messages is identified as having primarily to do with the actual or predicted outcome of the action that the recipient is advised to do. | 18 | 11.9 |
| Recipient/Context<br><br>The difference between the advice messages is identified as having primarily to do with the recipient, the situation (problem), or the interaction in which the advice was given. | 27 | 17.9 |
| No Identified Difference<br><br>The difference between the two advice messages is not specified beyond saying that one was better than the other, or it is stated that there is no difference. | 3 | 2.0 |

Clearly, the central finding from this frequency analysis is that source and style characteristics are central to participants' own distinctions between good and bad advice. Most important, this finding supports the claim (made from prior research) that advice givers need to consider their "qualifications" (such as expertise and closeness to the advice recipient) before giving advice and adapt their supportive behavior appropriately (perhaps avoiding advice in situations where expertise and closeness are low). The finding also supports the need (again, identified in prior research) for advice givers to give advice in a nonoffensive style (e.g., not overly directive or critical). The current finding also suggests that researchers have not gone wrong in focusing on source and style characteristics in prior studies.

Even if source and style characteristics do have the greatest influence on participants' judgments of advice as good or bad, research on content, recipient, and context factors should not be abandoned for several reasons. First, while stimulated recall tends to identify the most salient features of an experience, it often does not represent the actual relative influence of those and nonrecalled crucial variables (Motley, Faulkner, & Reeder, 2008). Other research still suggests a primary role for content factors in evaluating advice (Feng, 2006). Second, content and recipient/context factors still formed the basis for substantial minorities of participant comparisons. Third, taking a pragmatic perspective, it may be easier to formulate useful recommendations for advice givers based on content rather than on source or style. Source characteristics can be difficult to alter (e.g., if you aren't an expert on a problem, that's unlikely to change during a single interaction), and the research on stylistic aspects of advice has failed to provide much specificity about how to reduce face threat for advice recipients (MacGeorge, Feng, et al., 2004; MacGeorge et al., 2002). Content, by contrast, is probably easier for an advice giver to change, and there is a growing research base on which to make recommendations about content (Feng & Burleson, 2007; Feng & MacGeorge, 2006; Hung & Feeley, 2005; MacGeorge, Feng, et al., 2004).

To answer Research Question 2—whether participants and researchers identify similar key variables—we inspected participants' comparisons of good and bad advice for specific factors that appeared to be similar to or different from variables examined in previous research. Within the source/style category, participants mentioned the closeness or type of relationship ("[Advice] from my family member was less supportive than a friend"), the advisor's expertise ("The doctor was an expert on eating disorders and therefore credible"), and features of style that appeared to reference concerns for aspects of face (including both autonomy and esteem concerns, e.g., "left me with options," "said 'It's not your fault'" vs. "pushy," "condescending," "accusing"). They also distinguished between good and bad advice using terms such as "supportiveness," "empathy," "caring," "sensitivity," or "compassion." The distinction that seemed most unique (relative to variables examined in existing research) was made by one participant who contrasted advice based on the advice giver's experience with similar problems versus advice informed by familiarity with the specifics of the recipient's own situation. In this case, the latter was viewed as the good advice. This contrast suggests the potential utility of examining different bases for expertise.

Within the content category, participant comparisons frequently appeared to reflect the variables examined in the handful of studies on advice content. Some participants appeared to reference issues of usefulness, including whether the advice was "specific" or "logical." Others mentioned distinctions that related to feasibility, such as stating that the advice was "not possible" or "I didn't have to go too far out of my way." Participants also mentioned limitations; for example, one participant said that the advised action had "consequences worse than the benefits." Two participants made a content distinction that has not been directly referenced in prior studies, mentioning the morality or ethicality of the advised action, with statements such as "The first advice was morally reprehensible." Although this might be considered an aspect of advice limitation, it focuses more on the goodness or badness of the action itself, rather than its consequences. Thus the influence of moral or ethical judgments on advice evaluation is another area for future investigation.

In the recipient/context category, some recipients echoed variables previously examined, including distinctions based on whether advice was desired from a particular person or whether it had been solicited ("[I was] more willing to listen to one than the other," "I didn't ask for advice"). One participant suggested that the sequence in which advice was presented was important: "My friend tried to understand my point of view and gave me supports before she told me her advises [sic]." However, inspection of this category also provided perhaps the strongest evidence of a factor not previously examined: whether the advice acted to support the recipient's preferred plan of action. Multiple participants said that good advice was "what I wanted to hear" or "was already planning on doing." For example, one participant said, "Conversation 1 was more in line with my thoughts; I just needed reinforcement. Conversation 2 was something totally opposite of what I wanted to hear." Harry S. Truman, 33rd president of the United States, is quoted as having said, "I have found the best way to give advice to your children is to find out what they want and then advise them to do it." A number of participants in our study seemed to agree. Thus future research needs to address how this factor impacts advice evaluation. For example, is reinforcement always preferred to novel advice? Furthermore, it seems likely that engaging in problem analysis with the support seeker prior to giving advice would help advice givers reinforce the recipient's planned actions (because they would know what those actions are). Does the perception of reinforcement therefore mediate the effect of problem analysis on advice evaluation? Perhaps most critically, what can advice givers do if they feel they should not provide support or reinforcement for some action?

## Discussion—Extending Research on Advice Evaluations and Outcomes

Data from the current study suggest that previously unexamined factors, including expertise with the advice recipient's specific problem and the extent to which the advice "reinforces" the recipient's intended actions, may affect advice evaluations and associated outcomes. Overall, further research is needed to replicate and extend what is known, contributing to theoretical development and practical knowledge. As much as possible, experimental and naturalistic interaction studies should be used to examine hypotheses that have received initial support from self-report surveys. And given our increasingly multicultural society, it is important to continue examining the question of cultural differences in responses to advice (Feng, 2006).

## Advising the Advice Giver

Although people frequently give advice to distressed others, they do not necessarily do it well. In the present study, none of the 151 participants reported any difficulty recalling a piece of bad advice, and most of the instances they reported had occurred during the preceding month. However, the giving of bad advice is not inevitable. In this conclusion, we synthesize the existing research, the study reported in this chapter, and a bit of our expert opinion into some basic do's and don'ts for advice givers.

1. *Don't assume that every person who has a problem needs or wants advice.* In some situations, such as bereavement or other losses, there is nothing that can truly be "done" about the problem, and it will be more beneficial for you to concentrate on listening and conveying caring. In other cases, where the problem does permit a solution of some kind, you should still resist the urge to jump in. For example, if a friend has lost a job, or his girlfriend, there may be things he truly should do, such as revising his resume or not getting involved with someone else too quickly. However, he is less likely to appreciate your advice if you ignore how he's feeling or what he may already have done or planned to do. Remember that someone who really wants advice can ask for it.

2. *Hold back on giving advice if you aren't a well-qualified source.* Do you have any real expertise with regard to the person's problem? Do you have a close relationship with the person? Imagine a situation in which one college student, Anne, sees a classmate, Brenda, looking at a course catalogue. In casual conversation Brenda reveals that she is really worried about whether to begin

her career immediately or try to go to graduate school. If Anne doesn't herself know much about graduate school or the pros and cons of the different choices and doesn't know Brenda all that well, she runs a high risk of giving advice that is unsuited to Brenda's needs and may end up offending Brenda by butting in where she doesn't really belong. Anne is likely to do better if she listens to Brenda talk about her situation and expresses interest and concern where appropriate. Once Anne understands Brenda's situation a little more fully, some advice might be appropriate, assuming Anne has some kind of expertise on which to base that advice ("You know, my brother was trying to decide what to do, and he . . .").

3. *Do think very carefully about the action(s) you are going to advise, trying as much as possible to consider not just why you think the action is a good one but how the other person is likely to view it.* If your friend is unhappy at work, you may believe that he should try to negotiate his salary and hours with his boss. Presumably, you believe this would be effective, that your friend could do this, and that it wouldn't have any bad consequences. However, your friend may not see it that way, and if he doesn't, he's unlikely to appreciate the advice. You may need to explain why you think negotiating is a good strategy ("You know, there was an article in *Business Week* that said . . ."), why you believe that your friend can do it ("I remember when you argued with the principal about . . . and you won, man!), or why you think it won't hurt to try ("You know he won't fire you"). Of course, it wouldn't be a bad idea to start by asking your friend questions about his views on the situation. Remember, it's his life.

4. *Do exercise some sensitivity in how you phrase your advice.* Yes, there are people who claim they appreciate honesty, directness, bluntness, or even tough love. But it's also easy to cross that invisible line and end up making someone feel bossed around, patronized, or criticized—on top of any distress over the problem itself. If a friend has failed an exam, it may well be that she went out too much in the week before, but that doesn't mean you should say so, either directly or by implication. It might be best to avoid "Study harder next time" in favor of "When you get your exam back, go over it with your TA." If you feel that your friend really needs to hear "Study harder," you should probably convey lots of sympathy for her distress ("That sucks, really, really sucks. Come here and let me give you a hug"), and only later say, "I guess it's a tougher class than it seemed. Do you think some extra studying would help?" Also watch that you don't come off as a drill sergeant. Even when you know exactly what another person should do, a degree of respect for that person's independence is important. Contrast the statement "If you're going to get out of this financial hole, you have to cut back on buying clothes and eating out" with "My suggestion is that you try to reduce your spending. Is there something you could cut back on for a while?"

5. *Do remember that advice can be a powerful force for either ill or good, and use your best moral judgment.* In particular, because advice is a form of persuasion, you need to exercise your persuasive skill with some attention to the consequences. For example, you might cause your friends to follow more of your advice by expressing unreserved confidence in everything you advise ("I'm 100% certain! I know this will work!"), but if a friend follows some of your advice and it doesn't turn out to be a sure thing, that's bad for your friend and quite possibly for you too. However, advice is not just persuasion but also an important form of support when others need help solving their problems. In fact, most people *expect* advice from their close relationships. So even though it can be challenging to give good advice, we don't recommend that you give up and stop advising altogether. Instead, use the information in this chapter to give the best support and advice that you can.

## References

Bonaccio, S. (2006). *Determining the relative importance of antecedents to advice utilization during decision-making with and without missing information.* Unpublished doctoral dissertation, Purdue University, West Lafayette, IN.

Bonaccio, S., & Dalal, R. S. (2006). Advice taking and decision-making: An integrative review of the literature. *Organizational Behavior and Human Decision Processes, 101,* 127–151.

Brown, P., & Levinson, S. C. (1987). *Politeness: Some universals in language usage.* Cambridge, England: Cambridge University Press.

Burleson, B. R. (2008). What counts as effective support? Explorations of individual and situational differences. In M. T. Motley (Ed.), *Studies in applied interpersonal communication* (pp. 207–227). Thousand Oaks, CA: Sage.

Burleson, B. R., & Goldsmith, D. J. (1998). How the comforting process works: Alleviating emotional distress through conversationally induced reappraisals. In P. A. Anderson & L. K. Guerrero (Eds.), *Handbook of communication and emotion: Research, theory, applications, and contexts* (pp. 245–280). San Diego: Academic Press.

Burleson, B. R., & MacGeorge, E. L. (2002). Supportive communication. In M. L. Knapp & J. A. Daly (Eds.), *Handbook of interpersonal communication* (3rd ed., pp. 374–424). Thousand Oaks, CA: Sage.

Caplan, S. E., & Samter, W. (1999). The role of facework in younger and older adults' evaluations of social support messages. *Communication Quarterly, 47,* 245–264.

Cutrona, C. E., & Russell, D. W. (1990). Type of social support and specific stress: Toward a theory of optimal matching. In B. R. Sarason, I. G. Sarason, & G. R. Pierce (Eds.), *Social support: An interactional view* (pp. 319–366). New York: John Wiley.

Dakof, G. A., & Taylor, S. E. (1990). Victims' perceptions of social support: What is helpful from whom? *Journal of Personality and Social Psychology, 58,* 80–89.

Feng, B. (2006). *Features and effects of advice in supportive interactions in two cultures.* Unpublished doctoral dissertation, Purdue University, West Lafayette, IN.

Feng, B., & Burleson, B. R. (2007). *The effects of argument explicitness on responses to advice in supportive interactions.* Unpublished manuscript, Department of Communication, University of California, Davis.

Feng, B., & MacGeorge, E. L. (2006). Predicting receptiveness to advice: Characteristics of the problem, the advice-giver, and the recipient. *Southern Communication Journal, 71,* 67–85.

Goldsmith, D. J. (1994). The role of facework in supportive communication. In B. R. Burleson, T. L. Albrecht, & I. G. Sarason (Eds.), *Communication of social support: Messages, interactions, relationships, and community* (pp. 29–49). Thousand Oaks, CA: Sage.

Goldsmith, D. J. (2000). Soliciting advice: The role of sequential placement in mitigating face threat. *Communication Monographs, 67*(1), 1–19.

Goldsmith, D. J., & Fitch, K. (1997). The normative context of advice as social support. *Human Communication Research, 23,* 454–476.

Goldsmith, D. J., & MacGeorge, E. L. (2000). The impact of politeness and relationship on perceived quality of advice about a problem. *Human Communication Research, 26,* 234–263.

Hung, H. Y., & Feeley, T. H. (2005). *Evaluating advice in supportive social interaction: A replication of MacGeorge, Feng, Butler, and Budarz (2004).* Paper presented at the International Communication Association, New York.

Lehman, D. R., Ellard, J. H., & Wortman, C. B. (1986). Social support for the bereaved: Recipients' and providers' perspectives on what is helpful. *Journal of Consulting and Clinical Psychology, 54*(4), 438–446.

MacGeorge, E. L., Feng, B., Butler, G. L., & Budarz, S. K. (2004). Understanding advice in supportive interactions: Beyond the facework and message evaluation paradigm. *Human Communication Research, 30*(1), 42–70.

MacGeorge, E. L., Graves, A. R., Feng, B., Gillihan, S. J., & Burleson, B. R. (2004). The myth of gender cultures: Similarities outweigh differences in men's and women's provision of and responses to supportive communication. *Sex Roles, 50,* 143–175.

MacGeorge, E. L., Lichtman, R. M., & Pressey, L. C. (2002). The evaluation of advice in supportive interactions: Facework and contextual factors. *Human Communication Research, 28,* 451–463.

Motley, M. T., Faulkner, L. J., & Reeder, H. (2008). Conditions that determine the fate of friendships after unrequited romantic disclosures. In M. T. Motley (Ed.), *Studies in applied interpersonal communication* (pp. 27–50). Thousand Oaks, CA: Sage.

Servaty-Seib, H. L., & Burleson, B. R. (2007). Bereaved adolescents' evaluations of the helpfulness of support-intended statements: Associations with person centeredness and demographic, personality, and contextual factors. *Journal of Social and Personal Relationships, 24,* 207–223.

Sniezek, J. A., & Buckley, T. (1995). Cueing and cognitive conflict in judge-advisor decision making. *Organizational Behavior and Human Decision Processes, 62,* 159–174.

Sniezek, J. A., Schrah, G. E., & Dalal, R. S. (2004). Improving judgment with prepaid expert advice. *Journal of Behavioral Decision Making, 17,* 173–190.

Sniezek, J. A., & Van Swol, L. M. (2001). Trust, confidence, and expertise in a judge-advisor system. *Organizational Behavior and Human Decision Processes, 84,* 288–307.

Van Swol, L. M., & Sniezek, J. A. (2005). Factors affecting the acceptance of expert advice. *British Journal of Social Psychology, 44,* 443–461.

White, T. B. (2005). Consumer trust and advice acceptance: The moderating roles of benevolence, expertise, and negative emotions. *Journal of Consumer Psychology, 15,* 141–148.

Wilson, S. R., Aleman, C. G., & Leatham, G. B. (1998). Identity implications of influence goals: A revised analysis of face-threatening acts and application to seeking compliance with same-sex friends. *Human Communication Research, 25,* 64–96.

Witte, K. (1998). Fear as motivator, fear as inhibitor: Using the Extended Parallel Process Model to explain fear appeal successes and failures. In P. A. Anderson & L. K. Guerrero (Eds.), *Handbook of communication and emotion: Research, theory, application, and contexts* (pp. 423–450). San Diego: Academic Press.

---

AUTHORS' NOTE: The authors wish to thank Graham Bodie, Brant Burleson, Stacey Connaughton, Julie Delaney, Mohan Dutta, Rebekah Fox, Brian Kanouse, Robert Ogles, Suchitra Shenoy, and Glenn Sparks for assistance with data collection.

# 8

## Forgiving Communication and Relational Consequences

*Vincent R. Waldron*

*Douglas L. Kelley*

*Jessica Harvey*

*My boyfriend called me up one Saturday night after being out with his friends. He had been drinking, and wanted me to come over. I kept saying "no," and he was getting mad. At one point he hung up on me and never called back, so I just went to bed. The next day he called and acted as if nothing was wrong. I explained to him I was upset with him and why I was upset. He said "sorry," and would I forgive him. The situation did not appear to be very serious to him. I also did not believe his apology was very sincere. He just wanted the argument to be over. I told him I needed a couple of days to think about this. A few days later he called and was asking again for my forgiveness. I explained to him my reasons once again for being upset, and finally accepted his apology. Our relationship has suffered greatly because of this particular night.*

—Jill, age 23 (from Waldron & Kelley, 2008)

Our relationships with family members, romantic partners, friends, and coworkers are grounded in a set of assumptions and informal agreements. We are emotionally invested in these social arrangements, as they form the basis of our mutual trust, respect, and psychological safety. Yet nearly every partner in a long-term relationship experiences breaches in the "relational covenant" (Hargrave, 1994). In fact, our research with long-term romantic couples suggests that nearly all of them have experienced major transgressions or significant relational trauma (Waldron & Kelley, 2008). The capacity to negotiate forgiveness during these trying episodes may be among the most potent predictors of relationship longevity.

As Jill's account above indicates, our communicative responses, and those of our partners, may have crucial relational consequences. The boyfriend's forgiveness request insufficiently acknowledged Jill's distress. Assuming Jill's account is accurate, she used her communication to delay the process, clarify her own reactions, emphasize her reasons for being upset, and ultimately accept his (second) apology. The relational outcome, if not entirely satisfactory, was certainly determined in part by the way this couple negotiated forgiveness.

Of course, forgiving a partner after a hurtful transgression is a daunting task. When partners forgive, they willingly give up legitimate claims to hostile emotion and retaliation (Exline & Baumeister, 2000). Yet the forgiveness process may reduce emotional burdens, help individuals regain their spiritual footing, and restore a sense of relational justice. While it is possible, and sometimes absolutely necessary, to forgive someone while also choosing to terminate the relationship, it is not surprising that many researchers prefer to study the process of forgiveness as an important step in relationship repair and recovery (e.g., Fincham & Beach, 2002a; Gordon, Baucom, & Snyder, 2000). Marriage therapists have reported some success with clients who have been trained in techniques of forgiveness (Fincham & Beach, 2002b). However, therapists and researchers have called for more research on the *communication behaviors* used to seek and grant forgiveness. In response, communication scholars have launched a series of studies designed to identify these behaviors and link them to relational consequences (Kelley, 1998; Kelley & Waldron, 2005; Waldron & Kelley, 2005, 2008). This chapter draws on the results of three studies to identify the communication behaviors likely to be most effective when partners negotiate forgiveness. We will focus our attention on forgiveness in romantic relationships, although some of our recommendations may apply to other relationship types.

## Defining Forgiveness

Forgiveness is often conceived of as a psychological *decision* made by a harmed individual, but the *relational negotiation* leading up to the forgiveness decision is of more interest to communication scholars. Communication is the symbolic process by which individuals manage their relationships. Working from this perspective, we offer the following definition: *forgiveness is a relational process whereby harmful conduct is acknowledged by one or both partners, the harmed partner extends undeserved mercy to the perceived transgressor, one or both partners experience a transformation from negative to positive psychological states, and the meaning of the relationship is renegotiated, with the possibility of reconciliation.*

By "undeserved mercy" we mean that the damaged partner gives up his or her right to seek retribution, even though retribution might be a legitimate response to the wrongful act. Three additional elements are critical to this definition: (1) it is relationally based, (2) a wrong must be identified, and (3) there is a renegotiation of the relationship's meaning. Regarding the first, forgiveness prompts partners to renegotiate their relationship. It may (or may not) lead to some degree of reconciliation, but we assume that *forgiveness is a central part of productive relationship renegotiation.*

Second, we emphasize overt recognition of harmful behavior. Relational negotiations characterized by tolerance, acceptance, or excuses—but no acknowledged wrongdoing—more often lead to what some writers call false or "cheap" forgiveness (Volf, 2001). In our view, forgiveness is merciful, but at the same time, it promotes relational justice and mutual respect.

Finally, forgiveness is a process whereby partners create new meanings. As the forgiveness episode unfolds, they reexamine personal and relational values, create memories of the incident, and reconsider their future together. This sense-making process may result in a new sense of "who we are." It may lead to a stronger or weaker or simply different relational identity.

## Forgiving Communication: Message Strategies

As we have noted in more detail elsewhere (Waldron & Kelley, 2008), at least six communication processes are integral to the negotiation of forgiveness: (1) revealing and discovering transgressions, (2) communicating emotions, (3) sense making, (4) seeking forgiveness, and (5) granting forgiveness, with (6) a final process that we call *managing relational transition* occurring after forgiveness initially is granted (see Figure 8.1). Here we focus on the essential communicative activities of seeking and granting forgiveness.

## Forgiveness-Seeking Tactics

Kelley (1998) uncovered more than 20 forgiveness-seeking behaviors in a qualitative study of forgiveness narratives. These were factor analyzed to create a more concise five-category taxonomy. Each category includes several specific tactics (Kelley & Waldron, 2005).

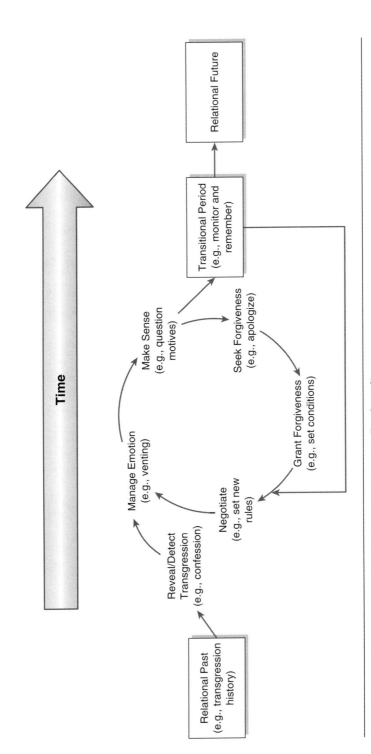

**Figure 8.1**  The Forgiveness Episode (From Waldron & Kelley, [2008])

1. *Explicit acknowledgment:* The offender acknowledges that harm has been committed, takes responsibility, and expresses remorse. The following example is from a husband who sought forgiveness from his wife after an extramarital affair:

> I told her I was 100% wrong. That the affair was my fault, in no way hers. That I was deeply sorry for the pain I had caused her. I asked if she would give me a chance and maybe some day forgive me.

2. *Nonverbal assurances:* The offender communicates sincerity and renewed commitment through nonverbal expression, including direct eye contact, touching, and tone of voice. One of our students wrote this about her boyfriend's request for forgiveness:

> I could tell that he was really sorry because he cried and sounded completely miserable. He looked at me and hugged me hard when I said things would be okay.

3. *Compensation:* The offender offers restitution in the form of promises of improved behavior, flattery, or a willingness to comply with the offended partner's wishes. An example came from a teenager who sought forgiveness for damaging her father's car in an accident:

> I told him how much I appreciated his calm response and how I would have been really upset if I were him. I said I would work hard to raise the money for the repairs.

4. *Explanation:* The offender offers mitigating details, excuses, and reasons to reframe the offense or deny intentional harm. Susan's boyfriend failed to show up at her house at the agreed-upon time because his previous girlfriend had called him in emotional distress. As Susan reported:

> He told me he hadn't intended to be late but she (the previous girlfriend) was crying over her family problems. He felt torn between listening to her and calling me. He wanted me to know that he has no feelings for her, just friendship, but he couldn't just leave her hanging in a bad situation. He wanted me to forgive him because the situation was not what it seemed.

5. *Humor:* The offender makes light of the situation or attempts to alter the aggrieved partner's mood. Jenny's longtime friend and roommate was hurt when Jenny forgot her birthday. Jenny tried self-deprecating humor:

> After not talking for 2 days, I came home from work one day with a funny belated birthday card for her and a gift certificate to her favorite restaurant. We were both relieved because we knew that our friendship would go back to the way it was. We went to dinner, and in a joking manner, I expressed to her how sorry I was and how selfish I was being since I was so wrapped up in my own life. She realized that was my way of expressing how sorry I was.

## Forgiveness-Granting Tactics

Waldron & Kelley (2005) studied the behaviors used by romantic partners when they granted forgiveness. They identified five types.

1. *Explicit forgiveness statements:* Explicit use of the word "forgive" or its variations, as in the statements "I forgive you" or "You are forgiven."

2. *Conditional forgiveness:* Variations on "I will forgive you if you meet conditions X, Y, and Z." As an example, one of our respondents said to her boyfriend, "I can forgive you this time but only if you promise to stop flirting at parties."

3. *Nonverbal displays:* Nonverbal expressions designed to communicate forgiveness and restoration of intimacy (e.g., offering a hug). One respondent told us, "I hugged him hard so he would know that it was okay and I accepted his apology. He knew I wasn't angry anymore."

4. *Discussion-based approaches:* Approaches designed to explore the reasons for the offense, the intentions of the partners, and the likelihood of future relational success. An example is the following: "I told him I wanted to talk about why he hurt me. I needed to know if he really understood my feelings. I wanted to put it [the offense] in the past, but I didn't want to be hurt all over again."

5. *Minimizing/forbearance:* Indicating that the offense was relatively unimportant; indicating understanding. "I told him I could sort of understand why he did it [failed to show up as planned] and it wasn't a big deal in our friendship."

## The Efficacy of Forgiving Communication

These tactical descriptions are useful starting points in that they help us think concretely about how forgiveness is enacted through communication behaviors. But several limitations are obvious. First, the tactical categories that emerged from our statistical analyses are incomplete descriptions of what is often a complex forgiveness negotiation. Inevitably some of the richness of "real" communication is lost in the effort to create precise measures and succinct descriptions. Second, the surveys on which these categories are based are completed by individuals. But we know that forgiveness unfolds in the context of *relationships,* including friendships, romances, families, and work teams. Finally, simple descriptions of possible communication tactics fail to capture the heart of the matter for most people who are seeking or granting forgiveness. That is, what communication approaches seem to work best? The goal of many (but not all) efforts to negotiate forgiveness is to improve a damaged relationship. Can forgiving communication restore the trust that was lost due to an affair? Can it help a family restore harmony after a child is caught in a serious deception? Can it help friends repair their relationship after a major argument? We won't be able to address every relational situation in this brief chapter. Instead, we will relate findings from several studies concerned with forgiveness in dating relationships and marriages. These studies were driven in part by the following research question.

*Research Question: Which types of forgiving communication are associated with positive relational outcomes after romantic partners experience a serious relational transgression?*

## Method

To answer this question, we draw on data from three sources. First, we examined 304 narratives describing forgiveness episodes in various relational contexts, including romantic ones. These data were coded for forgiveness-seeking/granting categories according to procedures first reported by Kelley (1998). Second, we summarized results of a survey of 187 romantic partners in an earlier study (Waldron & Kelley, 2005), drawing from previously unpublished data yielded by that study. In particular, we examined responses to open-ended questions about the use and efficacy of various communication tactics during forgiveness episodes. We used these data primarily to generate examples of what romantic partners considered to be effective communication.

Finally, we generated a third source of data via methods to be detailed below. Briefly for now, we interviewed 60 long-term romantic couples about the forgiveness practices used in their relationship and will report on the communication practices that helped them recover from serious transgressions. We considered these couples "experts" in the sense that they had forgiven at least one (and often several) relationship-threatening transgressions within their present relationship and reported being happily married after at least 30 years together.

### PARTICIPANTS

Kelley's original survey was completed by 107 student volunteers who produced 307 forgiveness narratives on open-ended questionnaires. The students received a small amount of extra credit for their work. The sample was 69% female and the average age was 26 years.

A second survey study used network sampling procedures to locate 187 members of romantic relationships. Average age for this sample was 31 years (range = 18–83 years). Fifty-two percent of the participants were males. Romantic relationships had lasted on average approximately 36 months. The forgiveness episode they described via questionnaire had occurred approximately 24 months into the relationship, on average. When asked to rate the intimacy of the relationship immediately prior to the transgression on a 1 (lowest) to 7 (highest) scale, 93% of participants selected 6 or 7.

Sampling for the interview study was purposive in the sense that we "went looking" for heterosexual romantic couples who (a) had been married more than 30 years, (b) had experienced significant relationship challenges, and (c) were willing to be interviewed in detail by university researchers. Couples were solicited through local media, senior centers, and local residential retirement communities. We interviewed mostly couples in our geographic area (metropolitan Phoenix). However, many of our couples had retired to Arizona from various locations across the United States. Most of the couples who originally volunteered were Caucasian, middle class, and of Judeo-Christian religious background, so we modified our sampling strategy to increase the ethnic, socioeconomic, and religious diversity. This resulted in an interview sample of 54 couples, all of whom had been married more than 30 years, with an average of 44 years (range = 30–80 years). Of these, 95% were in their first marriage and 95% were parents. Roughly 10% of the participants belonged to cultural minority groups, including Mexican American, Asian American, and African American.

## INTERVIEW PROCEDURES

We followed a format similar to the oral history interview used by other marriage researchers (e.g., Buehlman & Gottman, 1996). Interviews began with a written description of the study, discussion of informed consent and confidentiality issues, and a request for permission to record the interviews. Both researchers were present during most interviews, although some later ones were conducted by one researcher alone. We questioned the couple together for 20 to 25 minutes, then each partner alone for 15 minutes, and finally we brought them together again so they could share any concluding thoughts as a couple. The interview began with small talk and questions about how the couple met. Having established rapport, the interviewer asked the couples to identify particularly challenging times in their relationship. Challenges that did not involve a partner transgression and were thus irrelevant to forgiveness—for example, death of a child, job layoffs, transgressions by other family or friends—were skipped. The most important, clearly remembered challenge was then discussed in detail with each individual. We asked about (a) antecedents to the incident, (b) the nature of the transgression or trying incident, (c) the kind of communication used to seek and grant forgiveness, and (d) the short- and long-term relational responses and effects. When rejoined, the pair discussed additional details of the event and then answered questions about the longevity of their marriage and their advice to younger couples. We ended the interview by affirming the couple and their long relationship and thanking them for the privilege of hearing their story. (The entire interview protocol is available from the authors.)

## RESULTS AND APPLICATION

We present our results in the form of guidelines for doing forgiveness successfully. These guidelines were originally presented in our recent book on forgiving communication (Waldron & Kelley, 2008). They are presented with some caution. Each relationship involves unique circumstances. Our research results continue to evolve. Nonetheless, quantitative results from our surveys tell us what kinds of forgiveness-seeking tactics are associated (by our respondents) with positive relationship outcomes. We also found helpful a qualitative analysis of our interview transcripts. Harvey (2004) used qualitative methods of analysis, including the constant comparative method, to identify recurring patterns in couples' descriptions of recovery from challenging relational events. Finally, our analysis of open-ended responses to survey questions helped us identify additional exemplars of successful forgiveness tactics.

## FORGIVENESS-SEEKING TACTICS
## AND POSITIVE RELATIONSHIP OUTCOMES

Table 8.1 presents forgiveness-granting and forgiveness-seeking tactics and their association (as indicated by statistically significant correlations) with positive relational outcomes (for detailed statistics, see Kelley & Waldron, 2005; Waldron & Kelley, 2005). Serious transgressions nearly always result in sharp short-term reductions in relationship quality. In our studies, "positive" outcomes are improvements from this low point after forgiveness has been communicated. In some cases a "positive outcome" is a return to original levels of relationship functioning; other times it represents an increase over original levels. In the present study, positive outcomes included the interrelated dimensions of trust, intimacy, and relationship satisfaction. Although we have measured other relationship dimensions in our studies, including stability and global relationship quality, they tend to be highly correlated with these three indicators.

**Table 8.1**   Self-Reported Forgiveness Strategies and Romantic Relationship Outcomes

| Strategy | Examples | Outcome |
|---|---|---|
| Forgiveness-Seeking Strategies | | |
| 1. Explicit acknowledgment | Apology; remorse | Positive |
| 2. Nonverbal assurance | Eye contact; hugs | Positive |
| 3. Compensation | Gifts; repeated efforts | Positive |
| 4. Explanation | Reasons; discuss offense | None |
| 5. Humor | Joking; humoring | None |
| Forgiveness-Granting Strategies | | |
| 1. Explicit | "I forgive you" | Positive |
| 2. Conditional | "I forgive you, but only if . . ." | Negative |
| 3. Nonverbal displays | Facial expressions; touch | Positive |
| 4. Discussion | Talking about the offense | Positive |
| 5. Minimize | "No big deal"; "don't worry" | None |

SOURCE: Kelley & Waldron, 2005; Waldron & Kelley, 2005.

NOTE: "None" indicates that no significant correlations were detected in previous studies.

1. *Explicit acknowledgment is the forgiveness-seeking strategy most associated with relationship improvement after a transgression.* Taking responsibility and apologizing for harmful acts are behaviors that reinforce the moral code that undergirds a relationship. Wounded partners want us to acknowledge the hurt we have caused. In the example that opened this chapter, Jill's boyfriend failed to get this message. As she said, "The situation did not appear to be very serious to him. I also did not believe his apology was very sincere. He just wanted the argument to be over."

2. *Nonverbal assurance is associated with positive relational outcomes.* Respondents wrote that they could tell by "the look on his face" or the "the tears in his eyes" that the partner was truly repentant (and thus deserving of forgiveness). These behaviors acknowledge the gravity of the relational damage and may increase the victim's confidence that the transgression won't be

repeated. After her boyfriend responded coolly to her apology for flirting with another young man, Jana "cried and told him I deeply missed him. I didn't want my stupidity to ruin things for us." Her boyfriend was convinced by her emotional sincerity.

3. *Offers of compensation tend to be perceived positively by a wounded partner.* Particularly in family and work situations, the offer to compensate for harm can be positively received. The daughter who offers to pay for damaging the family car may be seen as displaying maturity. Regardless of whether the compensation is accepted, she may be perceived as "more forgivable" for having learned a lesson from the experience. Offering to make amends is an acknowledgment that your behavior has caused a loss to others. It is a tangible attempt to make things right.

4. *Humor is the message behavior least associated with relationship improvement after a transgression.* Humor may be an effort to direct attention away from the emotional hurt experienced by the partner. It may have a positive effect when used appropriately to reduce interaction arousal levels. However, when transgressions are serious enough to require forgiveness seeking, humor is rarely effective by itself. Humor deflects responsibility and fails to acknowledge the serious pain felt by the offended party. An exception to this rule may be self-deprecating humor, particularly among friends. As the "forgotten birthday" example made clear, humor can be a way of making it clear that responsibility lies with the self, that the transgression was another instance of an unfortunate pattern of mistakes made by the offender.

## USING TACTICS IN COMBINATION

Guidelines 5 and 6 refer not to the use of any one tactic but rather to the use of multiple behaviors to help aggrieved partners manage uncertainty and protect their identities. We see these patterns in responses to open-ended survey questions as well as in statistical results showing that most forgiveness episodes call for multiple communicative approaches.

5. *Message behaviors that help the aggrieved partner to predict the relational future are among the most efficacious forgiveness strategies.* This principle is consistent with the assumption that uncertainty management is an important motive in personal relationships (see, e.g., Afifi & Weiner, 2004). Serious transgressions create uncertainty about the relational future. Reconciliation is more likely when partners can predict the future, including the likelihood that relational rules will be followed. Forgiveness-seeking behaviors that manage uncertainty by (for example) explicitly acknowledging that a relational rule was

broken ("I broke our agreement about being on time for the kids' events"), proposing clearer relational rules ("What if I am always home by 5:30, no matter what?"), and sincerely pledging to follow rules ("I *really* do think this is important and promise to make it up to the kids in the future") all function to increase predictability. In essence, this set of responses combines the explicit acknowledgment, nonverbal assurance, and compensation approaches.

6. *Message strategies that protect the identity of the wounded partner are associated with positive outcomes.* Transgressions (including extrarelational affairs) can create embarrassment and guilt for the victim, in addition to provoking hurt and rage. As Affifi, Falato, and Weiner (2001) argued, communication tactics that alleviate threat to the identity of the wounded partner may have positive effects, even if they don't result in full reconciliation. Forgiveness-seeking approaches that avoid blaming the victim (e.g., direct confessions) are better than those approaches that intensify embarrassment or shame. For example, blaming your affair on the partner's lack of intimacy heightens the shame generated from adulterous behavior. The partner is less likely to be forgiving in such situations. Allowing a partner to discover a transgression through the reports of third parties is another means of increasing identity threat because an "audience" is added to the scenario. However, offenders may be more successful if they shape the perceptions of third parties by, for example, publicly accepting blame for the offense (a form of explicit acknowledgment) and repeatedly "begging for forgiveness" (a kind of compensation).

## FORGIVENESS-GRANTING TACTICS AND POSITIVE RELATIONAL OUTCOMES

Our data indicated that three forms of forgiveness-granting communication were reported to have positive relational effects after a transgression. One approach was associated with negative relational outcomes.

1. *Explicit statements of forgiveness are associated with positive relational effects.* Unequivocal statements, such as "I forgive you," were most associated with positive outcomes. Those who reported using these kinds of behaviors tended to report that the relationship recovered after a transgression. In some cases, the relationship actually improved beyond original levels of satisfaction. For some couples, the successful negotiation of forgiveness after a serious transgression was an important moment of relational maturation. It had become part of their narrative as a couple. As one husband noted: "The fact that we could get so angry at each other, accuse each of bad things, then find a way to forgive and move on—that is what makes us who we are as a couple. We can relive the bad times and know that we survived them. Things got better.

In fact, they got much better after we learned to forgive and not hold a long grudge. We don't forget the past, but it kind of helps us deal with the present when things get bumpy."

2. *Conditional offers of forgiveness are negatively associated with relational recovery.* This approach to forgiveness is associated with reduced trust and increased self-protection. It may be best used when partners are committed to preserving the relationship but remain fearful of repeated offenses. Those couples who allow long periods of time for the forgiveness process to unfold (sometimes) report that conditional forgiveness led to a gradual restoration of trust.

3. *Nonverbal displays are associated with positive outcomes.* Similar to the nonverbal assurances offered by forgiveness seekers, the nonverbal behaviors of those offering forgiveness are associated with positive outcomes. Facial expressions, hugs, and touches are among the behaviors described by those who felt that forgiveness helped their relationship recover from serious transgressions.

4. *Inviting your partner to discuss the offense may lead to positive outcomes.* In contrast to the silent treatment, partners who reported positive relational outcomes took an "invitational" approach (see Foss & Griffin, 1995). By asking questions and seeking the offender's perspective, they opened up possibilities for new understandings of the situation, the partner's motives, and possibilities for reconciliation (Foss & Griffin, 1995). The forgiver's willingness to engage in constructive communication may be the key here. As noted in Table 8.1, explanations offered by offenders were not associated with a particular outcome (perhaps because explanations differ in quality).

## PRACTICAL APPLICATIONS—FORGIVENESS PRACTICES OF LONG-TERM COUPLES

The couples we interviewed were "marriage experts" in the sense that they had remained married for many years, despite encountering very difficult circumstances. The couples survived affairs, financial irresponsibility, business failures, drug and alcohol abuse, serious differences in parenting, public embarrassments, vicious arguments, and other major transgressions (for details, see Waldron & Kelley, 2008). Of course, longevity is only one measure of success (and indeed is not always even an indicator, since it is possible to maintain a dysfunctional relationship for a very long time). Moreover, the forgiveness practices learned by older couples, in this case those married in the 1930s to the 1960s, may not be entirely applicable to younger couples. The forgiveness attitudes and practices of these couples were shaped by the cultural values of their generations. For example, couples married before the 1960s sometimes felt compelled to forgive their spouses, in part because divorce was a cultural or religious taboo. Despite obvious "cohort differences," we found cross-generational consistencies in the interviews. We focus on these as we share these couples' prescriptions for successful forgiveness. The generalizations reported here are based in large part on the work of Harvey (2004), who used the constant-comparative method to categorize the comments made by these couples in response to our questions about the practice of forgiveness. Essentially, she repeatedly read the interview transcripts, seeking recurring themes, expanding and revising the categories with each reading until she had what appeared to be a comprehensive set of prescriptions. Here we have summarized those prescriptions that were most frequently invoked or (to us) most generalizable to circumstances beyond those experienced by any given couple.

### Acknowledge Wrongdoing

Nearly all couples agreed that a key to negotiating forgiveness was taking responsibility for hurting your partner. The sufficient *acknowledgment* of wrongdoing appears to be both a necessary part of forgiveness and an important step in reasserting relational justice. As a communication process, a forgiveness interaction expresses, changes, or reinforces the moral order of our relationships. It is the process by which injustice is identified and owned up to. In some cases, offenders are forgiven unconditionally. Admitting wrongdoing and taking responsibility for transgressions is often enough to assure our partners that commonly agreed-upon values will be respected in the future—that "justice will prevail."

In many cases the responsibility for a transgression is mutual. As an example, Judith admitted continually overspending the family budget and hiding the creditor notices from her husband, Adam. As they discussed the matter, Adam realized that his sometimes harsh criticism encouraged Judith to be evasive about financial problems. Only when they both acknowledged their culpability could they move the forgiveness process along.

### Apologize Sincerely

Apology is the form of communication most likely to be associated with successful forgiveness. Usually issued with words like "I am sorry," apologies communicate remorse and acknowledge a shift in conversational power to the wounded partner. Only the victim can "accept" an apology. Whereas transgressions can shatter the victim's sense of control, apologies put them in a position to determine the nature of the relationship. As indicated previously, apologies must be authentic to advance the forgiveness process. Jill's scenario that opened this chapter illustrates the consequences of an apology that was insufficiently sincere.

### Address Emotion Explicitly

Serious transgressions result in shock, embarrassment, anger, and hurt. Communicating these emotions is an important part of the early stages of forgiveness. Communication is the means by which emotion is vented. "Get it out on the table," one wife advised, "don't hold it in." The offender's acknowledgment of the type and depth of emotion is important as well: "I know I hurt you badly." Sometimes couples help each other label emotions: "I didn't realize how ashamed I was until he asked why I hid the bills from him." For many couples, honest discussion of emotion was a prerequisite for progress.

### Request Outside Assistance

Many couples recommended outside assistance as an important step in the forgiveness process. Particularly during the early stages of relationships, serious transgressions overwhelmed the relational skills of the couples. Pastors, counselors, and older family members were among those consulted, particularly when the partners found it impossible to resolve issues of accountability or manage volatile emotions. For example, Couple #019 described the grudges that developed over repeated financial problems. They finally made progress by "talking with some of the other people that I've been very close to. How do they handle it? We'd go ask other people who have done these things." In this case, the friends helped identify the relational causes of the couple's financial distress and urged the partners to release feelings of resentment.

### Forgive and Remember

Some couples claimed that the key to a successful marriage was to "forgive and forget," to simply excise past transgressions from current discourse. However, as they discussed the history of their relationships, it became clear that forgetting was selective for most couples. Couples "actively forget" in the sense that they no longer experience the emotional pain when they remember the transgression, and they put discussions of blame in the past. Yet they "actively remembered" the lessons learned from past transgressions as they negotiated through a long-term process of forgiveness.

In fact, some couples use what might be called a *forgive and remember* approach. Mike, married to Darlene for 36 years, had three different times steered his family into deep financial trouble with bad investment decisions and ill-fated businesses. During the early years, Darlene entrusted financial decisions to Mike. Out of pride or unrealistic optimism, he hid the problems from Darlene. Mike was always convinced that things would "turn around soon." However, the couple indicated that their past financial difficulties are now a frequent topic of discussion. Mike says they need to relive the past, so he doesn't "hurt us again." Darlene realized that she needed to provide "reality checks" for Mike's well-intended but sometimes unrealistic financial schemes. She has forgiven her husband and is proud that their marriage survived very trying times. She believes the couple is now more honest and emotionally close. Mike and Darlene forgive but don't forget.

### Use Time to Advantage

An advantage of interviews with long-term couples is their appreciation for the importance of time. They told us that forgiveness can be an ongoing negotiation, one that sometimes takes months, years, and, in some cases, even decades. Ray (married to Doris for 32 years) recalled a time when he brawled with some local "punks." Doris was humiliated when she was forced to bail him out of their small-town jail, but as a traditional wife, she believed she should suffer in silence. As Doris told us, until recently she had nurtured a grudge over the incident. In fact, the couple revealed that only a few weeks before the interview (nearly two decades after the event), Doris had shared her feelings with Ray. In response, Ray belatedly acknowledged that he was wrong. Even as we interviewed them, the couple seemed to be mulling over the event and how it had affected their marriage. Doris has not fully released her feelings of resentment, but she feels the couple is on stronger emotional footing now. "With time" Doris feels she can fully forgive Ray. She feels more hopeful about the retirement years, because she is putting the past behind her.

Time is sometimes used strategically in forgiveness negotiations. Angry partners sometimes "need time" to cool off before deciding if and how to forgive. "Taking time" to think and reduce high arousal levels sometimes helps partners put a transgression in larger relational perspective. Hal described how he sometimes left the house briefly before realizing he needed to ask for forgiveness. "It gave us time to cool off. . . . I jump in the car and go roaring off and drive around a little bit and come back and realize that I was really [a] stupid idiot for doing that, you know."

### Invoke Spiritual Values

For some couples, the difficulty of forgiveness is eased by shared spiritual values. In some interpretations of Christian theology, forgiveness is viewed as a mandate from God. For these couples, the discourse of forgiveness involves a revisiting of sacred teachings. As one Christian wife said to her husband in front of us, "If God forgave all of our sins, I guess I can forgive you for being a jerk sometimes." In some cases, couples seemed overwhelmed by the gravity of the offense. Together they sought insight, comfort, and guidance from shared religious texts and spiritual principles. The invoking of "higher order" values and a "higher power" may have allowed them to transcend the emotions and confusions that accompanied the relational crises. Couple #A032 was originally overwhelmed when the husband admitted his infidelity and alcoholism: "I'm sorry," he said, "I want [you] to read the book of Mormon with me every day." So we did. We read it every day together for at least 3 years. . . . And we would read it every day and honestly it was bringing the Lord into our life and that's what brought us together."

### Revisit Communication Rules

Transgressions often call into question the implicit agreements that govern relationships and make them predictable. Forgiveness often involves a reassertion of those rules. The offender must assure the wounded party that rules will be followed in the future. One young woman told us she greatly distressed her parents by staying out all night and not checking in by phone (as was the custom in her family). She apologized for the upset she caused and pledged to "never do it again." In other cases, new rules are proposed. A wife felt she could forgive her husband for an affair only if he pledged to let her "know where he was at every minute of the day." By complying with this new rule, the husband would reduce her uncertainty and gradually restore her trust.

## Conclusion

Forgiveness is an increasingly discussed phenomenon in both the popular and scientific literatures. One explanation for its popularity might be a relentless increase in broken relationships due to increasing divorce rates, family stresses, substance abuse, and other pressures. Alternatively, the interest may arise from the acknowledgment that now, more than ever, close relationships are worth saving. We find the negotiation of forgiveness to be one of the more important communication processes used by partners to maintain and repair relationships. Of course, reconciling with a partner is only one of several reasons to practice forgiveness. The desire to be consistent with our personal values may encourage us to forgive. We may do so to feel better, mentally and even physically (see Witvliet, 2001, for a review of health consequences). Forgiveness may allow us to put a troubling incident firmly in the past, where it no longer saps our energy. Moreover, we may make the purely psychological decision to forgive a transgressor, even though we simultaneously decide to terminate the relationship with that person. At times, relationship termination is the best way to protect ourselves from harm.

From our own studies and those of others, we have concluded that there are "better" and "worse" ways to seek and grant forgiveness. Of course, the principles presented here are tentative, based on a relatively small set of studies. As our long-term couples noted, couples in distress often need outside assistance with the forgiveness process. We note further that physical and mental abuse always calls for outside intervention. In abuse situations, self-protection is always the primary course of action, although individuals may eventually choose, with outside help, to explore possible forgiveness. Finally, in our view, forgiveness is most centrally a matter of relational morality. Communication is the means by which we discover and confront wrongful behavior, make amends, negotiate its consequences, and "set things right" in our minds and in our relationships. By learning how to forgive more effectively, couples may find both hope and justice in their relationship's darkest moments.

# References

Afifi, W. A., Falato, W. L., & Weiner, J. L. (2001). Identity concerns following a severe relational transgression: The role of discovery method for the relational outcomes of infidelity. *Journal of Social & Personal Relationships, 18,* 291–308.

Afifi, W. A., & Weiner, J. L. (2004). Toward a theory of motivated information management. *Communication Theory, 14,* 167–190.

Buehlman, K., & Gottman, J. M. (1996). *The oral history interview and the oral history coding system.* Mahwah, NJ: Lawrence Erlbaum.

Exline, J. J., & Baumeister, R. F. (2000). Expressing forgiveness and repentance: Benefits and barriers. In M. C. McCullough, K. I. Pargament, & C. E. Thoresen (Eds.), *Forgiveness: Theory, research, and practice* (pp. 133–155). New York: Guilford Press.

Fincham, F. D., & Beach, S. R. H. (2002a). Forgiveness in marriage: Implications for psychological aggression and constructive communication. *Personal Relationships, 9,* 239–251.

Fincham, F. D., & Beach, S. R. H. (2002b). Forgiveness: Toward a public health approach to intervention. In J. H. Harvey & A. Wenzel (Eds.), *A clinician's guide to maintaining and enhancing close relationships* (pp. 277–300). Mahwah, NJ: Lawrence Erlbaum.

Foss, S. K., & Griffin, C. L. (1995). Beyond persuasion: A proposal for an invitational rhetoric. *Communication Monographs, 62,* 2–18.

Gordon, K. C., Baucom, D. H., & Snyder, D. K. (2000). The use of forgiveness in marital therapy. In M. C. McCullough, K. I. Pargament, & C. E. Thoresen (Eds.), *Forgiveness: Theory, research, and practice* (pp. 203–227). New York: Guilford Press.

Hargrave, T. D. (1994). Families and forgiveness: A theoretical and therapeutic framework. *Family Journal: Counseling and Therapy for Couples and Families, 2,* 339–348.

Harvey, J. (2004). *Trauma and recovery strategies across the lifespan of long-term married couples.* Unpublished master's thesis, Arizona State University West, Phoenix.

Kelley, D. (1998). The communication of forgiveness. *Communication Studies, 49,* 255–271.

Kelley, D., & Waldron, V. (2005). An investigation of forgiveness-seeking communication and relational outcomes. *Communication Quarterly, 53,* 339–358.

Volf, M. (2001). Forgiveness, reconciliation, and justice: A Christian contribution to a more peaceful social environment. In R. Helmick & R. L. Petersen (Eds.),

*Forgiveness and reconciliation: Religion, public policy, and conflict transformation* (pp. 27–49). Philadelphia: Templeton Foundation Press.

Waldron, V., & Kelley, D. (2005). Forgiveness as a response to relational transgression. *Journal of Social and Personal Relationships, 22,* 723–742.

Waldron, V., & Kelley, D. L. (2008). *Communicating forgiveness.* Thousand Oaks, CA: Sage.

Witvliet, C. V. (2001). Forgiveness and health: Review and reflections on a matter of faith, feelings, and physiology. *Journal of Psychology and Theology, 29,* 212–224.

# 9

## Verbal Coercion to Unwanted Sexual Intimacy

### How Coercion Messages Operate

*Michael T. Motley*

Sexual intimacy is often viewed as operating on a willingness continuum, with simultaneous mutual consent at one pole and physical force at the other. Occupying a wide band somewhere in between are various levels of *unwanted sexual intimacy* wherein sexual behaviors, while voluntary in the strict sense (i.e., not entirely forced), are nevertheless the result of having "given in" against one's will, or at least against one's preferences (e.g., Christopher, 1988).

Unwanted sexual intimacy is usually viewed as a social problem (e.g., Motley & Reeder, 1995; Struckman-Johnson, Struckman-Johnson, & Anderson, 2003). The large majority of college women have been the reluctant partner in episodes of unwanted sexual intimacy in one form or another (e.g., Hannon, Hall, Kuntz, Van Laar, & Williams, 1995; Struckman-Johnson et al., 2003). The same is true for college men (e.g., Muehlenhard & Linton, 1987; Struckman-Johnson et al., 2003). About one third of college women have been the reluctant partner in unforced but unwanted sexual intercourse (e.g., Christopher, 1988; Koss, Gidyez, & Wisniewski, 1987), and about half of college men have been (e.g., Muehlenhard & Cook, 1988). Moreover, almost all women characterize unwanted sexual activity as unpleasant, often extremely so (Muehlenhard & Cook, 1988), and many men are similarly disturbed by it (Grauerholz & Serpe, 1985; Hines & Saudino, 2003).

Research on unwanted sexual intimacy usually focuses on the values and personality characteristics of the yielding partner (e.g., Haworth-Hoeppner, 1998;

Muehlenhard, 1988) or on the coercion strategies and behaviors of the instigating partner (e.g., DeSouza & Hutz, 1996; Perper & Weis, 1987; Struckman-Johnson & Struckman-Johnson, 1991). While it is common for research to acknowledge verbal coercion strategies, approaches vary. Some researchers acknowledge a specific category for verbal strategies, the most common name for which is "verbal coercion" (e.g., Muehlenhard, Julsonnet, Carlson, & Flarity-White, 1989; Murnen, Perot, & Byrne, 1989). Other researchers include verbal behaviors such as "persuasion," "positive statements," "logic," "deception," and so on but without an explicit verbal coercion category (e.g., McCormick, 1979; Perper & Weis, 1987; Spitzberg, 1995). In either case, verbal coercion usually receives only tangential attention in research on unwanted sexual intimacy.

Verbal coercion may very well be worth focusing upon, however. Certainly, it is an extremely common approach, if not the most common (Muehlenhard et al., 1989), in attempts to induce unwanted sexual intimacy in general (Muehlenhard & Cook, 1988; Murnen et al., 1989) and unwanted intercourse in particular (Murnen et al., 1989). For the reluctant partner, these coercion efforts are disturbing even when they are unsuccessful (Kanin, 1957) and certainly so when they do indeed lead to unwanted sex (e.g., Christopher, 1988; O'Sullivan, Byers, & Finkelman, 1998). Between 34% and 59% of women report having yielded to unwanted sexual intimacy solely as a result of verbal coercion (Muehlenhard et al., 1989; Poppen & Segel, 1988), as do about 25% of men (Muehlenhard & Cook, 1988; Poppen & Segel, 1988). Similarly, about 13% of men report having yielded to unwanted intercourse primarily via verbal coercion, as do about 11% of women (Muehlenhard & Cook, 1988).

Apparently it is fairly common for individuals to establish a sexual-intimacy threshold within a particular episode with a particular partner but then to sacrifice it because of what the partner has said. Very simply, verbal coercion messages appear to be powerful. But how this influence operates—that is, how it is that these messages incline one to give in to unwanted sexual intimacy—is a bit of a mystery.

The present study sought to shed light on the verbal sexual coercion dynamic. In particular, it was assumed (based on pilot work) that many sexual coercion messages take this general form, implicitly or explicitly: "You should be willing to go further because [X] is present (or has occurred) in our relationship." And in such cases, an implied premise is that "when [X] is present in a relationship, sexual intimacy should advance beyond our present level." For example, it is easy to imagine one partner mentioning his or her high level of sexual arousal and either implicitly or explicitly suggesting that the other should *therefore* escalate the intimacy. In such a case, the implicit major premise is that once one partner reaches a high level of arousal, the other is expected or obligated to escalate the intimacy.

Preliminary probes suggested that this sort of "logic" might be common to many verbal coercion messages, that is, (a) major premise—"higher levels of sexual intimacy are expected when Condition X is present," (b) minor premise—"Condition X is present here," (c) conclusion—"therefore, you/we should escalate our sexual intimacy." And intuitively it seems that this kind of message cannot be effective unless *somebody* believes the major premise. For example, suppose Chris and Pat are engaged in physical intimacy while on a date, Pat's intimacy threshold is reached, and Chris mentions his or her own heightened arousal in an attempt to coerce Pat into escalated intimacy. Which of the partners—Chris, Pat, both, or neither—believes the implied major premise that one partner's heightened arousal warrants or requires the other's unwanted escalation of intimacy?

The present study focuses on the question of which partner(s) believe(s) the major premises implied within verbal coercion toward unwanted sexual intimacy (assuming that such premises are indeed common to verbal coercion). Given that question, it would seem that most any finding could at least supplement earlier research on the values, beliefs, and assumptions behind "moral" evaluations of unwanted sex generally (e.g., Black & Gold, 2003; McCormick, 1979). Moreover, certain findings could be enlightening regarding the dynamics of verbal coercion in particular. Most important, perhaps, certain answers might be able to serve a practical or applied function toward reducing the incidence of verbal coercion attempts or thwarting verbal coercion efforts when they occur.

More specifically, there is a limited range of outcomes and interpretations on the question of which partner(s) believe(s) verbal coercion premises, and most any of them could be illuminating, in the following ways: (a) if it were found that both partners believe the major premises, then the verbal coercion dynamic would seem closer to simple negotiation or reasoning than to typical connotations of "coercion"; (b) if the coercer genuinely believes the premise but the partner does not, then one might characterize the episode as a somewhat innocent persuasion effort on a values issue; (c) if the coerced believes the premises while the coercer does not, then the episode more closely matches typical connotations of coercion; and (d) finally, if it were found that neither partner believes the verbal coercion premises, then a variety of interpretations would be viable, perhaps depending upon other components of the belief system.

The study assumed no a priori prediction favoring any of these possibilities over the others. There was an intuitive hunch, based on pilot probes, that coercers' beliefs in their own messages' premises may be quite weak, either along with or relative to their targets' beliefs. And there was particular a priori interest in the practical application implications (e.g., as discussed above) if indeed coercers' beliefs in their own premises are weak. The study was conducted as a nondirectional investigation of relative premise agreement, however.

# Method

## PILOT: PRELIMINARY IDENTIFICATION
## OF COMMON COERCION MESSAGES

Identification of common coercion messages for later analysis was done via a relatively informal pilot study (to be partially replicated more formally in the main study below). A list of likely verbal coercion messages was begun via casual anecdotal interviews of undergraduates by an undergraduate assistant. Candidate coercion messages were put on an evolving questionnaire, usually administered to about 12 or so participants of both genders, asking whether they had experienced the individual messages in a sexual coercion situation and especially soliciting additional candidate messages via open-ended query. After the first round of these questionnaires, no new verbal coercion messages were suggested. After three rounds (36 females, 34 males), all messages that had been experienced by at least 8% of the participants were retained for the main part of the study. (After 8%, the relative frequencies dropped so dramatically that the remaining messages were deemed idiosyncratic.)

Only the 12 messages displayed in Table 9.1 emerged. While the simple identification of common verbal coercion messages is a very minor part of this study, these preliminary results deserve brief attention.

It appears that the messages represent four general strategies of sexual verbal coercion: (1) the large majority of the messages (specifically ##1–7 in Table 9.1) appear to be attempts to elicit *guilt* over not satisfying some ostensible "obliga-tion" to engage in sexual intimacy once some particular *condition* is present—for example, a lengthy relationship (#1), financial sacrifice (#2), and so forth; (2) a much smaller number (namely, ##8 and 9) appear to operate by *challeng-ing the sexual adequacy* of the reluctant partner, the challenge being to "prove," via escalated intimacy, that one is sexually competent; (3) messages ##10 and 11 *threaten consequences* if escalated intimacy does not occur, but these are not so much threatened consequences to the individual as to the relationship—for example, threats to terminate the relationship or to terminate assumptions of sexual exclusivity; and (4) finally, #12 (saying "I love you") may come close to an effort to make the partner *want to* escalate the intimacy, that is, "Knowing that I love you, you might like the idea of sharing intimacy with me." We could also characterize #12 as a variation on the guilt/obligation theme, with an implied premise that we owe it to be intimate with those who love us.

One may characterize the 12 messages differently, of course. But it is interest-ing that with the possible exception of #12 ("I love you"), none of these messages appears to operate by trying to seduce the reluctant partner to shift perspectives so that unwanted sex becomes wanted. That is to say, all of the common mes-sages seem to be based on strategies whereby the coercing partner is content with having guilted, threatened, or humiliated the partner into submitting.

Table 9.1        Common Verbal Coercion Messages For Escalated Sexual Intimacy

Coercing partner says or implies that

1. By this point in the relationship most would have gone further than his or her partner has.

2. Considering the amount of money spent, the reluctant partner is expected to go further than he or she has.

3. He or she is so aroused that it is unfair to stop and not go further.

4. The reluctant partner has led him or her on via suggestive behavior or remarks, so it is unfair to resist going further.

5. Since the reluctant partner initiated the date, relationship, or intimacy, it is expected that he or she should want to be willing to go further.

6. Since the reluctant partner has gone further with other partners in past relationships, he or she should be willing to go further with the coercing partner. (guilt/obligation)

7. Since the reluctant partner has gone further with the coercing partner on past occasions, it is unfair to not go further now.

8. The reluctance makes the coercing partner suspect that his or her gender is not the one the reluctant partner prefers.

9. The resistance suggests that the reluctant partner is in some way sexually inadequate.

10. The reluctance to go further may cause the coercing partner to terminate the relationship.

11. The reluctance will necessitate the coercing partner getting the desired level of intimacy from someone else.

12. He or she loves the reluctant partner.

With respect to the main objectives of this study, the purpose of the pilot study was to collect common coercion messages and to determine whether there were identifiable premises to warrant pursuit of the primary research question. To identify the premises for the main study, the author and an assistant generated semi-independent lists of premises from the 12 common messages. A few of the messages suggested more than one premise. A list of 15 premises was agreed upon and endorsed by a second assistant. The 15 premises targeted for the main study are presented in Table 9.2.

## MAIN STUDY: BELIEFS IN VERBAL COERCION MESSAGE PREMISES

### Participants

Participants were 50 female and 50 male students of various upper-division communication and psychology courses (none of which had discussed

**Table 9.2**       Premises Behind Common Verbal Coercion Messages

---

a. We are supposed to be willing to go quite far with physical intimacy after dating someone for a while. (#1 in Table 9.1)

b. We owe it to our date to go fairly far with physical intimacy if he or she has spent a lot of money on us. (#2)

c. It is cruel to not go further once one's date becomes highly aroused. (#3)

d. We owe it to our partner to go quite far with physical intimacy if we have flirted, used suggestive talk, made sexual innuendos, dressed provocatively, and so forth. (#4)

e. We owe it to our partner to go quite far with physical intimacy if we initiated the date, the relationship, or the intimacy. (#5)

f. We owe it to our partner to go quite far with physical intimacy if we have gone quite far with others at about the same point in the relationship. (#6)

g. We owe it to our partner to go at least as far with physical intimacy as we have gone in the past with that same partner. (#7)

h. One who resists advanced physical intimacy with a partner he or she has been dating for a while probably prefers the other sex. (#8)

i. One is probably sexually dysfunctional if one doesn't want to go further after being aroused. (#9)

j. When we do not allow physical intimacy to go very far, our partner is justified to terminate the relationship. (#10a)

k. When we do not allow physical intimacy to go very far, it ensures that the partner will terminate the relationship. (#10b)

l. If we do not want to go as far with physical intimacy as does our partner, then the partner is justified in seeking physical intimacy from someone else, even if he or she continues dating us. (#11)

m. We owe it to our partner to go far with physical intimacy if he or she truly loves us. (#12a)

n. When one is willing to go quite far with physical intimacy, it "proves" that he or she loves the partner. (#12b)

o. When one refuses to go very far with physical intimacy, it "proves" that he or she does not really love the partner. (#12c)

---

unwanted sex or verbal coercion) at the University of California, Davis, who had lived in the United States for at least the past 10 years.

### Questionnaire

All participants were administered the same questionnaire. Three kinds of measures were obtained:

Section I placed the participant in the role of the reluctant partner. Participants completed the section only if they answered affirmatively both that they had been in an intimacy situation where "your partner wants to take the physical intimacy further than you do" *and* they had "tried to resist going further." Those who completed the section were presented with the 12 verbal coercion messages described above. Each of these was presented as a two-part item: (1) whether the participant had ever experienced a partner having used the coercion message or strategy[1] (answered on a 5-point Likert scale—*yes, often* to *almost certainly no*) and (2) "If so, did this cause you to give in and go further?" (answered *yes/no* or *not applicable/hasn't happened*).

Section II was the same as Section I except that the context was that of the participant in the coercing role (i.e., "You want to take the physical intimacy a good bit further than your partner does" *and* "You tried to get your partner to go further"), with participants who could not identify skipping the section. For each of the 12 strategies, participants were asked, "Have you ever done this?" and "If so, did this cause your partner to 'give in' and go further?" (same response scales as Section I).

Section III contained 30 items (randomly ordered)—the 15 *premises* (as discussed above) presented in both a "male victim" and "female victim" version; for example, both "A man owes it to his date to go fairly far with physical intimacy if . . ." and "A woman owes it to her date to go fairly far with physical intimacy if . . ." For each of the 30 premise items, participants responded to three questions (randomly ordered in each case): (1) "Personally, I would agree/disagree" (7-point Likert scale from *strongly agree* to *strongly disagree*), (2) "I think most *WOMEN* would agree/disagree" (same scale), and (3) "I think most *MEN* would agree/disagree" (same scale). All participants completed Section III.

## ANALYSES AND RESULTS

### Sections I and II

Table 9.3 summarizes the data from Sections I and II of the questionnaire. These were the items asking whether participants had experienced the individual coercion messages in the reluctant partner role or had used them as the more eager partner. Seventy-eight percent of the female participants ($n = 39$) and 44% of the males ($n = 22$) reported having experienced being the reluctant partner who resists escalation. Table 9.3 reports only on these participants as coercion targets. Sixty-four percent of males ($n = 32$) and 22% of females ($n = 11$) reported having experienced the role of the more eager partner who tries to get the other to go further. Table 9.3 reports only on these participants as coercers.

All 12 verbal coercion messages were confirmed to be reasonably common, as was the verbal coercion phenomenon more generally. The large majority of participants who had experienced the more eager partner role and who tried to get their partner to go further had done so via one or more of these messages (namely, 100% of the 11 females and 84% of the 32 males in this assertive partner role). Moreover, the majority of participants who had experienced the reluctant partner role acknowledged having yielded on occasion to one or more of these specific messages (namely, 71% of the females and 86% of the males in this role).

**Table 9.3**  Participants' Relative Familiarity With the Coercion Messages

| Verbal Coercion Message Coercer Uses | Subject as Coercion Target | | | | Subject as Coercer | | | |
| --- | --- | --- | --- | --- | --- | --- | --- | --- |
| | Female Participants (n = 39) | | Male Participants (n = 22) | | Male Participants (n = 32) | | Female Participants (n = 11) | |
| | Heard (%) | Yielded (% of Heard) | Heard (%) | Yielded (% of Heard) | Used (%) | Worked (% of Used) | Used (%) | Worked (% of Used) |
| 1. Dated long time | 48.7 | 36.8 | 18.2 | 100.0 | 31.3 | 60.0 | 18.2 | 100.0 |
| 2. Money angle | 12.8 | 40.0 | 9.1 | 100.0 | 6.3 | 0.0 | 0.0 | - |
| 3. So aroused | 66.7 | 46.2 | 54.5 | 66.7 | 59.4 | 63.2 | 36.4 | 100.0 |
| 4. You led me on | 23.1 | 33.3 | 27.3 | 100.0 | 40.6 | 53.8 | 9.1 | 0.0 |
| 5. You initiated it | 10.3 | 50.0 | 45.5 | 60.0 | 6.3 | 0.0 | 27.3 | 33.3 |
| 6. You've done it with others | 20.5 | 37.5 | 27.3 | 66.7 | 21.9 | 42.9 | 9.1 | 0.0 |
| 7. You've done it with me before | 59.0 | 65.2 | 54.5 | 66.7 | 50.0 | 75.0 | 9.1 | 100.0 |
| 8. You must prefer other gender | 10.3 | 25.0 | 18.2 | 100.0 | 9.4 | 0.0 | 27.3 | 66.7 |
| 9. You're frigid/impotent | 17.9 | 28.6 | 36.4 | 75.0 | 15.6 | 40.0 | 27.3 | 100.0 |
| 10. I'll leave you | 20.5 | 37.5 | 4.5 | 100.0 | 12.5 | 25.0 | 18.2 | 50.0 |
| 11. I'll get it somewhere else | 20.5 | 37.5 | 9.1 | 100.0 | 12.5 | 50.0 | 18.2 | 50.0 |
| 12. "I love you" | 43.6 | 52.9 | 18.2 | 50.0 | 37.5 | 50.0 | 27.3 | 33.3 |

NOTE: See Table 9.1 for less abbreviated version.

Several of the messages appear to be more common as strategies used more by one sex than the other. In particular, ##1, 2, 3, 7, and 12 in Table 9.3 seem to be used more often by men than women, while ##5, 8, and 9 seem to be more common to women. For a few messages, targets and coercers had different accounts of which gender was more likely to use the strategy. Males, whether in the role of coercer or coerced, acknowledged more familiarity with ##4 and 6, while females in either role acknowledged more familiarity with ##10 and 11.[2]

Reports on the efficacy of coercion strategies are suspect, of course. It would seem likely that coercers might exaggerate the "success" of their strategies, while reluctant partners might be inclined to deny having yielded in response to verbal messages. Even so, it is apparent from Table 9.3 that many participants consider themselves to have yielded to unwanted sexual intimacy mostly as a result of certain coercion messages. On the whole, it appears that participants' overall perceptions have male targets yielding to verbal coercion more easily than female targets (i.e., compare male targets and female coercers' estimated yield rate with those of female targets and male coercers). Of course, there is no way of knowing whether this is because reluctant males are less adamantly reluctant than are reluctant females or because males, compared with females, find it difficult to reject a persistent partner—for example, perhaps due to relative inexperience with the reluctant partner role. In any case, the apparent efficacy of coercion messages by either gender upon the other is perceived to be fairly high.

Sections I and II of the questionnaire were designed merely to confirm whether the a priori verbal coercion messages were sufficiently common within participants' experience to warrant investigation of their corresponding premises in Section III of the study. Table 9.3 suggests that from the perspective of at least one role, all of the messages are fairly common (i.e., experienced by at least 10% of the participants) in sexual resistance situations. Thus all corresponding premises were retained for analysis in Section III.

### Section III: Premise System

Two sets of analyses were performed on the coercion message premises, one with the 15 premises assuming a female as the reluctant partner and coercion target (e.g., "She owes it to him to go further if . . .") and another with the 15 companion premises targeting males (e.g., "He owes it to her to go further if . . ."). In either case, the design was that of a $2 \times 3 \times 15$ analysis: Gender (male, female) $\times$ Belief Estimates (self, most men, most women) $\times$ Premise. The research question was aimed at comparisons of various combinations of the six Gender $\times$ Belief cells for each premise. A MANOVA ($2 \times 3 \times 15$) supported the viability of multiple pairwise comparisons on each data set.[3]

Means for all cells of both data sets are presented in Table 9.4, along with an abbreviated version of the results for all comparisons of a priori interest.

**Table 9.4**  Means: Strength of Belief in Premises

| Premises: Male "Coercer," Female Target | Means Female Participants | | | Means Male Participants | | | Multiple Comparisons | | | | |
|---|---|---|---|---|---|---|---|---|---|---|---|
| | Actual Participants a | Est. re Women b | Est. re Men c | Actual Participants d | Est. re Women e | Est. re Men f | a < c | a ~ b | a ~ d | c > d | d ~ e |
| 1. She should go far if dating a long time | 1.64 | 1.74 | 3.34 | 1.58 | 1.34 | 3.30 | *** | ns | ns | *** | ns |
| 2. Woman owes if $ spent | 1.38 | 2.18 | 4.26 | 1.76 | 1.76 | 3.92 | *** | ns | ns | *** | ns |
| 3. She owes it if he's aroused | 2.22 | 2.64 | 5.48 | 3.48 | 2.84 | 5.52 | *** | ns | ns | *** | ns |
| 4. She owes it if she's flirted and been suggestive | 2.30 | 2.64 | 5.36 | 3.88 | 3.12 | 5.48 | *** | ns | ns | *** | ns |
| 5. She owes it if she initiated it | 1.46 | 2.14 | 4.60 | 2.48 | 2.24 | 4.08 | *** | ns | ns | *** | ns |
| 6. She owes going as far as with others | 1.76 | 2.48 | 4.64 | 3.20 | 2.56 | 4.88 | *** | ns | ns | *** | ns |
| 7. She owes going as far as in past with him | 2.04 | 2.52 | 4.98 | 3.04 | 2.08 | 5.12 | *** | ns | ns | *** | ns |
| 8. Woman who resists prefers women | 1.50 | 1.62 | 3.18 | 1.60 | 1.20 | 2.60 | *** | ns | ns | *** | ns |
| 9. Aroused woman who wants to stop is inadequate | 1.52 | 1.58 | 3.38 | 1.96 | 1.28 | 3.00 | *** | ns | ns | *** | ns |
| 10. He's justified in terminating if she resists | 1.90 | 2.24 | 4.48 | 3.08 | 2.00 | 4.56 | *** | ns | ns | *** | ns |
| 11. Her resistance ensures he'll terminate | 2.68 | 3.10 | 3.84 | 3.00 | 3.44 | 3.60 | ** | ns | ns | * | ns |
| 12. He's justified to seek it elsewhere if she resists | 1.58 | 1.44 | 3.84 | 2.12 | 1.28 | 3.52 | *** | ns | ns | *** | ns |
| 13. She owes it if he loves her | 2.04 | 2.44 | 4.56 | 3.20 | 2.84 | 5.20 | *** | ns | ns | *** | ns |
| 14. Giving in proves that she loves him | 2.80 | 3.38 | 3.64 | 3.72 | 3.88 | 4.22 | * | ns | ns | ns | ns |
| 15. Resistance proves she doesn't really love him | 1.72 | 2.44 | 3.98 | 2.20 | 1.92 | 3.96 | *** | ns | ns | *** | ns |

|  | Male Participants | | | Female Participants | | | Multiple Comparisons | | | | |
|---|---|---|---|---|---|---|---|---|---|---|---|
| Premises: Female "Coercer," Male Target | Actual Participants A | Est. re Men B | Est. re Women C | Actual Participants D | Est. re Men E | Est. re Women F | A < C | A < B | A ~ D | C > D | D < E |
| 1. He should go far if dating a long time | 2.36 | 3.24 | 3.56 | 2.28 | 4.14 | 3.00 | ** | * | ns | ** | *** |
| 2. Man owes if $ spent | 2.40 | 3.44 | 2.40 | 1.54 | 2.44 | 1.88 | ns | * | ns | * | * |
| 3. He owes it if she's aroused | 3.20 | 4.04 | 3.84 | 2.24 | 3.20 | 2.74 | ns | * | ns | *** | * |
| 4. He owes it if he's flirted and been suggestive | 3.28 | 3.96 | 3.84 | 2.64 | 3.46 | 3.40 | ns | ns | ns | ** | * |
| 5. He owes it if he initiated it | 2.08 | 2.80 | 2.68 | 1.46 | 2.16 | 2.06 | ns | ns | ns | ** | ns |
| 6. He owes going as far as with others | 2.52 | 3.92 | 3.48 | 1.98 | 3.24 | 3.04 | * | *** | ns | *** | ** |
| 7. He owes going as far as in past with her | 3.68 | 4.60 | 4.44 | 2.76 | 3.94 | 3.84 | ns | * | ns | *** | ** |
| 8. Man who resists prefers men | 2.04 | 2.84 | 2.84 | 2.70 | 4.48 | 3.10 | * | * | ns | ns | *** |
| 9. Aroused man who wants to stop is inadequate | 2.92 | 4.64 | 3.76 | 2.72 | 4.74 | 3.54 | * | *** | ns | * | *** |
| 10. She's justified to terminate if he resists | 2.36 | 2.84 | 2.88 | 2.18 | 3.18 | 2.88 | ns | ns | ns | ns | ** |
| 11. His resistance ensures she'll terminate | 2.46 | 3.02 | 2.26 | 1.84 | 2.94 | 2.38 | ns | ns | ns | ns | ** |
| 12. She's justified to seek it elsewhere if he resists | 1.64 | 1.96 | 2.20 | 2.24 | 1.98 | 2.70 | ns | ns | ns | ns | ns |
| 13. He owes it if she loves him | 3.32 | 4.96 | 3.76 | 2.66 | 4.10 | 3.48 | ns | *** | ns | ** | *** |
| 14. Giving in proves that he loves her | 2.24 | 2.48 | 3.16 | 2.10 | 2.16 | 2.88 | * | ns | ns | ** | ns |
| 15. Resistance proves he doesn't really love her | 1.68 | 2.72 | 3.20 | 2.32 | 2.74 | 2.90 | *** | * | ns | * | ns |

NOTE: Means: 1 = *strongly disagree*, 7 = *strongly agree*. See Table 9.2 for less abbreviated versions of premises.
*p < .05. **p < .01. ***p < .001.

Means have been converted to be consistent with scale poles, whereby 1 = *strongly disagree* and 7 = *strongly agree*. On the whole, agreement with the verbal coercion premises (i.e., columns a, A, d, and D) is rather low. Nevertheless, various comparisons between the six Gender × Belief cells (i.e., the six columns) yield worthwhile observations. (Pairwise comparisons were via multiple-comparison *t* tests, e.g., Bruning & Kintz, 1977.)[4]

For *female-target premises,* data comparisons are as follows: (a) There is no significant difference between the degree to which the premises are believed by male and female participants (i.e., Table 9.4, column a ~ d). Given that all of the means are below the midpoint on the disagree/agree scale (i.e., < 4), most of them considerably so, the simple interpretation is that neither gender believes any of the premises very strongly. (b) Moreover, there is no significant difference between female targets' beliefs and their estimate of most other women's beliefs (i.e., column a ~ b). Thus it does not appear that the coercion messages operate by female targets thinking that they are "supposed to" believe the premises on the assumption that most women do. (c) There is no significant difference between male participants' beliefs and their projections about women's beliefs (i.e., column d ~ e). Thus it does not appear that male "coercers" use the messages on the assumption that women believe the premises. (d) On the other hand, significant differences for all premises are observed when comparing female targets' own beliefs with what they *think* most males believe (column a < c), presumably including their male coercion partner. Specifically, while female participants' belief in the various premises is quite low, they estimate males' belief to be quite high for many premises and significantly higher than their own for all premises. In other words, a given female target probably believes that her partner indeed believes the premises behind the coercion messages he uses. (e) Women's estimates of men's belief in the premises is grossly inflated, however (i.e., column c > d), with men's actual belief in the premises being significantly lower than women estimate in almost every case.

For *male-target* premises, the picture is similar: (a) There is no significant difference between male and female participants as to their general disagreement with the premises—that is, column A ~ D. (b) In general, unlike the female-target premises, there is no consistent pattern for male-target premises when comparing the targets' beliefs against their estimates of the coercer's beliefs (i.e., column A < C). If, however, we use Table 9.3 to highlight the coercion messages that are most likely to be used by female coercers, it turns out that for most of the corresponding premises—that is, Premises 1, 3, 5, 8, 9, 13, 14, and 15 of Table 9.4—male targets do indeed tend to think that women's belief in the premise is significantly greater than their own. This is the same target/coercer estimate relationship observed for female-target premises. (c) As with the female-target premises, it appears that the target's estimate of the coercer's beliefs is grossly exaggerated when compared with the coercer's true beliefs—that is, column C > D—at least for 11 of the 15 premises, including all but one of those relevant to the messages most commonly used by women. (d) Male targets estimate other males' belief in most of the premises to be considerably stronger than their own (column A < B). This is in contrast to the pattern noted above for women. We might speculate that male targets' assumption that most males' attitudes are more liberal than their own might provide a sort of peer pressure to conform to the assumed norms of their gender. (e) When looking at female coercers, we get a different impression from that of their male counterparts. Whereas male coercers estimated their targets' beliefs to approximate their own, female coercers estimate their targets' belief in the premises to be, in most cases, considerably stronger than their own (column D < E). Relatively speaking, female coercers employ premises that they don't believe but that they think (mistakenly—see column E vs. column A) their targets do believe.

*Post Hoc Observations—Double Standards*

Casual examination of participants' own beliefs in Table 9.4 (i.e., columns a and d) reveals at least a few alarming differences between attitudes toward a particular premise when it applies to one's own gender versus the same premise when applied to the other gender. As but one example, most women, relatively speaking, do not believe that an aroused *female* who resists escalated intimacy is frigid or otherwise sexually inadequate (Table 9.4, male coercer/female target, Premise 9) but believe more strongly that an aroused *male* who resists escalated intimacy is impotent or otherwise sexually inadequate (i.e., female coercer/male target, Premise 9). This kind of disparity is, of course, commonly known as a double standard, perhaps especially if the disparate beliefs or values are more charitable toward one's own gender. While it was not within the original rationale for the study to examine double standards, the data provided an opportunity to do so on a wide range of premises, double standard being operationalized as a significant difference between belief in (i.e., agreement with) male-target and female-target versions of the same premise. Space considerations preclude reporting the procedure and results of this analysis, but they are available from the author upon request.

# Discussion

This study has illuminated several dimensions of the use of verbal coercion toward unwanted sexual intimacy. At the most basic level, the study confirms the prevalence and effectiveness of verbal coercion efforts in situations where one partner desires more physical intimacy than the other. The large majority of individuals who find themselves in the more-eager-partner role try to get their reluctant partner to yield (69% of the women surveyed, 86% of the men), and of these, virtually all occasionally attempt verbal coercion of the reluctant partner (100% of women, 84% of men). And for those on the receiving end of this pressure, the majority will sometimes yield directly to verbal messages (71% of women, 86% of men). This is consistent with earlier studies having found verbal coercion to be common generally, and it provides even higher estimates when isolating participants who have experienced asymmetrical intimacy threshold situations.

The nature of the coercion messages themselves has become clearer as well. Earlier studies rarely provide specific examples of verbal coercion messages, typically identifying instead verbal behavior categories that are too vague to make specific messages self-evident (e.g., "logic," "coercion"). The present study identifies the specific coercion messages common to attempted sexual escalation episodes and offers one more approach to classifying underlying strategies.

Most of these messages seem to operate by inferring that the reluctant partner somehow "owes" an increased level of intimacy because of some condition that exists within the relationship (e.g., a lengthy period of dating, having been more intimate in the past) or within the immediate episode (e.g., heightened arousal, having been led on). *If* reluctant partners accepted the notion that these conditions obligate them to higher levels of intimacy, then the strategy presumably would instigate guilt over their lower threshold. But the present data suggest that reluctant partners in fact generally do not accept the obligation premise for any of these conditions. So actual guilt appears to play a lesser role in sexual verbal coercion than we may have thought.

A smaller set of messages seems to operate by challenging that heightened intimacy is needed in order to "prove" the reluctant partner's sexual preference, sexual adequacy, or love, the implication being that the more eager partner is dubious and in need of "evidence." But having found here that the more eager partner neither believes that the other's reluctance makes his or her sexuality or affection suspect, nor believes that increased intimacy provides evidence to the contrary, it appears that these are bogus challenges.

Another small set of messages simply threatens to terminate the relationship or to seek intimacy elsewhere if heightened intimacy is not forthcoming. As it turns out, neither partner believes that a low intimacy threshold warrants the termination of a relationship or its existing level of exclusivity. Logically, therefore, it would seem that carrying out the threat would compromise the integrity or character of the more eager partner. And in this case, it would seem that the threat itself would risk some degree of face loss for the more eager partner.

Since neither party believes the premises, coercion messages apparently do not operate by "coercing" reluctant partners via guilt, threats, embarrassment, or challenges to prove themselves. Rather, the use and effectiveness of these messages—messages whose premises neither party believes—seems best explained by what one partner *thinks* the *other* believes.

Looking first at the more eager partner, males in the coercer role assume the female's belief in the coercion message premises to be about as low as their own. That is, males appear to use what they consider to be admittedly weak and transparent arguments. Characterizations of this approach on ethical dimensions will be subjective, of course, but it is easy to suggest that common negative connotations of "coercion" may be too strong for this strategy. To use admittedly weak and presumably transparent arguments involves little if any intentional trickery, deception, or force, for example. With women in the coercer role, the situation is different, with women more frequently assuming their partner's belief in the premises to be significantly stronger than their own. Thus it is possible that the strategy is to "take advantage" of arguments the partner presumably believes, in which case the strategy would appear a bit more coercive.

In either case, however, the coercer is advancing what he or she considers to be admittedly weak arguments. But since the messages do make clear one's sincere wishes for heightened intimacy, albeit without providing a good reason for compliance, perhaps their intended rhetorical function is simply that—stating one's wishes for increased physical intimacy. The implied argument may provide a weak justification for the request in case the partner thinks too much is being asked, or it may provide an excuse for compliance in case the resistance is bogus or "token resistance"—that is, saying or implying "no" though actually willing (e.g., Abbey, 1982). In any case, it seems unlikely that strong versions of intentional coercion are operating when one uses admittedly weak and presumably transparent arguments. Moreover, it is reasonable to expect that if the partner continues to resist, the resistance should be more acceptable following an admittedly weak argument (compared with the relative potential for continued pressure or coercion after failing with a more sincere argument, for example).

Looking next at the more reluctant partners, we must wonder why they give in to arguments that neither they nor the message senders believe. Much of the answer appears to lie in the fact that they don't realize that their partner's belief is as weak as it is. For most all relevant messages, both reluctant females and reluctant males significantly overestimate the more eager partner's belief in their implied arguments. The source of these inflated estimates of the message user's beliefs is uncertain, of course. It could be part of an independent a priori stereotype of the other gender's beliefs, or it could be a charitable assumption that one's partner would not argue a premise he or she does not believe, or it could be a combination—for example, a generalization coming from having heard a number of past partners arguing the same premises with inferred sincerity. In any event, there is an additional misconception in the case of the typical reluctant male. Not only does he mistakenly assume that his position on the sender's premises is more conservative than hers, but also he assumes, mistakenly again, that his position is more conservative than that of most other males.

Thus, on the one hand, it does not appear that reluctant partners who yield on the basis of verbal messages do so via persuasion by a valid argument. Indeed, it is possible that yielding partners are sometimes "persuaded" by nothing more than the more eager partner's overt acknowledgment of a desire for heightened intimacy. Given this characterization of the episode, the verbal message would be serving merely to instigate "altruistic sex" (e.g., Muehlenhard & Cook, 1988)—that is, giving in to increased intimacy as a sort of favor just because the partner wishes it. On the other hand, even if one is not persuaded by the "logic" of the more eager partner's messages, the messages present a certain degree of pressure. There is at least a sort of "politeness" pressure that operates when one is asked to do something of which one is obviously capable—generally (Brown & Levinson, 1978), and within sexual resistance situations in particular (Motley & Reeder, 1995). And there is additional pressure when persuasion efforts are accompanied by ostensibly sincere arguments, especially those presented by persons we like or respect.

## PRACTICAL APPLICATIONS

Either explanation—yielding altruistically or yielding via relational pressures—represents a relatively mild form of pressure compared with more extreme unwanted sex variations (e.g., Christopher, 1988; Spitzberg, 1995). But it is pressure, nevertheless, and appears to be sufficient to instigate unwanted sex in many cases. Moreover, it is conceivable that it accounts in part for unwanted sex episodes, including verbal coercion variations, often reported as being unpleasant. Intuitively, it seems that this *pressure would be reduced, perhaps considerably, were the reluctant partner not under the mistaken impression that the eager partner believes the premises of his or her coercion messages.* Thus there should be practical applications and advantages to sharing the results of this study—for example, via popular press, interpersonal communication texts, lectures—with individuals who date. Suppose, for example, that both partners on a date knew what we know now. The more eager partner might be less likely to use these verbal messages if he or she suspected the other knew that the implied arguments were insincere (or knew that they are almost universally not believed). And if the arguments are used, there should be more acceptance of continued resistance, perhaps especially by more eager females, knowing that the partner does not believe the premises. Moreover, while not tested directly in this study, there might be more reluctance to use these messages if it were assumed that, sincere or not, transparent or not, the messages place pressure on the partner beyond that of a mere take-it-or-leave-it request for heightened intimacy.

Most important, however, reluctant partners almost certainly would *feel less pressure to comply* if they were informed that contrary to their usual assumptions, the premises usually are advanced insincerely. And in the case of the reluctant male, there should be additionally reduced pressure from the realization that his own disagreement with the message premises is indeed the norm. In short, saying no should be easier if reluctant partners were to realize that their own disagreement with the premises of verbal coercion messages is almost universally shared by those in their own position as well as those in their partner's position.

## CONCLUSION

Threshold asymmetry in physical intimacy situations is to be expected. In and of itself, this need not be especially problematic, or at least need not necessarily lead to unwanted sexual intimacy by the lower-threshold partner. Likewise, the mere acknowledgment of the more eager partner's desire for increased intimacy need not be problematic. By conventional accounts,[5] it is well within the boundaries of proper behavior for the more eager partner to "make a move" or verbally indicate a desire for increased intimacy, followed by resistance from the other partner, followed by respect for and acceptance of the resistance by the more eager partner, with this acceptance being made clear to the reluctant partner. Obviously, asymmetry does not always operate this ideally, however. If it did, there would be very little unwanted sexual intimacy and, for the rare exception, relatively little accompanying discomfort, it would seem. It is easy to understand what accounts for yielding and for discomfort in the most extreme forms of sexual coercion—physical force, threat of physical force, badgering, and similar situations wherein the more eager partner's failure to accept the resistance is clear.

In the less extreme versions, however, including verbal coercion as represented in the present study, the explanation is less certain. It is not clear what differentiates those episodes that operate as the more ideal situation (i.e., attempted escalation, resistance, and acceptance) from those that become uncomfortable (attempted escalation, resistance, verbal coercion, unwanted yielding, and discomfort).[6] The present study supplies part of the answer by noting that escalation efforts often are accompanied by verbal rationales and by finding that while reluctant partners disagree with those rationales, they grossly overestimate the degree to which the more eager partner believes them. This probably explains a key component of the pressure reluctant partners perceive from verbal coercion messages. It seems likely that much of this pressure would subside were the reluctant partner to learn what this study seems to have discovered—namely, that the sender doesn't believe the premise either.

## Notes

1. An example of exact wording: "Your partner tried to make you feel guilty about not going further because of the amount of money he or she had spent on you (e.g., on a particular date, gift, or in general). Have you experienced this?"

2. Statistical comparisons within Sections I and II are precluded by the nature of the data, since cells allow both related and independent measures.

3. In summary, all main effects except gender were significant at $p < .00001$, as were all interaction effects for both sets of premises. Details are available from the author.

4. Differences were negligible ($p >> .10$, $t$ test) when comparing beliefs and estimates of participants with versus those without experience using or yielding to the messages—whether for women who yielded, men who yielded, women who used the messages, or men who used the messages.

5. This is rarely, if ever, spelled out in studies of unwanted sex, but it is implied in many cases (e.g., Haworth-Hoeppner, 1998; Struckman-Johnson, 1988).

6. Variations not involving unwanted sex are ignored here intentionally, including bogus resistance/coercion/consent.

## References

Abbey, A. (1982). Sex differences in attributions for friendly behavior: Do males misperceive females' friendliness? *Journal of Personality and Social Psychology, 42,* 830–836.

Black, K. A., & Gold, D. J. (2003). Men's and women's reactions to hypothetical sexual advances: The role of initiator socioeconomic status and level of coercion. *Sex Roles, 49,* 173–178.

Brown, P., & Levinson, S. (1978). Universals in language usage. In E. N. Goody (Ed.), *Questions and politeness: Strategies in social interaction.* Cambridge, England: Cambridge University Press.

Bruning, J. L., & Kintz, B. L. (1977). *Computational handbook of statistics.* Glenview, IL: Scott, Foresman.

Christopher, F. S. (1988). An initial investigation into a continuum of premarital sexual pressure. *Journal of Sex Research, 25,* 255–265.

DeSouza, E. R., & Hutz, C. S. (1996). Reactions to refusals of sexual advances among U.S. and Brazilian men and women. *Sex Roles, 34,* 549–565.

Grauerholz, E., & Serpe, R. T. (1985). Initiation and response: The dynamics of sexual interaction. *Sex Roles, 12,* 1041–1059.

Hannon, J., Hall, D. S., Kuntz, T., Van Laar, S., & Williams, J. (1995). Dating characteristics leading to unwanted vs. wanted sexual behavior. *Sex Roles, 33,* 767–783.

Haworth-Hoeppner, S. (1998). What's gender got to do with it: Perceptions of sexual coercion in a university community. *Sex Roles, 38,* 757–779.

Hines, D. A., & Saudino, K. J. (2003). Gender differences in psychological, physical, and sexual aggression among college students using the Revised Conflict Tactics Scales. *Violence and Victims, 18,* 197–217.

Kanin, E. J. (1957). Male aggression in dating-courtship relationships. *American Journal of Sociology, 63,* 197–204.

Koss, M. P., Gidyez, C. A., & Wisniewski, N. (1987). The scope of rape: Incidence and prevalence of sexual aggression and victimization in a national sample of higher education students. *Journal of Consulting and Clinical Psychology, 55,* 162–170.

McCormick, N. B. (1979). Come-ons and put-offs: Unmarried students' strategies for having and avoiding sexual intercourse. *Psychology of Women Quarterly, 4,* 194–211.

Motley, M. T., & Reeder, H. M. (1995). Unwanted escalation of sexual intimacy: Male and female perceptions of connotations and relational consequences of resistance messages. *Communication Monographs, 62,* 355–382.

Muehlenhard, C. L. (1988). Misinterpreted dating behaviors and the risk of date rape. *Journal of Social and Clinical Psychology, 6,* 20–37.

Muehlenhard, C. L., & Cook, S. W. (1988). Men's self-reports of unwanted sexual activity. *Journal of Sex Research, 24,* 58–72.

Muehlenhard, C. L., Julsonnet, S., Carlson, M. I., & Flarity-White, L. A. (1989). A cognitive-behavioral program for preventing sexual coercion. *The Behavior Therapist, 12,* 211–214.

Muehlenhard, C. L., & Linton, M. L. (1987). Date rape and sexual aggression in dating situations: Incidence and risk factors. *Journal of Counseling Psychology, 34,* 186–196.

Murnen, S. K., Perot, A., & Byrne, D. (1989). Coping with unwanted sexual activity: Normative responses, situational determinants, and individual differences. *Journal of Sex Research, 26,* 85–106.

O'Sullivan, L. F., Byers, E. S., & Finkelman, L. (1998). A comparison of male and female college students' experiences of sexual coercion. *Psychology of Women Quarterly, 22,* 177–195.

Perper, T., & Weis, D. L. (1987). Proceptive and rejective strategies of U.S. and Canadian college women. *Journal of Sex and Research, 23,* 455–480.

Poppen, P. J., & Segel, N. J. (1988). The influence of sex and sex role orientation on sexual coercion. *Sex Roles, 19,* 689–701.

Spitzberg, B. H. (1995). *Communication predictors of sexual coercion.* Paper presented at the conference of the Speech Communication Association, San Antonio, TX.

Struckman-Johnson, C. (1988). Forced sex on dates: It happens to men too. *Journal of Sex Research, 24,* 234–241.

Struckman-Johnson, C., Struckman-Johnson, D., & Anderson, P. B. (2003). Tactics of sexual coercion: When men and women won't take no for an answer. *Journal of Sex Research, 40,* 76–87.

Struckman-Johnson, D., & Struckman-Johnson, C. (1991). Men and women's acceptance of coercive sexual strategies varied by initiator gender and couple intimacy. *Sex Roles, 25,* 661–676.

AUTHOR'S NOTE: The author gratefully acknowledges the contribution of his daughter, Shannon M. Motley, via prepilot investigations (not reported in this study), while an undergraduate at St. Mary's College.

# PART III

*Everyday Situations*

# 10

## What Counts as Effective Emotional Support?

### Explorations of Individual and Situational Differences

*Brant R. Burleson*

W hen feeling hurt, disappointed, or upset, virtually everyone would like to receive sensitive emotional support from caring others. But is what counts as sensitive emotional support like beauty—that is, in the eye of the beholder? Do people differ substantially in their views about the type of emotional support that makes them feel better, or do most people have similar ideas about what counts as helpful (and unhelpful) emotional support? This chapter contributes to answering this question by summarizing the results of three studies that explore how certain psychological and situational factors influence people's responses to various emotional support strategies.

## Emotional Support: Its Nature and Significance

Emotional support is viewed by both theorists and laypeople as a basic provision of close personal relationships (Cunningham & Barbee, 2000) and is an important determinant of satisfaction within these relationships. People value the emotional support skills of their relationship partners, and perceptions of emotional supportiveness have been found to play a critical role in the development and maintenance of friendships, romances, families, and work relationships (see review by Burleson, 2003a). When emotional support is provided skillfully (i.e., addresses a distressed other's feelings in a sensitive and effective way), it can yield numerous benefits for the recipient, including improvements in emotional states (Burleson & Goldsmith, 1998), coping (Stroebe & Stroebe, 1996), and even health (Wills & Fegan, 2001). Unfortunately, research indicates, many attempts to provide emotional support are *not* experienced as sensitive and effective by recipients. There is a burgeoning literature concerned with "support attempts that fail," "miscarried helping," and "cold comfort" (see Holmstrom, Burleson, & Jones, 2005) showing that well-meaning but insensitive attempts to provide emotional support are all too common and can be quite harmful to recipients, intensifying their emotional hurt, undermining their coping, and even damaging their health.

Providing effective, sensitive support thus requires more than good intentions; those who provide truly helpful support must know what to say (as well as what not to say). So what properties of messages are generally perceived as providing helpful, sensitive support? One useful approach to characterizing the features of more and less effective supportive messages makes use of the concept known as *person centeredness.*

In comforting contexts, person centeredness reflects the extent to which messages explicitly acknowledge, elaborate, legitimize, and contextualize the distressed other's feelings and perspective (Burleson, 1994). Thus messages low in person centeredness (LPC) deny the other's feelings and perspective by criticizing his or her feelings, challenging the legitimacy of those feelings, or telling the other how he or she should act and feel. Messages that exhibit a moderate degree of person centeredness (MPC) afford an implicit recognition of the other's feelings by distracting attention from the troubling situation, offering expressions of sympathy and condolence, or presenting non-feeling-centered explanations of the situation intended to reduce the distress (e.g., citing mitigating circumstances). In contrast, highly person-centered (HPC) comforting messages explicitly recognize and legitimize the other's feelings, help the other to articulate those feelings, elaborate reasons why those feelings might be felt, and assist the other to see how those feelings fit in a broader context. Examples of comforting messages that vary in level of person centeredness are presented in Table 10.1. Numerous studies have found that HPC messages are evaluated as more sensitive, effective, helpful, and appropriate than MPC and especially LPC messages (see review by Burleson, Samter, et al., 2005).

## Differences in Responses to Person-Centered Comforting

Important as these findings are, they do not mean that all people necessarily find HPC comforting messages superior to MPC or LPC messages in all

**Table 10.1**      Comforting Messages That Exhibit Low, Moderate, and High Levels
of Person Centeredness

---

Set 1: Messages that might be used to comfort a college student friend who is
somewhat irritated about not doing well on a quiz that counts 1% of the
class grade (mild problem severity and emotional upset)

**Low Person-Centered Message** *(Deny receiver's feelings by criticizing and
challenging him or her, telling receiver how to feel or act)*

Well, that's too bad, but maybe you're just not trying hard enough. Maybe that's
why you didn't do so well on the quiz. You're probably just gonna have to study
harder. You know, you shouldn't be so upset about it if you didn't study as hard
as you could have. I'm sure that you'll get better grades when you study harder.
But right now, can you just try to forget about the quiz? I mean, remember that
there are more important things in the world than stupid quizzes over class
readings. Anyway, it's a pretty dumb class; it's really not worth worrying about.
So just try to forget about it. Just think about something else.

**Moderately Person-Centered Message** *(Expressions of sympathy and condolence,
presenting non-feeling-centered explanations of the situation)*

Well, I'm really sorry you didn't do better on the quiz. I wish you'd done better on
it too. But I can see how this happened. College is really tough sometimes. It's really
too bad that you didn't do as well on this one. I've heard a lot of people don't do
well on those quizzes. You did better on all the other ones and will probably do well
on the rest of them. And hey, I heard you aced that biology midterm last week—
that was great! I know! Those guys that live over on Sylvia Street are having a party
tonight. Do you want to go get some dinner and then go to the party?

**Highly Person-Centered Message** *(Explicitly recognize and legitimize the other's
feelings, help the other to articulate those feelings, elaborate reasons why those feelings
might be felt, and assist the other to see how those feelings fit in a broader context)*

Well, I understand why you're feeling bummed out about the quiz. I can
appreciate why you're feeling down right now. I mean, not doing as well as you
want on an assignment is always hard. It's just so frustrating sometimes to work
really hard in a class and still not do as well as you want. The same thing
happened to me earlier this year, so I can guess how disappointed you must feel
about this. It's probably hard to look at it this way, but maybe you've learned
something from this that will help you do better on the next quiz. I'd be happy
to talk to you more about this, if you want.

*********************************************************************

Set 2: Messages that might be used to comfort a college student friend who is
moderately upset about having his or her car booted in a university garage
for parking in a reserved space and having to pay $350 in fines and fees to
have the boot removed (moderate problem severity and emotional upset)

---

*(Continued)*

**Table 10.1** (Continued)

---

**Low Person-Centered Message**

Well, you'll have to pay those fines and tickets, but it could be worse—they could have towed and impounded your car. They can do that when you park in a reserved space during the day. So, you got off comparatively easy—you should remember that and be grateful. And try not to make such a big thing out of it, because you'll only upset yourself. This is one of those things that is not really worth worrying about; just pay the fine so you can move on and forget about it. I guess next time you should be more careful about parking in the garage overnight.

**Moderately Person-Centered Message**

Well, I'm really sorry that your car got booted. I wish this hadn't happened, but it seems like one of those things that can just happen sometimes. This university is out to take students for every dollar it can. I see parking boots on people's cars all the time around campus. I guess they really mean it when they say they'll ticket at 7 a.m. Hey, I know! There's a party over on Waldron Street tonight. It might be just the thing to cheer you up. I can pick you up later so you don't have to drive.

**Highly Person-Centered Message**

Of course, you're really mad right now! This is *so* outrageous! I mean, you were only 5 minutes late moving your car; you'd figure they'd give you a break. But not here, I guess; sounds like you got hit by one of those ticket Nazis. It's no fun having to pay those fines and tickets, and it's not like you don't have better things to do with the money! I'd be angry too. I mean, I totally understand, especially since you might be short on cash right now. I'm happy to help you blow off some steam about this; just wish I could do more!

---

circumstances. In recognition of this, a growing number of studies have sought to determine whether people differ in the types of comforting messages they view as helpful and prefer to receive when they need support.

Knowing whether and why people differ in their responses to various comforting messages is important for several practical and theoretical reasons. From a pragmatic point of view, it is of obvious importance to determine whether groups of individuals systematically differ in their responses to distinct comforting approaches: clearly, helpers will want to know whether some groups of people respond more favorably to certain comforting strategies than do others; if so, types of support strategies can be matched with types of people to achieve the most desirable outcomes.

From a theoretical point of view, knowing whether and why people differ in their response to comforting approaches should help us to better understand the mechanisms through which comforting messages work to bring improvements in affect and coping behavior. For example, some theorists (e.g., Tannen,

1990; Wood, 2000) maintain that certain comforting strategies effectively reduce emotional distress in some groups of people but not in other groups; these theorists hold that comforting strategies are effective within certain groups because they are the conventionally recognized and accepted devices in those groups for conveying care and concern. In contrast, other theorists (Burleson & Goldsmith, 1998) maintain that certain comforting strategies (such as HPC messages) should work effectively with virtually all people because of how these strategies impact the psychological functioning of their recipients. Thus by examining the extent to which distinct groups of people respond similarly or differently to various comforting strategies, we not only can determine what comforting messages should work best with an intended recipient but also can gain insight into why these messages produce certain cognitive, affective, and behavioral outcomes.

## The Current Focus: Psychological and Situational Factors That Influence Responses to Person-Centered Comforting

In recent years, studies have examined whether people who belong to distinct *demographic groups* respond differently to various comforting messages. Demographic characteristics (e.g., age, sex, nationality) are an obvious place to begin looking for similarities and differences in responses to comforting messages, since considerable research indicates that people who belong to different demographic groups communicate in distinct ways (see Gudykunst & Matsumoto, 1996). And in fact, numerous studies have detected statistically significant differences in responses to comforting messages exhibiting different degrees of person centeredness as a function of recipient demographic characteristics such as age, sex, ethnicity, and nationality (see review by Burleson, 2003b). However, most of these demographic differences have been small in magnitude, usually accounting for only 1% to 3% of the variability in responses to these messages and never accounting for more than 10% of the variability.

More important, recent theory and research suggest that responses to comforting messages may differ more as a function of recipient psychological characteristics (e.g., personality traits and cognitive abilities) than as a function of demographic variables. Of course, demographic factors do not themselves directly influence responses to messages. Rather, certain demographic factors are generally associated with particular patterns of socialization and social experience, which, in turn, shape the personality traits and cognitive orientations of the people in these groups. Theoretically, then, responses to comforting messages should be influenced most directly by underlying psychological factors that mediate the effects of demographic differences on responses to messages.

Indeed, a limited number of studies (e.g., Burleson & Mortenson, 2003; Kunkel, 2002) have found that certain psychological variables (e.g., values, goal orientations) explain more variability than demographic variables in support message responses and also mediate the effects of demographic variables.

It is also possible that recipient responses to comforting messages may vary as a function of certain situational factors, such as the severity of the problem confronted by the recipient. To date, almost all research assessing responses to comforting messages has examined these in the context of moderate or severe problems that generally create intense, negative emotional upset. The question posed here is whether people who experience comparatively mild upsets are best comforted by the same support strategies found to be effective at helping people cope with moderate to severe upsets. When coping with mild upsets, support recipients may not give much attention to the content of highly sophisticated comforting strategies (such as HPC messages), and if they do, these strategies may be viewed as having undesirable implications (e.g., suggesting that the situation is more serious than the recipient thought; implying that the helper thinks the recipient is incapable of managing the situation). Thus it is possible that less person-centered comforting strategies may actually be more effective than more person-centered strategies when seeking to support someone experiencing a relatively mild upset.

*Do different types of people prefer different types of comforting messages when coping with different degrees of upset?* This chapter seeks answers to this question by reporting three studies that examine how certain psychological and situational factors affect responses to comforting messages that exhibit different levels of person centeredness. Two studies examined how the psychological factors of *communication values* and *self-concept* influenced responses to comforting strategies, while a third study assessed whether evaluations of comforting strategies varied as a function of *problem severity* and other situational factors.

## Study 1

Communication values are aspects of personality that reflect the importance people place on various communication skills; hence supportive communication value is the importance (i.e., value) that people place on the skill of providing support, especially emotional support. Studies have found that the value people place on the skill of comforting is associated with several important outcomes, including their degree of peer acceptance, their level of loneliness, and their development of mutually satisfying friendships and romances (Burleson, 2003a, 2003b). It seems reasonable to assume that people who place comparatively high value on the emotional support skills of relationship partners will respond more positively to HPC comforting messages and more negatively to LPC comforting messages. In contrast, people who place little value on comforting skill may differentiate little, if at all, among comforting messages that differ in person centeredness. To date, only one study (Burleson & Mortenson, 2003) has examined how the value placed on support skill influences responses to comforting messages that vary in person centeredness, and the results of that study were inconclusive. Thus Study 1 was designed to assess whether, and to what extent, responses to comforting messages of differing levels of person centeredness vary as a function of the value people place on emotional support skill.

## METHOD

Participants in Study 1 were 184 college students (89 men and 95 women) attending a large midwestern university. To assess value placed on supportive communication skills, participants responded to three items pertaining to comforting skill taken from Burleson and Samter's (1990) Communication Functions Questionnaire (CFQ). Participants rated (on 5-point scales) how important it was for a close, same-sex friend to be able to skillfully comfort them when upset (e.g., "Helps make me feel better when I'm hurt or depressed about something," "Can help me work through my emotions when I'm feeling upset or depressed"). Cronbach's alpha for the three comforting items was .80. A median split was conducted to create a group ($n = 91$) that placed relatively low value on comforting skill ($M = 3.30$) and a group ($n = 93$) that placed relatively high value on comforting skill ($M = 4.66$).

To obtain participants' evaluations of comforting messages that differed in level of person centeredness, participants read two randomly ordered situations in which a "good friend" was portrayed as experiencing moderate emotional distress. The situations depicted the friend as (a) coping with a recently announced parental divorce and (b) not receiving an anticipated academic scholarship. A list of nine randomly ordered messages followed each of the hypothetical scenarios, with three messages exhibiting a low level of person centeredness, three messages exhibiting a moderate level of person centeredness, and three exhibiting a high level of person centeredness. Participants were instructed to rate the quality of each strategy—that is, its sensitivity and effectiveness—on 5-point scales; acceptable reliabilities (.70–.82) were obtained.

## RESULTS

The effects of support value and message person centeredness on evaluations of the comforting messages were assessed by a $2 \times 3$ mixed-model ANOVA with repeated measures on the second factor. The between-groups factor was support value (low vs. high), the repeated factor was message person centeredness (low, moderate, and high), and the dependent variable was rated message quality (i.e., averaged sensitivity and effectiveness ratings). Means for this analysis are plotted in Figure 10.1. The main effect for support value was not significant, $F(1, 182) = 1.18, p > .25$. However, there was a strong main effect for message person centeredness, $F(2, 364) = 376.13, p < .001$, $\eta^2 = .67$, with HPC messages ($M = 3.53$) rated as better ($p < .001$) than MPC messages ($M = 2.79$), and MPC messages rated as better ($p < .001$) than LPC messages ($M = 2.16$). More important, there was a significant interaction between the factors of support value and message person centeredness, $F(2, 364) = 7.90, p < .001, \eta^2 = .04$. Decomposition of this interaction (utilizing polynomial trend analysis) revealed that, as anticipated, the linear effect for message person centeredness explained significantly more variance in message ratings among those with high support values ($\eta^2 = .75$) than among those with low support values ($\eta^2 = .58$), $F(1, 182) = 11.32, p < .001, \eta^2 = .06$. Participants high in support value rated HPC messages as significantly better than did those in low support value, $t(182) = 3.15, p < .002$ (see Figure 10.1). There was a near significant trend for participants low in support value to rate LPC messages as better than did those high in support value, $t(182) = 1.84$, $p < .10$. The two groups did not differ in their evaluation of MPC messages, $t(192) = 0.40$, ns.

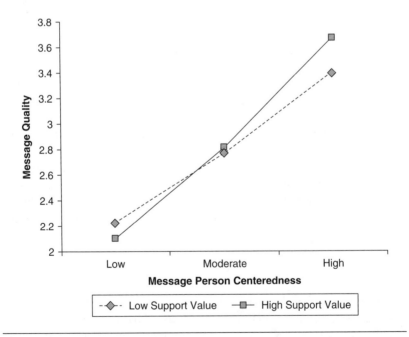

**Figure 10.1**    Effects of Person Centeredness and Support Values on Message Evaluations in Study 1

## DISCUSSION

The results of Study 1 indicate that people who highly value support skills rate HPC comforting messages more positively, and LPC messages less positively, than do people who place comparatively low value on support skills. However, the differences in message evaluations attributable to support value were relatively small, especially in comparison to the very large effect observed for message person centeredness. All participants—regardless of their support values—rated HPC messages as substantially better than MPC messages and rated MPC messages as substantially better than LPC messages (see Figure 10.1). The theoretical implications of these findings are intriguing; they suggest that people who highly value support skills pay more attention to the details of the comforting messages they receive than do those who place comparatively low value on support skills. The practical implication of the present findings is rather different, however: the present results strongly suggest that HPC messages will do the best job of providing comfort to all recipients, regardless of their support values.

## Study 2

Numerous scholars (e.g., Cushman, Valentinsen, & Dietrich, 1982) have suggested that self-concept—the way we think about ourselves—is a powerful influence on our communicative behavior. To date, however, little research has examined whether self-concept influences recipient responses to comforting messages that differ in degree of person centeredness. Two independent aspects of self-concept that appear relevant to how people respond to comforting messages are self-definitions as expressive and instrumental. People who see themselves as highly expressive believe themselves to be emotional, kind, warm, gentle, and sensitive to the feelings of others. People who see themselves as highly instrumental believe themselves to be independent, active, decisive, confident, and persistent (Spence & Helmreich, 1978). In contemporary American society, an expressive orientation is often associated with femininity, whereas an instrumental orientation is often associated with masculinity (Prentice & Carranza, 2002), though men and women vary widely in their self-perceived degrees of both expressiveness and instrumentality. Given the centrality of affect in their self-definitions, high expressives might be expected to evaluate HPC comforting messages more positively, and LPC messages less positively, than low expressives. In contrast, given their focus on solving practical problems, high instrumentals might be expected to evaluate MPC and, perhaps, even LPC messages more favorably than low instrumentals. To date, only one study (MacGeorge, Graves, Feng, Gillihan, & Burleson, 2004) has examined the influence of expressive and instrumental orientations on evaluations of comforting messages that differ in person centeredness; this study found that instrumentality was positively associated with evaluations of MPC comforting messages, whereas expressivity was positively associated with evaluations of HPC messages and negatively associated with evaluations of LPC messages. Study 2 sought to replicate and extend those results by providing a more detailed examination of how instrumental versus expressive orientations jointly influence responses to comforting messages with different degrees of person centeredness.

## METHOD

Participants were 387 college students (190 men and 197 women) enrolled in undergraduate communication courses at a large midwestern university. Participants completed the short form of Spence and Helmreich's (1978) Personal Attributes Questionnaire (PAQ), which provides assessments of both expressivity and instrumentality. Eight 5-point semantic differential scales were used to assess expressiveness (e.g., *not at all emotional* to *very emotional*; *not at all kind* to *very kind*), and another eight 5-point scales were used to assess instrumentality (e.g., *very passive* to *very active*; *not at all independent* to *very independent*), with participants indicating the point on the scales that best described themselves. In the current study, internal consistencies were .76 for expressivity and .78 for instrumentality. A median split was conducted to create a group ($n = 194$) relatively low in expressivity ($M = 3.51$) and a group ($n = 193$) relatively high in expressivity ($M = 4.29$). A second median split was conducted to create a group ($n = 196$) relatively low in instrumentality ($M = 3.18$) and a group ($n = 191$) relatively high in instrumentality ($M = 4.13$).

To obtain participants' evaluations of comforting messages that differed in level of person centeredness, participants read 1 of 18 different transcribed conversations ostensibly taking place between two college students (in fact, these were constructed by the researcher). In all versions of the conversations, a helper seeks to comfort a distressed same-sex friend (see Samter, Burleson, & Murphy, 1987, for a detailed description of this protocol). In 6 of the conversations, the helper used comforting messages exhibiting LPC; in 6 other conversations, the helper used messages exhibiting MPC; and in the remaining 6 conversations, the helper used messages exhibiting HPC. After reading the conversation, participants rated the message and helper for several qualities, including the perceived helpfulness of the messages (tapped by four items assessing message effectiveness [e.g., *very ineffective* to *very effective*] and five items assessing message supportiveness [e.g., *very insensitive* to *very sensitive*]). Internal consistency for this measure of perceived message helpfulness was quite good, $\alpha = .93$.

## RESULTS

A 2 (expressivity: low vs. high) × 2 (instrumentality: low vs. high) × 3 (message person centeredness: low vs. moderate vs. high) ANOVA was conducted to assess the effects of the independent variables on evaluations of message helpfulness. A strong, significant main effect was observed for message person centeredness, $F(2, 370) = 177.55$, $p < .001$, $\eta^2 = .49$, with HPC messages ($M = 3.85$) rated as more helpful ($p < .05$) than MPC messages ($M = 3.67$), and MPC messages rated as much more helpful ($p < .001$) than LPC messages ($M = 2.40$). The main effect for expressivity was not significant, $F(1, 370) = 0.29$, *ns*; nor was the main effect for instrumentality, $F(1, 370) = 0.78$, *ns*.

As anticipated, however, there was a significant interaction between expressivity and message person centeredness, $F(2, 370) = 4.06$, $p < .02$, $\eta^2 = .02$ (see Figure 10.2). Decomposition of this interaction indicated that, as predicted, high expressives viewed HPC comforting messages as more helpful ($M = 3.95$) than did low expressives ($M = 3.75$), $t(114) = 1.84$, $p < .05$ (one-tailed test), and LPC messages as less helpful ($M = 2.25$) than did low expressives ($M = 2.52$), $t(136) = 1.96$, $p < .05$; low and high expressives did not differ in their evaluation of MPC messages. Also as predicted, there was a significant interaction between instrumentality and message person centeredness, $F(2, 370) = 3.48$, $p < .05$, $\eta^2 = .02$ (see Figure 10.3). Decomposition of this interaction indicated that high instrumentals viewed MPC comforting messages as significantly more helpful ($M = 3.82$) than did low instrumentals ($M = 3.51$), $t(126) = 2.80$, $p < .01$; high and low instrumentals did not differ in their evaluations of LPC or HPC messages. The three-way interaction was not significant, $F(2, 370) = 1.06$, *ns*.

## DISCUSSION

The results of Study 2 indicate that people who see themselves as high in the trait of expressivity view HPC comforting messages as more helpful, and LPC messages as less helpful, than do people who see themselves as low in expressivity. In addition, people who see themselves as high in the trait of instrumentality view MPC comforting messages as more helpful than do those who see themselves as low in instrumentality. As in Study 1, however, the differences in message evaluations attributable to personality characteristics were relatively small, especially in comparison to the large effect observed for message person centeredness. All participants in Study 2—regardless of their expressive and instrumental orientations—rated HPC messages as more helpful than MPC messages and rated MPC messages as substantially more helpful than LPC messages.

These results are noteworthy for several reasons. First, they closely replicate the results reported by MacGeorge et al. (2004, Study 3) for the effects of expressivity and instrumentality on evaluations of comforting messages having

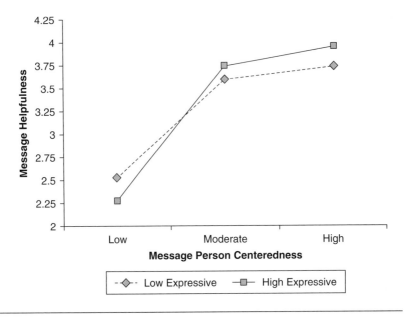

**Figure 10.2**    Effects of Person Centeredness and Expressive Orientation on Message Evaluations in Study 2

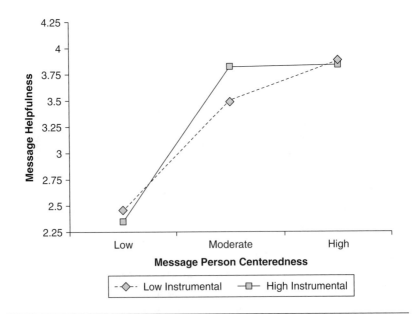

**Figure 10.3**    Effects of Person Centeredness and Instrumental Orientation on Message Evaluations in Study 2

different levels of person centeredness. Thus the present results emphasize the stable effects of these dimensions of personality on responses to comforting messages. Second, the present results underscore that distinct aspects of personality differentially affect responses to various comforting approaches; expressivity influenced evaluations of LPC and HPC messages, whereas instrumentality influenced evaluations of MPC messages. There appear to be good theoretical reasons for this pattern of results. MPC comforting messages are, in many ways, the most problem-focused support strategies; thus it seems reasonable that these would be more appealing to those having a high instrumental orientation. High expressives are particularly sensitive to the affective component of human experience (see Belansky & Boggiano, 1994), so it makes sense that they would especially appreciate HPC messages (which acknowledge, legitimate, and explore feelings) and that they might be put off by LPC messages (which deny or ignore feelings). Put differently, high expressives appear particularly motivated to attend to the details of the comforting messages to which they are exposed. Finally, although the two aspects of personality examined in this study had some effect on responses to diverse comforting messages, the present results also clearly indicate that HPC messages should do the best job of providing comfort to *all* recipients, regardless of their expressive and instrumental orientations.

## Study 3

Studies 1 and 2 focused on how responses to comforting messages varied as a function of the personality characteristics of their recipients. In contrast, Study 3 examines how aspects of the communicative situation influence responses to comforting messages that differ in person centeredness. Two aspects of the communicative situation receive scrutiny in Study 3: the severity of the problem experienced by the message recipient and the sex of the helper.

Considerable research on persuasion indicates that people process messages systematically (i.e., give the greatest attention to and are most influenced by message content) when the matter addressed by the message is personally relevant to them (see Petty, Rucker, Bizer, & Cacioppo, 2004). These findings suggest that, in the context of supportive communication, people will be particularly motivated to systematically process comforting messages when they experience a moderate to severe emotional upset (see Bodie & Burleson, 2008). Thus features of comforting message content, such as degree of person centeredness, should have a greater effect when recipients are coping with a moderate or severe emotional upset rather than a mild upset.

When recipients are less motivated to process the comforting messages they receive in a highly systematic manner (as, perhaps, when experiencing a mild upset), other features of the communicative situation, such as the sex of the helper, may act as environmental cues that influence recipient responses. Extensive research (see Cialdini, 2001) indicates that people utilize heuristics (simple decision rules) in responding to communicative situations when they are less motivated to process messages systematically. One heuristic that people may rely upon when they receive support in mildly upsetting situations is that women provide better (i.e., more sensitive, effective, and helpful) support than do men. Several lines of research suggest that this is a commonly used heuristic: there is a broadly shared cultural expectation that women will be ready providers of warm, nurturing support; women, compared with men, are more nurturing, "tender minded," expressive, and emotionally supportive; and women are more likely than men to provide more sophisticated forms of emotional support (including HPC comforting) to those in need (see review by Burleson & Kunkel, 2006). Indeed, several experiments that have exposed people to identical, standardized support messages (e.g., Uno, Uchino, & Smith, 2002) have found that recipients respond more favorably to these messages when they are attributed to female helpers rather than to male helpers.

Thus Study 3 evaluated the prediction that sex of the helper would influence judgments of comforting message quality when recipients confronted a mildly upsetting situation but not when they confronted a more intense upset. When dealing with more intense upsets, it was expected that judgments of message quality would be a sole function of message person centeredness; furthermore, it was expected that message person centeredness would explain more variance in judgments of message quality when recipients confronted a moderate rather than a mild upset.

## METHOD

Participants were 131 college students (59 men and 72 women) enrolled in undergraduate communication courses at a large midwestern university. To obtain evaluations of comforting messages, participants read about (and were asked to assume they were experiencing) one of six upsetting problem situations (e.g., not doing well on a test; receiving a parking citation). There were two versions for each of these situations: a mildly severe version (e.g., getting a C on a quiz that counted 1% of the course grade; receiving a $25 parking ticket) and a moderately severe version (e.g., getting a D in a course that required a B for admission into one's chosen major; getting one's car booted and having to pay $350 in fines and fees to get the car released). Participants next read a set of six comforting messages that were attributed to either a female or male helper; in each set, two messages exhibited low, moderate, and high levels of person centeredness. Participants rated each of the six messages on four 5-point items tapping perceptions of message helpfulness (e.g., helpful, effective). Internal consistencies of these message evaluations were good, with alphas ranging from .81 to .91 and averaging .86. Finally, participants completed three items intended to check the problem-severity manipulation (i.e., the perceived severity, seriousness, and degree of upset associated with the situation). The reliability of the items for the manipulation check was excellent, $\alpha = .90$.

## RESULTS

The manipulation of problem severity was successful, with the mildly severe problems being rated as significantly less serious ($M = 2.76$) than the moderately severe problems ($M = 4.18$), $t(129) = 8.94$, $p < .001$. Given the success of this manipulation, the effects of helper sex and message person centeredness in mild and moderately severe situations were evaluated through a 2 × 2 × 3 mixed-model ANOVA with repeated measures on the last factor. The between-groups factors were problem severity (mild vs. moderate) and helper sex (female vs. male), and the repeated factor was message person centeredness (low, moderate, and high). The dependent variable was evaluation of message helpfulness. There was a strong main effect for message person centeredness, $F(2, 254) = 161.08$, $p < .001$, $\eta^2 = .56$, with HPC messages ($M = 3.86$) rated as more helpful ($p < .001$) than MPC messages ($M = 2.86$), and MPC messages rated as more helpful ($p < .001$) than LPC messages ($M = 2.17$). The main effect for problem severity was not significant, $F(1, 127) = 1.76$, $p > .15$, nor was the main effect for helper sex, $F(1, 127) = 2.11$, $p = .15$.

There was, however, a near significant interaction between problem severity and message person centeredness, $F(2, 254) = 2.34$, $p < .10$, $\eta^2 = .02$ (see Figure 10.4). Decomposition of this interaction (utilizing polynomial trend analysis) revealed that, as anticipated, the linear effect for message person centeredness explained more variance in message ratings (at a near significant level) among those coping with a moderate upset ($\eta^2 = .76$) than among those coping with mild upset ($\eta^2 = .59$), $F(1, 127) = 2.84$, $p < .10$, $\eta^2 = .02$. In addition, there was a significant interaction between problem severity and helper sex, $F(1, 127) = 4.10$, $p < .05$, $\eta^2 = .03$ (see Figure 10.5). Decomposition of this interaction indicated, as predicted, that in the mild severity condition, female helpers were perceived as using more helpful messages than male helpers, $t(65) = 2.65$, $p < .01$, whereas in the moderate severity condition, there was no difference in the perceived helpfulness of the messages used by female and male helpers, $t(62) = 0.38$, $ns$. The interaction between helper sex and message person centeredness was not significant, $F(2, 254) = 0.39$, $ns$, nor was the three-way interaction between problem severity, helper sex, and message person centeredness $F(2, 254) = 0.42$, $ns$, which indicates that the effects of message person centeredness were not qualified by helper sex.

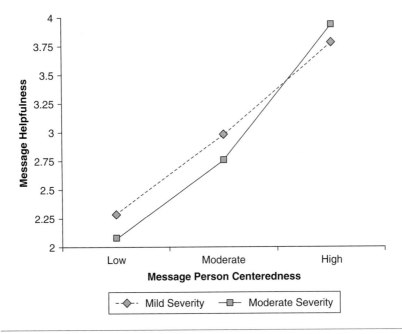

**Figure 10.4**   Effects of Person Centeredness and Problem Severity on Message Evaluations in Study 3

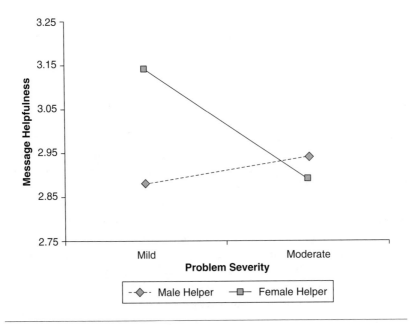

**Figure 10.5**   Effects of Problem Severity and Helper Sex on Message Evaluations in Study 3

## DISCUSSION

The results of Study 3 indicate that the person-centered quality of a comforting message has a somewhat greater impact on recipients when they are coping with a moderate rather than a mild upset, perhaps because the more intense upset motivates greater systematic processing of received messages. It is also possible that people may view less person-centered messages as appropriate in situations in which they only experience mild distress, though the data here clearly indicate that highly person-centered messages remain preferred even when participants imagine themselves coping with a mild upset (see Figure 10.4). When coping with a comparatively mild upset, a peripheral feature of the communicative context, the helper's sex, was found to influence judgments of message quality, perhaps because recipients make use of decisional heuristics (e.g., "women provide helpful support") when processing supportive behavior in the context of relatively mild upsets.

Although these situational variations in message evaluations are theoretically interesting, they should not obscure the fact that message person centeredness was, by far, the strongest influence on message evaluations. Regardless of problem severity and helper sex, HPC messages were rated as more helpful than MPC messages, and MPC messages were rated as more helpful than LPC messages (review Figure 10.4). The practical implication of these findings is straightforward: helpers should employ HPC comforting messages when seeking to assist a distressed other, regardless of the helper's sex and the severity of the problem faced by the other.

## Conclusion

The current studies were undertaken to explore how selected psychological and situational factors influence responses to comforting messages that exhibit different degrees of person centeredness. Previous research indicates that there are some variations in responses to person-centered comforting messages as a function of demographic factors such as sex, age, ethnicity, and nationality; however, the influence of these demographic variables is small, especially in comparison to the uniformly large effects observed for the person-centered quality of the messages. Similarly, the three studies reported here found that although certain psychological and situational factors had some effect on responses to various comforting messages, the influence of these factors is relatively minor, especially in comparison to the uniformly large effects for message person centeredness.

These results have considerable theoretical interest, since they suggest people generally attend to the features of comforting messages directed at them and the features of these messages exert a stronger influence on message outcomes than do situational or recipient characteristics. The modest effects observed for personality and situational factors in the current studies (as well as for demographic factors in previous studies), in conjunction with the large effects observed for message person centeredness, suggest that messages with different levels of person centeredness exert differential effects on recipients because they impact underlying cognitive and emotional processes in recipients. More specifically, it does not appear that HPC messages are simply conventional devices within certain social groups for indicating care and concern; rather, these messages appear to influence how recipients *think* about their feelings and the circumstances producing those feelings (Burleson & Goldsmith, 1998; Jones & Wirtz, 2006).

## PRACTICAL IMPLICATIONS

Our current knowledge concerning the effects of demographic, psychological, and situational factors on responses to comforting messages has some fairly direct pragmatic implications. To date, no factor (or combination of factors) has been found that renders HPC comforting messages less effective and helpful than MPC or LPC messages. This indicates that helpers should employ HPC comforting messages when seeking to assist a distressed other, regardless of the helper's characteristics (e.g., sex), features of the situation (e.g., problem severity), or recipient's characteristics (e.g., demographic, personality, or cognitive qualities). Of course, this recommendation is based on research examining how *most* people respond to messages under various conditions, and in the real world helpers may sometimes encounter the exception. Thus the helper's knowledge of the specific other to be comforted must be the ultimate guide for the selection and implementation of support efforts. Obviously, the point of providing support is to help a particular individual (and not to use a particular type of message); thus helpers must always remain sensitive to the particular others they seek to help and the qualities of the support situation in which they find themselves. Still, the available evidence indicates that most people respond most favorably to HPC comforting messages most of the time, and this means that in the absence of contraindications, helpers are most likely to effectively comfort a distressed other by using HPC messages.

Unfortunately, it appears that a great many people do not spontaneously use HPC comforting messages when seeking to provide support and, indeed, may be incapable of generating such messages even when motivated to do so (Burleson, Holmstrom, & Gilstrap, 2005; MacGeorge, Gillihan, Samter, & Clark, 2003). The implication that follows from this is particularly salient for those of us who define ourselves as communication educators as well as researchers: we need to develop and implement curricula that efficiently and effectively enhance the supportive communication skills of our students and other members of our communities. Elsewhere, I have sketched some of the issues that must be addressed in such curriculum development efforts (Burleson, 2003a). Developing such curricula will be no small task, and these efforts should be informed by theoretical models of both support skill and the message production process. The contributions of effective emotional support to our personal, physical, and social well-being make the development of such curricula a worthy undertaking, despite the challenges of doing so.

Until research on comforting effectiveness is completed, the following guidelines may facilitate the use of helpful comforting strategies. First, helpers help by getting a distressed person to talk about his or her feelings and the circumstances producing those feelings (Burleson & Goldsmith, 1998). Hence, what a helper wants to do is (a) create a conversational environment in which the distressed person feels comfortable talking about his or her troubles and (b) assist the distressed person in telling a story about the upsetting problem. To help achieve the first goal (creating a supportive conversational environment), the helper can *express genuine care and concern* ("Gee, you seem pretty upset. I really care about you. You matter to me; I hope you know that"). The helper might also *emphasize his or her availability* and *willingness to listen* ("I want you to know that I'm here for you. Let me hear you out. I've got plenty of time. I think you may need to talk about this, and I certainly want to listen"). And the helper can directly *support the expression of feelings*—something that many people have trouble with ("Say whatever you are feeling. It's okay to be emotional; it's okay to cry").

Once the distressed person begins telling his or her story, there are several things the helper can do to facilitate this process. First, the helper can *emphasize that the other should feel free to tell an extended story* about the upsetting event ("Go ahead, tell me about it. Take your time. I want to hear the whole story"). While the other person is telling the story, the helper can assist by *prompting continuation and elaboration* ("Um-hum. Yes. And then what happened? What happened after that?"). It is essential that a distressed person talk about his or her *feelings* and not just external events. The helper can assist with this by *asking explicitly about the other's thoughts and feelings about the situation* ("Wow. And how did you feel when that happened? What were you thinking when she said that?"). Helpers can also encourage the distressed person to talk about his or her feelings by *indicating understanding of the feelings expressed* ("Gee, if that happened to me, I'd be very upset too. Of course I understand"). "*Giving voice" to emotions and expressing empathy* for the other also helps encourage the expression of feelings (e.g., "That had to be really tough; no wonder you're upset").

However, expressions of emotion should *not* focus *extensively* on the helper's own emotional experiences. That is, the helper should *avoid* statements like "Gosh, I know exactly how you feel. Something like that happened to me and I felt . . . ," since this may draw attention away from the experiences and feelings of the distressed other. Helpers should also avoid *evaluating the other person,* or his or her feelings, or other people connected with the situation; *giving advice* about how to solve the problem; *telling the distressed person how he or she should think or act* in the situation; *trying to find the silver lining in the cloud; distracting the other's attention* from his or her painful feelings; and *ignoring the other's feelings.*

In sum, good comforting comes down to helping distressed others work through their troubled feelings about an upsetting event or situation. Good comforters are good listeners—active, involved listeners who are really there for the other and encourage the other in the telling of his or her tale.

# References

Belansky, E. S., & Boggiano, A. K. (1994). Predicting helping behaviors: The role of gender and instrumental/expressive self-schemata. *Sex Roles, 30,* 647–661.

Bodie, G. D., & Burleson, B. R. (2008). Explaining variations in the effects of supportive messages: A dual-process framework. In C. Beck (Ed.), *Communication yearbook 32.* Mahwah, NJ: Lawrence Erlbaum.

Burleson, B. R. (1994). Comforting messages: Features, functions, and outcomes. In J. A. Daly & J. M. Wiemann (Eds.), *Strategic interpersonal communication* (pp. 135–161). Hillsdale, NJ: Lawrence Erlbaum.

Burleson, B. R. (2003a). Emotional support skills. In J. O. Greene & B. R. Burleson (Eds.), *Handbook of communication and social interaction skills* (pp. 551–594). Mahwah, NJ: Lawrence Erlbaum.

Burleson, B. R. (2003b). The experience and effects of emotional support: What the study of cultural and gender differences can tell us about close relationships, emotion, and interpersonal communication. *Personal Relationships, 10,* 1–23.

Burleson, B. R., & Goldsmith, D. J. (1998). How the comforting process works: Alleviating emotional distress through conversationally induced reappraisals. In P. A. Andersen & L. K. Guerrero (Eds.), *Handbook of communication and emotion: Research, theory, applications, and contexts* (pp. 245–280). San Diego: Academic Press.

Burleson, B. R., Holmstrom, A. J., & Gilstrap, C. M. (2005). "Guys can't say *that* to guys": Four experiments assessing the normative motivation account for deficiencies in the emotional support provided by men. *Communication Monographs, 72,* 468–501.

Burleson, B. R., & Kunkel, A. W. (2006). Revisiting the different cultures thesis: An assessment of sex differences and similarities in supportive communication. In K. Dindia & D. J. Canary (Eds.), *Sex differences and similarities in communication* (2nd ed., pp. 137–159). Mahwah, NJ: Lawrence Erlbaum.

Burleson, B. R., & Mortenson, S. R. (2003). Explaining cultural differences in evaluations of emotional support behaviors: Exploring the mediating influences of value systems and interaction goals. *Communication Research, 30,* 113–146.

Burleson, B. R., & Samter, W. (1990). Effects of cognitive complexity on the perceived importance of communication skills in friends. *Communication Research, 17,* 165–182.

Burleson, B. R., Samter, W., Jones, S. M., Kunkel, A. W., Holmstrom, A. J., Mortenson, S. T., et al. (2005). Which comforting messages *really* work best? A different perspective on Lemieux and Tighe's "receiver perspective." *Communication Research Reports, 22,* 87–100.

Cialdini, R. B. (2001). *Influence: Science and practice* (4th ed.). Boston: Allyn & Bacon.

Cunningham, M. R., & Barbee, A. P. (2000). Social support. In C. Hendrick & S. S. Hendrick (Eds.), *Close relationships: A sourcebook* (pp. 272–285). Thousand Oaks, CA: Sage.

Cushman, D. P., Valentinsen, B., & Dietrich, D. (1982). A rules theory of interpersonal relationships. In F. E. X. Dance (Ed.), *Human communication theory* (pp. 90–119). New York: Harper & Row.

Gudykunst, W. B., & Matsumoto, Y. (1996). Cross-cultural variability of communication in personal relationships. In W. B. Gudykunst, S. Ting-Toomey, & T. Nishida (Eds.), *Communication in personal relationships across cultures* (pp. 19–56). Thousand Oaks, CA: Sage.

Holmstrom, A. J., Burleson, B. R., & Jones, S. M. (2005). Some consequences for helpers who deliver "cold comfort": Why it's worse for women than men to be inept when providing emotional support. *Sex Roles, 53,* 153–172.

Jones, S. M., & Wirtz, J. (2006). How *does* the comforting process work? An empirical test of an appraisal-based model of comforting. *Human Communication Research, 32,* 217–243.

Kunkel, A. W. (2002). Explaining sex differences in the evaluation of comforting messages: The mediating role of interaction goals. *Communication Reports, 15,* 29–42.

MacGeorge, E. L., Gillihan, S. J., Samter, W., & Clark, R. A. (2003). Skill deficit or differential motivation? Accounting for sex differences in the provision of emotional support. *Communication Research, 30,* 272–303.

MacGeorge, E. L., Graves, A. R., Feng, B., Gillihan, S. J., & Burleson, B. R. (2004). The myth of gender cultures: Similarities outweigh differences in men's and women's provision of and responses to supportive communication. *Sex Roles, 50,* 143–175.

Petty, R. E., Rucker, D. D., Bizer, G. Y., & Cacioppo, J. T. (2004). The elaboration likelihood model of persuasion. In J. S. Seiter & R. H. Gass (Eds.), *Perspectives on persuasion, social influence, and compliance gaining* (pp. 65–89). Boston: Allyn & Bacon.

Prentice, D. A., & Carranza, E. (2002). What women and men should be, shouldn't be, are allowed to be, and don't have to be: The contents of prescriptive gender stereotypes. *Psychology of Women Quarterly, 26,* 269–281.

Samter, W., Burleson, B. R., & Murphy, L. B. (1987). Comforting conversations: Effects of strategy type on evaluations of messages and message producers. *Southern Speech Communication Journal, 52,* 263–284.

Spence, J. T., & Helmreich, R. L. (1978). *Masculinity and femininity: Their psychological dimensions, correlates, and antecedents.* Austin: University of Texas Press.

Stroebe, W., & Stroebe, M. (1996). The social psychology of social support. In E. T. Higgins & A. W. Kruglanski (Eds.), *Social psychology: Handbook of basic principles* (pp. 597–621). New York: Guilford Press.

Tannen, D. (1990). *You just don't understand: Women and men in conversation.* New York: William Morrow.

Uno, D., Uchino, B. N., & Smith, T. W. (2002). Relationship quality moderates the effect of social support given by close friends on cardiovascular reactivity in women. *International Journal of Behavioral Medicine, 9,* 243–262.

Wills, T. A., & Fegan, M. F. (2001). Social networks and social support. In A. Baum, T. A. Revenson, & J. E. Singer (Eds.), *Handbook of health psychology* (pp. 209–234). Mahwah, NJ: Lawrence Erlbaum.

Wood, J. T. (2000). Relational culture: The nucleus of intimacy. In J. T. Wood (Ed.), *Relational communication: Continuity and change in personal relationships* (2nd ed., pp. 76–100). Belmont, CA: Wadsworth.

---

AUTHOR'S NOTE: The author wishes to acknowledge Melanie Taylor Harris for her assistance with data collection for Study 1, Amanda J. Holmstrom and Cristina M. Gilstrap for their assistance with data collection for Study 2, and Graham D. Bodie, Amanda J. Holmstrom, and Jessica J. Rack for their assistance with data collection for Study 3.

# 11

# Understanding the Communication and Relational Dynamics of Humor

*Jess K. Alberts*

*Jolanta A. Drzewiecka*

The study of humor has a long and varied history. It has been examined from a psychoanalytic perspective (Freud, 1905/1960), as a type of artful ambiguity (Oring, 1992), and to determine which of its structural and linguistic properties cause people to laugh (Berger, cited in Lewis, 1997; Morreall, 1989). This chapter, however, takes a very different approach; it addresses a specific type of humor that often proves to be problematic for its participants: humor that targets the listener or other individuals and groups.

In *Jokes and Their Relation to the Unconscious,* Freud (1905/1960) makes a distinction between two types of jokes or humor: jokes that are an end in themselves and jokes "with a purpose." He calls the first type innocent jokes whose purpose is what Davidson (1987) calls "pure entertainment." Riddles, puns, elephant jokes, and the like are all types of innocent jokes. The second type comprises "tendentious" jokes, which are those that "run the risk of meeting with people who don't want to listen to them" (Freud, 1905/1960, p. 90). Humor that targets individuals and groups is often tendentious and therefore can become problematic.

During interpersonal interaction, even tendentious humor can serve a variety of positive functions. It can lead to increased affinity (Norrick, 1993) and social attractiveness (McGhee, 1979) as well as a decrease in social distance (Graham & Rubin, 1987). However, not all such humor attempts have positive outcomes.

Sometimes humor can be used to express disapproval of individuals, groups, or specific behaviors (Stephenson, 1951) and thereby function as a form of social control. For example, humor can be used to sexually harass (Alberts, 1992b) or bully (Einarsen & Mikkelsen, 2003) individuals and as an expression of racism (Dundes, 1987).

Tendentious humor can serve these different functions because it contains elements of both play and aggression. Typically, such humor involves a potentially negative evaluation of a person or group that is framed as not serious or as play (Alberts, 1992b). For example, the famous Henny Youngman joke, "Take my wife—please!" is comprised of a negative evaluation of wives, perhaps his wife specifically, framed as a nonserious comment. Although much of the humor in a joke rests upon this dual nature, it also renders humor one of the more difficult conversational interactions communicators must navigate. For example, the person making a joke that targets the listener or a social group is faced with offering the humor attempt in a way that the recipient interprets the attempt as intended—as either primarily playful or as somewhat (or even very) serious. However, humor's duality and resultant ambiguity means that humor attempts may be subject to a high degree of failure. That is, the speaker may lack the ability to balance the elements of aggression and play in order to deliver an effort that is understood as humor, and whatever the speaker's intent, the aggressive content may lead the recipient to view it as a serious comment (i.e., an insult) and to respond negatively (Alberts, Kellar-Guenther, & Corman, 1996; Drew, 1987).

Responding to and negotiating the import of humor is fraught with complexities for the recipient as well. The recipient has to interpret an ambiguous utterance to determine the speaker's goal or purpose and respond appropriately. Since a sense of humor is considered one of the core cultural values in American society (Apte, 1987), how a recipient responds to a joke often is viewed as an indication of his or her sense of humor. Lack of amusement in response to a joke is perceived as a lack of a sense of humor generally as well as a personal failing. Thus the burden of proof usually falls on the recipient "to prove he can 'take a joke'" (La Fave & Mannell, 1976, p. 118). On the other hand, if the humor attempt is truly offensive and recipients laugh, they may be seen as agreeing with the negative evaluation of the individual or group targeted.

Tendentious humor also is challenging because it can function as a rhetorical device to influence or alter identities (Alberts et al., 1996; Fine, 1983), and laughing along may act to ratify the proposed identity. Identities are not stable (Banks, 1987; Fine & Kleinman, 1983); rather, they are defined and redefined through interaction (Collier & Thomas, 1988; Hecht, Collier, & Ribeau, 1993). Consequently, people continually negotiate their own and others' identities as they communicate (Brown & Levinson, 1978; McCall & Simpson, 1978). Thus humor episodes create situations in which definitions of identities are likely to become problematic and in need of negotiation, making the interaction complex and difficult for both parties.

Because tendentious humor can create negative identities, many people are sensitive to the potentially face-threatening and embarrassing elements inherent in it. Such humor often casts the recipient (or important others) in a negative light, as someone who is ridiculous, inept, or undesirable (Alberts, 1992b; Drew, 1987). Therefore, it is likely to threaten positive face needs, that is, the desire to be liked and respected by others (Cupach & Metts, 1994).

Tendentious humor's ability to threaten face needs, create negative identities, and embarrass recipients means it can result in negative outcomes. When humor attempts fail, anger, aggression, and pain can result. For example, a majority of the women interviewed for a study of sexual harassment cited humor as a source of sexual harassment and emotional distress on the job (Alberts, 1992a). In addition, jokes and teasing frequently contribute to the violence that leads to male convicts' incarceration (Berkowitz, 1993), and jokes at one's partner's expense is perceived to be the riskiest form of play by romantic partners (Baxter, 1992).

Given the complexities, ambiguities, and potentially negative outcomes inherent in these types of humor attempts, it behooves communicators to learn how to engage in them more effectively. Therefore, in this chapter we address how communicators can more competently engage in humor interactions. Based on a variety of research studies we have conducted on tendentious humor, we explore the factors that impact recipients' responses to humor attempts and offer suggestions for how humorists may more effectively communicate their humor attempts as well as how humor recipients may respond to humor they deem inappropriate or offensive.

## Performing Humor: Three Studies

Most studies of humor focus on how speakers tell jokes or construct humor attempts; few have addressed humor from the receiver's point of view. More important, relatively few studies have examined why humor goes awry (see Drew, 1987, for a notable exception). Therefore, in order to help explain why some humor attempts fail, three studies were conducted to analyze the factors that influence receivers' interpretations and responses to tendentious humor (Alberts, 1992a, 1992b; Alberts et al., 1996).

In the first study (Alberts, 1992b), 20 women who reported being sexually harassed were interviewed regarding their experiences with humor and other forms of sexual harassment. In the second study (Alberts 1992a), a discourse analysis of humor was performed to analyze the interactional features that impact receivers' responses to humor that targets them. Based on the data analysis, Alberts argued that responses are formulated in reaction to receivers' interpretations of the humorist's goal, based on multiple clues to meaning: background knowledge, communication content, and paralinguistic clues. In the final study (Alberts et al., 1996), questionnaire responses of 252 participants were subjected to chi-square and log-linear analysis to determine more specifically the factors that influence recipients' responses to tendentious humor that targeted them. The effect of topic, recipients' perceptions of the speaker's intent, and cues used by the recipients to determine intent were examined.

## FACTORS THAT AFFECT RECEIVER RESPONSES TO HUMOR ATTEMPTS

Across all three studies, Alberts (1992a, 1992b; Alberts et al., 1996) argued that humor recipients react to the intent they attribute to the "humorist" rather than specifically to the message characteristics that comprise the humor attempt, as had been claimed previously by other scholars (e.g., Drew, 1987). This claim was supported in the 1996 study (Alberts et al.) when log-linear analysis determined that recipients did not respond to humor attempts based primarily on message characteristics. That is, whether participants in the study responded positively, neutrally, or negatively to a humor attempt that targeted them was not associated with the topic of the joke. This suggested that it may not be so much what one jokes about as it is other situational, relational, and personal variables that influence responses to tendentious humor attempts.

Analyses revealed that participant attributions of intent and responses to humor attempts were influenced significantly by four specific cues: background knowledge, context, paralinguistic cues, and self. In the study, 43% of respondents said they relied upon background knowledge of the humorist or their relationship with one another to inform their judgments of intent. These respondents made comments such as "We joke with each other all the time" and "I knew he didn't mean it." Thirteen percent of participants reported they relied upon contextual cues. Context cues referred either to the social context (e.g., work, at home, or on a date) or to the conversational context, such as during a joking interaction. For example, respondents who made statements such as "We were joking back and forth" and "He was trying to divert attention from my mistake" were describing context cues. Seventeen percent of the respondents said they relied upon paralinguistic cues such as laughter, vocal tone, and "sounding serious." Finally, a fourth "cue" was reported that had not been anticipated. Approximately 27% of respondents claimed that their attributions were based primarily upon their own internal states or psychology. For example, one respondent said she believed the speaker meant the joke seriously;

when asked what cue she used in making that judgment, she wrote, "That's just the way I am. I have no sense of humor."

Global analysis of the factors that affect recipients' responses to humor revealed a three-way interaction between cue, perception, and response. Local significance tests suggested that background cues contributed the most to this interaction and that negative and neutral responses had the largest effects. Specifically, respondents were more likely to perceive humorous intent overall, and they were more likely to respond positively when they ascribed humorous intent. However, when participants perceived serious intent, they were more likely to respond negatively. Of the four cues, the self cue appeared to be the strongest mediator between respondents' perceptions of intent and their responses.

Participants also indicated that their responses to the humor attempts were influenced by the cue they used to determine intent. For example, reliance upon self as a cue to self cues was more likely to result in the participant responding negatively to the humor attempt, while dependence upon paralinguistic cues was more likely to end with the participant responding neutrally.

In addition, results indicated that recipients were more likely to ascribe humorous intent, which suggests individuals often recognize when speakers are trying to be humorous. However, perceiving humorous intent did not always lead to a positive response. Examination of the three-way interaction suggested that when humorous intent is perceived, the use of a paralinguistic cue is likely to lead to a positive response, while use of the self cue is likely to lead to a neutral response. Furthermore, when recipients perceived serious intent, they were more likely to respond positively when they used a self cue and negatively when they relied on paralinguistic cues. This suggests that people who say they laugh even when they believe the other person is serious do so because of their own tendency to find things funny. On the other hand, people who perceive a serious intent and respond negatively rely on external paralinguistic cues.

## Responding to Offensive or Inappropriate Humor: A Study of Ethnic Humor

In addition to understanding how one can perform humor more effectively, communicators also need to understand how to respond when they find a joke insulting, offensive, or demeaning. Appreciating a joke is a relatively simple endeavor—one only has to laugh. However, responding to an unappreciated joke is more complex. If the recipient wishes to maintain a relationship with the humorist, he or she must formulate a response that indicates the joke was not appreciated in a way that does not significantly harm the relationship or damage the joke teller's face. On one hand, the recipient does not want to convey approval, because that might indicate agreement with the negative or offensive content. At the same time, given the importance of a sense of humor in American culture, the recipient may wish to present himself or herself as someone who can take a joke, even if not this particular one. Fashioning such a response can be challenging.

In this section we report on a study we conducted that explored how individuals respond to ethnic jokes that target their own ethnic group. We chose to study recipients' responses to ethnic jokes because ethnicity is one of the most important and prevalent expressions of identity, and ethnic jokes are a part of everyday talk that can influence both individual and group experiences in a given culture. Typically, ethnic jokes use characteristics of the target's ethnicity in order to disparage that group, often in contrast to the joke teller's group. For this reason, ethnic jokes may be perceived as aggressive (Davies, 1982; Dundes, 1987). Other types of jokes that target an individual's or group's identity (e.g., lawyer jokes and dumb blonde jokes) similarly can be seen as aggressive attacks on one's identity. However, ethnic jokes also carry a force beyond other types of identity jokes, because while one may choose not to be a blonde or a lawyer, ethnicity is not so easily altered or hidden.

Specifically, we chose to examine Polish jokes. Although most of the jokes receivers find unappealing or demeaning certainly are not Polish jokes, nor are they necessarily even ethnic jokes, based on our findings we can offer suggestions for how a broad range of humor recipients might respond when faced with humor they find offensive or negative. Historically, Polish Americans have occupied one of the lowest ranks among white ethnic groups, and Polish jokes have been pervasive and notorious (Wytrawl, 1969). Nonetheless, because Polish jokes target a white ethnic group, they rarely are seen as "racist" (Drzewiecka & Alberts, 1995); thus they provide an excellent context in which to study how joke tellers and targets communicatively negotiate the meaning of ethnic jokes.

In our research, we sought to determine the communicative strategies targets/receivers of Polish jokes used to respond to and negotiate these ethnic jokes. However, to understand *why* participants responded as they did, we first examined how receivers of ethnic jokes interpret the joking interaction and the jokes.

## METHODS AND ANALYSIS

We interviewed 22 first-generation Polish immigrants (born in Poland) between the ages of 21 and 51. Participants had been in the United States between 3 and 15 years; 4 were students, others were employed in blue- and white-collar jobs. First-generation immigrants were selected because they are the most sensitive to their treatment as an ethnic group and are the likely targets of ethnic jokes (Aroian, 1992; Polzin, 1982). All of the participants reported that they frequently interacted with U.S. Americans, socially and professionally, and that they encountered Polish jokes during these interactions.

The interviews were semistructured, following the format of a guided conversation (Lofland & Lofland, 1995). This method elicits information from respondents without asking directed questions and allows them to tell their own stories. For example, participants were asked, "Have you heard any or have you heard about Polish jokes? Where were you? Who was there?" and "How do Polish jokes affect how you feel?" Interviews lasted between 30 minutes and 2 hours. The 22 interviews provided saturation of the data (Lincoln & Guba, 1985).

Interviews were transcribed and yielded over 130 transcription pages. A sample of the transcripts was coded to establish mutually exclusive categories that were then used to code the remaining data. First, units describing information relevant to the research questions were identified. Next, themes were allowed to emerge from the data and were coded into categories by one of the coauthors. (These themes are described and discussed below under results.)

Dependability was achieved when an independent coder confirmed emergent categories, and an auditing team examined and authenticated the process (Lincoln & Guba, 1985). Interview transcripts, process notes, and theoretical memos served as an audit trail used to establish confirmability (Lincoln & Guba, 1985).

## RESULTS: INTERPRETATIONS OF JOKING INTERACTIONS

When asked *why* people told them Polish jokes, respondents identified two conversational purposes the jokes might serve: 16 responses described the jokes as a *conversation starter,* and 21 responses described the jokes as a *put-down.* Responses in the conversation starter category indicate that U.S. Americans tell ethnic jokes to a Polish person to start a conversation or make a connection because it is the only thing they know about Poland. Participants stressed either nonmaliciousness of the joke telling or the mindlessness of the tellers who wanted to evoke laughter as a tension breaker and did not think that the jokes could be offensive. One respondent speculated, "It seems to me that a lot of people do it to start a conversation, but they probably do not realize that I may not like it." Another one wondered if he was told Polish jokes "maybe because I am a Pole, or they wanted to joke around, they wanted to see how I would react, whether I would be mad, what my reaction will be toward these jokes."

The more common category, conversational put-down, included responses that interpreted the joke's function as an attempt to humiliate the recipient. A respondent who had spent 14 years in the United States and reported that he had no problems in his relationships with U.S. Americans nonetheless perceived the jokes as an attempt "to humiliate us, to let us know that he is an American and he is better." The responses in this category often indicated that telling Polish jokes makes the joke tellers feel self-gratified—for example, "most of all because they want to feel better themselves." In addition, respondents inferred that jealousy and competition between U.S. Americans and immigrants, and superiority based on being born U.S. American, fueled the motivation for these jokes. Such respondents claimed, "Americans want to show that they dominate over others, and these are racist matters." Some participants interpreted the joke telling as an in-group versus out-group dynamic in conversational situations. Thus a man in his 50s who had lived in the United States for 8 years observed that the jokes are an expression of "local patriotism, staying together against the stranger." Similarly, a 21-year-old man observed that "every time they say something like that, when they tell a joke knowing that I am from Poland, they let me know that I will never be an American." He perceived Polish jokes as displaying antagonism toward immigrants: "I think that although all Americans have grandparents from Europe or Asia or wherever, they feel American and all the time they think that they are better than all these Mexicans or Blacks, or whoever, and they think that by saying these jokes, they are better." Other respondents in this group drew parallels between themselves and other ethnic groups in the United States.

Interestingly, when asked why they thought people told them Polish jokes, participants tended to ascribe essentially one of two motives: lack of awareness or hostility. Approximately 40% of the responses indicated that the joke recipient felt the joke teller was unaware that the joke might be offensive or was trying to engage in conversation. These recipients appear to acknowledge what a previous study (Drzewiecka & Alberts, 1995) discovered—that many U.S. Americans do not view Polish jokes as racist or offensive, even when they believe that jokes negatively portraying Jews, Hispanics, and African Americans are offensive.

### RESULTS: ETHNIC JOKE RESPONSE STRATEGIES

As speakers frequently are reminded, "The meaning of one's actions does not rest with oneself alone" (Emerson, 1969, p. 171). That is, other participants and audiences to a communication event help determine the meaning an event has. In the case of joking, recipient response to a joke defines whether the humor attempt functions as a joke in the specific interaction. To begin understanding how recipients help shape ethnic joking interactions, we analyzed the strategies recipients use to respond to these jokes. Respondents reported using 45 strategies in response to Polish jokes they were told. The 45 strategies were distributed in the following manner: verbal rejection (21), nonverbal rejection (5), ignore (6), laugh along (4), and ethnic retort (9).

The most common category, *verbal rejection*, describes responses that either rejected an *actual* joke itself or rejected an *offer* of a joke. In the first instance, subjects directly acknowledged that a joke had been told and rejected it; that is, they demanded an apology, challenged the joke teller's credibility, retorted in some way, asked the joke teller to stop, or used a threat or an appeal to the

U.S. Constitution. The following response is an example of a direct rejection: "I will not have it; first of all, I am from Poland and I will not have it; if you want to tell Polish jokes, you can go somewhere else."

In the second instance of *verbal rejection,* the rejection of a joke came right after the teller offered to tell a joke, so that the joke was never told. Some respondents directly refused to listen to a joke. A participant explained that "[when someone asks me whether I know Polish jokes,] I immediately warn and say: I know that you know a few of them; don't ever even try to tell me one." This category also included responses explaining to the teller why the jokes are not amusing to Poles.

The category of *nonverbal rejection* consisted of responses that acknowledged the joke and expressed dissatisfaction nonverbally without challenging the joke teller verbally. This response allowed the joke teller to save his or her face; at the same time, however, it let the joke teller know that the joke was not appreciated. The nonverbal responses included "making a dissatisfied face" or "an ironic smile."

A response was coded in the *ignore* category when the target reported that he or she ignored the joke, did not say anything, walked away, or showed a lack of reaction. A 21-year-old male who spent three extended visits in the United States before immigrating explained why he did not respond to a Polish joke by pointing to complex group dynamics. He said, "They were in a bigger group and I was by myself, and they could try to take revenge on me later and that would be distasteful." Later he added, "They are my friends and I like them, and I do not want to break my contacts with them because I do not have many friends." Thus he felt the joke could position him as a member of an out group and that it was important to maintain his in-group position and negotiate personal relationships by not rejecting the joke. His response shows that at least some recipients perceive there are potential significant costs to rejecting a joke.

The *laugh along* category included instances where the target reported that he or she laughed along with the joke teller, either sometimes, one time, or all the time. This category included responses such as "I laughed at them also" and "I laugh and I say 'Oh, this was a good one' or 'Oh, terrible.'" One respondent noted that he sometimes laughed at the jokes and observed his father laugh at them and that he felt included in the group in those moments. Another respondent, a 21-year-old woman, explained: "When I was younger, it really hurt me. I was mad and they were telling me even more jokes—'you know that she will be mad'—and when you laugh, they missed their goal." She further explained, "Even if something hurt me, I did not give them any satisfaction."

A response was coded as *ethnic retort* when the target reported acknowledging the joke and attacking the claim made in the joke, for example, attacking the claim that Poles are stupid by telling jokes about Americans or claiming the Americans are the ones who are stupid, not Poles. This strategy turned the joke to the advantage of Poles; that is, it made the point that Poles are different from Americans and Poles deserve *more* respect. A 21-year-old male explained how he tried to change the power dynamics: "I started to turn it around, I remember this joke to this day . . . : 'I will tell you a joke about Americans and you tell me whether you are mad or not.'" Another respondent reported saying, "Listen, I have known these jokes for a long time; you are younger than I am. When I was your age, I already heard these jokes in Austria, but it was about Americans."

Humor scholars and others have debated the import and impact of ethnic jokes. Some argue that they are relatively harmless, that they actually reduce aggression, and that Americans have become "too thin-skinned" (Derks, cited in Lewis, 1997; Kahn, 1993; MacHale, cited in Lewis, 1997), while others suggest that much ethnic-based humor is aggressive, mean-spirited, and has a negative impact (Davies, 1982; Dundes, 1987; Oring, 1992). In our study, the majority of participants appear to agree more with this latter claim. Of the 45 responses to the jokes, 42 in part or in whole framed the joke as if it were a negative event. The only category that captured positive responses was the laugh along category, and one of these responses indicated that the recipient laughed along even though she was hurt in order to prevent being even more vulnerable to joke tellers. Our joke recipients tended to view the jokes as a way for others to criticize them, hold them up to ridicule, and reinforce prejudice against them.

Why, then, do any recipients laugh at all or choose to ignore the joke? In part they may do so because they find the jokes to be amusing or at least inoffensive. In addition, as several respondents indicated, one's response can be a powerful strategy for renegotiating inclusion and reclaiming power in a group situation. Thus the respondent who said he didn't object because "they are my friends and I like them and I do not want to break my contacts with them" pointed out the group dynamics that may affect targets' responses to offensive humor. So some targets laugh in order to protect their positions within a group. Others may laugh along because such behavior signals inclusion. In addition, the laugh along and ignore strategies may be explained by the cultural importance of having a sense of humor in the United States (Apte, 1987; Norrick, 1993). These recipients seem to know implicitly what research studies have shown—similarity in humor appreciation is a strong factor in attraction and in some cases is even more important than attitude similarity (Cann, Calhoun, & Banks, 1997; Graham, 1995). However, if the joke targets the recipient's ethnic group, laughing along also might communicate acceptance of the dominant group's opinion and the recipient's position within the ethnic group.

In the majority of cases, participants enacted responses that attempted to redefine the joking interaction. That is, they sought to reframe the joke as a nonhumorous, even serious, event. The categories of verbal rejection and ethnic retort included the most direct attempts to define the jokes as not funny, either because the recipient argued that the claim made within the joke was invalid or because he or she viewed it as offensive. Nonverbal rejection strategies function in a similar way, but less directly.

Participants' responses in this study indicate that many of them were offended by the jokes directed at them. Even those who believe that the joke tellers told the jokes due to a lack of awareness, rather than hostility, felt negatively about the interaction. However, their response strategies were influenced at least in part by their goals for the interaction and their relationship with the other party or parties.

Those who were most concerned with maintaining their relationship with the joke teller(s) or their position within their peer group chose either to laugh along with the joke or to express their displeasure indirectly—through nonverbal rejection (such as a grimace or expression of displeasure) or by ignoring the joke entirely. Some of those laughing did so because they found the jokes amusing, but others laughed simply to try to fit in or to indicate their lack of sensitivity to the jokes.

Those who were most concerned with identity issues attempted to redefine the joking interactions—by attempting to deny the legitimacy of the joke, by characterizing the joke tellers as unintelligent, or by arguing that such jokes might be true of a certain class of Poles—but certainly not the respondent. The *ethnic retort* and *verbal* and *nonverbal rejection* strategies are attempts by the recipient to control the situation. One respondent resorted to a joke: "I asked them whether they knew any American jokes and told them an American joke." He claims he never had to listen to Polish jokes again. While *ethnic retort* and *verbal* (or perhaps even *nonverbal*) *rejection* may lead to termination or deterioration of interpersonal relations, *verbal rejection* also can include actively engaging the joke teller, encouraging the teller to learn and rethink his or her judgments.

## Practical Applications

Thus far in this chapter, we have explained the results of three studies we conducted focused on receiver interpretations and responses to tendentious humor. Next we offer strategies that can help both joke tellers and recipients participate more effectively in joking interactions of this nature.

### GUIDELINES FOR MORE EFFECTIVE JOKING

Based on the three studies examining factors that influence receiver responses, we provide the following suggestions for how to perform humor attempts more successfully. First, the finding that participants' responses to humor attempts were not affected significantly by the topic suggests that it may not be so much what one jokes about as it is other situational, relational, and personal variables that influence responses to humor attempts. Therefore, the task of joking well involves more than avoiding a specific list of topics. This does not deny, of course, that some types of humor may be inappropriate in particular contexts. Rather, it means that one cannot guarantee that any specific topic is "safe" if one is concerned with not offending others.

Although respondents indicated that the four cues (background knowledge, context, paralinguistic features, and self) did influence their perception of the humorist's intent, no specific cue was associated with a particular intent. Rather, humor recipients stated that the situational context, their background knowledge, the paralinguistic cues, and their own internal predispositions all influenced their perceptions of the humorist's intent. Thus a joke that may be appropriate in one context or within one relationship may not be appropriate in another. Consequently, joking successfully requires knowing which recipients and contexts are well suited to the humor attempt. Furthermore, how one delivers a joke (i.e., one's paralinguistic cues) also influences attributions of intent; this suggests that one may be more or less competent in displaying that one is "just joking." Overall, then, these findings imply that using humor to build rather than harm relationships involves awareness of and sensitivity to a variety of factors, some of which are not under the control of the joke teller.

The fourth cue, self, is especially problematic if one is trying to determine how to use humor successfully. The self cue reflected comments by the respondents that they perceived positive or negative intent because of their own predispositions toward humor. Approximately 10% of respondents said they find everything humorous, so they assume that humorists are just joking; 17% of the respondents wrote that they have no sense of humor, find joking unappealing, or have no sense of humor about themselves. This suggests that one may be unable to joke with some people at all, especially if they are the targets of the joke. The difficulty is that joke tellers may not know the receiver well enough to make a judgment concerning his or her attitudes toward humor. Because the self cue was associated with a greater likelihood that the recipient would respond negatively, one probably should not joke with individuals one does not know well and should be very careful even with those one knows intimately. Although some individuals do report that they respond positively because of their own natures, or "selves," it may be difficult to discern those who will respond positively because of their inherently jovial natures from those who report that they do not find joking about themselves humorous at all. Thus one may choose the context and carefully display appropriate paralinguistic cues, but if the recipient does not have sufficient background knowledge or if the humorist is unaware of the recipient's attitude toward tendentious humor, the humor attempt may elicit a negative perception or response.

Furthermore, these findings suggest why humor may be especially problematic in the workplace. Work may be the wrong context in which to joke with many people, and there may be insufficient background knowledge to allow recipients to form perceptions of humorous intent. As well, a greater possibility exists that one does not know one's colleagues well enough to predict their attitudes toward humor in general or toward the specific type of humor being displayed. Thus whatever one's intent, it may be difficult to predict or affect coworkers' responses to one's humor attempts.

The findings reported here may also provide some insight into why ethnic humor often is deemed funnier when told by an in-group versus an out-group member. First, in our studies, perceived intent influenced recipients' responses. Likely, a similar process operates in ethnic humor; that is, responses to ethnic humor may be influenced, in part, by recipients' perceptions of the joke teller's intent. In addition, background knowledge was the cue most frequently reported by recipients when ascribing intent. This cue may be an especially important one in the context of ethnic humor. Ethnic group members may assume similarity of background and knowledge with in-group members that they are unlikely to assume for out-group members. This background knowledge, in turn, may influence the likelihood that they will perceive humorous intent for in-group members.

## GUIDELINES FOR RESPONDING TO
## OFFENSIVE OR INAPPROPRIATE HUMOR

Based on our studies of tendentious humor, we believe receivers of humor attempts should consider two issues when formulating responses. First, they will benefit from assessing the humorist's intent. That is, based on the context, relationship history, and paralinguistic cues, recipients need to determine what they believe the speaker's goal is. In doing so, they should be aware that their own personal characteristics are likely to impact how they interpret others' intent and goals; thus their interpretations of intent may not be isomorphic with the speaker's intent. Second, they should decide their own goals for the interaction and the relationship. Specifically, they should assess the relational dynamics. That is, does the joke indicate a relational imbalance that they need to address? Does the joke or joking permanently harm or weaken an otherwise satisfying relationship, in which case the only way to save the relationship is to address or confront the joke in hopes of reaching an understanding (i.e., if the joker does not come around, the relationship might not be worth maintaining)? Finally, it is important to assess how important it is to respond to the offensive content.

If recipients perceive the humorist to have a relatively benign intent—such as truly attempting to be humorous, being unaware that the humor attempt could be offensive, or believing the joke to be okay because of their relationship— and they are most concerned with maintaining the relationship, they may choose to laugh along (at least a little). However, relationships are the most powerful sites of intimate contact and personal enlightenment; hence directly addressing the offensiveness of the joke and its personal and social implications might prove to be beneficial to both partners and their relationship. Alternatively, recipients may want to indicate their lack of pleasure through an indirect means such as ignoring the joke or nonverbally rejecting it (e.g., by groaning, rolling their eyes, or grimacing).

However, if recipients believe the humorist is intentionally being offensive or attempting to humiliate or embarrass them or if they are more concerned with addressing the offensive content than maintaining the relationship, they may wish to respond directly. Thus they may take a reactive stance and challenge the joke teller to think about the assumptions on which the joke is based. This can be done either by verbally rejecting the humor attempt and calling the speaker to task for voicing it or by asking the speaker how he or she would feel if a similarly demeaning comment were made about them or their identity group. Receivers may also talk about the effects of the joke on them and explain their emotions. Although such an approach is confrontational, it may serve to help reconfigure the interpersonal and conversational dynamics between the interactants.

Humor recipients who are offended or feel demeaned are placed in a difficult situation. It may well be impossible for them to protect both their own and the humorist's face. Thus they should assess to what degree they believe the attempt is designed to humiliate or demean them or others as well as determine what their primary goal is: to reject the offending humor, to maintain their relationship with the offending partner, or to renegotiate that relationship.

## Conclusion

Although humor can be fun and its skillful use can improve relationships, the potential for harm accompanies many efforts. Puns and simple jokes may have little potential for offense; however, because tendentious jokes are inherently aggressive, at least in part, their enactment can lead to tension and frayed relationships if managed poorly. Both humorists and their recipients are well served by understanding the factors that impact how humor is interpreted as well as how it, and responses to it, can impact individuals and relationships. That is, even when humor is funny, it is not necessarily fun.

## References

Alberts, J. K. (1992a). A strategic/inferential explanation for the social organization of teasing. *Journal of Language and Social Psychology, 11*, 153–177.

Alberts, J. K. (1992b). Teasing and sexual harassment: Double bind communication in the workplace. In L. A. Perry, H. Sterk, & L. Turner (Eds.), *Constructing and reconstructing gender* (pp. 185–197). Albany: State University of New York Press.

Alberts, J. K., Kellar-Guenther, Y., & Corman, S. R. (1996). That's not funny: Understanding recipients' responses to teasing. *Western Journal of Communication, 60,* 337–357.

Apte, M. L. (1987). Ethnic humor versus "sense of humor." *American Behavioral Scientist, 30,* 27–41.

Aroian, K. J. (1992). Subordination of immigrants: Historical trends and critical analysis. *Journal of Intergroup Relations, 19,* 30–43.

Banks, S. P. (1987). Achieving "unmarkedness" in organizational discourse: A praxis perspective on ethnolinguistic identity. *Journal of Language and Social Psychology, 6,* 171–189.

Baxter, L. A. (1992). Forms and functions of intimate play in personal relationships. *Human Communication Research, 18,* 336–363.

Berkowitz, L. (1993). *Aggression: Its causes, consequences, and control.* New York: McGraw-Hill.

Brown, L., & Levinson, S. (1978). Universals in language usage: Politeness phenomena. In E. Goody (Ed.), *Questions and politeness* (pp. 256–289). Cambridge, England: Cambridge University Press.

Cann, A., Calhoun, J. G., & Banks, J. S. (1997). On the role of humor appreciation in interpersonal attraction: It's no joking matter. *Humor, 10,* 77–89.

Collier, M. J., & Thomas, M. (1988). Cultural identity: An interpretive perspective. In Y. Y. Kim & W. B. Gudykunst (Eds.), *Theories in intercultural communication annual* (pp. 99–120). Newbury Park, CA: Sage.

Cupach, W. R., & Metts, S. (1994). *Facework.* Thousand Oaks, CA: Sage.

Davidson, C. (1987). An introduction to race and nationality. *Teaching Sociology, 15,* 296–302.

Davies, C. (1982). Ethnic jokes, moral values, and social boundaries. *British Journal of Sociology, 33,* 383–401.

Drew, P. (1987). Po-faced receipts of teases. *Linguistics, 25,* 219–253.

Drzewiecka, J. A., & Alberts, J. K. (1995). *"Have you heard the one about . . .": An exploration of ethnic jokes and intercultural interactions.* Paper presented at the Speech Communication Association Convention, San Antonio, TX.

Dundes, A. (1987). *Cracking jokes: Studies of sick humor cycles and stereotypes.* Berkeley, CA: Ten Speed Press.

Einarsen, S., & Mikkelsen, E. G. (2003). Individual effects of exposure to bullying at work. In S. Einarsen, H. Hoel, D. Zapf, & C. L. Cooper (Eds.), *Bullying and emotional abuse in the workplace: International perspectives in research and practice* (pp. 127–144). London: Taylor & Francis.

Emerson, J. P. (1969). Negotiating the serious import of humor. *Sociometry, 32,* 169–181.

Fine, G. A. (1983). Sociological approaches to the study of humor. In P. E. McGhee & J. H. Goldstein (Eds.), *Handbook of humor research* (pp. 159–183). New York: Springer-Verlag.

Fine, G. A., & Kleinman, S. (1983). Network and meaning: An interactionist approach to structure. *Symbolic Interaction, 6,* 97–110.

Freud, S. (1960). *Jokes and their relation to the unconscious.* New York: Norton. (Original work published 1905)

Graham, E. E. (1995). The involvement of humor in the development of social relationships. *Communication Reports, 8,* 158–169.

Graham, E. E., & Rubin, R. B. (1987, November). *The involvement of humor in the development of social relationships.* Paper presented at the Speech Communication Association Convention, Boston.

Hecht, M. L., Collier, M. J., & Ribeau, S. A. (1993). *African American communication: Ethnic identity and cultural interpretation.* Newbury Park, CA: Sage.

Kahn, J. P. (1993, October 24). Can't we take a joke anymore? *Boston Sunday Globe,* n.p.

La Fave, L., & Mannell, R. (1976). Does ethnic humor serve prejudice? *Journal of Communication, 26,* 116–123.

Lewis, P. (1997). Debate: Humor and political correctness. *Humor, 10,* 453–513.

Lincoln, Y. S., & Guba, E. G. (1985). *Naturalistic inquiry.* Newbury Park, CA: Sage.

Lofland, J., & Lofland, L. H. (1995). *Analyzing social settings: A guide to qualitative observation and analysis.* Belmont, CA: Wadsworth.

McCall, G. J., & Simpson, J. L. (1978). *Identities and interaction* (Rev. ed.). New York: Free Press.

McGhee, P. E. (1979). *Humor, its origins and development.* San Francisco: W. H. Freeman.

Morreall, J. (1989). Enjoying incongruity. *Humor, 2,* 1–18.

Norrick, N. R. (1993). *Conversational joking: Humor in everyday talk.* Indianapolis: Indiana University Press.

Oring, E. (1992). *Jokes and their relations.* Lexington: University Press of Kentucky.

Polzin, T. (1982). The Polish Americans. In D. L. Cuddy (Ed.), *Contemporary American immigration* (pp. 59–85). Boston: Twayne.

Stephenson, R. M. (1951). Conflict and control functions of humor. *American Journal of Sociology, 56,* 569–574.

Wytrawl, J. A. (1969). *Poles in American history and tradition.* Detroit, MI: Endurance Press.

---

AUTHORS' NOTE: Some of the data reported in this chapter resulted from the thesis work of J. Drzewiecka under the guidance of J. Alberts.

# 12

## Facework and Nonverbal Behavior in Social Support Interactions Within Romantic Dyads

*Nathan Miczo*

*Judee K. Burgoon*

In a perfect world, there would be no need for social support. We would never fail an important exam, have trouble with a coworker, or learn that a parent had been diagnosed with a chronic illness. Yet every day we face stressors and crises that challenge our ability to cope with our environment. When that happens, we often turn to close relational partners for assistance, and attempts to provide that assistance are known as social support. Social support, in turn, is linked to subsequent emotional and even physical outcomes (Cohen, Gottlieb, & Underwood, 2000; Stroebe & Stroebe, 1996).

In this chapter we consider how social support is accomplished by presenting a study of verbal and nonverbal facework during supportive interactions. Supportive *interactions* are communication episodes involving a person experiencing distress (hereafter, the support *seeker*) and the person attempting to alleviate that distress (hereafter, the support *provider*) (Albrecht, Burleson, & Goldsmith, 1994). Supportive *messages* are verbal and nonverbal acts, such as comforting and advice, that are intended to be helpful (Goldsmith, 1994; Hupcey, 1998; Shumaker & Brownell, 1984) and usually come from the support provider, often in response to prompts by the support seeker. For example, consider a woman returning home after a stressful day at the office and attempting to initiate a supportive interaction by saying, "What a day." Her husband may respond with a supportive message that encourages her to self-disclose (e.g., "Would you like to talk about it?") or an unsupportive message that discourages discussion (e.g., "Now what?").

## Supportive Messages as Coping Assistance

Supportive messages are intended to help the seeker cope with some form of psychological distress. According to Lazarus and associates (Lazarus, 1999; Lazarus & Folkman, 1984), psychological distress arises when individuals appraise a situation as relevant to their goals (*primary appraisal*) and as exceeding their abilities to cope with the demands imposed by the stressor (*secondary appraisal*). Responses to stress include coping efforts aimed at altering the stressful situation (*problem-focused coping*) or at altering the negative emotional states engendered by the situation (*emotion-focused coping*). Talking to another person can be a helpful part of the coping process for a number of reasons (Clark, 1993). It forces distressed individuals to produce coherent discourse about the event and also facilitates their adoption of multiple perspectives as they elaborate explanations and details for support providers. As a result, distressed persons may glean new insight into the problem or experience alterations in how they feel about it.

Burleson and Goldsmith (1998) offer a complementary perspective, suggesting that support providers can provide "coping assistance" (Thoits, 1986) by indicating that it is permissible for support seekers to experience and express their negative feelings; by encouraging them to articulate what they are feeling; by exploring coping options together; and by refraining from wanting to "fix" the problem, instead encouraging support seekers to arrive at their own insights into the problem through extended talk. This should promote a less stressful or more controllable primary appraisal of the situation—especially to the extent that support seekers are willing and able to engage in discussion of their feelings and providers signal acceptance of those emotions. Secondary appraisal should be facilitated to the extent that partners discuss the situation itself, evaluating prior and ongoing coping activities and exploring future options for coping.

## Dilemmas of Support

However, seeking and providing support is often easier said than done. Support episodes can pose a number of dilemmas, many of which center on impression management concerns (Albrecht & Adelman, 1987; Goldsmith, 2004; Goldsmith & Parks, 1990). Dilemmas for the seeker include the possibility of being perceived as dependent, the possibility of alienating the partner because of the negative self-disclosures (Lane & Hobfoll, 1992; Perrine, 1993), and the possibility of feeling obligated to accept the provider's advice. For the provider, dilemmas include ascertaining what the seeker desires (Trobst, Collins, & Embree, 1994), the possibility of offering support that is rejected (Rosen, Mickler, & Collins, 1987), and feeling constrained to provide support in the first place. Given these dilemmas, supportive interactions require effort in their own right. O'Brien and DeLongis (1996) refer to such activity as relationship-focused coping "aimed at managing, regulating, or preserving relationships during stressful periods" (p. 782).

## Facework

Appreciating the impact of relationship-focused coping upon supportive interaction outcomes can be facilitated by acknowledging the role of participants' identity concerns, or face. Face refers to the social identity that people display during interaction (Cupach & Metts, 1994; Goffman, 1967). Face overlaps with but is distinguishable from such constructs as self-presentation and impression management, which involve the "process of controlling how one is perceived by other people" (Leary, 1996, p. 2). Though at times we work very hard to establish a particular kind of face via impression management behaviors, face is something we have even in our mundane, routine interactions with familiar others. More important, perhaps, the face that we actually display during any given interaction does not just depend upon our own efforts. Saying that face is a *social* identity means that we depend upon others to uphold it. *Facework,* then, is defined as communication designed to create, support, enhance, or challenge these interactional identities. For example, during a job interview people may strive to present themselves as competent and hardworking but perhaps also easygoing and able to take direction. They are using impression management to attempt to lay claim to a particular kind of face. Facework refers to the way in which the interviewer (who also has a face he or she is trying to project) accepts the interviewee's identity without question, probes it gently for its legitimacy, or tries to tear it down. In general, we tend to accept our partner's face unless we have a good reason to reject it.

A connection between facework and social support has long been recognized in social support research (e.g., Goldsmith, 1992, 1994). Of particular interest to the present discussion, Lim and Bowers (1991) have developed a *communication model of facework* (CMF). The CMF asserts that human beings have three basic kinds of social identity (henceforth, three types of face) that they desire to have supported during interactions. *Fellowship face* is the desire to be included, to feel a sense of belonging, or to feel like an in-group member—that is, to be accepted for *who one is*. *Competence face* is the desire to have one's abilities and accomplishments be respected, to be appreciated, or to have one's status recognized—that is, to be recognized for *what one has done*. The difference between these two is the difference between the desire for the unconditional acceptance for who one is and the desire for recognition for what one does. The last face want, *autonomy face*, refers to the desire not to be imposed upon, to have control over one's environment and freedom of choice.

Presumably, each type of face is addressed by corresponding message strategies, including those that promote face and those that threaten face (Lim & Bowers, 1991). Fellowship face is addressed by solidarity. Positive fellowship/ solidarity messages include expressions of empathy and cooperation (e.g., "I understand what you're trying to say"). Face-threatening fellowship/solidarity messages include small talk and exclusion (i.e., communication that denies the existence of a relationship with the hearer) (e.g., "It's none of your business"). Competence is addressed through *approbation*, or conveying that one appreciates the other's efforts. Face-enhancing competence/approbation messages include support and expressions of admiration (e.g., "You did a very good job"), while face-threatening competence/approbation messages include ridicule or disapproval (e.g., "It's ridiculous"). Autonomy face is addressed through *tact*, which expresses respect for the other's autonomy. Messages that support autonomy/tact include experimenting (i.e., asking the other to volunteer) and responsibility sharing (e.g., "Could we sit together and work on the way to improve it?"). Face-threatening autonomy/tact messages include orders and invoking obligations (e.g., "Write the paper again"). Based on the results of an empirical investigation, Lim and Bowers (1991) argued that competent communicators must manage all three types of facework simultaneously during interaction. (The foregoing examples in this paragraph are from Lim & Bowers, 1991, pp. 412–439.)

## Nonverbal Messages of Social Support

Nonverbal communication plays a vital role in defining relationships and managing interactions (Burgoon, Buller, & Woodall, 1996; Burgoon, Olney, & Coker, 1987). As such, nonverbal messages are often an integral accompaniment to verbal facework. Two types of nonverbal behavior seem especially relevant to supportive interactions. One of these is involvement. Involvement is feeling and signaling "attentiveness, interest, and participation in interaction" (Prager, 1999, p. 299). Jones (2004) argued, in effect, that involvement plays an important role in helping a support seeker feel connected to a provider. Higher involvement is indicated by such behaviors as closer proximity, forward lean, higher gaze frequency, more open body orientation, facial animation, vocal variety, back-channeling, short response latencies, and absence of nervous vocalizations and adaptors (Burgoon & Le Poire, 1999). The second nonverbal behavior of interest is pleasantness (i.e., positive affect), defined as a desire to please the partner by communicating warmth and affiliation during interaction (Guerrero, 2005). Pleasantness is expressed through smiles, nods, facial agreeability, and "warmer" voices. Together, these cues convey a sense of psychological closeness and engagement, as well as a focus upon and concern with the partner.

There is good reason to believe that these two dimensions are relevant to the social support context. Involvement and pleasantness items have figured prominently in the coding systems used to study supportive interactions (Barbee & Cunningham, 1995). Furthermore, a number of empirical studies have included items related to involvement and pleasantness as dimensions of supportive interactions (Jones & Guerrero, 2001; Yankeelov, Barbee, Cunningham, & Druen, 1995). These studies support the conclusion of Jones and Guerrero (2001) that "researchers need to include verbal as well as nonverbal features of comforting behavior" (p. 590). The present investigation builds upon that conclusion by incorporating more detailed measures of nonverbal involvement and pleasantness.

## HYPOTHESES

A great deal of research supports the contention that as stressfulness increases, support seekers make more direct and active attempts to elicit coping assistance (Collins & Feeney, 2000; Dunkel-Schetter & Skokan, 1990). In the Collins and Feeney study, direct support seeking included such behaviors as emotional or instrumental disclosure, asking for assistance, providing details of the problem, and nonverbal expressions of distress. While this mix of behaviors confounds facework strategies, as well as verbal and nonverbal messages, it provides the basis for the prediction that *the more that support seekers appraise their problem as stressful and uncontrollable, the greater their levels of facework (fellowship/solidarity, competence/approbation, and autonomy/tact) and nonverbal behavior (involvement and pleasantness)* (Hypothesis 1, H1).

Research and theory support the idea that interaction partners tend to reciprocate one another's behaviors (Burgoon, Stern, & Dillman, 1995). In a study of supportive interactions between friends, Agne and White (2004) found positive correlations between seeker and provider solidarity and approbation. Cutrona, Hessling, and Suhr (1997) also found that romantic partners reciprocated each other's behavior, leading to the expectation that *the facework strategies and nonverbal behavior of support seekers and support providers are positively related* (Hypothesis 2, H2).

The third set of expectations concerns interaction outcomes. In general, the more support that is provided, the more the provider is perceived by the seeker as having been helpful. According to Goldsmith, McDermott, and Alexander (2000), helpfulness is the most commonly studied outcome in the evaluation of supportive interactions. They also uncovered a dimension that included empathy and understanding. Given that face concerns are relevant to both partners, however, it would be useful to examine both partners' interaction outcomes as a function of facework and nonverbal messages. Assuming that supportive interactions involve relationship-focused coping, satisfaction with the interaction is a third relevant outcome. Agne and White (2004) found relationships between some types of facework strategies and seeker and provider satisfaction. It is predicted that *seekers' and providers' evaluations of (a) their own interaction satisfaction, (b) provider helpfulness, and (c) provider empathy are positively related to both their own and their partner's levels of facework and nonverbal behavior* (Hypothesis 3, H3).

The perspective developed here is predicated on the notion that supportive messages are effective when they facilitate the appraisal process. Interestingly, this idea has received very little research attention. Collins and Feeney (2000) found that support seekers who perceived their partners as more caring experienced improvements in mood, but that may not have translated into altered perceptions of the problem. The present investigation will examine both partners' postinteraction appraisals, since these appraisals may shape future interactions between the pair. Given the virtual absence of social support research linking supportive communication (i.e., facework and nonverbal behaviors) to problem appraisals, the following research question is advanced:

*Research Question 1: What relationships do facework strategies and nonverbal behavior have to postinteraction appraisals of problem stressfulness and controllability?*

## METHOD

### Participants

Participants were 140 individuals (70 couples) currently involved in an exclusive heterosexual romantic relationship who responded to advertisements for a study examining how relational partners discuss personal issues. Participants ranged in age from 18 to 76 years old ($M = 26.01$, $SD = 10.98$). The majority of the sample was white/Caucasian (90%), with minimal representation of other ethnic groups (4.3% black/African American, 3.6% Hispanic/Latin American, and 2.1% "other"). Most of the participants were either undergraduate students at a medium-sized midwestern university (69.3%) or people with postgraduate education (15.7%).

Participants reported having been a couple for an average of 5.08 years ($SD = 8.86$ years; range from 6 months to 42.83 years), with 58.6% reporting seriously dating, 14.3% engaged to be married, 25.7% married, and 1.4% not classified. In accordance with the selection criteria, there were no individuals who reported their relationship status as casually dating.

*Procedures*

After expressing interest in the study, couples were mailed a packet of questionnaires, which, except for demographic items, are not relevant to the present investigation. Approximately a week later, they were scheduled to participate in a video- and audiotaped interaction. Upon arrival at the interaction site, couples signed consent forms and were then separated to complete the preinteraction questionnaire, which began with each individual writing out a brief description of a recent event or situation that was stressful, but in which the stress was not due to the partner. They then responded to questions regarding stressfulness and controllability. Next they were reunited and assigned to either the "support seeker" or "support provider" role, counterbalanced by sex. They were instructed to discuss the support seeker's event as they would normally for 10 minutes.

After 10 minutes, partners were separated again to complete the postinteraction questionnaire. This questionnaire asked each person to briefly describe the event or situation that he or she had just discussed (i.e., the support seeker's problem). They were then asked to rate the event in terms of how stressful and controllable it was for the seeker, using the same scales that were used in the preinteraction questionnaire. The second part of the postinteraction questionnaire contained measures of communication satisfaction and perceptions of provider helpfulness and empathy (as well as an additional measure not relevant to the current investigation). Each member of the couple was paid $10 compensation for his or her participation, debriefed, and excused.

*Measures*

*Stressfulness:* To assess perceived stressfulness, four items were adapted from Collins and Feeney (2000) and constructed as 5-point semantic differential scales (e.g., *not very stressful* to *very stressful, not very upsetting* to *very upsetting*). Higher scores indicated greater perceived stressfulness (for preinteraction ratings of full sample, $\alpha = .53$, $M = 3.85$, $SD = 0.66$; for postinteraction ratings of the support seeker of his or her own problem, $\alpha = .68$, $M = 3.57$, $SD = 0.78$; for postinteraction ratings of the support provider of the seeker's problem, $\alpha = .56$, $M = 3.88$, $SD = 0.67$).

*Uncontrollability:* Two items were used to assess perceptions of uncontrollability: *under my control/not under my control*, and *something I cannot affect/something I can affect* (per McAuley, Duncan, & Russell, 1992; Russell, 1982). Higher scores indicated greater perceptions of the event/situation as more uncontrollable (for preinteraction ratings of full sample, $\alpha = .64$, $M = 2.85$, $SD = 1.08$; for postinteraction ratings of the support seeker of his or her own problem, $\alpha = .89$, $M = 4.25$, $SD = 0.50$; for postinteraction ratings of the support provider of the seeker's problem, $\alpha = .89$, $M = 4.15$, $SD = 0.49$).

*Communication satisfaction:* Hecht's (1978) 19-item Communication Satisfaction Inventory (Com-Sat) was used to assess participants' satisfaction with their support interaction (e.g., "I was very satisfied with the conversation," "I would like to have another conversation like this one"). Higher scores indicated greater satisfaction with the conversation (for support seekers, $\alpha$ = .89, $M$ = 4.25, $SD$ = 0.50; for support providers, $\alpha$ = .89, $M$ = 4.15, $SD$ = 0.49).

*Provider empathy:* Empathy was assessed via eight items devised originally to measure empathy in a business meeting (Plank, Minton, & Reid, 1996). Items were reworded to be appropriate for the social support context and reworded slightly for seeker and provider (e.g., "My partner really understood my feelings about this problem," "I really understand my partner's feelings about this problem") (for support seekers, $\alpha$ = .86, $M$ = 4.33, $SD$ = 0.49; for support providers, $\alpha$ = .73, $M$ = 4.36, $SD$ = 0.67).

*Provider helpfulness:* Two items were utilized to address perceptions of the extent to which the provider was helpful during the discussion (e.g., "My partner was helpful in the discussion of my problem," "I was helpful in the discussion of my partner's problem") (for support seekers, $\alpha$ = .80, $M$ = 4.25, $SD$ = 0.47; for support providers, $\alpha$ = .86, $M$ = 3.88, $SD$ = 0.74).

*Coding facework in the interactions:* In an effort to apply facework variables to the social support context, we attempted to create a set of scales that could be used by independent raters, drawing especially from the Burleson and Samter (1985) measure of comforting sensitivity and the original Lim and Bowers (1991) typology. The eventual coding scheme was dubbed the Face Interaction Support Coding Scheme (FISCS).[1]

Given the conceptual similarity between comforting and fellowship facework, the Burleson and Samter items were adapted to create a nine-item measure of fellowship/solidarity. It is important to note that while solidarity messages were described above as addressing fellowship and group inclusion, our FISCS system operationalized solidarity messages exclusively as addressing the support seeker's feelings; for example, "*Provides an elaborated acknowledgment and explanation of the seeker's feelings,*" "*Helps the seeker gain a perspective on his or her feelings (e.g., attempts to help the seeker see these feelings in relation to a broader context or the feelings of others).*" Given our interest in examining the facework of both partners, we developed a scale for the support seeker that would be as close as possible to that used for the provider. Items were rewritten accordingly; for example, "*Provides an elaborated acknowledgment and explanation of his or her own feelings,*" "*Helps the provider gain a perspective on his or her own feelings (e.g., attempts to help the provider see these feelings in relation to a broader context or the feelings of others)*" as examples of high face support for the seeker.

To create measures of competence/approbation and autonomy/tact, nine items were written that ranged from low to high support for that particular type of face. Content for these subscales was derived from an examination of existing social support coding schemes, as well as the Lim and Bowers (1991) typology. As with the measure of solidarity/approbation, two versions were created, one for providers and one for seekers. Notably, while approbation messages were described above as addressing competence and achievements, our FISCS system operationalized approbation messages exclusively as addressing competence to handle the situation that instigated support seeking. Examples of high competence/approbation face support for the provider are *"Expresses approval of some aspects of how the seeker is handling the situation (with minimization of the problem)"* and *"Expresses admiration of how the seeker is handling the situation without any reservation,"* while examples for the seeker are *"Expresses approval of how he or she is handling the situation (with minimization of the problem)"* and *"Expresses admiration of how he or she is handling the situation without any reservation."* Examples of high tact/autonomy face support for the provider are *"States what he or she can or is willing to do without implying that the seeker has to accept the offer"* and *"Offers to share responsibility for coming up with ways to handle the situation,"* while examples for the seeker are *"States what he or she can or is doing without implying that the provider has to agree with the assessment"* and *"Offers to share responsibility for coming up with ways to address the situation."*

Participants' audiotaped interactions were coded by pairs of graduate student coders (two coding the provider, two coding the seeker), each of whom rated the level of facework exhibited by the provider and the seeker during the interaction from audiotapes. Each pair of coders received 4 hours of training, including discussion of the conceptualization and logic of the scheme, review of specific items, and practice coding of three dyads from the sample. Given the 10-minute length of the interaction, coders made assessments of 5-minute blocks. Subsequently, those two ratings for each coder were averaged for each item. Reliability was checked after each pair had completed 23% (16 of 70 dyads) of the sample. These initial checks indicated that reliable subscales could be obtained by recoding the first six items of each subscale. (Interrater and interitem reliabilities for the subscales across the full sample can be found in Miczo, 2004.)

*Coding nonverbal involvement and pleasantness:* The dimensions of involvement and pleasantness were measured using scales developed by Burgoon and associates (Burgoon et al., 1998; Burgoon & Le Poire, 1999). Involvement concerns the degree to which a person is engaged during an interaction and incorporates components of immediacy, expressiveness, composure, conversation management, and altercentrism (being focused on the partner) (Burgoon et al., 1996) and was assessed with six items (e.g., "very nonimmediate/very immediate," "very inattentive/very attentive"). Pleasantness refers to the affective tone of an interactant's behavior, with greater pleasantness expressed through such behaviors as smiling, vocal warmth, and relaxed laughter. It was assessed with three items (e.g., "very unpleasant/very pleasant," "very cold/very warm"). Items were rated with 7-point semantic differential scales, with higher scores indicating greater involvement and pleasantness. Two graduate student coders rated each interactant separately from videotapes of the interaction. Coders received 2 hours of training, which included discussion of concepts and practice coding using interactions unrelated to the present study. (Final interitem and interrater reliabilities across the full sample can be found in Miczo, 2004.)

## Results

Hypothesis 1 predicted that support seekers' nonverbal behavior and use of facework is positively related to their own appraisal of the problem as more stressful and more uncontrollable. This hypothesis was tested using Pearson correlations (see Table 12.1). There was a significant correlation between stressfulness and fellowship/solidarity. There were also near significant negative relationships between stressfulness and autonomy/tact and stressfulness and involvement. That is, the more seekers rated their problem as stressful, the more likely they were to be demanding of the provider and the less involved they were in the conversation, a finding that is contrary to what was hypothesized. With respect to controllability, there was a near significant correlation between uncontrollability and fellowship/solidarity. Perceiving the problem as uncontrollable was associated with a greater focus on feelings and emotions. Overall, H1 received limited support inasmuch as more of the significant correlations were among the interaction behaviors than with seekers' appraisals. However, the a priori stressfulness of the problem did lead to using more fellowship/solidarity appeals and to somewhat dampened involvement.

Hypothesis 2 predicted positive relationships between the facework behavior of the seeker and provider. Table 12.2 presents the correlations between the partners. Overall, a number of relationships were significant, of moderate magnitude, and in the hypothesized direction. More specifically, two points can be made. First, correlations between partners on the same interaction behaviors were all significant. Second, when examining relationships between the verbal behaviors, there were different patterns for support seekers' and providers' approbation and tact messages. The seekers' use of tact was related to all three of the provider's facework message types, while providers' levels of approbation were correlated with all three of the seeker's facework message types. Taken together, these results provide support for H2 with respect to matched pairs of behaviors.

The third hypothesis predicted that ratings of (a) interaction satisfaction (i.e., communication satisfaction), (b) provider helpfulness, and (c) provider empathy are related to both partners' facework messages and nonverbal behaviors. As can be seen in Table 12.1, support seekers were more satisfied when they had used solidarity messages and were more pleasant and when the provider

**Table 12.1** Correlations Between Appraisals, Behavior, and Outcomes for the Support Seeker

| | 1 | 2 | 3 | 4 | 5 | 6 | 7 | 8 | 9 | 10 | 11 |
|---|---|---|---|---|---|---|---|---|---|---|---|
| | | | | | Hypothesis 1 | | | | | | |
| *Preinteraction Appraisals* | | | | | | | | | | | |
| 1. Prestress | — | | | | | | | | | | |
| 2. Precontrol | .16 | — | | | | | | | | | |
| *Interaction Behavior* | | | | | | | | | | | |
| 3. Solidarity | .40** | .20† | — | | | | | | | | |
| 4. Approbation | -.07 | .07 | -.09 | — | | | | | | | |
| 5. Tact | -.20† | .09 | .02 | .18 | — | | | | | | |
| 6. Involvement | -.20† | -.15 | .07 | .20† | .33** | — | | | | | |
| 7. Pleasantness | -.16 | -.02 | .09 | .31** | .27* | .73** | — | | | | |
| | | | | | Hypothesis 3/Research Question 1 | | | | | | |
| *Interaction Outcomes* | | | | | | | | | | | |
| 8. Poststress | .56** | .24* | .17 | .00 | -.17 | -.06 | -.06 | — | | | |
| 9. Postcontrol | .01 | .84** | .17 | .06 | .05 | -.13 | -.01 | .22† | — | | |
| 10. Satisfaction | .06 | .05 | .30* | .12 | -.01 | .13 | .20† | -.03 | .03 | — | |
| 11. Helpfulness | .24* | -.00 | .32** | .15 | .10 | .04 | .01 | .12 | -.12 | .67** | — |
| 12. Empathy | -.08 | .25* | .32** | .23† | .24* | .08 | .23† | -.08 | .23† | .65** | .49** |

NOTE: Preinteraction ratings refer to appraisals of one's own problem; postinteraction ratings refer to appraisals of the seeker's problem.

**p < .01. *p < .05. †p < .10, two-tailed.

**Table 12.2**     Correlations Between Appraisals, Behavior, and Outcomes for Seeker and Provider

| | 1 | 2 | 3 | 4 | 5 | 6 | 7 | 8 | 9 | 10 |
|---|---|---|---|---|---|---|---|---|---|---|
| **Support Provider** | | | | | | | | | | |
| *Interaction Behavior* | | | | Hypothesis 2 | | | | | | |
| 1. Solidarity | .26* | .05 | .27* | .13 | .03 | .17 | .21† | .23† | .33** | .17 |
| 2. Approbation | .32** | .28* | .31** | .23† | .27* | .07 | .29* | .24* | .22† | .32** |
| 3. Tact | .11 | .13 | .31** | .16 | .15 | .04 | .08 | .14 | .22† | .17 |
| 4. Involvement | -.08 | -.09 | .01 | .43** | .31** | -.00 | .00 | .13 | .01 | .01 |
| 5. Pleasantness | -.05 | .12 | .07 | .44** | .59** | -.04 | .11 | .10 | -.06 | .16 |
| *Interaction Outcomes* | | | | | Hypothesis 3/Research Question 1 | | | | | |
| 6. Poststress | .17 | -.07 | -.05 | -.06 | -.04 | .26* | .02 | .04 | .21H | .06 |
| 7. Postcontrol | .23† | .09 | .20† | -.01 | .21† | .24* | .33** | -.10 | .03 | .14 |
| 8. Com-Sat | .24* | .13 | .08 | .25* | .24* | -.12 | -.10 | .45** | .48** | .30* |
| 9. Helpfulness | .05 | .25* | .11 | .25* | .28* | -.09 | -.03 | .33** | .41** | .20 |
| 10. Empathy | .08 | .20 | .10 | .23† | .29* | -.16 | -.18 | .23† | .25* | .12 |

NOTE: Com-Sat = Communication satisfaction.

$**p < .01$. $*p < .05$. $†p < .10$, two-tailed.

had used both solidarity and approbation messages (H3a). Seekers perceived providers as more helpful when they used solidarity messages (Table 12.1) and when the provider used any of the three types of facework (Table 12.2) (H3b). Seekers' ratings of provider empathy were related to their own use of all three facework message types and pleasantness (Table 12.1), as well as the provider's use of approbation (Table 12.2) (H3c). Providers' perceptions of satisfaction were correlated with their own use of solidarity, $r = .28$, $p < .05$, approbation, $r = .36$, $p < .01$, and tact, $r = .32$, $p < .01$, as well as the seeker's use of solidarity, involvement, and pleasantness (Table 12.2) (H3a). Providers' perceptions of their own helpfulness were related to their own use of solidarity, $r = .29$, $p < .05$, approbation, $r = .32$, $p < .01$, tact, $r = .30$, $p < .01$, and pleasantness, $r = .23$, $p < .01$, as well as the seeker's use of approbation, involvement, and pleasantness (Table 12.2) (H3b). The providers' perceptions of their own empathy were related to their own use of approbation, $r = .26$, $p < .05$, tact, $r = .26$, $p < .05$, and pleasantness, $r = .23$, $p < .01$, as well as the seeker's use of involvement and pleasantness (Table 12.2) (H3c). Overall, H3 received substantial support.

Research Question 1 concerned relationships between partners' facework and nonverbal behavior on the one hand and postinteraction appraisals of the seeker's problem on the other. The seeker's postinteraction ratings of stressfulness were not significantly correlated to any aspect of either partner's behavior. Seekers' ratings of uncontrollability, however, were correlated to the provider's use of fellowship/solidarity and competence/approbation facework messages (Table 12.2). For providers, postinteraction ratings of the stressfulness of the seeker's problem were not related to any aspect of either partner's behavior. However, postinteraction appraisal of the problem as uncontrollable was associated with providers' use of approbation, $r = .26$, $p < .05$, and seekers' use of solidarity, tact, and pleasantness (Table 12.2).

## Discussion

Adopting a facework-based approach, this study examined relationships between relational partners' appraisals and their communicative behavior during supportive interactions. H1—that as seekers evaluated their problem as more stressful and less controllable they would display more facework, involvement, and pleasantness during the interaction—received mixed support. Stressfulness and controllability were both positively correlated to fellowship/solidarity, suggesting that individuals experiencing more distress (arising from primary and secondary appraisals) were oriented toward emotion-focused coping (i.e., talking about their feelings in an elaborated fashion). Contrary to what was hypothesized, stressfulness was associated with less autonomy/tact and nonverbal involvement. Perhaps, as stressfulness and anxiety increased, seekers became more self-focused, which may be exhibited by reduced conversational involvement and becoming more demanding of the provider.

The second hypothesis predicted behavioral reciprocity between seeker and provider. This hypothesis received a great deal of support, though most correlations were moderate in magnitude. In every case, the association between matched behaviors was significant. Patterns for competence/approbation and autonomy/tact differed, with provider competence/approbation being correlated to all of the seeker's behavior and seeker autonomy/tact being related to all of the provider's facework behavior. Consistent with the idea of supportive dilemmas (Goldsmith & Parks, 1990), seekers may be especially sensitive to criticism of how they are handling the situation, whereas providers may be sensitive to being imposed upon to solve the problem.

The third hypothesis predicted that partners' perceptions of provider helpfulness, provider empathy, and their own satisfaction would be related to the use of facework and nonverbal behavior. In general, seekers' outcomes were related to their own use of fellowship/solidarity and providers' use of fellowship/solidarity and competence/approbation. Thus when both partners elaborated the seeker's feelings (i.e., solidarity) and when the provider praised the current coping efforts of the seeker (approbation), seekers were more satisfied with the interaction and saw the provider as more helpful and empathic. Providers' outcomes were associated with their own use of all three facework message types, as well as seekers' use of involvement and pleasantness. Providers who (a) were focused on the feelings of the seeker (solidarity), (b) praised his or her current coping efforts (approbation), (c) made suggestions in a more tentative fashion (i.e., tact), and (d) had partners who were more positively engaged in the conversation were more satisfied and saw themselves as having been more helpful and empathic. These results support the stress and coping paradigm's assertion that people focus on both emotion- and problem-focused coping.

The research question concerned relationships between partners' behaviors and postinteraction appraisals of the seeker's problem. For seekers, the provider's use of competence/approbation and fellowship/solidarity were associated with greater appraisals of uncontrollability. For providers, their own use of competence/approbation and the seeker's use of fellowship/solidarity, autonomy/tact, and pleasantness were also related to providers rating the problem as more uncontrollable after the interaction. These results contradict the general notion that messages that attend to face will lead partners to reappraise the situation as less severe or as something the seeker can control. Rather, discussion of the problem (or at least the kind of discussion partners can have in a laboratory setting) can bring to light the limits of the seeker's capabilities. This is both an area for future inquiry and a caveat to future researchers.

## Limitations

Interpretation of findings must be balanced against a consideration of the limits of the study. The first limitation stems from the requirements of the transactional approach, which places partners in clear-cut roles and dictates the nature of their interaction (Pierce, Sarason, Sarason, Joseph, & Henderson, 1996). Individuals may respond to these demand characteristics by trying to be more helpful and supportive to their partner than might otherwise be the case. Second, the sample was predominantly white, college-aged, and not married. While the sample size was comparable to other interaction studies in the support literature,[2] in absolute terms it was somewhat small and precluded an examination of potential influencing factors (e.g., sex, time period). Third, the 10-minute length of the interaction creates an artificial environment. For some couples, 10 minutes may seem an interminably long time to spend on one member's problem, while for others, the time span prevented them from exploring feelings and coping options to their conclusion. Furthermore, short versions of measures were used in some cases (e.g., stressfulness, controllability), which necessarily leave some facets of the construct untapped. Finally, there were issues surrounding the development of the FISCS to measure facework. In an effort to bolster reliability, strict parallelism could not be maintained between the two versions of the scheme. While the scheme seems to be a promising avenue for future research on supportive communication, it will require further revision.

## Practical Applications

It is a truism among communication scholars that messages operate on two levels: a content level (which concerns what is said) and a relational level (which concerns how it is said). The stress and coping paradigm (Lazarus & Folkman, 1984) and Thoits's (1986) notion of support as "coping assistance" suggest that the content of support interactions revolves around the problem being experienced by the seeker, his or her feelings about that situation, and current and future coping options. An emerging consensus among communication researchers studying support interactions is that the goal of the seeker is to reappraise the problem, while the goal of the provider is to facilitate the reappraisal process. The communication model of facework (Lim & Bowers, 1991) directs attention to how relationship-focused coping should be conducted by attending to face concerns surrounding acceptance of feelings, praise of coping efforts, and tentativeness in making suggestions. The following recommendations are guided by this model in light of the findings of the present investigation.

For seekers:

1. *Discuss your feelings.* Events are often appraised as stressful because they threaten concerns and goals that are particularly important to us. It's distressing to fail an exam or fight with a coworker, because we strive to be good students or good employees. While it may be a natural reaction to a threat to withdraw and become defensive, such reactions can block us from working through the emotions and gaining a new perspective on our troubles. The first step in working through emotions is being willing to acknowledge them. Beyond that, you must help your partner understand why you're feeling the way you are, which may involve explaining the situation and disclosing the desires or concerns that are threatened by that situation. Your goal during the interaction is to help your partner take your perspective, and in the process of doing that, you might both gain new insight into the problem.

2. *Respect your partner's autonomy.* Remember that only you can appraise a situation for its relevance to your own goals and concerns. Your partner cannot do it for you. Researchers have sometimes cautioned providers against wanting to fix the seeker's problem, but seekers themselves can make the same mistake, looking to providers to do more than they can. Respecting partners' autonomy face means letting them know that you value their insight and comments but without demanding or implying that they have to provide anything other than a listening ear. This may be the first time they've heard about the problem or realized how much it meant to you, and so they may be dealing with their own reactions to your situation or worrying about their ability to be helpful. No one likes feeling like they're being forced to do something, including offering social support.

3. *Be involved and pleasant.* Nonverbal communication plays a powerful role in shaping our interactions. When we're very anxious or worried, we have a tendency to become more self-focused, which is often displayed nonverbally by becoming less engaged and more negative during conversations. Abundant research suggests that this has a negative impact upon our partner. We need to remain pleasant toward our support-providing partner, even though we feel upset or distressed with the problem situation. In this study, support seekers who were more involved and pleasant had partners who were more satisfied with the interaction and saw themselves as more helpful and empathic. Remember that during a support interaction, you are the focus of the discussion; you will likely set the affective tone for the conversation that your partner will pick up on. Genuine involvement (the desire to engage in discussion) and pleasantness (being kind and caring) will usually be recognized by your partner through your nonverbal behaviors.

For providers:

1. *Encourage the support seeker's discussion of feelings.* Keep in mind that your goal is to assist the seeker in reappraising the situation and that a major way this is done is by working through feelings. Your responsibility is to create a conversational climate that encourages the seeker to disclose those feelings, even though they may be negative. Encourage the seeker to express feelings. Since people often frown upon the discussion of negative emotions, support seekers may gauge your reactions to see if they have "permission" to continue, so use back-channeling (such as head nods or "uh-huh") to prompt them to continue. At other times, you may be able to say something along the lines of "How did that make you feel?" Above all, resist the urge to jump in with offers and suggestions for how the seeker should be feeling or handling the situation. It may be difficult to see your partner in distress, but oftentimes the best way to ensure that he or she will work through that distress is to practice good listening skills. Good listening skills involve such things as paying attention to your partner (being quiet and not allowing yourself to get distracted by other things around you), asking questions (not just assuming you know what your partner is talking about), and paraphrasing (repeating back what you've heard in your own words).

2. *Praise the coping efforts of the support seeker.* A great deal of emphasis so far has been placed upon seekers' emotional responses to their situation, but don't overlook the fact that people experiencing distress are probably trying to cope with both their feelings and the problem itself. In discussing those problem-focused coping efforts, your partner is most likely trying to present himself or herself as handling the situation as competently as possible. You may not always agree with your partner's assessment, but it is important not to ridicule or trivialize their efforts. Remember that anything your partner has done so far to cope with the problem cannot be undone. Express your understanding of everything he or she has done so far, praise those efforts, and then indicate your openness to working with your partner to find ways to address the situation in the future.

3. *Be pleasant and acknowledge the support seeker's autonomy.* In this study, pleasantness by the support provider and his or her respect for the partner's autonomy had more to do with support providers' perceptions of having been helpful and empathic than with the support seekers' perceptions. Furthermore, providers' respect for the partner's autonomy was related to their own satisfaction with the interaction. Recall that respecting the partner's autonomy means not telling him or her how to handle the problem but rather involves making suggestions that allow him or her to volunteer to try ways to handle the situation and offering to share responsibility for coming up with ways to handle it.

Providers who used these tactics perceived themselves as having been more helpful and having better understanding of the seeker. Having a pleasant and cordial attitude toward the partner, which manifests itself in certain behaviors like smiling and tone of voice, leads to the same perceptions. Being cautious about offering solutions, and remaining pleasant, also will likely foster the kind of conversational climate that encourages the support seeker to open up, allowing both partners the opportunity to explore the problem.

## Conclusion

The results of the present investigation are promising and warrant further exploration and study. It seems clear that facework is a viable framework to the study of supportive communication. The facework perspective, with or without FISCS, reinforces two long-held but undertested suppositions of the support paradigm. First, during actual interactions, partners engage in both problem- and emotion-focused discussions of coping activities. Second, dilemmas of support result in partners being differentially sensitive and responsive to their roles. The present study also supports the notion that both partners contribute to the outcomes of a social support interaction. Even though one partner's problem is the focus of the discussion, both partners depend on each other to work through it.

## Notes

1. Details of the coding scheme are available from the authors upon request.

2. Note the following sample sizes: 60 (Pasch & Bradbury, 1998); 86 (Gurung, Sarason, & Sarason, 1997); 93 (Cutrona, Hessling, & Suhr, 1997); 93 (Collins & Feeney, 2000).

## References

Agne, R. R., & White, C. H. (2004). The nature of facework in discussion of everyday problems between friends. *Southern Communication Journal, 70,* 1–14.

Albrecht, T. L., & Adelman, M. B. (1987). Dilemmas of supportive communication. In T. L. Albrecht & M. B. Adelman (Eds.), *Communicating social support* (pp. 240–254). Newbury Park, CA: Sage.

Albrecht, T. L., Burleson, B. R., & Goldsmith, D. (1994). Supportive communication. In M. L. Knapp & G. R. Miller (Eds.), *Handbook of interpersonal communication* (2nd ed., pp. 419–449). Thousand Oaks, CA: Sage.

Barbee, A. P., & Cunningham, M. R. (1995). An experimental approach to social support communications: Interactive coping in close relationships. *Communication Yearbook, 18,* 381–413.

Burgoon, J. K., Buller, D. B., & Woodall, W. G. (1996). *Nonverbal communication: The unspoken dialogue* (2nd ed.). New York: McGraw-Hill.

Burgoon, J. K., Ebesu, A., White, C., Koch, P., Alvaro, E., & Kikuchi, T. (1998). The multiple faces of interaction adaptation. In M. T. Palmer & G. A. Barnett (Eds.), *Progress in communication sciences* (Vol. 14, pp. 191–220). Stamford, CT: Ablex.

Burgoon, J. K., & Le Poire, B. A. (1999). Nonverbal cues and interpersonal judgments: Participant and observer perceptions of intimacy, dominance, composure, and formality. *Communication Monographs, 66,* 105–124.

Burgoon, J. K., Olney, C. A., & Coker, R. A. (1987). The effects of communicator characteristics on patterns of reciprocity and compensation. *Journal of Nonverbal Behavior, 11,* 146–165.

Burgoon, J. K., Stern, L. A., & Dillman, L. (1995). *Interpersonal adaptation: Dyadic interaction patterns.* Cambridge, England: Cambridge University Press.

Burleson, B. R., & Goldsmith, D. J. (1998). How the comforting process works: Alleviating emotional distress through conversationally induced reappraisals. In P. A. Andersen & L. K. Guerrero (Eds.), *Handbook of communication and emotion: Research, theory, applications, and contexts* (pp. 245–280). San Diego: Academic Press.

Burleson, B. R., & Samter, W. (1985). Consistencies in theoretical and naive evaluations of comforting messages. *Communication Monographs, 52,* 103–123.

Clark, L. F. (1993). Stress and the cognitive-conversational benefits of social interaction. *Journal of Social and Clinical Psychology, 12,* 25–55.

Cohen, S., Gottlieb, B. H., & Underwood, L. G. (2000). Social relationships and health. In S. Cohen, L. G. Underwood, & B. H. Gottlieb (Eds.), *Social support measurement and intervention: A guide for health and social scientists* (pp. 3–25). New York: Oxford University Press.

Collins, N. L., & Feeney, B. C. (2000). A safe haven: An attachment theory perspective on support seeking and caregiving in intimate relationships. *Journal of Personality and Social Psychology, 78,* 1053–1073.

Cupach, W. R., & Metts, S. (1994). *Facework.* Thousand Oaks, CA: Sage.

Cutrona, C. E., Hessling, R. M., & Suhr, J. A. (1997). The influence of husband and wife personality on marital social support interactions. *Personal Relationships, 4,* 379–393.

Dunkel-Schetter, C., & Skokan, L. A. (1990). Determinants of social support provision in personal relationships. *Journal of Social and Personal Relationships, 7,* 437–450.

Goffman, E. (1967). *Interaction ritual: Essays on face-to-face behavior.* New York: Pantheon.

Goldsmith, D. J. (1992). Managing conflicting goals in supportive interaction: An integrative theoretical framework. *Communication Research, 19,* 264–286.

Goldsmith, D. J. (1994). The role of facework in supportive communication. In B. R. Burleson, T. L. Albrecht, & I. G. Sarason (Eds.), *Communication of social support: Messages, interactions, relationships, and community* (pp. 29–49). Thousand Oaks, CA: Sage.

Goldsmith, D. J. (2004). *Communicating social support.* Cambridge, England: Cambridge University Press.

Goldsmith, D. J., McDermott, V. M., & Alexander, S. C. (2000). Helpful, supportive and sensitive: Measuring the evaluation of enacted social support in personal relationships. *Journal of Social and Personal Relationships, 17,* 369–391.

Goldsmith, D., & Parks, M. R. (1990). Communicative strategies for managing the risks of seeking social support. In S. Duck & R. C. Silver (Eds.), *Personal relationships and social support* (pp. 104–121). Newbury Park, CA: Sage.

Guerrero, L. K. (2005). Observer ratings of nonverbal involvement and immediacy. In V. Manusov (Ed.), *The sourcebook of nonverbal measures* (pp. 221–235). Mahwah, NJ: Lawrence Erlbaum.

Gurung, R. A. R., Sarason, B. R., & Sarason, I. G. (1997). Personal characteristics, relationship quality, and social support perceptions and behavior in young adult romantic relationships. *Personal Relationships, 4,* 319–339.

Hecht, M. L. (1978). The conceptualization and measurement of interpersonal communication satisfaction. *Human Communication Research, 4,* 253–264.

Hupcey, J. E. (1998). Social support: Assessing conceptual coherence. *Qualitative Health Research, 8,* 304–318.

Jones, S. (2004). Putting the person into person-centered and immediate emotional support: Emotional change and perceived helper competence as outcomes of comforting in helping situations. *Communication Research, 31,* 338–360.

Jones, S. M., & Guerrero, L. K. (2001). The effects of nonverbal immediacy and verbal person centeredness in the emotional support process. *Human Communication Research, 27,* 567–596.

Lane, C., & Hobfoll, S. E. (1992). How loss affects anger and alienates potential supporters. *Journal of Consulting and Clinical Psychology, 60,* 935–942.

Lazarus, R. S. (1999). *Stress and emotion: A new synthesis.* New York: Springer.

Lazarus, R. S., & Folkman, S. (1984). *Stress, appraisal, and coping.* New York: Springer.

Leary, M. R. (1996). *Self-presentation: Impression management and interpersonal behavior.* Boulder, CO: Westview Press.

Lim, T.-S., & Bowers, J. W. (1991). Facework: Solidarity, approbation, and tact. *Human Communication Research, 17,* 415–450.

McAuley, E., Duncan, T. E., & Russell, D. W. (1992). Measuring causal attributions: The revised causal dimension scale (CDSII). *Personality and Social Psychology Bulletin, 18,* 566–575.

Miczo, N. (2004). *A facework-based approach to the elicitation and provision of support in romantic dyads.* Unpublished doctoral dissertation, University of Arizona, Tucson.

O'Brien, T. B., & DeLongis, A. (1996). The interactional context of problem-, emotion-, and relationship-focused coping: The role of the big five personality factors. *Journal of Personality, 64,* 775–813.

Pasch, L. A., & Bradbury, T. N. (1998). Social support, conflict, and the development of marital dysfunction. *Journal of Consulting and Clinical Psychology, 66,* 219–230.

Perrine, R. M. (1993). On being supportive: The emotional consequences of listening to another's distress. *Journal of Social and Personal Relationships, 10,* 371–384.

Pierce, G. R., Sarason, B. R., Sarason, I. G., Joseph, H. J., & Henderson, C. A. (1996). Conceptualizing and assessing social support in the context of the family. In G. R. Pierce, B. R. Sarason, & I. G. Sarason (Eds.), *Handbook of social support and the family* (pp. 3–23). New York: Plenum Press.

Plank, R. E., Minton, A. P., & Reid, D. A. (1996). A short measure of perceived empathy. *Psychological Reports, 79,* 1219–1226.

Prager, K. J. (1999). Nonverbal behavior in intimate interactions. In L. K. Guerrero, J. A. DeVito, & M. L. Hecht (Eds.), *The nonverbal communication reader: Classic and contemporary readings* (2nd ed., pp. 298–304). Prospect Heights, IL: Waveland Press.

Rosen, S., Mickler, S. E., & Collins, J. E., II. (1987). Reactions of would-be helpers whose offer of help is spurned. *Journal of Personality and Social Psychology, 53,* 288–297.

Russell, D. (1982). The causal dimension scale: A measure of how individuals perceive causes. *Journal of Personality and Social Psychology, 42,* 1137–1145.

Shumaker, S. A., & Brownell, A. (1984). Towards a theory of social support: Closing conceptual gaps. *Journal of Social Issues, 40,* 11–36.

Stroebe, W., & Stroebe, M. (1996). The social psychology of social support. In E. T. Higgins & A. W. Kruglanski (Eds.), *Social psychology: Handbook of basic principles* (pp. 597–621). New York: Guilford Press.

Thoits, P. A. (1986). Social support as coping assistance. *Journal of Consulting and Clinical Psychology, 54,* 416–423.

Trobst, K. K., Collins, R. L., & Embree, J. M. (1994). The role of emotion in social support provision: Gender, empathy and expressions of distress. *Journal of Social and Personal Relationships, 11,* 45–62.

Yankeelov, P. A., Barbee, A. P., Cunningham, M. R., & Druen, P. B. (1995). The influence of negative medical diagnoses and verbal and nonverbal support activation strategies on the interactive coping process. *Journal of Nonverbal Behavior, 19,* 243–260.

---

AUTHORS' NOTE: The authors would like to thank Chad Frederick, Mary Haynes, Jillian Helmer, Christa Knapp, and April Dawn Roth for coding assistance.

# 13

## Interpersonal Emotional Competence

### Sandra Metts

### Brandon Wood

F ew aspects of the human condition are more pervasive than emotion. Emotions are the theme of art, music, drama, and comedy. They inspire and frustrate; they empower and devastate; they make us laugh and make us cry. But for all their complexity and mystique, emotions are not beyond our understanding, nor are they beyond our control. Although emotions are relatively brief episodes of physiological arousal, the interpretation of this arousal and our expressive response are the result of cognitive processes (Frijda, 2000). An integral part of these cognitive processes is our ability to understand the social and relational context in which the emotion was experienced and the possible implications of whether and how we communicate the emotion.

Recognizing that emotions can be understood and communicated effectively is an important first step in becoming more emotionally skilled in how we respond to our own emotions and those of others.

The purpose of this chapter is to summarize a program of research focused on *interpersonal emotional competence* and to illustrate its association with several aspects of close relationships. First, we lay the foundation for our research by reviewing two domains of inquiry that informed our work: emotional intelligence (EI) and communication competence. Second, we summarize the construction of the Interpersonal Emotional Competence Scale (IECS), which integrates these two approaches to emotion, knowledge, and ability. Third, we present the results of several studies using the IECS to examine the role of emotional competence in several areas of interpersonal relationships. Finally, we offer several suggestions to enhance emotional competence in interpersonal contexts.

# Review of Emotional Intelligence and Communication Competence

## EMOTIONAL INTELLIGENCE

EI entered public awareness from the popular success of Robert Goleman's books *Emotional Intelligence* (1995) and *Working With Emotional Intelligence* (1998). Goleman (1998) defines EI as "the capacity for recognizing our own feelings and those of others, for motivating ourselves, and for managing emotions well in ourselves and in our relationships" (p. 317). He describes two domains of competence within his model: personal competence and social competence (pp. 26–27). Personal competence includes *self-awareness* (emotional self-awareness, accurate self-assessment, self-confidence), *self-regulation* (self-control, trustworthiness, conscientiousness, adaptability, innovation), and *motivation* (achievement orientation, commitment, initiative, optimism). Social competence includes *empathy* (understanding others, developing others, service orientation, leveraging diversity, political awareness) and *social skills* (leadership, communication, influence, change catalyst, conflict management, building bonds, collaboration and cooperation, and team capabilities).

Although Goleman's definition of EI is consistent with most academic definitions (Neubauer & Freudenthaler, 2005), the multidimensional set of skills, abilities, and competencies included within his model seem to have little theoretical coherence (Matthews, Roberts, & Zeidner, 2004). Indeed, the skills are predominantly professional competencies (leadership, management, and motivation), with little attention to emotional competencies, other than "emotional self-awareness" and some aspects within the "empathy" category. Nonetheless, and despite a lack of peer-reviewed research, Goleman has been trailed by a barrage of popular press publications (over 400 books can be found on amazon.com) all claiming in one way or another to define EI and provide strategies for becoming more emotionally intelligent, typically in the workplace.

Despite its popular association with Goleman, a construct called EI had been established in the scientific community before his first book was printed (Matthews, Zeidner, & Roberts, 2002). We summarize briefly the two most frequently used scientific approaches to EI, the "mixed model" of Bar-On and the "ability-based model" of Salovey and Mayer.

Mixed models of EI, as represented in the empirical work of Bar-On (and Goleman's descriptive model), conceptualize EI as a diverse group of dispositions and abilities that include personality traits and social skills that facilitate general life success. Mixed models generally use self-report instruments in order to assess respondents' perceptions of their psychological states and behavioral tendencies. Bar-On's (1997) emotion quotient inventory (EQ-i), for example, includes 133 Likert-type scales to measure intrapersonal skills (e.g., self-regard, emotional self-awareness, self-actualization), interpersonal skills (e.g., empathy, interpersonal relationships), adaptability (e.g., problem solving, flexibility), stress management (e.g., stress tolerance, impulse control), and general mood (e.g., happiness, optimism). In 2000, Bar-On revised his model and reframed five subcomponents (i.e., self-actualization, independence, social responsibility, optimism, and happiness) as facilitators of emotional and social intelligence rather than constituent components.

The EQ-i is a commonly employed self-report measure for EI. However, its broad domain of interest and strong statistical overlap with aspects of personality (e.g., Big Five Personality traits) have led some scholars to question whether it actually measures EI and offers substantially new insights that could not be gathered with existing measures of personality and social competence (Brackett & Geher, 2006; Neubauer & Freudenthaler, 2005).

Salovey and Mayer's (1990; Mayer, Caruso, & Salovey, 1999) approach to EI is considered an ability-based (rather than mixed) model because it focuses on cognitive abilities entailed in emotional awareness, regulation, and utilization but intentionally excludes attributes of personality, trait dispositions, and mood tendencies. Mayer and Salovey have worked to validate a performance-based measure of abilities that avoids what they see as limitations of self-report measures. Most recently they have offered the 140-item MSCEIT instrument (Mayer-Salovey-Caruso Emotional Intelligence Test; Mayer, Salovey, & Caruso, 2000; Mayer, Salovey, Caruso, & Sitarenios, 2001, 2003). The MSCEIT measures four "branches" of EI: perception of emotion, emotional facilitation of thought, understanding of emotion, and regulation/management of emotion. These components are presumed to be hierarchical in that the most basic cognitive processes are involved in perceiving emotion, which then underlies the more advanced cognitive processes necessary in using emotion to facilitate thought, which is necessary for understanding emotion meaning and for the most sophisticated level of cognitive processing used in regulating and managing emotion.

The MSCEIT is administered online and computer scored. Items within each component are given a "correct" answer according to group consensus (the most common response among a sample) or expert scoring (responses of emotion researchers). A respondent's answer is then compared with this score and coded as correct or incorrect (Mayer et al., 2003). Figure 13.1 illustrates the dimensions and sample testing format.

The MSCEIT is recognized for its contribution in providing clear criteria for the assessment of emotional ability (i.e., right or wrong answers), thereby holding it to the same rigor as IQ (Mayer & Salovey, 1997; Roberts, Zeidner, & Matthews, 2001). But it has also been criticized (Matthews et al., 2002, 2004). For example, Zeidner, Roberts, and Matthews (2004) question whether emotional and social information are two discrete forms of input as Mayer et al.

**Figure 13.1**    Abilities and Assessment of the Branches of the MSCEIT

---

### Branch 1: Perception of Emotion

*Abilities*

- identify one's own feelings
- identify emotions in other people, artwork, language, sound, appearance & behavior
- express emotions and emotional needs accurately
- discriminate between honest/dishonest and accurate/inaccurate expression of others

### Sample Assessment

This person feels

No   1   2   3   4   5   Extreme
Happiness                    Happiness

No   1   2   3   4   5   Extreme
Fear                         Fear

---

### Branch 2: Emotional Facilitation of Thought

*Abilities*

- prioritizing emotional information
- using emotions for judgment and memory
- awareness of mood swings
- using emotional states such as happiness to facilitate inductive reasoning and creativity

### Sample Assessment

Q. What mood(s) might be helpful to feel when meeting in-laws for the very first time?

|          | Not Useful |   |   | Useful |   |
|----------|:----------:|:-:|:-:|:------:|:-:|
| Tension  | 1 | 2 | 3 | 4 | 5 |
| Surprise | 1 | 2 | 3 | 4 | 5 |
| Joy      | 1 | 2 | 3 | 4 | 5 |

---

### Branch 3: Understanding Emotions

*Abilities*

- label emotions and understand the relationship between words and emotions
- interpret the meaning of emotions in relationships
- understand complex, simultaneous, and blended emotions
- recognize emotional transitions

### Sample Assessment

Scenario: Tom felt anxious and became a bit stressed when he thought about all the work he needed to do. When his supervisor brought him an additional project, he felt ___. (Select the best choice.)

   a) Overwhelmed
   b) Depressed
   c) Ashamed
   d) Self-conscious
   e) Jittery

| Branch 4: Regulation/Management of Emotion | Sample Assessment |
|---|---|
| *Abilities*<br><br>• stay open to feelings<br>• engage or detach from an emotion<br>• monitor emotions in relation to self and others<br>• manage emotion in oneself and others by moderating negative emotions and enhancing pleasant ones | Debbie just came back from vacation. She was feeling peaceful and content. How well would each action preserve her mood?<br><br>Action 1: She started to make a list of things at home that she needed to do.<br>Very Ineffective    Very Effective<br><br>1      2      3      4      5<br><br>Action 2: She began thinking about where and when she would go on her next vacation.<br>Very Ineffective    Very Effective<br><br>1      2      3      4      5<br><br>Action 3: She decided it was best to ignore the feeling since it wouldn't last anyway.<br>Very Ineffective    Very Effective<br><br>1      2      3      4      5 |

NOTE: The assessment items are taken from the MSCEIT Web page: emotionaliq.org/test.htm.

(1999) maintain. They propose that both may work in tandem, particularly in higher-order situations such as understanding emotions and regulating/managing emotions for self and others.

Criticism has come also from Salovey and his colleagues. They acknowledge, for example, that since "correct" answers on the MSCEIT are determined by the most popular response, truly creative responses to emotional challenges would be penalized for being nonnormative (Lopes, Cote, & Salovey, 2006). Salovey and Grewal (2005) also advocate additional EI research in order "to understand the motivational underpinnings of using certain skills depending on the particular interpersonal context" (p. 285).

Salovey and Grewal's (2005) comment raises an issue fundamental to the theoretical and methodological discussions in the EI literature—namely, is EI, in theory and practice, equivalent to traditional notions of cognitive intelligence, or is it a set of abilities that include social knowledge and motivation as well. Operationalizational procedures are the researcher's prerogative, of course. But we believe that understanding the role of emotion in interpersonal contexts requires examination of both emotional and social knowledge, as well as the abilities and motivation necessary to enact this knowledge. Thus consistent with the position of some emotion theorists who find the term "emotional intelligence" too focused on "mental ability" (e.g., Buckley & Saarni, 2006) and consistent with research confirming the importance of knowledge, skill, and motivation in interpersonal communication (Spitzberg, 2003), we use the term "interpersonal emotional competence" to characterize our domain of interest.

We believe that social, communicative, and emotional competencies are difficult domains to separate. Emotion meaning, emotion expression, and responses to our own and others' emotions are integrated processes, arising from and folding back into the interpersonal communication process (Metts & Planalp, 2002). Thus we believe that emotional competence overlaps with the broader set of knowledge, skills, and motivation known as "communication competence."

## COMMUNICATION COMPETENCE

Despite the conceptual interface between the constructs of EI and communication competence, no integrative model and corresponding measurement currently exist. Contributions relevant to understanding the association between these constructs, however, are evident in the work of several communication scholars, most notably in the areas of emotional self-awareness, responding to the emotions of others, and emotion expression.

Emotional self-awareness is evident in the Affective Orientation (AO) scale (Booth-Butterfield & Booth-Butterfield, 1990, 1994), which assesses "the degree to which people are aware of their emotions, perceive them as important, and actively consider their affective responses in making judgments and interacting with others" (1994, p. 332). The cognitive abilities tapped by AO are reminiscent of several components of EI, particularly facilitation of thought and understanding/analyzing emotions. The program of research on emotional support (see Burleson, 2003, 2008; Burleson & Goldsmith, 1998) contributes to our understanding of how support givers respond more or less competently to the emotional distress of others. Finally, variation in emotional expression style is addressed by Planalp and Knie (2002) in their application of message design logics (O'Keefe, 1988) to emotional expression. They integrate expression dimensions (e.g., communicative goals, skills needed) across the levels of message design logics: expressive, conventional, and rhetorical.

The conceptual and methodological overlap between emotional competence and communication competence is most clearly illustrated in a comprehensive review of the research in interpersonal communication competence by Spitzberg and Cupach (2002). Their summary profile (Table 15.3, pp. 587–588) illustrates the distribution of emotional self-awareness, responsiveness, and expression across the macro-skills categories of the communication competence construct. For example, within *Altercentrism,* 4 of the 39 competencies are related to emotion: emotional sensitivity, emotional support, empathy, and intimacy/warmth. Within *Composure,* 2 of the 25 skills are related to emotion: coping with feelings and emotional control. Within *Expressiveness,* 7 of the 21 skills are related to emotion: affective skills, confrontation/anger expression, emotional control, emotional expressivity, emotionality, expressiveness/expressivity, and facial expressiveness/vocal behavior.

In sum, although the constructs of EI and communication competence are theoretically linked, a practical self-report measure of interpersonal emotional competence is not available. We turn now to a summary of the scale construction process we used to accommodate this need.

## Constructing the Interpersonal Emotional Competence Scale (IECS)

### SCALE CONSTRUCTION

#### Generating Items

One of the coauthors and a research assistant generated items reflecting theoretical dimensions of EI and emotional communication. Particular attention was given to *self-awareness, managing emotion expression, empathy,* and *responding appropriately to the emotions of others.* Additional items were borrowed from existing scales for related constructs (e.g., Emotional Expressiveness Questionnaire of King & Emmons, 1990; Toronto Alexithymia Scale of Bagby, Parker, & Taylor, 1994; Affective Orientation Scale of Booth-Butterfield & Booth-Butterfield, 1990, 1994; Interpersonal Communication Competence Scale of Rubin & Martin, 1994; and several empathy scales from Mehrabian & Epstein, 1971; Weaver & Kirtley, 1995).

After pilot tests and revisions, 45 of the original 98 items were selected for inclusion in the IECS. Factor analysis on a convenience sample of undergraduates yielded a complex but theoretically interpretable factor structure composed of three conceptual dimensions, two with more specific subscales.

The first conceptual dimension was labeled *emotional attention* and represents the tendency to be conscious of emotional information and to consider it as salient and relevant within social interaction. This dimension contained three intercorrelated subscales: *emotion as a guide* (e.g., "If I am unsure about a decision, I pause to consider how I feel about my choices"; alpha = .84), *empathy* (e.g., "I seem to feel the emotions that others are feeling"; alpha = .91), and *emotional self-awareness* (e.g., "I am aware of my emotions as I experience them"; "I don't pay much attention to my emotions" [reverse scored]; alpha = .81).

The second conceptual dimension was labeled *emotional expression* and represents concerted effort to manage emotional expression and appraise the possible consequences of emotional expression. Two intercorrelated subscales emerged within this dimension: *expression management* (e.g., "I am usually able to express my emotions without losing control"; "When I am upset, I tend to speak first and think about it later" [reverse scored]; alpha = .81) and *reflected expression appraisal* (e.g., "My friends often say to me that I have good control of my emotions"; "After a conversation, I tend to reflect on how I expressed my feelings"; alpha = .79).

The third conceptual dimension was labeled *co-construction of affective meaning* because it reflected the theme of mutual engagement in efforts to process emotional meaning (e.g., "Talking with friends about my emotions helps me sort them out"; "My friends seem to trust me to help them talk about their feelings"; "I prefer to deal with my emotions in private" [reverse scored]; alpha = .87). Although empathy, emotional self-awareness, and expression management were correlated with the co-construction component, confirmatory factor analysis supported its integrity.

# The IECS and Interpersonal Relationships: Three Studies

## STUDY 1: DO CLOSE OTHERS RECOGNIZE AND RESPOND TO EMOTIONAL COMPETENCE?

Our first study was motivated by two fundamental questions: (1) *Is a person's interpersonal emotional competence recognized by close others who interact with him or her on a regular basis?* and (2) *Are close relationships with emotionally competent people perceived to be more satisfying than relationships with less emotionally competent people?* In order to answer these questions, we used a convenience sample of 47 matched pairs of friends or romantic partners ($N = 84$; mean age 21.8 years). A target person completed the IECS, and a friend or romantic partner completed a version adapted for outsider ratings (e.g., "He/she tends to 'pick up' or feel the happiness of others"; "He/she expresses his/her emotions appropriately"; "After I confide in him/her about something bothering me, I feel emotionally stronger"). Friends and romantic partners also completed the Relational Assessment Scale (Hendrick, Dicke, & Hendrick, 1998) (e.g., "This person meets my needs as a friend/romantic partner") and five items of interaction enjoyment constructed for this investigation (e.g., "When I have free time, I prefer to spend it with this person rather than with other people I know" (1 = *strongly disagree* to 5 = *strongly agree*). Factor analysis confirmed that the expanded scale was unidimensional and reliable (alpha = .83).

*Results*

Results indicated that friends and romantic partners do, indeed, rate the target's level of emotional competence in ways consistent with the target's own assessment. Within the *emotional attention* dimension, all three subscales were significantly correlated with outsider ratings: *Emotion as Guide* ($r$ = .33), *Empathy* ($r$ = .38), and *Emotional Self-Awareness* ($r$ = .22). Within the *emotional expression* dimension, both subscales were significantly correlated with outsider ratings: *Expression Management* ($r$ = .39) and *Reflected Expression Appraisal* ($r$ = .37). Finally, *co-construction of affective meaning* was significantly correlated with outsider ratings ($r$ = .44). It is not surprising that *emotional self-awareness* demonstrated the lowest correlation with outside ratings. Unless a person is exceptionally open in revealing this awareness, others would not necessarily recognize it as clearly as the person experiencing the emotion.

In addition, the relational satisfaction/interactional enjoyment scale was highly correlated with the target's overall emotional competence score ($r$ = .51) and particularly with *empathy* ($r$ = .54) and *co-construction of affective meaning* ($r$ = .60). This finding underscores the relational and interactional appreciation others experience when a partner or friend is skilled in recognizing their emotional needs and helping them appraise the implications of their emotional experiences.

## STUDY 2: CONVERSATIONAL COMPETENCE

As we noted previously, EI and communicative competence overlap, at least conceptually. It is not clear the extent to which they overlap in practice. Brackett, Rivers, Shiffman, Lerner, and Salovey (2006) found that the MSCEIT was associated with judges' ratings on two of four interaction dimensions ("being a team player" and "overall social competence") after viewing a short (6 minutes) videotaped conversation, but this held only for men. We speculate that emotionally competent people, relative to less competent, are better able to manage their emotions and those of others during interactions because they more fully understand and skillfully employ the implicit norms of conversation. Thus we hypothesized that *interpersonal emotional competence would predict conversational knowledge.*

A convenience sample of 241 university students (mean age 21.8 years) completed a measure of conversational knowledge taken from the Trait Version of the Conversational Knowledge Scale (CKS; Spitzberg, 1990), designed to measure knowledge of effective and appropriate conversational practices. The CKS contains 25 items, but those that refer explicitly to emotion-related skills were eliminated to avoid overlap with the IECS (e.g., "I am good at 'reading' people to know what they are thinking or *feeling*"), and 4 items that did not load during factor analysis were eliminated. Twelve items constituted the final scale (e.g., "I believe I am very knowledgeable about how to interact with people") (1 = *never or almost never true of me* to 5 = *always or almost always true of me*).

### Results

Regression analysis indicated that all of the higher-order blocks contribute to perceived knowledge about conducting effective and appropriate conversations. More specifically, however, within *emotional attention, empathy* and *emotional self-awareness* were significant predictors, but *emotion as a guide* was not. Within *emotional expression, expression management* was a significant predictor, but *reflected expression appraisal* was not. Remarkably, even after the variance contributed by emotional attention and emotion expression was removed, *co-construction of affective meaning* contributed another 12% of the variance in conversational knowledge. These findings confirm our expectation that people who believe they are attentive to their own and others' emotions and believe they are competent in controlling the expression of their emotions also tend to believe they are aware of the norms and practices associated with the routine management of conversation. Even more striking, appreciation for the value of using interaction to understand and possibly reappraise emotional experience for self and others is a particularly salient factor in conversational knowledge.

## STUDY 3: EMOTIONAL COMPETENCE, SOCIAL INTEGRATION, AND CONFLICT STYLES

The finding of Study 1 that close others recognize and appreciate the emotional competencies of their friend or romantic partner is important, but it does not assure us that the competencies we have identified are associated with successful maintenance of larger social networks. Research using the EQ-i indicates that EI is correlated with interpersonal adjustment (Summerfeldt, Kloosterman, Antony, & Parker, 2006) and life satisfaction (Livingstone & Day, 2005). We therefore predicted that *scores on the IECS would be positively correlated with the degree to which one enjoys activities with others, exerts the effort to maintain a social network, and does not feel socially isolated.*

In addition, the finding of Study 2 that emotionally competent individuals also report greater knowledge about conversational practices in general does not tell us whether emotional competence is associated with more challenging emotional situations. As a specific case, we examined the relationship of emotional competence to the management of conflict episodes. We predicted that *emotionally competent individuals would be more likely to report engaging in constructive conflict strategies (e.g., compromising and collaborating) compared with individuals who are less emotionally competent.*

A convenience sample of 224 university students (mean age = 20.9 years) completed the IECS and two other measures: a measure of social engagement (e.g., "I have a strong sense of self" and "I feel that I lead an energetic and full life"; alpha = .81) and a measure of social autonomy ("I prefer being alone rather than in the company of other people" and "When I meet people I don't know, it doesn't matter much whether they like me or not"; alpha = .67). Participants also completed the Blake and Mouton (1964) Conflict Styles scale to assess their conflict style: competing, accommodating, avoiding, compromising, or collaborating.

### Results

The first hypothesis was partially supported. As we would expect, *co-construction of affective meaning* was positively correlated with social engagement ($r = .31$) as were two aspects of *emotional attention: empathy* ($r = .22$) and *emotional self-awareness* ($r = .20$). In addition, *co-construction of affective meaning* ($r = -.19$), *empathy* ($r = -.18$), and one dimension of *emotional expression, reflected expression appraisal* ($r = -.21$), were negatively correlated with social autonomy. Taken together, these results suggest that people who recognize and respond to their own and others' emotions, and who use interactions to more fully understand the nature of emotional experience, are also more likely to value the quality of their social network and be satisfied with their social life. By contrast, those who are not able or motivated to respond to the emotions of others (empathy), to use interactions to understand emotional experience (co-construction of affective meaning), or to reflect on how their emotion expressions might be perceived by others (reflected emotional appraisal) tend to be socially isolated—either as a cause or as an effect of their emotional limitations.

The conflict hypothesis was also partially supported. One dimension of *emotional attention* and one dimension of *emotional expression* distinguished three of the five conflict styles. Specifically, the means for *emotional self-awareness* were significantly higher for those who reported using the compromising ($M = 3.51$) and collaborating ($M = 3.47$) styles compared with those who reported using the avoiding style ($M = 2.91$). *Expression management* was significantly higher for those who reported using the compromising ($M = 3.55$) and competing ($M = 3.53$) styles compared with those who reported using the avoiding conflict style ($M = 2.94$).

Apparently, confidence in the ability to recognize emotions and manage their expression encourages efforts to reach mutually satisfying conflict resolutions rather than avoid conflict. Interestingly, however, high scores on self-reported ability to manage the expression of emotions found in both the compromising and competing conflict styles reminds us that, like any skill, emotional expression can be used to achieve a variety of goals. This finding is consistent with Clark, Pataki, and Carver's (1996) research indicating that people can and do strategically control their emotion expression to influence others' perceptions of them—for example, expressing anger to appear dominant or intimidating.

## SUMMARY

Taken together, these findings suggest that interpersonal emotional competence is socially advantageous. Not only is it recognized by friends and romantic partners, but it is also associated with their level of relationship satisfaction and interactional enjoyment. Although close others cannot assess the knowledge that a friend or partner has regarding emotions he or she is experiencing, we suspect that this knowledge underlies the demonstrable skills exhibited in competent expression, empathetic responses, and processing emotion meanings for self and others during interaction. In addition to understanding the nature of one's emotional arousal, the ability to empathize with the emotions of others, manage emotion expression, and co-construct affective meaning through interaction are all associated with more general conversational competence. Finally, interpersonal emotional competence is systematically related to productive and satisfying social relationships and to the tendency to compromise and collaborate during conflict. Ironically, however, people who believe themselves to be skillful in managing the expression of their emotions seem to use that skill toward different goals during conflict—to reach a compromise or to emerge as the "winner."

Our investigation into the role of emotional competence in the processes and outcomes of interpersonal relationships is still in progress, and we acknowledge the limitations of these preliminary studies. Most apparent, perhaps, are the usual limitations imposed by convenience samples of college students and by self-report measures of competence. We believe, however, that self-report scales can be an appropriate measure when seeking information about someone's internal emotional states and attitudes or behaviors across a variety of situations that cannot be experimentally induced (Matthews et al., 2004). This is not to say that the IECS does not invite revision. Most notably, the factor within the *emotional attention* dimension that we labeled *emotion as a guide* was uninformative across our studies. Although previous research characterizes the practice of consulting one's emotions while making decisions as competent (e.g., Booth-Butterfield & Booth-Butterfield, 1990), our findings suggest reconsideration of this dimension. We suspect that less emotionally competent respondents endorsed this practice in its extremes ("Yes, emotions *always* guide my behaviors" or "No, I *never* let emotions guide my behaviors"). However, more emotionally competent respondents viewed it as sometimes productive and sometimes not, so the competent response would be "It depends." Thus this dimension was too unstable to distinguish levels of competence within our samples. We plan to revisit the conceptual and operational definition of this dimension.

With these caveats in mind, we turn now to a discussion of how the information contained in this chapter might be put to practical use for readers interested in improving their interpersonal emotional competence.

## Practical Applications

Despite the claims of many popular-press books, there are not 5 or 7 or even 10 easy steps to EI/emotional competence. However, we can offer several suggestions that might enhance the likelihood that people will be more emotionally competent in interpersonal contexts.

We believe that a fundamental step toward mastering the skills of interpersonal emotional competence is to demystify emotion. As we indicated when we began this chapter, emotions are first experienced as physiological arousal, but the interpretation and behavioral response to this arousal is ultimately a cognitive process. As Lazarus (2006) notes:

> [Emotions] are, in effect, logical and depend on reason or thought, even though the reasoning may be faulty or based on unrealistic premises. . . . Blaming our foolishness on emotion and calling it irrational is attributing the problem to the wrong cause. (pp. 17–18)

Lazarus is reminding us that we are responsible for assessing the logic behind our emotional experience, as difficult or unpleasant as that process may be. By contrast, Goleman (1995) asserts that "we have two minds, one that thinks and one that feels" (p. 20). Such a position implies that emotion knowledge and experience are somehow independent of rational thought and not subject to the constraints of logical analysis and control. When taken literally, this position invites a sense of entitlement for unfettered (and sometimes harmful) emotional expression. Consider the following exchange:

Why did you say that cruel thing to me?

Because I couldn't help it; I was just so angry.

The justification "I couldn't help it" exonerates the person who spoke unkindly only if arousal "causes" anger and anger "causes" a vitriolic display. According to contemporary views, cognition intercedes in this process and people can reflect on their feelings to understand them and manage their expression. More specifically, emotion attention, understanding, regulation, and expression are the result of three steps in the appraisal process: primary appraisal (positive or negative arousal), secondary appraisal (quality and intensity of the emotion and coping strategies), and reappraisal (a reevaluation of emotion and coping strategies) (Smith & Lazarus, 1993). Consistent with this perspective and the salience of emotional awareness and expression in our three studies, we offer suggestions for how to use the appraisal process in order to enhance interpersonal emotional competence.

First, we suggest pulling the stages of secondary appraisal and reappraisal into conscious awareness when appropriate. In some circumstances, secondary appraisal and reappraisal are not especially important, because the initial interpretation of arousal is automatic and virtually instantaneous. We realize quickly that the pleasant sensations we feel when laughing with a friend are cues of happiness and that the unpleasant sensations we feel when learning that a grandparent is ill are sadness. In more complex or ambiguous circumstances, however, the competent action is to consciously process the meaning of the arousal before responding. For example, when initial appraisal tells us that arousal is intense and unpleasant, we can move to secondary appraisal and actually think through a series of evaluation questions: "Do I really feel anger, or might I be feeling guilt, embarrassment, or hurt rather than anger?" "Have I done something that would make me feel guilty, or have I failed at something that is making me embarrassed?" "Do I feel devalued or betrayed, and that makes me feel hurt?"

Second, once the nature of the emotion has been assessed, we can pause to reflect on how to cope with that emotion. Sometimes immediate expression is an appropriate response—for example, expressing love or happiness when felt and suitable to the situation. However, when emotions are complicated, strong, and negative, such as guilt, anger, envy, or jealousy, we may need to consider ways of coping that might include moderating the intensity of the emotion or changing something in the environment that is evoking it. These reassessments may influence whether and how an emotion is expressed. If expression is warranted, controlled verbal statements are generally preferred—for example, "I'm angry (or annoyed, hurt, afraid, or jealous) right now because . . ." A controlled verbal expression of emotion is not an outburst; it is a description that helps the listener to understand and, hopefully, empathize with our emotional state. By contrast, indirect expression through raised voice, sarcasm, or unkind statements only serves to arouse negative emotional responses in others, which then fold back into the pattern of negative arousal.

Controlled verbal expressions are particularly important when the listener is a friend, coworker, romantic partner, or family member who is the proximate cause of the emotion. Such expressions provide him or her with the opportunity to acknowledge (and perhaps validate) the emotion, to change and correct the behavior that elicited the emotion, or to apologize or explain their behavior. Such responses facilitate the reappraisal process. During reappraisal, we reconsider our emotions and, in some cases, even realize that we can find an alternative interpretation of others' behaviors or messages. For example, the intense anger felt toward a romantic partner after a betrayal may actually be hurt or sadness because we feel devalued. Sometimes reappraisal involves the difficult but functional transformation of vengeful feelings into forgiveness (Metts & Cupach, 2007).

Of course, characterizing controlled expression as competent presumes that a speaker's goal is to continue the interaction and sustain relational harmony. Interpersonal trust facilitates emotional openness, and openness facilitates trust (Boone & Buck, 2003), but only to the extent that emotional openness is responsive to the needs of both partners and the relationship. When we express emotions for self-serving purposes such as exerting control, ascribing blame, inducing guilt, or repairing wounded self-esteem, the interaction can escalate into conflict or intensify a conflict already in progress (Laux & Weber, 1991; Schutz, 1999). Although it may be difficult to stop and think about motives during ongoing interaction, considering our motives for expressing emotion is sometimes important. "Do I really want her to understand why I am feeling jealous, or am I expressing it as anger so I can control her behavior?" "Do I really want to be open about my feelings for the sake of closeness, or do I just want to retaliate because he hurt me?" Whenever the responses to these questions reflect a self-serving bias, we have moved from emotion expression as self-disclosure to emotion expression as a strategic move in interpersonal competition (Buck, Losow, Murphy, & Costanzo, 1992).

In addition to our suggestions for using the appraisal process, we offer a suggestion that stems from a consistent finding in our research. People who engage in the process of working through their own and others' emotions during conversation (co-construction of affective meaning) were also rated emotionally competent by friends and partners, were in satisfying relationships, and were more socially integrated and involved. This suggests that we should approach emotional experience as a certain type of information that is amenable to analysis and problem solving (e.g., Burleson & Goldsmith, 1998). Indeed, the ability and willingness to talk about emotions, whether emerging within or experienced outside the relationship, not only facilitates understanding of these emotions but serves the secondary function of enriching the relationship in the same way that self-disclosure, social support, and affiliative actions do.

This process can be facilitated by using simple openers. For example, when others want to process their emotions, rather than simply stating, "Oh, that's too bad" or "You're overreacting," employ questions that help the appraisal process—for example, "Why do you think you got so angry?" or "Why do you think you love (or don't love) her?" When you feel the need to talk about your own emotions, anticipate what you hope to accomplish. If you need simply to vent frustration or to externalize sadness, verbalize that need: "Can I dump on you for a few minutes?" But if you are trying to understand a complicated emotional state, say so: "I'm so confused; can I talk to you about something?" Certainly there is no script available for all situations of co-constructing emotional meaning, but it is a conversational episode that can be guided by general principles of effective and appropriate interaction.

## Conclusion

So often, in an effort to make the theoretical tangible, scholars lose sight of the human condition, the collage of emotional experiences that emerge from and recede into our daily lives. We do not intend the cognitive and skills-based approach reflected in this chapter to trivialize the personal experience of emotion. However, we believe that finding a balance between theoretical rigor and practical utility is the best way to promote emotional competence. Toward this end, we have reviewed the major traditions in emotion theory and communication competence in order to frame our research on interpersonal emotional competence. We have offered suggestions for improving emotional competence based on existing research and our own findings. Emotions are powerful shaping forces in our interpersonal lives, and we hope that our efforts in this chapter to unravel their mystery will make them more manageable but no less intriguing.

## References

Bagby, R. M., Parker, J. D., & Taylor, G. J. (1994). The twenty-item Toronto Alexithymia Scale–I: Item selection and cross-validation of the factor structure. *Journal of Psychosomatic Research, 38,* 23–32.

Bar-On, R. (1997). *Emotional Quotient Inventory: Technical manual.* Toronto, Ontario, Canada: Multi-Health Systems.

Bar-On, R. (2000). Emotional and social intelligence: Insights from the Emotional Quotient Inventory. In R. Bar-On & J. Parker (Eds.), *The handbook of emotional intelligence: Theory, development, assessment, and application at home, school, and in the workplace* (pp. 363–388). San Francisco: Jossey-Bass.

Blake, R. R., & Mouton, J. (1964). *The managerial grid.* Houston, TX: Gulf.

Boone, R. T., & Buck, R. (2003). Emotional expressivity and trustworthiness: The role of nonverbal behavior in the evolution of cooperation. *Journal of Nonverbal Behavior, 27,* 163–182.

Booth-Butterfield, M., & Booth-Butterfield, S. (1990). Conceptualizing affect as information in communication production. *Human Communication Research, 16,* 451–476.

Booth-Butterfield, M., & Booth-Butterfield, S. (1994). The affective orientation to communication: Conceptual and empirical distinctions. *Communication Quarterly, 42,* 331–344.

Brackett, M. A., & Geher, G. (2006). Measuring emotional intelligence: Paradigmatic diversity and common ground. In J. Ciarrochi, J. P. Forgas, & J. D. Mayer (Eds.), *Emotional intelligence in everyday life* (2nd ed., pp. 27–50). New York: Psychology Press.

Brackett, M. A., Rivers, S. E., Shiffman, S., Lerner, N., & Salovey, P. (2006). Relating emotional abilities to social function: A comparison of self-report and performance measures of emotional intelligence. *Journal of Personality and Social Psychology, 91,* 780–795.

Buck, R., Losow, J. I., Murphy, M. M., & Costanzo, P. (1992). Social facilitation and inhibition of emotional expression and communication. *Journal of Personality and Social Psychology, 63,* 962–968.

Buckley, M., & Saarni, C. (2006). Skills of emotional competence: Developmental implications. In J. Ciarrochi, J. P. Forgas, & J. D. Mayer (Eds.), *Emotional intelligence in everyday life* (2nd ed., pp. 51–76). New York: Psychology Press.

Burleson, B. R. (2003). Emotional support skills. In J. O. Greene & B. R. Burleson (Eds.), *Handbook of communication and social interaction skills* (pp. 551–594). Mahwah, NJ: Lawrence Erlbaum.

Burleson, B. R. (2008). What counts as effective emotional support? Explorations of individual and situational differences. In M. Motley (Ed.), *Studies in Applied Interpersonal Communication* (pp. 207–227). Thousand Oaks, CA: Sage.

Burleson, B. R., & Goldsmith, D. J. (1998). How the comforting process works: Alleviating emotional distress through conversationally induced reappraisals. In P. A. Andersen & L. K. Guerrero (Eds.), *Handbook of communication and emotion: Research, theory, applications, and contexts* (pp. 245–280). San Diego: Academic Press.

Clark, M. S., Pataki, S. P., & Carver, V. (1996). Some thoughts and findings on self-presentation of emotions in relationships. In G. Fletcher & J. Fitness (Eds.), *Knowledge structures in close relationships: A social psychological approach* (pp. 247–274). Hillsdale, NJ: Lawrence Erlbaum.

Frijda, N. H. (2000). The psychologists' point of view. In M. Lewis & J. M. Haviland Jones (Eds.), *Handbook of emotions* (2nd ed., pp. 59–74). New York: Guilford.

Goleman, D. (1995). *Emotional intelligence: Why it can matter more than IQ.* New York: Bantam Books.

Goleman, D. (1998). *Working with emotional intelligence.* New York: Bantam Books.

Hendrick, S. S., Dicke, A., & Hendrick, C. (1998). The relationship assessment scale. *Journal of Social and Personal Relationships, 15,* 137–142.

King, L. A., & Emmons, R. A. (1990). Conflict over emotional expression: Psychological and physical correlates. *Journal of Personality and Social Psychology, 58,* 864–877.

Laux, L., & Weber, H. (1991). Presentation of self in coping with anger and anxiety: An intentional approach. *Anxiety Research, 3,* 233–255.

Lazarus, R. (2006). Emotions and interpersonal relationships: Toward a person-centered conceptualization of emotions and coping. *Journal of Personality, 74,* 9–46.

Livingstone, H. A., & Day, A. L. (2005). Comparing the construct and criterion-related validity of ability-based and mixed-model measures of emotional intelligence. *Education and Psychological Measurement, 65,* 757–779.

Lopes, P. N., Cote, S., & Salovey, P. (2006). An ability model of emotional intelligence: Implications for assessment and training. In V. U. Druskat, F. Sala, & G. Mount (Eds.), *Linking emotional intelligence and performance at work: Current research evidence with individuals and groups* (pp. 53–80). Mahwah, NJ: Lawrence Erlbaum.

Matthews, G., Roberts, R. D., & Zeidner, M. (2004). Seven myths about emotional intelligence. *Psychological Inquiry, 15,* 179–196.

Matthews, G., Zeidner, M., & Roberts, R. D. (2002). *Emotional intelligence: Science and myth.* Cambridge: Massachusetts Institute of Technology Press.

Mayer, J. D., Caruso, D. R., & Salovey, P. (1999). Emotional intelligence meets traditional standards for an intelligence. *Intelligence, 27,* 267–298.

Mayer, J. D., & Salovey, P. (1997). What is emotional intelligence? In P. Salovey & D. J. Sluyter (Eds.), *Emotional development and emotional intelligence* (pp. 3–31). New York: Basic Books.

Mayer, J. D., Salovey, P., & Caruso, D. R. (2000). Competing models of emotional intelligence. In R. J. Sternberg (Ed.), *Handbook of human intelligence* (2nd ed., pp. 396–420). New York: Cambridge University Press.

Mayer, J. D., Salovey, P., Caruso, D. R., & Sitarenios, G. (2001). Emotional intelligence as a standard intelligence. *Emotion, 1,* 232–242.

Mayer, J. D., Salovey, P., Caruso, D. R., & Sitarenios, G. (2003). Measuring emotional intelligence with the MSCEIT V2.0. *Emotion, 3,* 97–105.

Mehrabian, A., & Epstein, N. (1971). A measure of emotional empathy. *Journal of Personality, 40,* 525–543.

Metts, S., & Cupach, W. R. (2007). Responses to relational transgressions: Hurt, anger, and sometimes forgiveness. In B. H. Spitzberg & W. R. Cupach (Eds.), *The dark side of interpersonal communication* (2nd ed., pp. 243–274). Mahwah, NJ: Lawrence Erlbaum.

Metts, S., & Planalp, S. (2002). Emotional communication. In M. L. Knapp & J. A. Daly (Eds.), *Handbook of interpersonal communication* (3rd ed., pp. 339–373). Thousand Oaks, CA: Sage.

Neubauer, A. C., & Freudenthaler, H. H. (2005). Models of emotional intelligence. In R. Schulze & R. D. Roberts (Eds.), *Emotional intelligence: An international handbook* (pp. 31–50). Cambridge, MA: Hogrefe & Huber.

O'Keefe, B. (1988). The logic of message design: Individual differences in reasoning about communication. *Communication Monographs, 55,* 80–103.

Planalp, S., & Knie, K. (2002). Integrating verbal and nonverbal emotion(al) messages. In S. R. Fussell (Ed.), *Verbal communication of emotions: Interdisciplinary perspectives* (pp. 55–77). Mahwah, NJ: Lawrence Erlbaum.

Roberts, R. D., Zeidner, M., & Matthews, G. (2001). Does emotional intelligence meet traditional standards for an intelligence? Some new data and conclusions. *Emotion, 1,* 196–231.

Rubin, R. B., & Martin, M. M. (1994). Development of a measure of interpersonal communication competence. *Communication Research Reports, 11,* 33–44.

Salovey, P., & Grewal, D. (2005). The science of emotional intelligence. *Current Directions in Psychological Science, 14,* 281–285.

Salovey, P., & Mayer, J. D. (1990). Emotional intelligence. *Imagination, Cognition, and Personality, 9,* 185–211.

Schutz, A. (1999). It was your fault! Self-serving biases in autobiographical accounts of conflicts in married couples. *Journal of Social and Personal Relationships, 16,* 193–208.

Smith, C. A., & Lazarus, R. (1993). Appraisal components, core relational theme, and the emotions. *Cognition and Emotion, 7,* 233–269.

Spitzberg, B. H. (1990). The construct validity of trait-based measures of interpersonal competence. *Communication Research Reports, 7,* 107–115.

Spitzberg, B. H. (2003). Methods of interpersonal skill assessment. In J. O. Greene & B. R. Burleson (Eds.), *Handbook of communication and social interaction skills* (pp. 93–134). Mahwah, NJ: Lawrence Erlbaum.

Spitzberg, B. H., & Cupach, W. R. (2002). Interpersonal skills. In M. L. Knapp & J. A. Daly (Eds.), *Handbook of interpersonal communication* (3rd ed., pp. 564–611). Thousand Oaks, CA: Sage.

Summerfeldt, L. J., Kloosterman, P. H., Antony, M. M., & Parker, J. D. A. (2006). Social anxiety, emotional intelligence, and interpersonal adjustment. *Journal of Psychopathology and Behavioral Assessment, 28,* 57–68.

Weaver, J. B., III, & Kirtley, M. D. (1995). Listening styles and empathy. *Southern Communication Journal, 60,* 131–140.

Zeidner, M., Roberts, R. D., & Matthews, G. (2004). Emotional intelligence bandwagon: Too fast to live, too young to die? *Psychological Inquiry, 15,* 239–248.

# 14

## *Television Viewing and Relational Maintenance*

### *Christina G. Yoshimura*

### *Jess K. Alberts*

The television is a mainstay of U.S. households. According to Nielsen Media Research (2006), the television is turned on for an average of 8 hours and 14 minutes per day in U.S. households, and each household member watches an average of 4 hours and 35 minutes a day. Even though engagement in computer activities has caused television watching to decrease somewhat among viewers aged 18 to 34, television watching has not declined significantly for most people (Comstock & Scharrer, 1999; McRae, 2006), and the average U.S. household is, in fact, watching more television today than at any other time in history (Nielsen Media Research, 2006).

In addition to being pervasive, television also is multifunctional. That is, it fulfills a variety of purposes for individuals, couples, and families. It is a source of information and entertainment, it helps shape personal identities, and it serves important social functions, such as enabling individuals to connect with family, friends, and society (McQuail, 1987). We propose that an additional function that television viewing may serve is as a site where couples can maintain, or even enhance, their relationships.

Television watching is a potentially important context for interaction because television works in multiple ways to shape intimate relationships, including romantic ones. How characters perform their relationships on television helps shape individual and cultural views of romantic relationships. That is, most people have limited access to others' relationships, so they often rely on media versions of relationships to learn how other couples behave

(Finucane & Horvath, 2000). Second, viewers can learn about one another's beliefs and attitudes by their reactions to televised events (Lull, 1990). Finally, watching television together requires that viewers negotiate many elements, such as shared space, program choice, and use of the remote control (Copeland & Schweitzer, 1993). Thus television viewing is a frequent activity that may be a worthwhile context for studying couples' relationships.

One important aspect of couples' relationships is relational maintenance, that is, the strategic and routine behaviors couples perform in order to keep their relationships at a desired level of satisfaction or intimacy (Ayres, 1983; Canary & Stafford, 1992; Guerrero, Eloy, & Wabnik, 1993). Relational maintenance is vital, because poorly maintained or unsatisfactory relationships can have significant negative effects on physical and mental health. For example, criticism and negativity, which are common in failing relationships, are linked to poor health outcomes (Fiscella & Campbell, 1999). In addition, divorced individuals are at a higher risk for psychiatric illnesses—men being 4 times and women 2½ times more likely to experience mental health problems after a divorce than are their counterparts who remain married (Svedin & Wadsby, 1998).

Much of the advice couples receive on how to maintain their relationships suggests they engage in "special events" behaviors, such as sending flowers, setting aside a date night, or going away together (e.g., Rainey & Rainey, 2004). They usually are not told, however, what they can do during the course of their everyday routine that might enhance their relationships. Yet most relationships presumably succeed or fail based on daily interaction patterns, not how often gifts are exchanged or couples go out together (Plante & Sullivan, 2000). Similarly, while couples are encouraged to "communicate," this usually addresses the management of conflicts or problems rather than communication and relational maintenance during routine activities. Moreover, admonitions for couples to communicate typically advise that they set aside time in a quiet place for focused conversation. Not only is this logistically difficult for some couples, but it also can be counterproductive. Some partners may actually wind up engaging in poor communication due to acute anxiety or pressure to maintain the conversation and communicate "well." Given these drawbacks to advising special and isolated activities for communication, it might be helpful to find ways that satisfied couples can engage in relational maintenance behaviors within the routines of their everyday lives.

The study reported here attempts to do just that. In it, we seek to examine how couples enact relationship maintenance in their daily lives. More and more, scholars recognize that an important way to understand people's relationships is through studying their everyday interactions (e.g., Duck, 1994; Goldsmith & Baxter, 1996). In fact, Duck (1995) argues that the essence of a relationship lies in the interactions that partners share, indeed, that we "talk our relationships into being" (p. 535).

In order to understand how couples maintain their relationships outside of special or isolated contexts, this study examines the conversational interactions of romantic partners during their routine joint leisure time—which we broadly define as awake time away from paid employment and which we assume may be a relatively opportune occasion for relationship construction and maintenance. As identified here previously, television is a frequent leisure activity for American adults. Adults aged 18 to 64 spend 37% of their leisure time watching television, adults over 64 spend at least 50% of leisure time watching television (Cornish, 1991; Robinson, 1991), and talk *about* television has been found to make up 10.5% of couples' interaction while at home (Alberts, Yoshimura, Rabby, & Loschiavo, 2005).

## Discourse Approaches to Studying Relational Maintenance Interaction

Conversations with one's relational partner about the relationship serve as digestive juices that help partners assess, clarify, and frame their views of the relationship and therefore affect the nature of the relationship itself (Duck & Pond, 1989). However, it is not only talk *about* the relationship that affects how partners view the relationship. All talk between relational partners may function to help them create joint understandings of the relationship and help them to formulate and negotiate accounts, history, and a framework of their lives together (Duck, 1995; Duck & Pond, 1989). Casual, everyday talk is a large part of what helps us make sense of our interactions and impose continuity upon them (Duck & Pond, 1989; Sigman, 1991). Thus offhand and routine comments about television programs may at first glance seem simply to fill a silence or answer a question. However, they may also establish and maintain a sense of shared reality and may reinforce the continuity of interactions that create joint formulations of the relationship.

One occasion that provides opportunities for these joint formulations is television watching. Research indicates that during the majority of the time people are watching television, they are also engaged in another activity—eating, talking, reading, doing homework or paperwork, and so forth (Clancey, 1994). Thus when individuals are "watching television," their attention may vary—from high focus and concentration on the television to focus on other things while the television becomes mere background noise (Lee & Lee, 1995). Or as Comstock and Scharrer (1999) put it, viewers engage in two types of television watching: *monitoring* and *viewing*.

Monitoring involves varying levels of concentration divided between the television program and other stimuli. Viewing, on the other hand, implies "a theater-like physical disposition in which the screen is watched continuously" (Comstock & Scharrer, 1999, p. 84) while one focuses almost completely on the set. Because viewers do not pay attention to others when this occurs, few maintenance behaviors are likely to occur while viewing. Therefore, monitoring is the type of television watching referred to in this study. During monitoring, couples are receptive to cues from one another, are generally in close enough proximity to engage in conversation, and may have conversational topics introduced to them through stimulus from the television programming. That is, television monitoring is a part of many couples' routine daily life that may influence relationship maintenance.

## Studying Relational Maintenance

Researchers typically define relational maintenance as *preserving or sustaining a desired relationship state or definition* (Ayres, 1983; Canary & Stafford, 1992; Guerrero et al., 1993). Early typologies of maintenance behaviors focused on the strategic behaviors individuals used to maintain their relationships. These studies revealed a number of general behaviors (Ayres, 1983; Bell, Daly, & Gonzalez, 1987; Dindia & Baxter, 1987), which Stafford and Canary (1991) reduced to five: *positivity, openness, assurances, social networks,* and *sharing tasks.* In a study of various types of relationships, Canary, Stafford, Hause, and Wallace (1993) extended the typology to include five more strategic maintenance behaviors: *joint activities; cards, letters, and calls; avoidance; antisocial;* and *humor.*

Attention later turned to examining routine maintenance behaviors individuals enact daily *without* significant premeditation or attention to specific goals, such as ingrained patterns within a relationship (Gilbertson, Dindia, & Allen, 1998). In Dainton and Stafford's (1993) study, participants reported using many maintenance behaviors in a routine manner. In particular, positivity, openness, assurances, social networks, sharing tasks, joint activities, talk, mediated communication (cards, letters, calls), avoidance, and antisocial behaviors were found to function as both strategic *and* routine maintenance behaviors (Dainton & Stafford, 1993).

Even with the incorporation of routine behaviors into the typologies, maintenance research has relied almost exclusively upon participants being conscious of the behaviors they use to maintain their relationships; otherwise, participants would not have been able to report them. We believe it is possible, however, that relationships are also maintained by behaviors people are not even aware of using. Specifically, types of everyday talk in and about relationships may act to maintain relationships, without one even noticing (Duck, 1994, 1995; Sigman, 1991), especially in the context of another activity such as television watching. For this reason, it is possible that earlier self-reporting and role-playing studies have not captured relational maintenance behaviors that occur at a very low level of awareness. Therefore, we chose to examine couples' naturally occurring conversations during joint television watching to determine whether television watching provides an occasion for relational maintenance and, if so, what type of relational maintenance is likely to occur.

## METHOD

### Participants

For this study we collected data from 10 romantic couples in a large southwestern metropolitan area. The couples ranged in age from early 20s to late 60s and had been together from 2 to 33 years. A variety of socioeconomic and education levels were represented, with household incomes ranging from approximately $30,000 to over $60,000 and education levels ranging from high school to master's degrees. The couples were Caucasian; 8 were heterosexual, 1 was gay, and 1 was lesbian. As one of the goals in this data collection was to find satisfied couples to study, all couples were highly satisfied in their relationship. College students recommended couples, who were then paid $100 for their participation.

### Procedures

The couples were given wireless microphones and asked to wear them at all times when they were at home alone. Conversations were transcribed, then divided into thought units, defined here as an utterance segment that expresses a complete and autonomous idea (Sillars, 1986). Important features of everyday conversation can occur in minute segments of talk and might be missed if the unit of analysis were as large as the conversational turn or even the sentence. One of the coauthors did the unitizing, with a trained student unitizing 25% of the data to check reliability. A Cohen's kappa of .90 was achieved.

Due to the large amount of data collected, one weekday and one weekend day were randomly chosen from each of the 10 couples, resulting in 20 total days of conversation to be analyzed. Television watching was operationalized according to Comstock's (1991) definition of monitoring. All sections of the transcripts that evidenced television watching were coded for this project; generally several hours on each day were sampled.

### Coding

The coding was based on the communicative force of each unit; that is, we coded the action implied by each thought unit (Austin, 1975). As Nofsinger (1991) points out, any observer can see what people are *saying;* as researchers, the goal is to discern what they are *doing*. Thus we sought to locate the symbolic, communicative behaviors individuals enacted. Coding according to the communicative action of the utterance best guided the analysis toward this goal.

We began by applying a ubiquitous typology of maintenance strategies assembled by Canary et al. (1993). It consists of several categories of behaviors that individuals self-reported using to maintain their relationships. After several practice coding sessions on portions of the data not used in this study, nine of these categories were found to be applicable to the data: *positivity, openness, assurances, social networks, shared tasks, avoidance, antisocial, humor,* and *miscellaneous.* (Definitions of all coded categories are provided below.)

We added four additional categories to our coding scheme based on relevant relational maintenance research and our own experience in coding the data: *general small talk, TV small talk, back-channel,* and *uncodable.* The general small talk category captured utterances not serious or deep enough to be considered *openness* but which still functioned to share general information (e.g., "Honey, they were out of milk at the store today"). This behavior has been identified as a relational maintenance strategy by Haas and Stafford (1998). Since we were looking specifically at television watching in this study, and since we found in our initial coding that a significant portion of general small talk centered specifically on television programming or characters, we added an additional category of *TV small talk* to our coding system. This enabled us to separate out small talk that was individually or relationally focused from that which was television focused. Finally, we included the category of *back-channel* communication to account for the numerous utterances participants used to indicate that they had heard their partner (such as "uh-huh" or "yeah"), but which did not add unique content to the conversation, and we also added an *uncodable* category to account for utterances that were inaudible on our tapes.

One of the coauthors coded the data, and a trained coder independently coded 20% of the data to check the reliability of the coding scheme. Simple intercoder agreement was .86, and the Cohen's kappa reliability was .79. According to Fleiss (1981), a reliability level greater than .75 is excellent, so the coding scheme was deemed reliable.

## RESULTS

Analysis of the data confirmed our impression that joint television watching provides a potentially fruitful context for relational maintenance behaviors in two ways. Most obviously, at times the events that occurred during the television programs themselves seemed to prompt couples to engage in maintenance behaviors, such as *self-report* or *humor*. For example, one spouse reported to the other, "That special I want to see is on next." At other times, the context of television watching itself encouraged couples to perform maintenance behaviors. Because joint television watching requires that spouses be in proximity to one another, conversations occur that might not if the couple were involved in separate activities. In addition, since television watching often requires relatively little energy and focus, it allows secondary, and sometimes joint, activities to occur. These activities, such as cooking or folding laundry, frequently led couples to engage in maintenance behaviors, as might be expected. The analysis also found that couples engage in a wide variety of communication behaviors while jointly watching television (see Table 14.1).

**Table 14.1**    Maintenance Behaviors, Frequency of Use, and Percentage of Use

| Maintenance Code | Frequency | Percentage |
|---|---|---|
| 1.  Positivity: polite, pleasant, or upbeat comments | (53) | (1.30) |
| a.  Probes for positivity | 3 | 0.07 |
| b.  Compliments | 8 | 0.20 |
| c.  Favors | 3 | 0.07 |
| d.  Courtesy | 36 | 0.88 |
| e.  Affectional expressions | 3 | 0.07 |
| 2.  Openness: direct discussions about the relationship or personal issues | (0) | (0.0) |
| a.  Probes for openness | 0 | 0.0 |
| b.  Self-disclosure | 0 | 0.0 |
| c.  Meta-relational communication | 0 | 0.0 |
| d.  Advice | 0 | 0.0 |
| 3.  Assurances: comments that indicate relational continuity or affirmation | (116) | (2.84) |
| a.  Probes for assurances | 0 | 0.0 |
| b.  Overtly stated assurances | 0 | 0.0 |
| c.  Planning | 116 | 2.84 |
| 4.  Sharing/negotiating tasks: verbal narration or navigation of household chores/projects | 93 | 2.28 |
| 5.  Social networks: discussion of people or interactions in couples' social networks | 386 | 9.46 |

*(Continued)*

**Table 14.1** (Continued)

| Maintenance Code | Frequency | Percentage |
|---|---|---|
| 6. Humor—laughter or statements delivered humorously | (188) | (4.61) |
|   a. Positive | 70 | 1.71 |
|   b. Sarcasm | 22 | 0.54 |
|   c. Laughter | 96 | 2.35 |
| 7. TV small talk—discussion directly about television programming | 1,176 | 28.81 |
| 8. General small talk—verbal communication, not as "deep" as openness | (1,509) | (36.97) |
|   a. Probe for general small talk | 331 | 8.11 |
|   b. Self-report | 812 | 19.84 |
|   c. General observation | 164 | 4.02 |
|   d. Partner's experiences | 129 | 3.16 |
|   e. Narratives about news or nonmutually known others | 75 | 1.84 |
| 9. Avoidance—evasion of certain topics or issues | 1 | 0.02 |
| 10. Antisocial—socially unfriendly or unacceptable utterances | 35 | 0.86 |
| 11. Uncodable—no clear meaning or referent | 282 | 6.91 |
| 12. Miscellaneous—comments not codable within this scheme | 8 | 0.20 |
| 13. Back-channel communication—"filler" utterances indicating attention or understanding ("mm-hmm") | 233 | 5.71 |

## General Small Talk

We found that the behavior enacted most frequently was *general small talk,* which is defined as verbal exchange between partners regarding general information, not including information about the relationship or deep personal issues. This category was composed of three subcategories: *self-report, partner experiences,* and *narratives.*

*Self-report* was the largest subcategory of general small talk, followed by *probes for general small talk.* Self-report describes utterances that reveal one's internal states, feelings, or opinions. At times, self-report was occasioned by direct comments about the television, as evidenced in Example 1. In this instance, a photocopier shown on television led directly to self-report:

Example 1:

1. M:  I bet that's a cheap copier.

2. F:  Oh yeah, don't you think so? I mean, it all depends what you need it for, you know? . . . Like we don't need an expensive one. We just copy stuff for our files, that's all.

3. M:  Yeah, the girls are buggin' me to get a new one.

Self-report also occurred on occasions when at least one of the partners engaged in a secondary activity. For instance, as they watched TV, one couple sorted through clothes they had bought during the day and discussed their opinions of the clothes while also discussing the television show.

Finally, self-reports often occurred after a period of silence while the couple watched television. In these instances, the last comment made concerned the television program being observed. Then, after a pause, one of the partners would attempt to resume the conversation either by self-reporting (e.g., "I am not feeling so hot") or probing for a self-report from the other partner (e.g., "Are you enjoying this?"). Focusing on the television seemed to relieve viewers from the need to converse, at least for a time. After the focus on the television was over, viewers often attempted to restart the conversation through self-report:

Example 2:

1. M1:  Oh, synchronized swimming [referring to television program].

2.     (Pause of one minute, 11 seconds)

3. M1:  Oh, my back, . . . my aching back.

4.     (Pause of 52 seconds)

In these cases, self-reports appeared to function as bids for engagement, though, as in Line 3 above, they were not always successful.

Television fosters self-report by providing topics that couples may seize upon as relevant to their lives and experiences (as in Example 1), by allowing secondary activities to occur during television watching, and by allowing participants to pause their conversation after which they may attempt to restart it through self-report (Example 2). Probes for general small talk, that is, comments that sought to elicit self-reports form the partner, were observed throughout the interactions as well.

*Partners' experiences* consisted of comments on the other partner's experiences or attempts to direct or control the partner's behavior. Examples of this include "Chuck. Wake up" or "You have to start over." These comments occurred most often during secondary activities that couples performed while watching television.

*Narratives* about news or nonmutually known others formed the least frequently occurring subcategory of general small talk. During breaks in talk about the programs they were watching, couples shared information they acquired throughout the day or through the reading they were doing while also watching television. One such instance occurred when a couple began to share information they had learned during the day regarding the stock market. This sharing did not seem to be triggered by anything on television; rather, the presence of the television and the experience of joint watching provided the opportunity for couples to talk.

### TV Small Talk

Much of couples' communication while watching television was about topics *other than* the television. But it is not surprising that they engaged in considerable *TV small talk* as well. Couples made frequent, direct comments about the television programs, which underscores the fact that television watching is, indeed, a joint experience. Sharing impressions of the television program and asking questions to clarify one's understanding of the television program connected the couple even as they focused, in part, on the stimulus of the television. Small talk about the television included such comments as "What'd he say?" "How come a high school fight never happened like this for me?" and "See the Quaker church?"

### Discussing Social Networks

After *TV small talk* and *general small talk,* the next most frequently used behavior was *discussing social networks.* This category includes talk about friends, family, or other social network members known by both parties. This type of talk occurred most often over several talk turns, not in isolated comments about others. Most often, the thrust of the conversation was the couple's concern for someone in their social network. The following is a typical instance of *discussing social networks:*

Example 3:

1. F: Well, she wants to intern first for like a semester, which would [be] her last semester at school.

2. M: Yeah, but he may not have internships.

3. F: Yeah. . . . You know, because I mean in all honesty, Nikki doesn't have experience in that, you know. I mean, she'll be coming to him green, but . . .

*Humor*

The next most frequently enacted behavior was coded through both laughter and humorous comments. Couples frequently laughed aloud together while watching television programming, often in the absence of any conversation between them. Humorous comments made by the couple were classified as positive or sarcastic, with more positive than sarcastic comments evidenced in the data. Positive humorous comments often occurred in the context of an activity secondary to television watching, such as cooking dinner. For example, one woman commented to her partner, upon realizing that she had burned some food, "You didn't know you were getting Cajun, did you?" Often the statements seemed to be related to the television only in that it had brought the couple into proximity with one another.

*Assurances*

Although the category of *assurances* (comments that indicated relational continuity or relational affirmation) was next highest in frequency, it was the subcategory of *planning* that accounted for all assurances. Haas and Stafford (1998) included planning as a subcategory of assurances in their typology because planning implies a future relationship and continued togetherness, which act to assure partners of the state of their relationship. The planning evidenced in the data ranged from very short term (deciding what to do that day) to long term (planning a trip to Europe).

*Sharing/Negotiating Tasks*

Utterances that functioned to assign or ask for assistance with household chores, or to discuss how to complete them, represented the *sharing/negotiating tasks* category. These consisted of comments such as, "Do you want to get the croutons out of the pantry, please?" and "Well, you're gonna make sure that, uh, your favorites are taken to the dry cleaners and . . . have 'em laundered, okay?" Such utterances generally occurred as the couples were preparing food or cleaning in an area near the television.

*Positivity*

Comments that were pleasant or polite, that is, *positivity*, occurred rarely and were evidenced mainly through expressions of *courtesy*, such as a simple "Thank you" or "Excuse me." *Compliments*, when given, were mainly about food, such as "Good dinner." *Affectional* expressions, when used, often occurred at the beginning or the end of an utterance (such as "Good dinner, hon"). Finally, *favors* occurred when partners expressed that they were doing something for the other that they didn't have to do, such as "I'll take that for you." Although the use of *positivity* was infrequent, almost every couple had some utterances that fell into this category.

### Remaining Categories

Although they were observed in the data, comments in the *antisocial* and *avoidance* categories occurred very infrequently. *Antisocial* statements included socially unfriendly comments or statements of criticism or complaint, were rare, and were manifest in utterances such as "About time you did some work around here" and "Your memory's goin' bad." Even more rare was *avoidance*, defined as direct evasion of certain topics or issues, which occurred only once in the data studied—in the utterance "Do I have to talk about the trip to Europe right now?"

The only behavior in the coding scheme for this study that was not observed was *openness*, which is defined as direct discussion about the relationship or about weighty personal issues. Baxter and Wilmot (1985) have found that couples view discussions about the state of their relationship as potentially destructive and inefficient, and they argue that discussion of the relationship is a taboo subject in most established relationships. So perhaps such serious discussions are rare generally in established romantic relationships, but if not, they apparently are particularly rare during television watching.

*Back-channel communication*, such as "uh-huh" and "mm-hmm," accounted for 5.71% of the data, and *miscellaneous* comments accounted for 0.20%, both within expected ranges. Although 6.91% of the data were *uncodable*, this is understandable given the context of their collection. The couples studied did not have extensive experience with the equipment, and some taping glitches were to be expected.

The total amount of talk about television programming (28.81%) was significantly outweighed by the talk about other topics (58.34%) that occurred while couples watched television. Talk coded as miscellaneous, back-channel, or uncodable totaled 17.85% and could not be classified as talk about television or about other topics. These proportions illustrate that the greater focus during television watching is not on the television programming itself but rather on other topics of relevance to the couples. Thus even though maintenance behaviors occur during direct comments about television programming, more maintenance behaviors occur in talk about other topics that occurs in the context of television watching.

### New Maintenance Behaviors

In addition to the a priori maintenance behaviors included in our coding scheme, we noticed another interaction pattern that recurred across talk turns, namely, turns in which one partner expressed an opinion and, in the next turn, the other partner agreed with the opinion. Most frequently, this type of joint opinion expression occurred over three talk turns, with one person initiating a view, the other person agreeing with the view, and then the first person reaffirming the view yet again (as in Example 4).

Example 4:

1. M:  If he goes down there, he'll become a slave.

2. F:   Exactly.

3. M:  They'll grab him.

In a few instances, this pattern was evident over an even longer sequence of talk turns. For instance, in Example 5, the couple discuss a friend who they think should settle for a lower salary because of the substantial benefits a new job would provide.

Example 5:

1. F:   Like he said when he was here, he could move to Arizona for the same salary, but he could never move beyond that. But you know what, he makes good money. He doesn't need to make a ton of money.

2. M:  I told him that. I pointed that out to him in Vegas. You know Steve . . .

3. F:   Money is only worth so much.

4. M:  I know, I know, you know, I know, you make $65,000 a year, I know, but you know what? You also get a car provided for you, you get benefits provided for you. You got retirement provided for you.

5. F:   Oh, yeah.

Over these talk turns (and several more that followed), the couple asserted and reasserted their joint view of their friend's situation, indicating that this is a view that they both hold strongly. This joint expression of views likely plays a part in creating a dyadic identity, or relational culture, as Wood (1982) defines it. Thus expressing joint views is another potentially relationally enhancing behavior common to television watching.

## DISCUSSION

Some of the findings detailed above may not seem particularly surprising—couples mainly engage in small talk while watching television but do not have important relationship talks while doing so—but it is always preferable to have "commonsense" expectations confirmed (or disconfirmed) empirically. Less intuitive, presumably, are the findings that couples' conversations while watching television are more frequently about topics other than the programs they are watching and that couples use television programming to enact antisocial behaviors and avoidance relatively rarely when jointly watching television. These findings were not necessarily expected or intuitive. Consequently, this study has provided us with greater understanding of how couples engage with one another during the routine activity of television watching. It also provides one of the first accounts of observed (rather than reported) relational behavior in couples in a natural setting.

## Television and Relational Maintenance

The findings reported here also suggest that a number of the existing maintenance categories are true not only of individuals' perceptions of their routine maintenance behavior but also of their actual behavior. This provides important evidence of the utility of maintenance typologies for describing couples' behavior. Specifically, we determined that the context of joint television watching may especially foster relational maintenance behaviors such as *positivity, assurances, sharing/negotiating tasks, discussing social networks, humor,* and *small talk.* More important, these behaviors occurred not *in spite of* the activity of television watching but at least partially *as a result of* the activity itself.

These findings indicate that television does not silence couples. Rather, couples can use television watching as a forum to show affiliation with one another, to discuss their individual and joint lives, and to make plans. These behaviors serve to reinforce the fact that, even when couples focus attention on the television, they still recognize that they are in the company of one another and seek to maintain a tie through the television program's stimulus. At times, the couple may even use the television program as a means to share information unrelated to the television. Such communication, which links the television program to events or issues in the couple's everyday life, can serve as social grease that helps the couple move from interacting through the television to relating directly about their own lives and experiences. Such a sequence indicates that the television program can be used to encourage relational interaction on multiple levels and that partners are able to move easily between these types of exchanges. Television, then, provides an opportunity for enacting maintenance both via talk about the programming being watched and via talk irrelevant to the program yet relevant to the couples' lives.

It also appears that the simple *environment* of television watching may encourage various maintenance behaviors. Behaviors such as discussing social networks or sharing tasks often seemed linked not so much to the television program as to simply being in close proximity to one another. The ability of joint television watching to establish copresence and a context for interaction should not be underestimated. Similarly, since planning occurred independent of stimuli from television programming, it is possible that television simply mediated the flow and duration of planning. Perhaps having the television as another site to divert one's attention allowed couples to pause during stressful planning interactions and to focus on the television as a time-out.

Therefore, although television has long been thought of as an activity that isolates others and restricts genuine interaction, this study found the opposite. Joint television watching can bring couples into a context where they are able to connect with one another in a way that more individualistic activities do not allow, both through stimuli from the television program and through the environment of television watching itself. We do not contend that television watching is the only site for relational maintenance that is needed in couples' relationships—far from it. Communication and activities not evidenced in this study (like revealing personal self-disclosures or spending time in one another's social circles) are no doubt important to relational satisfaction and commitment. We simply argue that joint television watching is *one* activity from which couples may receive relational benefits or satisfaction.

Dainton and Stafford (1993) make a compelling claim that relational benefits accrue not only when people strategically invoke maintenance behaviors but also when they are used routinely, without conscious decision making. We believe that much of the behavior identified in this study was routine in nature and that not all relational communication can be considered relational maintenance. However, since the couples in this study all reported high relational satisfaction before, during, and after the completion of this study, we believe that these routine communication behaviors while watching television must at least be considered in terms of their potential positive impact on relationships. Based on the relational communication observed in this study, joint television watching must be considered as a potential context for proactive relational maintenance talk.

### Practical Application of the Findings

What, then, should couples do based on our findings? We recommend that couples take advantage of the context of joint television watching to strategically initiate communication that could serve a relational maintenance function. Specifically, we propose that strategic introduction of the relational maintenance behaviors of joint activities, small talk, openness, positivity, assurances, sharing tasks, and avoidance could easily and effectively function to enhance the relational benefits of joint television watching.

*Joint activities:* Perhaps counterintuitive to previous studies on relationships, we believe that couples should be *encouraged* to watch television, so long as they do so together. With most households containing more televisions than people in the household (Nielsen Media Research, 2006), there may be a tendency for family members to watch different televisions so that they can each view their preferred programs. We think they would be much better served by negotiating the programs they wish to see (or recording one for later viewing) and spending their time together. Such time together allows couples to engage in other everyday, routine maintenance behaviors that can bond partners in a relationship.

*Small talk:* Second, we encourage couples to engage in television *monitoring* (which allows for divided attention between the television and other stimuli) rather than television viewing (which requires full focus on television programming). Alberts et al. (2005) found that one of the more important roles relational partners may play is as an audience for the articulation of each other's experiences and thoughts. Stafford (2003) notes that talk about little things, or about a person's day, should certainly be considered as one way that satisfying personal relationships are maintained.

Thus an important part of relational communication may simply be co-presence and general talk. Commercial breaks and lulls in television programming provide pockets of time when couples can share thoughts and details that, while not immediately consequential to the couple or their relationship, reinforce their connection and each person's ability to speak and be heard. Instead of focusing exclusively on the television, couples should emphasize brief talk and general comments throughout their joint television monitoring in moments when television programming is of low interest.

*Openness:* In contrast to small talk, the relational maintenance behavior of openness features personal and consequential disclosures. Although we didn't find evidence in our data that this naturally occurred during couples' joint television watching, we did see opportunities where it could have if members of the couple had probed one another for details or extended their general comments. Specifically, one couple was watching a movie where a main character has a coming-of-age moment when he defends his beliefs from a classmate by engaging in a physical fight. The male of the couple commented, "How come a high school fight never happened like that for me?"

This comment was coded in our data as "television small talk" because it contained no elaborated disclosure and was not responded to by the female of the couple. However, if she had paused the movie (or simply turned her attention away from the programming), she might have followed up on this comment by asking, "What was high school like for you?" or "What would a fight like that have meant for you?" Conversely, the male who originally made this comment could have followed it up on his own with information important to him about his high school experiences or disclosures about his own coming-of-age moments. In this study, opportunities for personal disclosures were generally not taken, but we would encourage couples to consider taking advantage of these moments for increased understanding and intimacy.

*Positivity and assurances:* Aside from instances of planning, assurances and positivity were rarely evidenced in this study. Yet studies of relational maintenance show that focusing upon making interactions enjoyable, being cheerful, and stressing commitment to the future of a relationship are important relational maintenance behaviors. Although conscientious couples could choose to insert more positive and assuring communication into their joint television watching in many ways, we'd like to suggest that one way this might occur is through comparisons with characters and relationships shown in television programming.

People naturally compare their own relationship and their relational partners against others in their social landscape (Kelley & Thibaut, 1978). That we do this on some level while we watch characters and relationships on the television is not unusual, yet the comments we choose to make articulating these comparisons may be useful as relational maintenance. For instance, noting "That person on TV has beautiful hair, just like you do" or "That person's skiing is nothing compared to what you can do on the slopes" can be a way to insert positivity into everyday television watching. Assurances such as "One day we'll be married just as long as that couple sitting outside on their porch" stem from the stimuli on the television but are explicitly linked to the commitment that the relational partners speaking have for one another. Certainly our relationship or partner may not always stack up favorably against the portrayals in television programming, but when they do, choosing to focus on those positive comparisons can be one way to strategically communicate positivity.

*Sharing tasks:* Performing household responsibilities and helping equally with tasks that need to be accomplished have long been recognized as important behaviors for maintaining satisfactory relationships. In this study, many couples chose to pair their household tasks with the recreation involved in television watching. Specifically, couples in this study folded laundry, cooked dinner, washed dishes, and cared for pets during moments of joint television watching. Couples may find sharing household tasks less aversive and arduous if these tasks are undertaken together while the television simultaneously provides entertainment. We suggest that other tasks that could easily be shared while watching television include sorting mail, paying bills, creating grocery lists, dusting and tidying, and planning tasks that are better undertaken away from television watching.

*Avoidance:* Along with more positively valenced behaviors, evading one's partner or particular topics can sometimes be a productive relational maintenance strategy. Because focus is divided between the television and the interaction, some people may find it easier to share information in small doses during television watching (such as during television commercials) and then provide a break from this information while focusing back on television programming. Others may find that they can share the comfort of copresence with a relational partner during television watching when verbal interaction is not desired or productive. The television can serve as a strategic diversion when members of a couple require some time and distance from one another or a particular topic. Certainly, our previous suggestions are clear in encouraging couples to positively and productively interact while jointly watching television; however, should avoidance seem appropriate, it would be beneficial for couples to recognize the television as a source of distance as well.

Finally, we suggest that partners simply become more mindful of the relationship-enhancing activities that occur as they watch television with one another. Reframing television watching as a chance to explore new stimuli together rather than as time wasted may more positively shape couples' view of their relationship. Although individual benefits can be accrued from couples' engaging in separate activities during recreational time (such as one person hiking while the other surfs the Internet), the relational benefits of recreational time spent in a joint activity like television watching should not be underestimated. Recognition of the benefits of television watching may also make couples more active in consciously choosing to engage in television-related relational maintenance while watching television.

## Limitations and Conclusion

One limitation of this study is that sequential moves could not be tabulated adequately because the data were coded according to thought units. While there were advantages to coding by thought unit—having discovered the expression of joint views as a potential maintenance strategy, for example—future research applying a sequential analysis to the couples' conversational talk could further elucidate the nature of this process as well.

Specifically, while the thought unit is well suited to studying maintenance behaviors in discourse (Rabby, 1996), some behaviors (such as discussing social networks) tend to involve many more thought units than others (such as assurances). It may take only 1 thought unit to say "I love you" but 40 thought units to discuss a friend's relational dilemma. Therefore, the current analysis may not capture an accurate portrayal of the frequency with which each of these behaviors is enacted. It may be useful to recode the data by turn or by topic to determine how many times the couple shifts behaviors, which would result in a more accurate count of the number of times each behavior was enacted.

Another limitation of the study is that no comparison conditions were examined. We cannot say, for example, whether the communication behaviors observed during television watching are substantially different from those that occur during couples' other mundane activities such as dining together or driving together. Since we studied only satisfied couples who engaged in the activities outlined here, we cannot say that the behaviors we observed are more common to satisfied or dissatisfied couples or that the behaviors observed during television watching directly impact the relationship. Any of these comparisons should be worth pursuing in future studies.

Despite these limitations, we believe this study provides support for the belief that maintenance communication occurs in everyday, mundane contexts and suggests that joint television watching is an important context in which relational maintenance may take place. We believe that observation of relational behaviors in a natural setting adds new depth to relational data previously gathered through self-report. In addition, we believe the evidence that individuals show affiliation by expressing joint views is noteworthy and should be investigated more closely as a maintenance behavior across relational contexts.

# References

Alberts, J. K., Yoshimura, C. G., Rabby, M. K., & Loschiavo, R. (2005). Mapping the topography of couples' daily conversation. *Journal of Social and Personal Relationships, 22,* 299–322.

Austin, J. L. (1975). *How to do things with words.* Cambridge, MA: Harvard University Press.

Ayres, J. (1983). Strategies to maintain relationships: Their identification and perceived usage. *Communication Quarterly, 31,* 61–67.

Baxter, L. A., & Wilmot, W. W. (1985). Taboo topics in close relationships. *Journal of Social and Personal Relationships, 2,* 253–269.

Bell, R. A., Daly, J. A., & Gonzalez, M. C. (1987). Affinity-maintenance in marriage and its relationship to women's marital satisfaction. *Journal of Marriage and the Family, 49,* 445–454.

Canary, D. J., & Stafford, L. (1992). Relational maintenance strategies and equity in marriage. *Communication Monographs, 59,* 243–267.

Canary, D. J., Stafford, L., Hause, K. S., & Wallace, L. A. (1993). An inductive analysis of relational maintenance strategies: Comparisons among lovers, relatives, friends, and others. *Communication Research Reports, 10,* 5–14.

Clancey, M. (1994). The television audience examined. *Journal of Advertising Research, 34*(4), S1–S10.

Comstock, G. (1991). *Television in America.* London: Sage.

Comstock, G., & Scharrer, E. (1999). *Television: What's on, who's watching, and what it means.* San Diego: Academic Press.

Copeland, G., & Schweitzer, K. (1993). Domination of the remote control during family viewing. In J. R. Walker & R. V. Bellamy (Eds.), *The remote control in the new age of television* (pp. 155–168). Westport, CT: Praeger.

Cornish, J. (1991). How Americans use time: An interview with sociologist John P. Robinson. *The Futurist, 25,* 23–27.

Dainton, M., & Stafford, L. (1993). Routine maintenance behaviors: A comparison of relational type, partner similarity, and sex differences. *Journal of Social and Personal Relationships, 10,* 225–271.

Dindia, K., & Baxter, L. A. (1987). Strategies marital partners use to maintain and repair their relationship. *Journal of Social and Personal Relationships, 4,* 143–158.

Duck, S. (1994). Steady as (s)he goes: Relational maintenance as a shared meaning system. In D. J. Canary & L. Stafford (Eds.), *Communication and relational maintenance* (pp. 45–60). San Diego: Academic Press.

Duck, S. (1995). Talking relationships into being. *Journal of Social and Personal Relationships, 12,* 535–540.

Duck, S., & Pond, K. (1989). Friends, Romans, countrymen; Lend me your retrospections: Rhetoric and reality in personal relationships. In C. Hendrick (Ed.), *Review of social psychology and personality: Vol. 10. Close relationships* (pp. 17–38). Newbury Park, CA: Sage.

Finucane, M. O., & Horvath, C. W. (2000). Lazy leisure: A qualitative investigation of the relational uses of television in marriage. *Communication Quarterly, 48,* 311–321.

Fiscella, K., & Campbell, T. L. (1999). Association of perceived family criticism with health behaviors. *Journal of Family Practice, 48,* 128–134.

Fleiss, J. L. (1981). *Statistical methods for rates and proportions.* New York: Wiley.

Gilbertson, J., Dindia, K., & Allen, M. (1998). Relational continuity constructional units and maintenance of relationships. *Journal of Social and Personal Relationships, 15,* 774–790.

Goldsmith, D. J., & Baxter, L. A. (1996). Constituting relationships in talk: A taxonomy of speech events in social and personal relationships. *Human Communication Research, 23,* 87–114.

Guerrero, L. K., Eloy, S. V., & Wabnik, A. I. (1993). Linking maintenance strategies to relationship development and disengagement: A reconceptualization. *Journal of Social and Personal Relationships, 10,* 273–283.

Haas, S. M., & Stafford, L. (1998). An initial examination of maintenance behaviors in gay and lesbian relationships. *Journal of Social and Personal Relationships, 15,* 846–855.

Kelley, H. H., & Thibaut, J. W. (1978). *Interpersonal relations: A theory of interdependence.* New York: Wiley.

Lee, B., & Lee, R. S. (1995). How and why people watch TV: Implications for the future of interactive television. *Journal of Advertising Research, 35,* 9–18.

Lull, J. (1990). *Inside family viewing: Ethnographic research on television's audiences.* New York: Routledge.

McQuail, D. (1987). *Mass communication theory* (2nd ed.). Newbury Park, CA: Sage.

McRae, P. (2006). The death of television and the birth of digital convergence: (Re)shaping media in the 21st century. *Studies in Media and Information Literacy, 6*(2). Retrieved June 9, 2006, from http://www.utpjournals.com/simile/issue22/macraefulltext.html

Nielsen Media Research. (2006, September 21). *Nielsen Media Research reports television's popularity still growing* (Press Release). Retrieved June 9, 2007, from http://www.nielsenmedia.com/

Nofsinger, R. (1991). *Everyday conversation.* Newbury Park, CA: Sage.

Plante, T., & Sullivan, K. (2000). *Getting together and staying together: The Stanford University course on intimate relationships.* Available from http://www.authorhouse.com/BookStore/ItemDetail~bookid~3663.aspx

Rabby, M. K. (1996). *Maintaining relationships via e-mail.* Unpublished master's thesis, University of Pennsylvania State, State College.

Rainey, D., & Rainey, B. (2004). *Rekindling the romance: Loving the love of your life.* Nashville, TN: Thomas Nelson.

Robinson, J. P. (1991). Quitting time. *American Demographics, 13,* 34–36.

Sigman, S. J. (1991). Handling the discontinuous aspects of continuous social relationships: Toward research on the persistence of social forms. *Communication Theory, 1,* 106–127.

Sillars, A. L. (1986). *Procedures for coding interpersonal conflict.* Unpublished paper.

Slater, M. D., Henry, K. L., Swaim, R. C., & Anderson, L. L. (2003). Violent media content and aggressiveness in adolescents: A downward spiral model. *Communication Research, 30,* 713–736.

Stafford, L. (2003). Maintaining romantic relationships: Summary and analysis of one research program. In D. J. Canary & M. Dainton (Eds.), *Maintaining relationships through communication* (pp. 51–77). Mahwah, NJ: Lawrence Erlbaum.

Stafford, L. S., & Canary, D. J. (1991). Maintenance strategies and romantic relationship type, gender, and relational characteristics. *Journal of Social and Personal Relationships, 8,* 217–242.

Svedin, C. G., & Wadsby, M. (1998). The presence of psychiatric consultations in relation to divorce. *Acta Psychiatrica Scandinavica, 98,* 414–422.

Wood, J. T. (1982). Communication and relational culture: Bases for the study of human relationships. *Communication Quarterly, 30,* 75–83.

---

AUTHORS' NOTE: Grants from Arizona State University and the College of Public Programs supported this project.

# *Index*

# About the Editor

**Michael T. Motley** (PhD, Pennsylvania State University, 1970) is a Professor in the Department of Communication at the University of California, Davis, where he teaches in the areas of interpersonal communication and quantitative research methods. Before UC Davis, he had full-time teaching positions at Pennsylvania State University, California State University at Fresno, California State University at Los Angeles, and Ohio State University. In addition to *Studies in Applied Interpersonal Communication,* he has authored *Orientations to Language and Communication, Overcoming Your Fear of Public Speaking: A Proven Method,* and *Improving Communication* (with S. Osborn). He has published scores of articles in the major journals of the communication discipline, as well as in *Scientific American, Psychology Today,* and major journals in the fields of psychology, speech pathology, language, and psycholinguistics. He has also written about a dozen book chapters and well over 100 research papers. Most of his earlier work was in the areas of public speaking anxiety and language cognition. Most of his later work has been in interpersonal communication. Five of his publications have received best-article awards from professional associations, and 13 of his convention papers have received special recognition. For the quantity of his collective work, he has been recognized as among the Top 1% of Communication Scholars of the 1970s, 1980s, and 1990s. He has held several division-level offices in national and regional professional associations and served for 3 years as the National Communication Association's representative to the American Association for the Advancement of Science. He is also active as a consultant and expert witness in court cases involving the interpretation of warning labels, instructions, and other documents. He is widowed from his wife of 27 years (Deirdre), is proud of his grown, successful, and loving daughter and son (Shannon and Shane), and is again happy in a committed relationship (Virginia). He is an accomplished and active jazz musician (alto and tenor sax), an avid intermediate snow and water skier, and a bonsai hobbyist.

# About the Contributors

**Jess K. Alberts** (PhD, University of Texas, 1986) is a Professor at Arizona State University. Her research and teaching focus on relational communication, humor, and conflict in personal and professional contexts. In addition to scholarly essays and book chapters, she is coauthor of *Human Communication in Society* and *Adolescent Relationships and Drug Use.* She has received awards for her teaching, research, and service contributions to the university, and she recently was named President's Professor in acknowledgment of her contributions to undergraduate teaching.

**Judee K. Burgoon** (EdD, West Virginia University, 1974) is a Professor of Communication, Family Studies and Human Development at the University of Arizona, where she is Site Director for the Center for Identification Technology Research, Director of Research for the Center for the Management of Information, and Associate Director of the Media Interface Network Design Lab in the Eller College of Management. She has authored seven books and monographs and over 250 articles, chapters, and reviews related to deception, nonverbal and relational communication, computer-mediated communication, research methods, and media use. Her current research, funded by the Department of Defense and National Science Foundation, is examining ways to automate analysis of nonverbal and verbal communication to uncover dyadic interaction patterns and detect deception.

**Brant R. Burleson** (PhD, University of Illinois, Urbana-Champaign, 1982) is a Professor in the Department of Communication at Purdue University. His research centers on communication skill acquisition and development, the effects of communication skills on relationship outcomes, the role of emotion in communication and relationships, and supportive forms of communication such as comforting. He has authored more than 130 articles and chapters and has edited several publications, including *The Handbook of Communication and Social Interaction Skills, Communication of Social Support,* and *Communication Yearbook.* He has received several major awards for his research, including the Distinguished Scholar Award from the National Communication Association in 2006.

**William R. Cupach** (PhD, University of Southern California, 1981) is a Professor of Communication at Illinois State University. His research pertains to problematic interactions in interpersonal relationships, including such contexts as embarrassing predicaments, relational transgressions, interpersonal conflict, and obsessive relational pursuit. In addition to numerous articles and monographs, he has coauthored or coedited 10 books. He previously served as Associate Editor for the *Journal of Social and Personal Relationships* and is a past President of the International Association for Relationship Research.

**Jolanta A. Drzewiecka** (PhD, Arizona State University, 1999) is an Associate Professor at Washington State University. Her primary research interests include critical intercultural communication; ethnic, racial, and cultural identity; immigrant identity; and discourse. She teaches intercultural communication, globalization, cultural studies, critical intercultural communication, and qualitative research methods.

**Larissa J. Faulkner** (PhD, University of Iowa, 2004) is an Instructor in the Department of Communication, Popular Culture, and Film at Brock University (Canada). Her primary areas are critical studies, children's popular culture, and rhetoric.

**Bo Feng** (PhD, Purdue University, 2006) is an Assistant Professor of Communication at the University of California, Davis. Her research examines the processes through which people seek, provide, and respond to various forms of support such as advice and emotional support. She has recently begun to study the delivery of medical recommendations during physician-patient interactions. Her work has appeared in *Human Communication Research, International and Intercultural Communication Annual, Southern Journal of Communication,* and *Sex Roles.*

**Jessica Harvey** (MA, Arizona State University West, 2003) is a doctoral student in the Department of Communication at the University of Washington. Her research interests focus on adolescence and the role of family communication and the media in the socialization process of young people. Her MA thesis examined the relational challenges and recovery strategies of long-term married couples.

**Douglas L. Kelley** (PhD, University of Arizona, 1988) is an Associate Professor of Communication Studies at Arizona State University's West Campus, where he studies communication patterns in families and personal relationships. His recent published work has appeared in *Family Communication, Journal of Social and Personal Relationships,* and *Communication Quarterly.* With Vincent R. Waldron he is author of the scholarly text *Communicating Forgiveness* (Sage) and a general audience book, *Marriage Is For-Giving.*

**Erina L. MacGeorge** (PhD, University of Illinois, 1999) is an Associate Professor of Communication at Purdue University. Her research examines communication and coping, including advice, comforting, and prayer, and she has recently begun to focus on coping with health issues such as miscarriage. Her work has appeared in *Communication Monographs, Human Communication Research, Communication Research, The Handbook of Interpersonal Communication,* and *Sex Roles.*

**Sandra Metts** (PhD, University of Iowa, 1983) is a Professor in the School of Communication at Illinois State University, where she teaches undergraduate and graduate classes in interpersonal communication, emotion theory, language, and aging. Her research focuses on politeness theory, facework, relational transgressions, forgiveness, and emotional competence. She is the coauthor of *Facework* (1994) and has published numerous journal articles and chapters in academic books. She serves on several editorial boards and is currently an Associate Editor for the *Journal of Social and Personal Relationships.*

**Lisa A. Miczo** (PhD, University of Arizona, 2000) is an Associate Professor of Communication at Western Illinois University. Her research and teaching focus on the roles that interpersonal and nonverbal communication play in relationships and upon identities and life outcomes. In addition to publications on topics of emotion, nonverbal communication, and family communication, she has received multiple research and teaching awards.

**Nathan Miczo** (PhD, University of Arizona, 2004) is an Associate Professor of Communication at Western Illinois University. His research and teaching include interpersonal and health communication, with a particular focus on the intersection of these two areas. He has several publications, including journals such as *Health Communication, Qualitative Health Research, Human Studies,* and *Journal of Family Communication.*

**Heidi Reeder** is an Associate Professor at Boise State University. Her research has been published in communication and interdisciplinary journals such as *Communication Monographs, Sex Roles, Journal of Applied Communication Research,* and *Journal of Social and Personal Relationships.* Her scholarship is focused on gendered behavior and identity, theories of commitment, and friendships between men and women.

**Rachel M. Reznik** (PhD, Northwestern University, 2006) is an Assistant Professor in the Communication Arts and Sciences Department at Elmhurst College. Her research focuses on conflict in close relationships. She has published in such journals as *Communication Yearbook, Human Communication Research,* and *Journal of Social and Personal Relationships.*

**Michael E. Roloff** (PhD, Michigan State University, 1975) is a Professor of Communication Studies at Northwestern University. He researches in the area of conflict management. He wrote *Interpersonal Communication: The Social Exchange Approach* and coedited *Persuasion: New Directions in Theory and Research* (with Gerald R. Miller), *Interpersonal Processes: New Directions in Communication Research* (with Gerald R. Miller), *Social Cognition and Communication* (with Charles R. Berger), and *Communication and Negotiation* (with Linda Putnam). He has published in journals such as *Communication Monographs, Communication Research, Human Communication Research, International Journal of Conflict Management, Journal of Language and Social Psychology, Journal of Social and Personal Relationships,* and *Personal Relationships.* He is also the Senior Associate Editor of *The International Journal of Conflict Management.* He served as Editor of *The Communication Yearbook* and currently is Coeditor of *Communication Research.*

**Brian H. Spitzberg** (PhD, University of Southern California, 1981) is a Professor in the School of Communication at San Diego State University. His areas of research include interpersonal communication competence, conflict, jealousy, infidelity, intimate violence, sexual coercion, and stalking. He is author or coauthor of three scholarly books, coeditor of three scholarly books, and author or coauthor of numerous scholarly articles and chapters, including the award-winning book written with William Cupach titled *The Dark Side of Relationship Pursuit: From Attraction to Obsession and Stalking.* He also serves as an active member of the San Diego District Attorney's Stalking Case Assessment Team and is an active member of the Association of Threat Assessment Professionals.

**Elizabeth R. Thompson** (BA, Purdue University, 2007) is a graduate student in the School of Public Policy at Pepperdine University. Her graduate work focuses on international relations and economic policy.

**Vincent R. Waldron** (PhD, Ohio State University, 1989) is a Professor of Communication Studies at Arizona State University's West Campus, where he is also affiliated with the gerontology faculty. His research concerns communication practices in personal and work relationships. His work has appeared recently in the *Journal of Social and Personal Relationships,* the *Journal of Applied Gerontology,* and *Communication Yearbook.* With Douglas Kelley he has recently coauthored the scholarly text *Communicating Forgiveness* (Sage) and a general audience book, *Marriage Is For-Giving.*

**Brandon Wood** is completing his master's degree in the School of Communication at Illinois State University, where he serves as Co-director of Forensics and teaches classes in public speaking and interpersonal communication. He is the recipient of the 2005 National Forensics Association Rhetorical Criticism award. His research focuses on the role of emotional competence in instructional and interpersonal settings, forensics, and psychoanalytic rhetoric.

**Christina G. Yoshimura** (PhD, Arizona State University, 2004) is an Assistant Professor at the University of Montana. Her research focuses on family communication, with an emphasis on family dynamics in times of transition or stress. Her work has been published in the *Journal of Social and Personal Relationships* as well as in books such as *Widening the Family Circle* and Ponzetti's (2003) *International Encyclopedia of Marriage and Family.*